Civil Society in the Age of Monitory Democracy

Studies on Civil Society
Edited by **Dieter Gosewinkel**, *Wissenschaftszentrum Berlin*
and **Holger Nehring**, *University of Sheffield*

Civil Society stands for one of the most ambitious projects and influential concepts relating to the study of modern societies. Scholars working in this field aim to secure greater equality of opportunity, democratic participation, individual freedom, and societal self-organization against both the overbearing and over social deficits of globalizing neoliberalism. This series deals with the multiple languages, different layers, and diverse practices of existing and emerging civil societies in Europe and elsewhere and asks how far the renewed interest in the concept can contribute to the gradual evolution of civil society in the wider world.

Volume 1
The Languages of Civil Society
Edited by Peter Wagner

Volume 2
Civil Society: Berlin Perspectives
Edited by John Keane

Volume 3
State and Civil Society in Northern Europe:
The Swedish Model Reconsidered
Edited by Lars Trägårdh

Volume 4
Civil Society and Gender Justice: Historical and
Comparative Perspectives
Edited by Karen Hagemann, Sonya Michel, and Gunilla Budde

Volume 5
Markets and Civil Society: The European Experience in
Comparative Perspective
Edited by Victor Pérez-Díaz

Volume 6
The Golden Chain: Family, Civil Society, and the State
Edited by Jürgen Nautz, Paul Ginsborg, and Ton Nijhuis

Volume 7
Civil Society in the Age of Monitory Democracy
Edited by Lars Trägårdh, Nina Witoszek, and Bron Taylor

CIVIL SOCIETY IN THE AGE OF MONITORY DEMOCRACY

Edited by
Lars Trägårdh, Nina Witoszek, and Bron Taylor

berghahn
NEW YORK · OXFORD
www.berghahnbooks.com

Published in 2013 by

Berghahn Books

www.berghahnbooks.com

© 2013 Lars Trägårdh, Nina Witoszek, and Bron Taylor

Library of Congress Cataloging-in-Publication Data

Civil society in the age of monitory democracy / edited by Lars Trägårdh,
Nina Witoszek, and Bron Taylor.
    p. cm.
    Includes bibliographical references and index.
    ISBN 978-0-85745-756-1 (hbk. : alk. paper) —
    ISBN 978-0-85745-757-8 (institutional ebook)
    1. Civil society. 2. Civil society—History. I. Trägårdh, Lars.
II. Witoszek, Nina. III. Taylor, Bron Raymond.
JC337.C5636 2012
300—dc23

                                                            2012019050

British Library Cataloguing in Publication Data

A catalogue record for this book is available from the British Library

Printed in the United States on acid-free paper

ISBN: 978-0-85745-756-1 hardback
ISBN: 978-1-78238-149-5 paperback
ISBN: 978-0-85745-757-8 institutional ebook
ISBN: 978-1-78238-150-1 retail ebook

CONTENTS

ACKNOWLEDGMENTS

This volume has been inspired by the work of an international research team, CERES21 (ceres21.org). Although the primary objective of the CERES21 think-tank has been to study political, economic, and cultural innovation for a sustainable future across three continents, one of the seminars—organized at the European Institute in Florence in 2009—illuminated an increasing role of civil society in shaping the new world order. We realized that the dream of a sustainable world is a mere illusion without a substantial input from the civic sphere.

We wish to thank the Norwegian Research Council for its generous financial support and, thus, for making this book possible. We are also grateful to Professor Philipp Schmitter, who both hosted our discussions and responded to our project with an appropriate mixture of skepticism and enthusiasm. Finally, we owe a special note of thanks to Nina D. Brochmann, Line Sundt Næsse, Armando J. Lamadrid, Carlos A. Lamadrid, Rebecka Andersen, and Martin Lee Mueller whose help was invaluable in the last stages of preparing the manuscript.

Introduction

Lars Trägårdh and Nina Witoszek

In the 2008 James Bond film *Quantum of Solace,* international business tycoon Dominic Greene schemes to buy up swaths of South American desert with the aim to control the water supply of an entire continent. Greene is not a stock turbo-capitalist. On the contrary, he is a world-renowned developer of green technology, and his operations are staged under the flag of idealistic Non-Governmental Organizations (NGOs). We are metaphorically—and literally—in a jungle of blurred boundaries, where civil society is no longer an adversary of states or corporations; rather it is their secret sharer.

The Janus face of the twenty-first century's civil society is as fascinating as it is disturbing. The students of Gandhi's non-violent mobilization against British imperialism, or the American Civil Rights movement, or the reinvention of civil society during Polish Solidarnosc and Eastern European Velvet Revolutions have gotten used to a positively charged, romantic image of "civil society" and the variety of associational activity usually subsumed under this heading. These came to be linked to an emancipatory ethos, non-violent struggle, and solidarity—those indispensable "hormones" of a well-functioning democratic order. To this day, radical social critics like Naomi Klein and Michael Hardt—or even apostles of "camp socialism" like Slavoj Žižek—hope that, if capitalism is to be civilized and the earth healed, it will mainly happen thanks to the mass mobilization of the grass roots movements. Amartya Sen has gone so far as to hold that that the only way towards limiting violence and ensuring peace in the world is via civil society.[1]

At the same time, there is increasing evidence to the effect that organizations independent of the state often are a smokescreen for suspect interests, the allies of big business, the veiled agents of neoliberal economic agendas, and biopolitic governmentality—not to mention the agents of "corrupt humanitarianism."[2] The array of satirical acronyms inspired by non-governmental organizations speaks for itself: BONGOs (business organized NGOs), PONGOs (politically organized NGOs), BRINGOs (briefcase NGOs), DONGOs (donor organized NGOs), GONGOs (government organized NGOs), RONGOs (Royal NGOs), MONGOs (my own NGOs).[3]

The plethora of designations for non-governmental agents suggests not just a flourishing industry, but a growing conceptual confusion. Today the concept of civil society has been defined, redefined, and re-theorized in so many ways that it is a titanic challenge to capture its many manifestations and mutations. Philippe Schmitter has proposed a "panoramic" working definition, which we endorse as a preliminary point of departure:

> Civil society ... can be defined as a set or system of self-organized intermediary groups that: (1) are relatively independent of both public authorities **and** private units of production and reproduction, i.e. of firms and families; (2) are capable of deliberating about and taking collective actions in defense/promotion of their interests or passions; (3) do **not** seek to replace either state agents or private (re-) producers or to accept responsibility for governing the polity as a whole; (4) **do** agree to act within pre-established rules of a "civil," i.e. mutually respectful, nature. Civil society, therefore, is not a simple but a compound property. It rests on four conditions or, better, behavioral norms: (1) dual autonomy, (2) collective action, (3) non-usurpation, (4) civility.[4]

We shall return to the historical genealogy of the idea of civil society and the theoretical tensions that characterize its usage in both political and academic parlance, but first we wish to briefly sketch the current context of the global "civil society speak."

Civil Society on Trial

Empirically speaking, contemporary civil society presents something of a maze, containing at its center normative contradictions as well as a theoretical puzzle. On the one hand, broad sections of civil society in authoritarian regimes like Burma, Iran, or China, are composed of quixotic human rights idealists who incarnate civil courage, intelligence, and moral dedication. In China, there are 10,000 signatories of the Charter 2008, a dissident Magna Carta of democracy modeled on its Eastern European prototype Charter 77. In Cuba, there is Yoani Sanchez, the author of the blog "Generation Y," who, together with her husband Reinaldo Escobar, have been broadcasting their criticism of the authoritarian regime and thus have kept thousands of virtual dissidents in a state of hopeful mobilization. By contrast with the anti-Castro hardliners, their objectives appear to be more modest—and possibly more profound at the same time—more in line with the visions of their Eastern European predecessors. "They are not polemicists or pundits as much as poets and storytellers," as one commentator put it.[5] Like their Eastern European counterparts—Michnik, Havel, or Kis—these "lonely democratic riders" are less concerned with proposing new policies than addressing ordinary people and chronicling the costs of the repressive policies already in place: from the fate of sex workers to the daily struggle for bread and water. Similarly in the Iranian Islamic Republic there is a strong women's movement, which describes itself as feminist, but whose work is a continuation of the anti-totalitarian struggle of Solzhenitsyn, Sakharov, or the Polish Committee for Workers Defense (KOR).

The postmodern world, however, is on the whole less Promethean and more Protean. In many parts of the globe, instead of an inclusive and tolerant civil society emerging virtuous and triumphant, primordial tribal allegiances tempt self-appointed, populist spokesmen. Their ranks include those who cannot bear the strains of liberty, higher prices, unemployment, and inequality, and return to *ethnos*, feeling secure and at home among their own. In this regard, it is tempting to compare the ambiguity of the current civil society movements with nineteenth and twentieth century nationalism. A similar complexity pertained then with a "good" civic nationalism intimately linked to democratization and self-rule, and a "bad" ethnic nationalism serving as an ideology for demagogic leaders forging powerful movements based on fascist, racist, and xenophobic ideas.[6]

For today's tribalists, like yesterday's nationalists, the new attractive options of citizenship and cosmopolitanism have little meaning without deep structures of belonging. Many forms of what may pass as "civil society" today—from the ultra-Polish Radio Maria to the transnational Al Qaeda—attract racists, extremist nationalists, and religious fundamentalists who have increasingly used global communications and transnational networks to advocate intolerance and violence. Al Qaeda's media empire recruits the young warriors with rap music, Hollywood aesthetics, and clever branding. The biggest "civil society" in Egypt—the Muslim Brotherhood—is an organization, which, at the beginning of the twenty-first century, combines philanthropic, educational, and health initiatives and the effective promotion of hatred of the Western world.

Today, civil society is both powerful and impotent. On the one hand, it appears to affect the world's security politics, influence the process of cultural assimilation and migration, and make a tangible impact on the limits to scientific research and moral progress, from biotechnology to women's emancipation and freedom of speech. But the real effect civil society has on world affairs in crucial areas—affecting climate change or making an impact on Middle East politics—remains debatable. Rasmus Hansson, the director of the World Wide Fund for Nature (WWF) Norway, insists that "the environmental sector that emerged in the late 1960s has grown into the biggest new political project in the west during the twentieth century, and it continues to grow in the twenty-first century." Basic achievements like cleaner air and water, more efficient production and resource use, and laws that limit poisonous substances and over-exploitation of resources are the product of NGO's pressure to hold states, business, and individuals responsible for the environmental effects of their activities. But, continues Hansson: "Western Environmental NGOs (ENGOs) are now in the process of being overtaken by their own success. They may have reached the point where they no longer have a constructive role in Western societies—unless they are willing and able to make the potentially controversial transformation needed to remain important political drivers."[7]

The impasse facing civil society enthusiasts and the search for a way forward constitutes one central theme of this book. The latter can best be seen as a contribution to an emerging discussion on both how we (re-)theorize civil society and consider its practical import on a global scale in the age of WikiLeaks. In short, *les pouvoirs intermédiaires*, as Tocqueville and Montesquieu called them, are in an urgent need of redefinition.

John B. Keane, whose chapter opens this volume, makes a step in this direction when he codifies a term to cover some of the more recent developments concerning the links between democracy and civil society. His "monitory democracy"—a concept which he himself is still interrogating—is possibly one of the more fertile terms to describe the big transformation that is taking hold in regions like Europe and South Asia and in countries otherwise as different as the United States, Japan, Argentina, and New Zealand. Monitory democracy is a new historical form of democracy, defined by the rapid growth of many different kinds of extra-parliamentary, power-scrutinizing mechanisms. According to Keane: "These monitory bodies take root within the 'domestic' fields of government and civil society, as well as in 'cross-border' settings once controlled by empires, states, and business organizations. In consequence, the whole architecture of self-government is changing. The central grip of elections, political parties, and parliaments on citizens' lives is weakening. Democracy is coming to mean much more than elections, although nothing less."[8]

As is the case with all successful metaphors—from "small is beautiful" to "global village"—it is easy to find fault with Keane's concept. His "monitory democracy" gestures towards independent-minded, authority testing citizens, though we know all too well that public opinion is not necessarily a foundation of informed common sense but often a polluted reservoir of popular prejudice. Similarly, Keane's notion of "global civil society" borders on a dustbin category: it includes cosmopolitans and tribalists, civilians and barbarians, Manicheans and holists, barefooted idealists and beneficiaries of multimillion dollar businesses.[9] Still, there is something apt and reinvigorating about the monitory democracy trope: there is a sense in which Keane's "universal monitoring" has become the symbol of the twenty-first century—a tool of the new, emerging, and emergent centers of power. Monitory democracy means that the Norwegian Telenor, which attempts to enter the North Korean market, faces a dilemma in a society whose public sphere is familiar with the concept of corporate social responsibility. According to Amnesty International, taking this responsibility seriously implies a refusal to collaborate with the last totalitarian regime. The director of Telenor, who sees the Norwegian involvement as contributing to opening up of North Korea, has yet to convince the native "monitoring electorate" and the Norwegian media that this is the case.

There are many commentators and researchers who are skeptical about the democratizing or "greening" of potential of monitory democracy in the world ridden by crisis. John Clark—one of the contributors of this volume—challenges the heroic view of a global civil society. Confronting the NGO's apparent visibility with the current multiple crises, he sees signs of decline rather than success (see chapter 2). There are also claims to the effect that the causes of civil society have been taken over by philantrocapitalism, which has undermined NGOs in their historical role in building solidarity and acting as an accountability agent.[10] The very cyberspace that has colonized our world has created conditions where power-holders, big business, and civil society both press upon and control one another to an unprecedented degree. Finally, there has emerged a new mutation of civil society, consisting of a charismatic individual with a huge, virtual following of enthusiastic internauts—a phenomenon whose ultimate democratizing potential remains to be seen. Witness an increasing number of highly influential MONGOs, such as the one created by the Chinese cultural idol, Han Han. Apart from being a Robin Hood of the Chinese Internet who dares to take the side of the underdog, Han Han specializes in writing sizzling literary bestsellers, winning car races and ladies' hearts, and setting new trends and fashions. His political messages are censored (i.e. "harmonized") by the authorities, but they do comment on sensitive subjects like corruption, toxic milk scandals, or arrogance of the power holders—and thus serve to percolate *la reigne de la critique* to the masses.

The most striking emblem of civil society's "monitory" ambitions has become WikiLeaks, one of the most sophisticated—and confusing—forms of NGOs in the twenty-first century. Its mission runs: "WikiLeaks has combined high-end security technologies with journalism and ethical principles. Like other media outlets conducting investigative journalism, we accept (but do not solicit) anonymous sources of information. Unlike other outlets, we provide a high security anonymous drop box fortified by cutting-edge cryptographic information technologies. This provides maximum protection to our sources. We are fearless in our efforts to get the unvarnished truth out to the public."[11]

This sounds like monitory democracy at its best. One cannot deny WikiLeaks' role in disclosing high-level corruption in Kenya, the toxic waste scandal in Africa, or the abuses in Guantanamo Bay. But there is also evidence to the effect that WikiLeaks leaders sport a rather autocratic outfit and, in many cases, seem to copy the strategies of their opponents. On the whole, the apparently dramatic impact of the "new media"—the rock of monitory democracy—remains to be revalued (see chapters by Bill McKibben and by Paddy Coulter and Cathy Baldwin in this volume). There are also reasons to look again at the democratic potential of what has been called "twitter against tyrants." In most countries run by authoritarian regimes there is an untapped mass of activists, dissidents, and anti-government intellectuals who have barely heard of Facebook. Furthermore, one may well raise the question if the foundations of a true social movement—from Gandhi in India, through the Civil Rights Movement in the U.S., to Solidarnosc in Poland—must not lay in a durable personal commitment anchored in friendship. Historically it has been this "Eros of friendship"—a moral, spiritual process and face-to face contact which matures and solidifies through sharing hazards and building of deep loyalties—that has reinforced civil activists' motivation and kept their cause alive. As Jozef Tischner, the legendary chaplain of Solidarnosc, put it, "Solidarity is the willingness to bear one another's cross."[12] No army of virtual dissidents—who can always retreat from the battlefield without bearing personal costs—is able to create a magical "warm circle" where collective dreams and bonds are not part of a blogosphere but translate into concrete physical actions. Admittedly, there has been an Orange "mobile phone" revolution in Ukraine and a Jasmine "hackers uprising" in Egypt. And while there is no doubt that the new virtual tools are significant as channels of information and mobilization, can they fully replace voices, arguments, and charisma of real people? Even the most impassioned blog or SMS will not have the same effect as a blood and flesh leader or priest who—speaking directly to his audiences—sustains their actions and strengthens their will to continue their struggle.

Civil Society and the State: Theoretical Conundrums

The confusing and contradictory image of civil society that emerges from this empirical mosaic presents a considerable theoretical challenge. What does, in fact, constitute civil society as a theoretical concept? We propose here that one way of approaching this question is to consider two historical points of entry with regard to the contemporary civil society rhetoric. They both imagine a utopian society beyond the state and beyond politics, a realm of spontaneous social order based on friendship and warm and fuzzy human relationships. Here there is a common theme that unites thinkers on the left and on the right: from the left a vision inspired by the legacy of glorious revolutions and passionate revolts; from the right a dream of a society liberated from the meddling of an invasive state. Marx imagined an international civil society as the end point of a dialectical process, including bourgeois revolution and proletarian dictatorship, when the state—even the workers' state—had given way to universal freedom. Per analogiam, libertarian thinkers on the right like Hayek dreamt about a spontaneous order where the state had shrunk into insignificance, setting society and man free.

Current narratives on civil society embody both these variants of a common theme. On the left one finds an enduring infatuation with the romance of revolution, the cleansing effects of mass protest, the camaraderie on the barricades, the passions following the felling of the tyrant, the deep bonds of friendship and community born in revolutionary intoxication, and a disgust with ordinary politics. In the words of Havel, a dream of an "anti-political politics" built on the humanity of the people as opposed to the professional propaganda of career politicians: "a politics 'from below.' Politics of people, not of the apparatus. Politics growing from the heart not from a thesis."[13] The euphoria attending the 2011 uprisings in North Africa and the Middle East derived its energy from this enduring fantasy with its links back to the French revolution, and beyond that to heroic, if mostly futile, revolts on the part of long suffering slaves and serfs around the world.

On the right, the fascination with civil society has had fewer links to revolution than to an anti-statist sentiment. The American Revolution was, after all, not simply about battling tyranny of the old brutal kind. It was far more modern, a revolt already rooted in Adam Smith's vision of a market society and an expression of Hegel's civil society, at heart about taxation as much—or more—as it was about bloody repression. The Tocquevillian testament, with its reification of America as the land of citizens joined in free association, was an enshrining of a liberal utopia of civil society. In this reading, the central organizing trope is what Margaret Somers calls "a meta narrative of Anglo-American citizenship theory" in which the State is always seen as hovering "on the brink of being a source of tyranny."[14] This story has tended to push to the fore a vision of a social order in which the role of the state was minimized. *Les extrêmes se touchent:* libertarianism of the right meets up with anarchism of the left.

What is missing from both the left-wing revolutionary romance and the right-wing liberal "tea party" are the more sobering insights provided by Hegel—arguably still the most profound theorist of "civil society" as a concept of political theory. For Hegel, civil society was the social realm where individuals and groups sought to satisfy needs, fulfill desires, and protect interests.[15] It included both what we today think of as the market and the associational life that in contemporary parlance has become synonymous with the more narrow understanding of what constitutes civil society, with a focus on non-profit and non-governmental organizations.

Inspired by Adam Smith, Hegel envisioned the market as a legitimate, necessary, and ultimately positive force, enabling the pursuit of gain, pleasure, and self-expression, leading at the aggregate, societal level to an increased "wealth of the nation." At the same time, however, he also argued that the internal contradictions of civil society produced by this relentless pursuit of particular interest—atomistic individualism, inequality, poverty, and social disorder—could never be resolved by civil society itself. Only the state, Hegel argued, could promote and safeguard the general or universal interest of society as a whole, achieving a higher purpose of rationality that he described as the "unity and interpenetration of universality and individuality."[16]

In other words, for Hegel civil society was not intrinsically "good" or "civil," and he certainly did not view the state as inherently "bad." Rather, he conceived of civil society and the state in more dynamic, relational, and evolutionary terms. From the individual's point of view, he suggested a movement from the inward looking privacy of the family, through the forging of an intermediary social identity transcending private self-interest in the corporations and associations of civil society, to the universalist rationality embodied by the state. From a societal perspective, he stressed the institutions mediating and resolving conflict within civil society and connecting civil society to the state, rather than a reification of civil society in terms of opposing, overcoming, or transcending the state.

In the contemporary world, the Hegelian idea of civil society has largely lost out to the anti-statist notion that informs most ideas of global civil society or, for that matter, most national conversations that invoke the concept of civil society. But as an empirical fact, the Nordic countries have perhaps come the closest to constituting a democratic, neo-Hegelian political order, as Lars Trägårdh argues in his chapter of this book. Characterized by a democratic corporatist system whose hallmark is precisely the routinized institutions that connect state and civil society in a peculiar form of governance, these societies exhibit both a large and vital civil society providing political input and social voice from a particularized society, and a equally strong state, given the task to represent and safeguard national community and universal social welfare.[17]

Comparing and contrasting the Nordic and the American state/civil society nexus thus helps illuminate the more general discussion of what is at stake in the current civil society debate. One finding is that we can identify two major parts of civil society that, for many reasons, must be treated analytically and politically as separate and different. On the one hand, there are those that primarily have a political function in providing "voice" to any number of groups in society, including interest groups and social movements. This is the part of civil society that has sustained the ongoing democratization process, aiming to liberate and empower the historically disenfranchised and to provide a critical counterforce to the powers that be, states as well as private firms. One the other hand, there are the multiform charities, faith-based institutions, and non-profit organizations that are engaged in providing relief, support, and social services to those in need, both at home and abroad (often in the form of NGOs active in the development industry).

It is clear that social and political movements devoted to making rights claims and charity and service oriented organizations stand in tension in relation to each other. Indeed, to some extent, the classic social movements in Western Europe, and most especially in the Nordic countries, aimed to eradicate the need for private charity, and civil society and family-based social services by establishing state guaranteed social rights based on citizenship in the form of a universalist welfare state. To put it differently, the goal for *one part* of Nordic civil society (the social movements) was to liberate the individual from the ties of dependency that prevailed in the family and in the charitable institutions of *the other part* of civil society. This should be contrasted with the adversarial vision of civil society that centers on the idea that family and civil society based provision of social services though charities is preferable given the overarching aim to keep the state at arm's length.

While the Nordic, neo-Hegelian instantiation of the state/civil society dynamic by all accounts is remarkably successful as measured in terms of social trust, confidence in institutions, efficient economies, relative equality, and social mobility, on a global level it is the Anglo-American conception of civil society and its proper functions and relations to the state that dominates today. This was apparent during the heyday of dissident movements in former Communist Eastern Europe and it has since been especially true for how the concept has been deployed in relation to the global aid and development industry.

As Jens Stillhoff Sörensen has argued, the ascendency of civil society as a fashionable concept in the development and aid sector was intimately linked to the paradigmatic shift from a state-centered approach to development to a neoliberal focus on the market. With the loss of faith in state-to-state aid and the rise of a broader neoliberal trend dating back to the Thatcher-Reagan era, the "Washington consensus" brought with it a new focus on civil society NGOs as both the vehicle and target for aid: a semi-utopian faith in the market and civil society was joined to a deep skepticism of the Keynesian state-centered approach. However, in the first decade of the twenty-first century, this faith in the magic of civil society has been declining, not least in the wake of the 9/11 attacks and the rise of the "war on terror." To some extent the state is making a comeback, though this is a return that is largely restricted to the security related functions of the state and does not include Nordic style ambitions to promote state-guaranteed social security.[18]

Furthermore, it becomes increasingly clear that to speak of a global civil society (cf. John Keane) in the absence of a "global state" is problematic at best. In so far as civil society is in fact constituted by, and inseparable from, the modern state—even if it occasionally spawns and fosters a critique of that state—it is clear that the Hegelian emphasis on the relations between the state and civil society, and the ties that bind them together, is as relevant as ever.[19]

Civil society seems plainly incapable of replacing the state. Instead of pitting one against the other—a rhetorical and tactical ploy of Eastern European dissidents and of American neoliberals—may it perhaps be more fruitful to focus on the ways in which the interplay of state and civil society results in a productive mode of governance?

The Empirical Mosaic of Civil Society

Against the backdrop of the theoretical challenges posed by the current empirical mosaic, this book proposes to contribute to the field of civil society studies in several areas. First, it will offer a broad panorama of empirical investigation of Asian, African, and European societies, ranging from the totalitarian Islamic Republic in Iran and the repressive Burmese regime, through the "managed" democracy of Russia and the authoritarian market society of China, through the emerging democracy of Kenya, the restive Muslim world, and on to the Scandinavian welfare state. Second, it will attempt to delineate the evolution of civil society against the backdrop of a wide range of twenty-first century trends and forces, from the rise of new media and WikiLeaks, to global warming, the impacts of the "war on terror," and the financial crisis of 2008. Finally, it will aim to provide theoretical perspectives which illuminate or reconceptualize modern civic movements, taking as points of departure Keane's analysis of "monitory democracy," the juxtaposition of the liberal and Hegelian conceptions of state-civil society interaction, Hannah Arendt's theory of totalitarianism and, finally, creative rereading of Montesquieu's scenario of the balance of powers.

The book begins with three chapters that provide a framing tension for the book. First out is John Keane with his elaboration of civil society and monitory democracy, suggesting a new and crucial role for civil society both nationally and globally. He proposes what he sees as a fundamental revision of the way we think about representation and democracy in our times. According to Keane, "epochal transformations" have been taking place, and he argues that representative democracy has begun to change into what he calls a "post-representative" democracy. His chapter explores some of the reasons why this change happened. Keane suggests that notions such as the "end of history" (Fukuyama) or a third wave' (Huntington) fail to capture how "political tides have begun to run in entirely new directions." The author's thesis is "that the world of actually existing democracy is experiencing an historic sea change, one that is taking us away from the assembly-based and representative democracy of past times towards a form of democracy with entirely different contours and dynamics."

In the next chapter John Clark provides, as a counterpoint to Keane's celebratory account of civil society's potential, a more somber analysis of "the return of the state." He sees a deep challenge to global civil society in the age of three crises: financial meltdown, global warming, and the "war on terror." While, Clark contends, there exists a significant literature on how civil society influences these crises, to date there has been little analysis of how the crises shape civil society. The chapter charts the various ways that civil society organizations (CSOs) have been impacted, ranging from the crowding out of CSO voices by government spokespeople in debates that were once a civil society preserve, to overzealous multilateral anti-terrorism strategies that have squeezed the space for CSOs. Combined, this "age of crisis" has had a significant impact on the political freedoms, public credibility, influence, and financial base of civil society.

In chapter 3 Paddy Coulter and Cathy Baldwin consider the role of new media on the formation and action of civil society. They argue that since their arrival in the early 1990s, new digital media have offered unparalleled opportunities for CSOs working for sustainable development to mobilize their supporters and lobby governments. Some observers have a strongly positive view of such media, convinced that they promote social and economic inclusion, while others reject such a view as unwarranted "techno-deterministic optimism." Based on a review of such perspectives, analysis of well-documented case studies from the developing world—including the Grameen Village Phone in Bangladesh, the Kothmale Radio web browsing in Sri Lanka, and the use of new and traditional media by the Treatment Action Campaign in South Africa—and interviews with senior figures in leading international civil society organizations, Coulter and Baldwin conclude that new information and communications technologies (ICTs) influence development projects and sustainability efforts in much more complex ways than are commonly recognized.

These three chapters, which all seek to pinpoint broader structural trends, are followed by a series of chapters that form the empirical core of the book. In chapter 4, Kathryn Stoner Weiss engages with Keane's analysis by examining the existence, role, and efficacy of contemporary Russian civil society in monitoring state actors and institutions. If we assume that meaningful democratic practice requires that state actors and organizations be held accountable to the citizenry, and given that formal democratic institutions are weak in Russia, Stoner Weiss raises the question if, in fact, non-state actors in Russia act as independent agents that balance state power. Her answer to this question is, despite the fact that Russia is clearly not a democracy, a qualified "yes." Public interest groups exist independently of the state in contemporary Russia, and often, they successfully provide public goods and services. They fall far short, however, of the "monitory" ideal that Keane envisions in European democracies. This is largely a result of the fact that in Russia—perhaps unlike many established democracies—the assumption on the part of state actors in particular (but also many Russians) is that it is the state that must monitor and restrain society, and not the other way around. Moreover, the author concludes, suspicion of non-state political monitoring activity has been pervasive long after the fall of communism and its monitoring function is severely circumscribed, although not completely absent.

Turning from Russia to China, James Miller seeks to focus his analysis on one important subset of civil society, namely the faith-based organizations (chapter 5). He asks what role do national and transnational religions play in civil society in China today. By tracing the history of bureaucratic control of religion by the state and its underlying ideological assumptions and motivations, religious movements are revealed as both alternatives to, and servants of, the changing ideology of the modern Chinese state. From this perspective, the chapter assesses the extent to which newly invigorated religious movements in China can be understood as aspects of an emerging "monitory democracy" in Chinese civil society. In particular, the chapter examines the ways in which religious movements can be understood not simply as functional elements of a putative civil society in China today but, more significantly, as providing alternative ways to meet the widely-noted "crisis of belief" in a China that faces severe social and environmental instability.

While both Russia and China can be thought of as emerging or "managed democracies," Burma represents a case of a more solidly repressive regime. Still, Burma—or Myanmar—is on the cusp of political changes under continued military influence that could affect civil society, as defined herein, in its monitory role. In chapter 6, David Steinberg's main thesis is that in spite of functioning under a soft-authoritarian military administration, we can speak of the aspects of indigenous and foreign international civil society that have been operating in the twenty-first century. The interplay between international and local NGOs, the relationship to central authority and GONGOs, and some international prohibitions against working with the government are all analyzed in comparison with such organizations in China. The author discusses the dangers of treating civil society as a panacea for authoritarian regimes and makes recommendations to the donor communities.

In chapter 7, Bron Taylor looks afresh at Kenya's Green Belt Movement, which became internationally famous when in 2004 its founder, Wangari Maathai, was awarded the Nobel Peace Prize. Since 1977, in Kenya and elsewhere in Africa, the movement has planted millions of trees in an effort to restore ecosystems, promote sustainable livelihoods, empower women, and promote democracy. Increasingly, Maathai has drawn a close connection between all these objectives and the quest for a peaceful society. This skeletal understanding of Maathai and the movement she inspired are well known internationally. However, a more careful analysis reveals many conflicts and complications, and that while many of the movement's contentions have been vindicated and strategies effective, it faces many challenges that undermine its objectives. These challenges include, among others, incomplete diagnoses and inadequate prescriptions in response to the unfolding crisis. This raises important epistemological and ethical questions for grassroots civil society movements, suggesting that they will be more effective if they blend local and international concerns in the pursuit of environmental sustainability and social justice.

In the next chapter (8) Zeynep Atalay turns her attention to transnational civil society in the Muslim world. Over the last three decades, she argues, civic action in the Muslim World has undergone a major transformation. Not only have the previously informal religious communities started mobilizing in the form of non-governmental organizations, but they are also joining forces and forming transnational coalitions. Such coalitions allow the isolated and dispersed organizations to speak in one voice; to devise common action plans and agendas; to facilitate communications, information transfer, and resource sharing; and to increase legitimacy with their own communities and governments. This chapter—based on the three year long field work conducted in Turkey, Germany, U.S., Malaysia, and Cambodia—traces the progress of the first and most extensive Muslim civil society coalition: Union of the NGOs of the Islamic World (UNIW). Atalay discusses the ways in which both the UNIW and its members draw together the discourse of civil society and the language of religion in order to achieve their stated goal of salvaging the *Umma*, and the ways in which the pragmatic advantages of partnering with a large scale coalition mobilize hundreds of Muslim NGOs to action from all around the globe.

Gouging the question of Islam and civil society, Haideh Daragahi and Nina Witoszek offer an analysis of the women's movement in Iran as an example of a novel civic revolt within the framework of a Muslim totalitarian government (chapter 9). Drawing their inspiration from the work of Hannah Arendt, the authors refer to gender apartheid and the suppression of women's freedoms as totalitarian ploys to isolate, stigmatize, and scapegoat part of society by invoking religion and the supremacy of Sharia law. The chapter draws attention to the history of the unique, Iranian feminist anti-totalitarianism that constitutes a significant civic mobilization in today's Iran. The authors argue that Western observers have largely overlooked this unique, women-driven "revolution." Not only does it aim at establishing an advanced, modern democracy in the Islamic Republic; it may have consequences, not just for the countries or regions where Islam is gaining ground, but also for Europe and the rest of the Western world. The pressing question remains: if democracy is to finally win in Iran, how to ensure that women freedoms will be respected and institutionalized?

The two chapters that follow discuss the polar opposite of the analysis of the authoritarian and managed democracy in the countries in Africa and Asia. Lars Trägårdh and Asle Toje take up the case of Nordic countries, often heralded as particularly successful examples of constructive state/civil society interaction and cooperation. First, Lars Trägårdh provides in chapter 10 a theoretical and historical account of Nordic state/civil society interaction, focusing on the institutional underpinning of democracy and governance in the Nordic countries. In the historical section, Trägårdh's focus is on the development and legacy of the popular movements that preceded formal modern democracy and subsequently became key players in a neo-corporatist political system that linked state and civil society. Furthermore, he provides a distinction between what has been called the "voice" (or "monitory") and "service" functions of civil society. In the theoretical section, he compares the Nordic and American experiences and challenges the dominant Anglo-American—liberal or neoliberal—account of "civil society" and its relation to the state by invoking what he calls a "neo-Hegelian" conception of state and civil society.

By contrast, in the following chapter (11) Asle Toje offers a critique of such close intertwining of state and civil society, focusing on the negative consequences of the corporatist arrangement in Norway, with a special focus on the development aid industry. Using clientelism as the point of entry, Toje employs five interconnected concepts: (i) *institutional capture*, (ii) *rent seeking*, (iii) *agenda chasing*, (iv) *partisan politics*, and (v) *moral hazard*, in an attempt to flesh out the main hazards of collusion between civil society and the funding government. In Norway this practice has been expanded to an extent where many non-governmental organizations, particularly those working with foreign aid, are nearly fully funded by the government. The chapter will also provide examples from the state-financed research institutions that, alongside the government bureaucracy, make up a neo-corporative triangle. Toye's main argument is, in the simplest terms, that the inherent dangers of a state-funded civil society are greater—both for the government and for non-governmental organizations—than is generally acknowledged.

The book ends with two contributions that return to the theoretical challenges and structural trends that were pinpointed in the first three chapters. Atle Midttun, engaging with and attempting to complement and expand on Keane's model, suggests in chapter 12 an approach inspired by Montesquieu and his classical idea of the "balance of powers." The article explores how civic initiatives and organizations, with their flexibility and engagement, may play a vital entrepreneurial role in facilitating new governance arrangements across political divides. Midttun proposes this new analytical perspective through a close reading of a case study of the Extractive Industry's Transparency Initiative (EITI). He seeks to show how civic initiatives, using free media in open societies, can play a vital role in monitoring and rebalancing the powers of markets and politics gone astray. The conclusion is that in a new triad of balancing powers—industry, governance, and civil society—civil society is not so much supposed to deliver concrete results; rather it is an entrepreneurial agent of innovation, pressing state powers and market forces to employ new political and business solutions.

We have chosen to conclude this volume with Bill McKibben's reflections on the role that the Internet plays in the reconfiguration of civil society (chapter 13). Drawing on his experience as the creator of one of the most successful environmental mobilizations in the world via his website 350.org, McKibben argues that the rise of the Internet has offered new opportunities for political mobilization against the governments' sluggishness in abating a climate shift. He concludes that while new technologies allow for the easy and powerful agglomeration of local actions into global movements, they fail to fundamentally affect the shift at the governmental level.

Our contributions suggest a number of observations and questions, which can be summarized as follows:

(1) The sheer plethora of modern forms of associational life implies that civil society has emerged as a significant power on the international as well as the national arenas; we have entered a new age of "monitory democracy" in which the public sphere has gone global even though democratic governance structures largely remain wedded to the nation-state. This has produced a mismatch in which the power of global civil society is limited by the absence of a global state that could serve as partner in "making democracy work."

(2) Furthermore, it appears that in the current socio-political context, civil society is as much the victim as the agent of monitory democracy. While the new technologies have enabled the Wikileaks of the world to serve as more potent watchdogs of governmental and corporate corruption and abuse of power, they have also allowed governments and corporations to widen and deepen its surveillance and control of citizens and consumers along with criminals and terrorists. To invoke Foucault, we increasingly live in a kind of two-way Panopticon, where civil society and the citizenry on the one hand, and the agents of governments and corporations on the other, monitor each other's actions. (We shall return to this question in the Epilogue).

(3) A further theme is the rise of the new media, by most accounts a powerful agent of mobilization in civil society. The question here is to what extent new media primarily facilitates the role of civil society as a cultural innovator and a tool for social networking, rather than functions as a vehicle for social movements to voice political protest. Some argue

that civil society is less and less the agent of direct democratization or moral rearmament; rather, it is entangled in various forms of collusion with the economic or political power holders which raises the question as to whether these alliances detract from or contribute to emancipatory processes in the world.

(4) There is a need for more analytical attention to the tension between independent, democratic, and sometimes adversarial civil society actors that express bottom-up political interest and voice, and those more professional and hierarchically organized organizations that focus on the top-down provision of service ranging from charity and development aid, to non-profit schools, hospitals, and care for the old and weak. This is linked to the crucial question of the relationship between civil society and the state. Should the normative ideal be to seek maximum autonomy and construe civil society as "the big society" promoted in the 2010s by the British conservatives? Or should our model be inspired by the Nordic case, which flaunts a less adversarial and more cooperative relationship with a state as the ultimate guarantor of equal access to basic social goods?

Here we see how a liberal or Anglo-American understanding of the "good society" which views the state with suspicion, is pitted against political traditions that reverse this perspective and see civil society as rooted in special interests and mired in unequal and hierarchical structures. This applies to governments like the Russian or the Chinese, that perceive civil society as messy and subversive, a bringer of chaos and corruption. But it is also a view common among the champions of the welfare state. They view parts of civil society, such as charities and philanthropies, as expressing and imposing unequal power relations in the name of giving and charity. In this perspective, modern Nordic history can be viewed as the struggle to expand the universal welfare state with its rights tradition while minimizing the space and need for *caritas*. Paradoxically that has, in practice, entailed a kind of "civil war" in civil society, where social movements aiming to expand universal social rights clash with the traditional charities and philanthropic foundations. Interestingly, however, we can today see signs of a return of charity and philanthropy in the Nordic countries. This happens partly in response to demographic and economic pressures that put the squeeze on the welfare state, and partly an expression of the primacy of the neoliberal model with its hostility to the state and its preference for civil society based provision of social services. This has, of course, implications far beyond the Nordic countries, suggesting the increasingly hegemonic position of a neoliberal conception of civil society formed around a negative view of the state, and the correspondingly romantic view of civil society and its potential to realize "civility" beyond the coercive logic of the state.

(5) As some of our contributors have implicitly argued, the notion of monitory democracy may have an extra ring to it, though not in the sense John Keane intended. This is due to the Janus face of the new technology. On the one hand it has made civil society today a ubiquitous and transnational agent of moral blackmail—pressing politicians and industry for good governance, democracy, gender equality, and sustainable development. Characteristically, this adversarial role is most buoyant in liberal and authoritarian societies such as U.S. and China. In the social democracies of the Scandinavian type and in the radical autocracies such as Iran or Burma, the oppositional status of civil society seems to have been diminished, and various forms of collusion with the state are more manifest. More importantly, webcams, tracking devices, and interlinked databases are increasingly leading to the shrinking of the public sphere. The MIT *Technology Review* has referred to a "surveillance state" which, paradoxically, is most sophisticated in countries that love freedom such as the United Kingdom and the U.S.[20] As has been pointed out, Google knows "roughly who you are, roughly what you care about, and roughly who your friends are."[21] Similarly, there is evidence to the effect that Facebook provides advertisers with information that even their current minimal privacy policies are supposed to protect.[22] Former French President Nicolas Sarcozy went as far as to speak of the Internet as a "wilderness" which he intended to "colonize with official government overseers."[23] Last, but not least, the Chinese government has a special "stability maintenance" budget which is second only to military spending. "Stability maintenance" means monitoring people—petitioners, aggrieved workers, professors, religious believers, and bloggers. In response, the Chinese have created a popular movement called "rights maintenance" (*weiquan*).

To conclude: In order to make sense of the countless civic actions across the continents—and to propose clarifying distinctions—one needs to carefully scrutinize the objectives and modus operandi of the main actors in the public sphere. To return to our original definition: One of civil society's four behavioral norms mentioned by Philippe Schmitter is "civility." WikiLeaks' Julian Assange has thought along the same lines when he insisted that his ultimate goal is "to make the world more civil" by making secretive organizations like the US State Department and Department of Defense accountable for their actions.[24] Finally, Ralf Dahrendorf has argued that: "The citizen is a proud creature ready to stand up for the basic values of the open society, ready to go to battle for them if need be. Is the discovery of citizenship, of civil society, of civic sense, and civil behavior a response to the experience of disintegration, to widespread antisocial behavior, and to the crude competition between individuals?" For Dahrendorf, civil society has to do with morality because: "citizens have to be civil and civilized. Expressions like civil courage and civil pride are rightly associated with it."[25]

The wealth of civic mobilizations today—much dependent on existing political structures and cultural traditions—calls for new theoretical approaches that shall better guide us in the existing labyrinth and allow for a more accurate interpretation of human actions. For one, it is clear that there is a species of "civil society" which today, in a direct way, contributes either to global anarchy or to genocide and ecocide. This variety of civil society—skipped over by most contributors in this volume—is at times labeled as "uncivil," suggesting that the ancient distinction between "civilians" and "barbarians"—however well exorcized from the academic lexicon—haunts in the background. Is there a need for a conceptual distinction between the two strong factions of civic movements which today shape the fate of the planet?

Such a distinction implies injecting a normative aspect into the Hegelian definition of civil society. Admittedly, there are hazards connected with arguing for the idea of civil movements as founded on "civility." A normatively charged conception of civil society threatens to romanticize what is actually a field defined by contestation among many actors, many of whom—perhaps most—would claim to act and speak for some ethical or political ideal. Furthermore, as we have argued, while some civil society actors may indeed strike most of us as altruistic, even saintly, and some others, conversely, as obviously selfish or downright evil, most fall somewhere in the middle, peddling self-interest dressed up as selfless idealism. The alternative to a normatively front-loaded, positive definition is an understanding of the civil society concept as value-neutral, referring to an arena for competition and conflict where different groups struggle for the primacy of one set or another of political, ethical, or religious values or ideals. In this view, one person's freedom fighter is another person's terrorist.

However, this position is also problematic, tending toward a moral relativism that is poorly equipped to deal with the major challenges of today—not least for civil society activists themselves for whom the struggle against authoritarian regimes, economic inequality, or environmental disaster is the proverbial struggle of "good" against "evil." Indeed, it may well be that one needs to distinguish between a cool analytical definition of civil society that is value-neutral, and thus useful in the social sciences, and a more impassioned understanding essential to activists for whom the fire of belief is vital to long-term, committed action against all odds.

To corroborate this last proposition, there is increasing evidence to the effect that the ideas of "civil" and "civilized" are universal, however compromised the concept of "civilization" has become in the last hundred years. Almost all modern cultures have some notion of a "civilized behavior," which is about restraints: on libido dominandi, on greed, on rapacious exploitation of the other, on predatory or violent behavior, and on insatiability. Altruism means restraining oneself for the sake of living with the Other. Ding Zilin, a 74-year-old retired Chinese professor of philosophy and the founder of the "Mothers of Tjananmen," would have agreed with this argument. In stressing "civility" and nonviolence as part of her vision, Ding Zilin claims Vaclav Havel, his civil courage and his ideal of "living in truth," have inspired her. Certainly in the current, multiple crisis that threatens a global *civilizational breakdown*, only a social vision embracing a mixture of civility and nonviolent, creative subversion, offers the way out of the present predicament.

Notes

1. See Naomi Klein, "Reclaiming the Commons," *The New Left Review*, 9 May 2001; Klein, *The Shock Doctrine. The Rise of Disaster Capitalism* (New York: Metropolitan Books 2008); Slavoj Žižek, *Living in the End Times* (London: Verso, 2010); Michael Hardt and Antonio Negri, *Multitude: War and Democracy in the Age of Empire* (New York: Penguin, 2004); Michael Hardt and Antonio Negri, *Commonwealth* (Cambridge, M.A.: Harvard University Press, 2011); Amartya Sen, *Identity and Violence: The Illusion of Destiny* (New York and London: W. W. Norton & Company, 2006).
2. See Roger Kimball, "Introduction: The Perils of Humanitarianism," *The New Criterion: "Corrupt Humanitarianism,"* Special Pamphlet (2005).
3. The concepts of civil society and non-governmental organizations (NGOs) are often used interchangeably—the fact that does not contribute to a lesser confusion. In his exploration of "*Civic, civil, or servile?*" (Geneva: International Standing Conference on Philanthropy, 1994) Robin Guthrie defines Civil Society functionally as: "what citizens do together in their own right at the bidding of no higher authority, for the common good, and apart, generally speaking, from direct party political affiliation or alignment. The civil society is, traditionally, not concerned with power, although it may be ranged against the excessive concentration or abuse of power in any quarter." By contrast, legal persons create NGOs, but their aspiration to maintain a non-governmental position makes them resemble, or emulate civil society. The NGOs tacit connection with the existing state (and donor's) jurisdiction gives them a dual identity that will be explored in more detail by some of our contributions.
4. Philippe Schmitter, "Ten Propositions Concerning Civil Society and the Consolidation of Democracy" (Stanford, 2006, unpublished paper). An earlier version was published at the Institute for Advanced Studies in Vienna, under the title "Some Propositions about Civil Society and the Consolidation of Democracy" in *Political Science Series*, vol. 10 (1993).

5. Daniel Wilkinson, "Thee New Challenge to Repressive Cuba," *New York Review of Books*, 19 August 2010.
6. Ernest Gellner, *Nations and Nationalism* (Oxford: Blackwell Publishers, 1983).
7. Rasmus Hansson, "NGOs: Suffocated by Success or Ditched by Development?" Unpublished lecture, Arne Næss Symposium 2007, The University of Oslo.
8. John Keane, Letters to the Editor, *The National Interest*, no 107, May/June 2010.
9. Only in the U.K. it generates over one hundred billion pounds a year, more than large swaths of the private sector.
10. Michael Edwards, *Just Another Emperor: the Myths and Realities of Philantrocapitalism.* (New York: Demos, 2008)
11. See WikiLeaks home page (Accessed 10 January 2012): http://wikileaks.org/About.html
12. Jozef Tischner, *Etos Solidarnosci*, (Krakow: Znak, 1981).
13. Vaclav Havel, "Anti-Political Politics" in *Civil Society and the State*, ed. John Keane (London: Verso, 1988): 398.
14. Margaret Somers, "Narrating and Naturalizing Civil Society and Citizenship Theory: The Place of Political Culture and the Public Sphere," *Sociological Theory* vol. 13, no. 3, (1995): 229–274, 259.
15. G.W.F. Hegel, "Elements of the Philosophy of Right," in *Elements of the Philosophy of Right*, ed. Allen Wood (Cambridge: Cambridge University Press, 1991).
16. Hegel, "Elements of the Philosophy of Right", *Elements of the Philosophy of Right*, 276.
17. Lars Trägårdh, "Rethinking the Nordic Welfare State through a neo-Hegelian Theory of State and Civil Society" in *Journal of Political Ideologies* vol. 15, no. 3, (2010): 227–239; See also Trägårdh's chapter in this book.
18. Jens Stillhoff Sörensen, "Introduction: Reinventing Development for the Twenty-First Century?" *Challenging the Aid Paradigm*, ed. Jens Stillhoff Sörensen (London: Palgrave Macmillan, 2010).
19. Jean Cohen, "Civil Society and Globalization: Rethinking the Categories" in *State and Civil Society in Northern Europe: The Swedish Model Reconsidered*, ed. Lars Trägårdh (New York: Berghahn Books, 2007).
20. Dan Farmer and Charles Mann, "Surveillance Nation" in *MIT Technology Review*, April (2003)
21. Charles Petersen, "Google and Money," *New York Review of Books*, 10 December 2010.
22. Emily Steel and Geoffrey SA. Fowler, "Facebook Online Privacy Breach," *Wall Street Journal*, 18 October 2010.
23. Virginia Heffernan, "The Trouble with E-mail," *New York Times*, 9 May 2011.
24. This may well be the case, though some cynical observers argue that in the Internet domain, technology has outpaced the ethics, and it seems justified to ask whether the ethics can ever catch up again. See Christian Caryl, "Why WikiLeaks Changes Everything," *New York Review of Books*, 13 January 2011.
25. Ralf Dahrendorf, *After 1989: Morals, Revolution, and Civil Society* (New York: St. Martin's Press, 1997): 59.

Chapter 1

CIVIL SOCIETY IN THE ERA OF MONITORY DEMOCRACY

John Keane

Introduction

This opening chapter proposes a fundamental revision of the way we think about representation and democracy in our times. It pinpoints an epochal transformation that has been taking place in the contours and dynamics of democracy as it is experienced within many global settings; it tables the claim that from roughly the mid-twentieth century, representative democracy in territorial state form started to morph into a new historical form of "post-representative" democracy, and explores some of the reasons why this change has happened. The chapter supposes that "end of history" perspectives and maritime metaphors (Huntington's "third wave" of the sea simile has been the most influential) are too limited to grasp the epochal change—too bound to the surface of things, too preoccupied with continuities, and aggregate data to notice that political tides have begun to run in entirely new directions. My conjecture is that the world of actually existing democracy is experiencing an historic sea change, one that is taking us away from the assembly-based and representative models of democracy of past times towards a form of democracy with entirely different contours and dynamics.

It is hard to find an elegant name for it, let alone to describe in a few words its workings and political implications. The strange-sounding term *monitory democracy* is the most exact for describing the big transformation that is taking hold in most regions of the world. Monitory democracy is a new historical form of democracy, a variety of "post-electoral" politics defined by the rapid growth of many different kinds of extra-parliamentary, power-scrutinizing mechanisms.[1] These monitory bodies take root within the "domestic" fields of government and civil society, as well as in "cross-border" settings once controlled by empires, states, and business organizations. In consequence, the whole architecture of self-government is changing. The central grip of elections, political parties, and parliaments on citizens' lives is weakening. Democracy is coming to mean much more than free and fair elections, although nothing less. Within and outside states, independent monitors of power begin to have major tangible effects on the dynamics and meaning of democracy. By putting politicians, parties, and elected governments permanently on their toes, monitory institutions complicate their lives and question their power and authority, often forcing them to chop and change their agendas—sometimes by smothering them in political disgrace.

Whether or not the trend towards this new kind of democracy is a sustainable, historically irreversible development remains to be seen, like its two previous historical antecedents—the assembly-based democracy of the ancient world and modern representative democracy in territorial form—monitory democracy is not inevitable. It did not have to happen, but it nonetheless happened, whether it will live, fade away, or die suddenly remains untreated in this.[2] Certainly when judged by its institutional contours and inner dynamics, monitory democracy is the most complex form of democracy yet. Those with a taste for Latin would say that it is the *tertium quid*, the not fully formed successor of the earlier historical experiments with assembly-based and representative forms of democracy. In the name of "the public," "public accountability," "the people," "stakeholders," or "citizens"—the terms are normally used interchangeably in the age of monitory democracy—power-scrutinizing institutions spring up all over the place, both within the fields of government and beyond, often stretching across borders. Elections, political parties, and legislatures neither disappear nor decline in importance, but they most definitely lose their pivotal position in politics. Contrary to the orthodox claims of many political scientists, democracy is no longer simply a way of handling the power of elected governments by electoral and parliamentary and constitutional means, and no longer a matter confined to territorial states.[3] Gone are the days when democracy could be described (and in the next breath attacked) as "government by the unrestricted will of the majority."[4] Whether in the field of local, national, or supranational government, or in the world of business and other non-governmental organizations and networks—some of them stretching down into the roots of everyday life and outwards, towards the four corners of the earth—people and organizations that exercise power are now routinely subject to public monitoring and public contestation by an assortment of extra-parliamentary bodies.

Here is one striking clue for understanding what is happening: the age of monitory democracy—beginning in 1945—has witnessed the birth of nearly one hundred new types of power-scrutinizing institutions unknown to previous democratic systems. As we shall see, defenders of these watchdog inventions often speak of their importance in solving a basic problem facing contemporary democracies: how to promote their unfinished business of finding new ways of democratic living for little people in big and complex societies, in which substantial numbers of citizens believe that politicians are not easily trusted, and in which governments are often accused of abusing their power or being out of touch with citizens, or simply unwilling to deal with their concerns and problems. By addressing such concerns, the new power-scrutinizing inventions break the grip of the majority rule principle—the worship of numbers—associated with representative democracy. Freed as well from the measured caution and double-speak of political parties, some inventions give a voice to the emotionally charged concerns of minorities that feel left out of official politics. Some monitors, electoral commissions, anti-corruption bodies, and consumer protection agencies for instance, use their alleged neutrality to protect the rules of the democratic game from predators and enemies. Other monitors, for instance in such fields as the environment, pensions, and healthcare, publicize long-term issues that are neglected, or dealt with badly, by the short-term mentality encouraged by election cycles. Still other monitory groups are remarkable for their evanescence; in a fast-changing world, they come on the scene, stir the pot, then move on like nomads, or dissolve into thin air.

By making room for opinions and ways of life that people feel strongly about, despite their neglect or suppression by parties, parliaments, and governments, these monitory inventions have the combined effect of raising the level and quality of public awareness of power, including power relationships "beneath" and "beyond" the institutions of territorial states. It is little wonder that in many countries the new power-monitoring inventions have changed the language of contemporary politics. They prompt much talk of "empowerment," "high energy democracy," "stakeholders," "participatory governance," "communicative democracy," and "deliberative democracy" while helping spread a culture of voting and representation into many walks of life where previously things were decided by less-than-democratic methods. Monitory democracy is the age of surveys, focus groups, deliberative polling, online petitions, and audience and customer voting. Whether intended or not, the spreading culture of voting, backed by the new mechanisms for monitoring power, has the effect of interrupting and often silencing the soliloquies of parties, politicians, and parliaments. The new power-scrutinizing innovations tend to enfranchise many more citizens' voices, sometimes by means of *unelected representatives* skilled at using what Americans sometimes call "bully pulpits."[5] The number and range of monitory institutions have so greatly increased that they point to a world where the old rule of "one person, one vote, one representative"—the central demand in the struggle for representative democracy—is replaced with the new principle of monitory democracy: "one person, many interests, many voices, multiple votes, multiple representatives."

Caution must be exercised when trying to grasp the long-term significance of these new systems of public checks and balances on power; in operative terms, they are certainly not cut from the same cloth, in part because they spring up in many different contexts. It is worth pointing out that the new monitory inventions are not exclusively "American," "European," "OECD," or "Western" products. Among their more remarkable features is the way they have rapidly diffused from all points around the globe. They mushroom in a wide variety of different settings and there are even signs, for the first time in the history of democracy, of mounting awareness of the added value of the art of invention—as if the democratic ability to invent is itself a most valuable invention.

Monitory mechanisms operate in different ways, on different fronts. Some scrutinize power primarily at the level of *citizens' inputs* to government or civil society bodies; other monitory mechanisms are preoccupied with monitoring and contesting what are called *policy throughputs*; still others concentrate on scrutinizing the *policy outputs of* governmental or non-governmental organizations. Quite a few of the inventions concentrate simultaneously upon all three dimensions. Monitory mechanisms also come in different sizes and operate on various spatial scales, ranging from "just round the corner" bodies with merely local footprints to global networks aimed at keeping tabs on those who exercise power over great distances.

Given such variations, it should not be surprising that a quick, short list of the post-1945 inventions resembles—at first sight, to the untrained eye—a magpie's nest of randomly collected items. The list includes: citizen juries, bioregional assemblies, participatory budgeting, advisory boards, and focus groups. There are think tanks, consensus conferences, teach-ins, public memorials, local community consultation schemes, and open houses (developed for instance in the field of architecture) that offer information and advisory and advocacy services, archive and research facilities, and opportunities for professional networking. Citizens' assemblies, democratic audits, brainstorming conferences, conflict of interest boards, global associations of parliamentarians against corruption and constitutional safaris (famously used by the drafters of the new South African constitution to examine best practice elsewhere) are on the list. So too are the many inventions of India's banyan democracy: railway courts, *lok adalats*, public interest litigation, and *satyagraha* methods of civil resistance. Included as well are consumer testing agencies and consumer councils; online petitions and chat rooms; democracy clubs and cafés; public vigils; and peaceful sieges, summits, and global watchdog organizations set up to bring greater public accountability to business and other civil society bodies. The list of innovations extends to deliberative polls, boards of accountancy, independent religious courts, expert councils (such as the "Five Wise Men" of the Council of Economic Advisers in Germany), public "scorecards," public consultation exercises, weblogs, electronic civil disobedience, and websites dedicated to monitoring the abuse of power (such as Bully OnLine, a U.K.-based initiative that aims to tackle workplace bullying and related issues). The list of new inventions also includes self-selected opinion polls ("SLOPs") and unofficial ballots (text-messaged straw polls, for instance), international criminal courts, truth and reconciliation commissions, global social forums, and the tendency of increasing numbers of non-governmental organizations to adopt written constitutions with an elected component.

Let us pause, for evidently the list of inventions is disjointed, and potentially confusing. Clear-headed thinking is needed to spot the qualities that these inventions share in common. Monitory institutions play various roles. They are committed to providing publics with extra viewpoints and better information about the performance of various governmental and non-governmental bodies; because they appeal to and depend upon publics, monitory institutions (to scotch a possible misunderstanding) are not to be confused with top-down surveillance mechanisms that operate in secret, for the private purposes of organizations of government or civil society. Monitory mechanisms are geared as well to the definition, scrutiny, and enforcement of public standards and ethical rules for preventing corruption, or the improper behavior of those responsible for making decisions, not only in the field of elected government, but in a wide variety of power settings. The new institutions of monitory democracy are further defined by their overall commitment to strengthening the diversity and influence of citizens' voices and choices in decisions that affect their lives. Regardless of the outcome of elections, and sometimes in direct opposition to the principle of majority rule, monitors give a voice to the losers and provide independent representation for minorities, especially to indigenous, the disabled, and other peoples who can never expect to lay claim to being a majority.

Political Geography

What is distinctive about monitory democracy is the way *all fields* of social and political life come to be scrutinized, not just by the standard machinery of representative democracy, but by a whole host of *non-party, extra-parliamentary, and often unelected bodies* operating within, underneath, and beyond the boundaries of territorial states. In the era of monitory democracy it is as if the principles of representative democracy—public openness, citizens' equality, selecting representatives—are superimposed on representative democracy itself. This has many practical consequences, but one especially striking effect is to alter the patterns of interaction—political geography—of democratic institutions.

Once upon a time, in the brief heyday of representative democracy, the thing called democracy had a rather simple political geography (figure 1). Within the confines of any given state, democracy meant (from the point of view of citizens) following an election campaign and on the great day of reckoning turning out to vote for a party or independent candidate. He—it was almost always men—was someone local, a figure known to the community, a local shopkeeper, professional, someone in business, or a trade unionist, for instance. Then came democracy's great ceremony: the pause of deliberation, the calm of momentary reflection, the catharsis of ticking and crossing, before the storm of result. "Universal peace is declared," was the sarcastic way the nineteenth-century English novelist George Eliot (1819–1880) put it, "and the foxes have a sincere interest in prolonging the lives of the poultry." Her American contemporary, Walt Whitman (1819–1892), spoke more positively of the pivotal function of

---

Figure 1: Territorially-bound Representative Democracy

polling day as the great "choosing day"; the "powerfulest scene"; a "sword-less conflict" mightier than Niagara Falls, the Mississippi River, or the gey-sers of Yellowstone a "still small voice vibrating"; a time for "the peaceful choice of all"; a passing moment of suspended animation when "the heart pants, life glows."[6] If blessed with enough votes, the local representative joined a privileged small circle of legislators whose job was to stay in line with party policy, support or oppose a government that used its major-ity in the legislature, to pass laws and to scrutinize their implementation, hopefully with results that pleased as many of the represented as possible. At the end of a limited stint as legislator, the buck passing stopped. Foxes and poultry fell quiet. It was again time for the swordless conflict of the great choosing day. The representative either stepped down into retire-ment from political life, or faced the music of re-election.

This is obviously a simplified sketch of the role of elections, but it serves to highlight the different, more complex political geography of monitory democracy. It is important to recognize historical continuities, of course. Just as representative democracies preserved assemblies, so monitory democracies preserve legislatures, political parties, and elec-tions which continue to be bitterly fought and closely contested affairs. But such is the growing variety of interlaced, power-monitoring mecha-nisms that democrats from earlier times, if catapulted into the new world of monitory democracy, would find hard to understand.

The new democracy demands a shift of perspective, a break with con-ventional thinking in order to understand its political geography. For this purpose, let us imagine for a moment, as if from an aerial satellite, the contours of the new democracy. We would spot that its power-scrutiniz-ing institutions are less centered on elections, parties, and legislatures; no longer confined to the territorial state; and spatially arranged in ways much messier than textbooks on democracy typically suppose (see figure 2). The vertical "depth" and horizontal "reach" of monitory institutions is striking. If the number of levels within any hierarchy of institutions is a measure of its "depth," and if the number of units located within each of these levels is called its "span" or "width," then monitory democracy is the deepest and widest system of democracy ever known. The political geog-raphy of mechanisms like audit commissions, citizens' assemblies, web-based think tanks, local assemblies, regional parliaments, summits, and global watchdog organizations defies simple-minded descriptions. So too does the political geography of the wider constellation of power-checking and power-disputing mechanisms in which they are embedded—bodies like citizen assemblies and juries, audit and integrity commissions, and many other watchdog organizations set up to bring greater public ac-countability to business and other civil society bodies.

Figure 2: Monitory Democracy

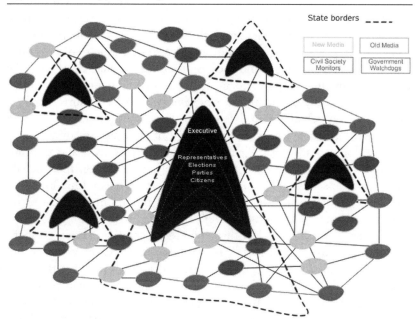

Some Misconceptions

Both the novelty and complexity of monitory democracy make it vulnerable to a handful of misconceptions. It is important to give careful consideration to these possible misunderstandings, if only to prepare the way for a richer, more nuanced, and politically relevant account of a fundamental shift that is well under way in the real world of democracy.

Representation

While it is often said that the struggle to bring greater public accountability to government and non-government organizations that wield power over others is in effect a struggle for "grassroots democracy," "participatory democracy," or "popular empowerment," the metaphors rest on a misunderstanding of contemporary trends.

The age of monitory democracy is not heading backwards; it is not motivated by efforts to recapture the (imagined) spirit of assembly-based democracy—"power to the people"—as some supporters of groups like Students for a Democratic Society (SDS) liked to chant at political demonstrations during the 1960s. Many contemporary champions of "deep" or "direct" democracy still speak as if they are Greeks, as if what really counts for a democracy is "the commitment and capacities of ordinary people to make sensible decisions through reasoned deliberation and [they are] empowered because they attempt to tie action to discussion."[7] The reality of monitory democracy is otherwise, in that all of the new power-scrutinizing experiments in the name of "the people" or citizens' empowerment rely inevitably on *representation*, that is, claims made by some actors on behalf and in defense of others. These experiments often draw their legitimacy from "the people,"[8] but they are not understandable as efforts to abolish the gap between representatives and the represented, as if citizens could live without others acting on their behalf, find their true selves, and express themselves as equals within a unified political community no longer burdened by miscommunication or by misgovernment.

Monitory democracy in fact thrives on representation. Take the much-discussed example of citizens' assemblies. In the early years of the twenty-first century, among the most talked about cases was the Citizens' Assembly on Electoral Reform in the Canadian province of British Columbia. Backed by the local legislature, the Citizens' Assembly worked for the best part of a year as an independent, non-partisan body charged with the task of casting a critical eye over the province's electoral system. The Assembly had 161 members; it included 1 woman and 1 man drawn randomly from each of the province's 79 electoral districts, plus 2 aboriginal citizen representatives, as well as 1 representative from the province's Legislative Assembly. The member representatives of the Citizens' Assembly were not elected, but drawn by lot. In contrast to the Greek trust in the deities as underwriters of decisions determined by lot, the Assembly members were chosen at random by a computer, from a pool that was supposed to reflect the age, gender, and geographical makeup of British Columbian citizens. Granted its own budget, the Citizens' Assembly was designed to operate outside the system of political parties, and to keep its distance from the legislature, organized lobby groups, and journalists. Its duty was to act as an unelected body of temporary representatives of all British Columbians.

Elections

Another misconception, related to the changing status and significance of elections, prevents many people from spotting the novelty of monitory democracy. Since 1945, when there were only a dozen democracies left on the face of the earth, party-based democracy has made a big come-back, so much so that it tricked scholars like Fukuyama and Huntington into thinking that nothing had changed, except for a large global leap in the number of representative democracies. They can be forgiven: fol-lowing the widespread collapse and near extinction of democracy during the first half of the twentieth century, it is indeed true that most parts of the world have since become familiar with the basic institutions of elec-toral democracy. Conventional party-centered forms of representation do not simply wither away. Millions of people have grown accustomed to competition among political parties, periodic elections, the limited-term holding of political office, and the right of citizens to assemble in public to make their views known to their representatives in legislatures and executives that operate within the jurisdictional boundaries of territorial states. In contexts as different as Sri Lanka, Nigeria, Trinidad and Tobago, Malta, and Botswana, the mechanisms of electoral democracy have taken root for the first time. In other contexts, especially those where electoral democracy is well embedded, experiments have been conducted to im-prove the rules of the electoral game, for instance by introducing primary elections into political parties, tightening restrictions on campaign fund-raising and spending, improving voting facilities for disabled citizens, and banning party hopping (a decision taken by the Brazilian Supreme Court in 2007).

For all these reasons, it seemed perfectly reasonable for Huntington and other scholars to speak of the spectacular rebirth and extension of representative forms of democracy in recent decades as a "third wave" of democratization. Enter monitory democracy: a brand new historical type of democracy that operates in radically different ways from textbook accounts of "representative," "liberal," or "parliamentary" democracy, as it is still often called. In the age of monitory democracy, democracy is prac-ticed in new ways. Where monitory democracy exists, institutions like periodic elections, multi-party competition, and the right of citizens to voice their public approval or disapproval of legislation remain familiar fixtures. To repeat: under conditions of monitory democracy, the whole issue of who is entitled to vote, and under which conditions, continues to attract public attention, and to stir up troubles. Think of the legal and political controversies sparked by the question of who owns the software of unreliable electronic voting machines manufactured by companies such as Election Systems and Software. Or consider the disputes trig-gered by the withdrawal of votes for people such as felons; or by claims that groups such as diasporas, minority language speakers, the disabled, and people with low literacy and number skills are disadvantaged by the secret ballot; or the loud public complaints about how still other constituencies, such as women, young people, and the biosphere, are either poorly represented, or are not properly represented at all.

Struggles to open up and improve the quality of electoral and legislative representation are by no means finished. But slowly and surely, the whole architecture of democracy has begun to change fundamentally. So too has the meaning of democracy. No longer synonymous with self-government by an assembly of privileged male citizens (as in the Greek city-states), or with party-based government guided by the will of a legislative majority, democracy has come to mean a way of life and a mode of governing in which power is subject to checks and balances—at any time, in any place—such that nobody is entitled to rule arbitrarily, without the consent of the governed, or their representatives. An important symptom of the redefinition of democracy is the advent of election monitoring. During the 1980s, for the first time in the history of democracy, founding elections in new or strife-torn polities began to be monitored systematically by outside teams of observers. The practice was admittedly an older invention, first used in the 1850s when Prussian, French, British, Russian, Turkish, and Austrian representatives jointly supervised a plebiscite in Moldavia and Wallachia; but in the new circumstances of monitory democracy, the methods of election monitoring assume a much more powerful and publicly visible role, on a global scale. "Fair and open" methods—the elimination of violence, intimidation, ballot-rigging, and other forms of political tomfoolery—are now expected of all countries, including the most powerful democracy on the face of the Earth, the United States, where observers from the Organization for Security and Co-operation in Europe (OSCE) played a role for the first time, in the presidential elections of November 2004.

Civil Society

In the era of monitory democracy, the franchise struggles that once tore whole societies apart have lost their centrality. As the culture of voting spreads, and as unelected representatives multiply in many different contexts, a brand new issue begins to surface. The old question that racked the age of representative democracy—*who* is entitled to vote and *when*—is compounded and complicated by a question for which there are still no easy answers: *where* are people entitled to vote, *for whom*, and *through which representatives?*

The intense public concern with publicly scrutinizing matters once thought to be non-political is unique to the age of monitory democracy. The era of representative democracy (as Tocqueville spotted) certainly saw the rise of self-organized pressure groups and schemes for "socializing" the power of government, for instance through councils of soldiers, workers' control of industry, and Guild Socialist proposals. Yet few of these schemes survived the violent upheavals of the first half of the twentieth century, which makes the contrast with monitory democracy all the more striking. The sea change in favor of extra-parliamentary monitors is evident in the unprecedented level of interest in the old eighteenth-century European term "civil society"; for the first time in the history of democracy, democrats around the world now routinely use these two words. The change is also manifest in the strong trend towards the independent public scrutiny of all areas of government policy, ranging from public concern about the maltreatment and legal rights of children and bodily habits related to exercise and diet, through to the development of habitat protection plans and efforts to take democracy "upstream" to ensure that the future development (for instance) of nanotechnology and genetically-modified food is governed publicly in the interests of the many, not the few. Experiments with fostering new forms of citizens' participation and elected representation have begun to penetrate markets; a notable early example, an invention of the mid-1940s, is the German system of co-determination, known as *Mitbestimmung*, in which employees in firms of a certain size are entitled to elect their own representatives onto the management boards of companies.

In the age of monitory democracy, there is rising awareness as well of the possibility and desirability of exercising rights of criticism and casting a vote in public service organizations, for instance in the areas of health and social care design and patient choice. The experience of voting for representatives even extends into large-scale global organizations. An example is the International Olympic Committee (IOC): once an exclusive private gentlemen's club, during the 1980s it became the target of muckraking journalism. Scandals ensued; public outcries followed. Under pressure, against considerable odds, the IOC began to apply monitory mechanisms to its own corrupted structures. Some things didn't change; by 2002, the IOC body of 115 co-opted members included only 12 women; in that year, not one woman was among the 66 new member nominations. But some things did change. Visits by IOC members to candidate cities were banned. An IOC Ethics Commission and a World Anti-Doping Agency were formed. Reports of income and expenditure were published for the first time. IOC meetings were thrown open to the media. A so-called Nominations Committee was set up for the purpose of more fairly deciding IOC membership, which was restricted to an eight-year term, renewable through election. Olympic athletes were granted the right to elect their own representatives to the

IOC directly. The upper age limit of IOC members was reduced from 80- to 70-years-old. And the rules of representative government were for the first time applied to its inner workings, at least on paper. The co-opted members of the IOC were required hereon to meet in Session at least once a year. What is interesting is that, unlike, say, the United Nations General Assembly, the Session members were expected to act as the IOC's representatives in their respective countries, not as delegates of their country within the IOC. The Session became something of a post-national or global assembly, a body charged with electing a President for an eight-year term, renewable once for four additional years. The Session also determined the membership of a powerful Executive Board. Elected by secret ballot, by a majority of votes cast, for terms of four years, the Executive Board came to function as the inner body ultimately responsible for managing the common affairs of the IOC including the recommendation of new IOC members, monitoring the codes of conduct of existing members, and the overall performance of the IOC itself.

Watchdogs

The vital role played by civil societies in the invention of power-monitoring mechanisms seems to confirm what might be called James Madison's Law of Free Government: no government can be considered free unless it is capable of governing a society that is itself capable of controlling the government. The Law (sketched in the *Federalist Papers*, number 51) has tempted some people to conclude—mistakenly—that governments are quite incapable of scrutinizing their own power. The truth is sometimes otherwise. In the era of monitory democracy, experience shows that governments, for their own sake as well as the good of their own citizens, can be encouraged to submit their own powers to independent public scrutiny.

Government "watchdog" institutions are a case in point. Their stated purpose is the public scrutiny of government by semi-independent government agencies (it is worth remembering that the word scrutiny originally meant "to sort rubbish," from the Latin *scrutari*, meaning "to search," and from *scruta*, "rubbish"). Scrutiny mechanisms supplement the power-monitoring role of elected government representatives and judges, even though this is not always their stated aim; very often they are introduced under the general authority of elected governments, for instance through ministerial responsibility. In practice, things often turn out differently. Government scrutiny bodies tend to take on a life of their own, especially when they are protected by legislation, given adequate resources, and managed well. Building on the much older precedents of royal commissions, public enquiries, and independent auditors checking the financial probity of government agencies—inventions that had their roots in the age of representative democracy—the new scrutiny mechanisms add checks and balances to avoid possible abuses of power by elected representatives. Often they are justified in terms of enhancing the efficiency and effectiveness of government, for instance through improved decision making that has the added advantage of raising the level of public trust in political institutions among citizens considered as "stakeholders." The process displays a double paradox. Not only are government scrutiny mechanisms often established by governments who subsequently fail to control the workings of these same mechanisms, for instance in cases of corruption and the enforcement of legal standards; the new mechanisms also have democratic, power-checking effects, even though they are normally staffed by judges, professional experts, and other un-elected officials who themselves operate at several arms' length from the rhythm of periodic elections.

The independent "integrity systems" that came to enjoy an important public profile in various states in Australia during the 1970s and 1980s are good examples. Following repeated media exposure of fraud and corruption among politicians and police, in some cases with links to business and organized crime, monitory agencies were established to bring new eyes, ears, and teeth to the public sector. The aim was to crack down on intentional wrongdoing or misconduct by elected representatives and appointed officials; fingers were also pointed at the lax and self-serving complaints systems operated by the police, who are to democratic governments what sharp edges are to knives. Misgivings were also expressed about the reluctance of elected ministers to oversee publicly sensitive police operational matters. During the 1970s two royal commissions in the state of South Australia made changes that subsequently led to the establishment in 1985 of the first Police Complaints Authority. Other states followed suit, culminating in Queensland's Criminal Justice Commission (later the Crime and Misconduct Commission). Established in 1990 as a combined anti-corruption and criminal detection body, it was charged with the job of exposing corruption within the public sector, undertaking crime research, gathering evidence of organized crime, and tracking and recovering criminal proceeds.

Cross-Border Democracy?

In the age of monitory democracy, there are strong prejudices against the very idea of "cross-border" or "international" democracy. These prejudices date from, and have their roots in, the era of territorially bound representative democracy, and in consequence almost all leading scholars of democracy today defend the supposed truth of such propositions as "democracy requires statehood" and "without a state there can be no democracy."

One interesting thing about monitory democracy is that it helps to confront these prejudices head on; its latticed patterns of power monitoring effectively scramble the distinction between "domestic" and "foreign," the "local" and the "global." Like other types of institutions, including business and universities, democracy too is caught up in a process of "glocalization." This is another way of saying that its monitory mechanisms are dynamically inter-related, to the point where each monitor functions simultaneously as both part and whole of the overall system. In other words, in the system of monitory democracy parts and wholes do not exist in a strict or absolute sense. Its units are better described as sub-wholes—"holons" is the term famously coined by Arthur Koestler—that function simultaneously as self-regarding and self-asserting entities that push and pull each other in a multi-lateral system in which all entities play a role, sometimes to the point where the part and the whole are blurred beyond recognition.

The example of summits, a remarkable mid-twentieth century invention, helps bring this abstract language down to earth. Among the many ironies associated with the birth and development of monitory democracy is that summits began as exercises in big power politics, as informal ad hoc meetings of heads of state, leaders of government, or foreign ministers—the kind of meetings that first took place during the fragile Soviet/American/British alliance against Hitler. Some people have reported that the word "summit" was first used to describe the so-called "percentages agreement" at the October 1944 meeting in Moscow, when Churchill and Stalin speculated about their ratios of influence in the post-war world. Whatever its origins, the word "summit" soon morphed into a term with mountain climbing connotations, exactly as Churchill himself thought should happen when advocating the tactic of high-level informal meetings in international relations. He spoke of "summit diplomacy" and the benefits of a "parley at the summit," which is the sense that prevailed in Geneva in 1955, when the mountain climbing word "summit" was used for the first time to describe a Cold War meeting of the political leaders of the United States, the Soviet Union, France, and Britain.

From the end of World War II until the time of the famous Vienna Summit meeting between Kennedy and Khrushchev (June 3–5, 1961), there were over 100 such summits, each using broadly similar methods.

The meetings were preoccupied with the dynamics of the Cold War, and so had both a global reach and a strong bipolarity about them. Whether used as tools of amity or enmity, the early summits were also marked by a strong measure of predictability. The rule was that no statesman was willing to risk the certainty of humiliation. Hence, the great attention paid to dramaturgy. The effect—like the old rituals of European monarchy—was to reinforce the sense among audiences that these were top-down affairs, proof that the world was run by just a handful of men.

During the last decades of the twentieth century, the wholly surprising thing about summits was their dramatic transformation into sites where the power of elected representatives was publicly contested. Summits morphed into monitory mechanisms. The altered meaning and function of summits was evident at a series of high-level meetings between Reagan and Gorbachev, including the 1986 Reykjavik gathering, where—without prior consultation with NATO and other bodies—the abolition of ballistic missiles and strategic nuclear weapons—meaning all nuclear weapons—was proposed. From then on, summits began to be used by leaders to force their bureaucracies into major policy shifts in a wide variety of contexts. That had the knock-on effect of politicizing government, making it clear to wider audiences, both inside and outside government, that different political options existed.

The tendency of summitry to remain cloaked in secrecy and pageantry backfired. Summits began to attract the attention of thousands of journalists eager to report stories and images of exclusive and powerful clubs. Beginning with the G7 Summit in Bonn in May 1985 (which attracted 30,000 demonstrators demanding greater global justice), its annual meetings provided an opportunity for civil society organizations and protesters to press their concerns related to matters as diverse as international trade and terrorism to energy development and cross-border crime—in effect, by turning rulers into culpable representatives. Similar trends were visible from the time of the 1988 IMF and World Bank meetings in Berlin, which attracted up to 80,000 well-briefed and well-organized protesters, and in the subsequent string of UN-sponsored summits that sparked off preparatory meetings, teach-ins, and planned mobilizations that descended on the Children's Summit (1990), the Earth Summit (1992), the Conference on Human Rights (1993), and the Conference on Women (1995). Perhaps the most spectacular attempt to transform top-down governmental summits into new channels of bottom-up representation of the interests of civil society happened in July 2005 with Live 8—the name alluded to the G8 group of states—a network of "global awareness" concerts calling upon political leaders to "Make Poverty History."

Political Efficacy

It is sometimes said that the public business of power scrutiny changes very little, that states and corporations are still the "real" centers of power in deciding not only who gets what in the world but also when and how. Evidence that this is not necessarily so is suggested by the fact that all of the big public issues that have erupted around the world since 1945, including civil rights for women and minorities, opposition to nuclear weapons and American military intervention in Vietnam and Iraq, poverty reduction, and the greening of politics, have been generated not by political parties, elections, legislatures, and governments, but principally by power-monitoring networks that run parallel to—and are often aligned against—the conventional mechanisms of party-based parliamentary representation.

The powerful civil rights movement that sprang up during the 1950s in the United States was among the pacesetters. Its inventive tactics—bus boycotts, improvement associations, co-coordinating committees, sit-ins, kneel-ins, "jail-no-bail" pledges, freedom rides, citizenship schools, freedom singing, voter registration drives, mock elections—were positive proof that monitory bodies could have effects upon existing power relations by forcing many citizens to sense the contingency of those relations, often through bitter battles, sometimes resulting in surprising victories for citizens bent on humbling the powerful. The tactics eventually produced two historic pieces of legislation. The Civil Rights Act, signed by President Johnson on 2 July 1964, barred racial discrimination in public accommodations, education, and employment. The Voting Rights Act, signed by Johnson on 6 August 1965, abolished literacy tests, poll taxes, and other restrictions on voting, in addition to authorizing federal government intervention in states and individual voting districts that continued to use such tests to discriminate against African Americans. The enactment of the two vital pieces of legislation was an example of monitory democracy in action. The laws proved that the powerless had the power to change things, and that change had to begin in the home, the workplace, and in other public fields of everyday life, before spreading across the whole of the political and social landscape of the American democracy.

Why Monitory Democracy?

Now that we have tackled some misconceptions about the main contours and dynamics of monitory democracy, let us pause to ask one short question: how can its unplanned birth be explained?

The forces that resulted in the various power-scrutinizing inventions described above are certainly complicated; as in earlier phases of the history of democracy, generalizations concerning origins are as difficult as they are perilous. In lieu of a more detailed analysis, two things can safely be said. More obviously, the new type of democracy has had both its causes and causers. Monitory democracy is not a monogenic matter—a living thing hatched from a single cell. It is rather the result of multiple pressures that have conspired over time to reshape the spirit, language, and institutions of democracy as we know it today. The other thing about which we can be certain is that one word above all describes the most powerful early trigger of the new era of monitory democracy: war.

In the history of democracy, war and the pity and suffering of war have often been the midwife of new democratic institutions. That rule certainly applied to the first half of the twentieth century, the most murderous ever recorded in human history. Two global wars plus terrible cruelties shattered old structures of security, sparked pushes and shoves and elbowing for power, as well as unleashed angry popular energies that fed major upheavals—revolutions, usually in the name of "the people," against representative democracy. Bolshevism and Stalinism in Russia, Fascism in Italy, Nazism in Germany, and military imperialism in Japan were effectively twisted and perverted mutations of democracy, which was typically misunderstood within these regimes as a mere synonym for popular sovereignty. These were regimes whose leaders acknowledged that "the people" were entitled to mount the stage of history—regimes whose hirelings then set about muzzling, maiming, and murdering both opponents and supporters among flesh-and-blood people. Western democracy was denounced as parliamentary dithering and muddling, as liberal perplexity, bourgeois hypocrisy, and military cowardice. A third of the way into the twentieth century, parliamentary democracy was on its knees. It seemed rudderless, spiritless, paralyzed, doomed. By 1941, when President Roosevelt called for "bravely shielding the great flame of democracy from the blackout of barbarism,"[9] when untold numbers of villains had drawn the contrary conclusion that dictatorship and totalitarianism were the future, only eleven electoral democracies remained on the face of the earth.[10]

It was exactly the possibility of annihilation that galvanized minds and gritted determinations to do something, both about the awful destruction produced by war, and the dictatorships and totalitarian regimes spawned by those wars. The great cataclysms that culminated in World War II demonstrated to many people the naïveté of the old formula, that people should obey their governments because their rulers protected their lives and possessions. The devastating upheavals of the period proved that this protection-obedience formula was unworkable, that in various countries long-standing pacts between rulers and ruled had been so violated that rulers could no longer be trusted to rule. The problem, in other words, was no longer the mobocracy of "the people," as critics of democracy had insisted from the time of Plato and Thucydides until well into the nineteenth century. The terrible events of the first half of the twentieth century proved that mobocracy had its true source in thuggish leaders skilled in the arts of manipulating "the people." That being so, the problem was no longer the mob, and mob rule—ruling itself was the problem.

The problem of ruling stood at the center of an important—though unfortunately little studied—batch of political reflections on democracy in the years immediately after 1945.[11] The intellectual roots of monitory democracy are traceable to this period. They are, for instance, evident in the contributions of literary, theological, and intellectual figures otherwise as different as Albert Camus, Sidney Hook, Thomas Mann, Jacques Maritain and, most strikingly, in a work that soon became a classic, Reinhold Niebuhr's *The Children of Light and the Children of Darkness* (1945). Each of these authors voiced fears that the narrow escape of parliamentary democracy from the clutches of war and totalitarianism might just be a temporary reprieve; several writers even asked whether the destruction of parliamentary democracy by war and totalitarian power served as confirmation that global events were now pushing towards a Camusian "end of the world" (Camus). All these authors agreed that among the vital lessons provided by recent historical experience was the way majority-rule democracy could be utterly corrupted, to the point where its mechanisms were used and abused by the enemies of democracy, in the name of the "sovereign people," to destroy the plural freedoms and political equality for which democracy avowedly stood. Deeply troubled, each author called for new remedies for the maladies of representative democracy, beginning with the abandonment of sentimental optimism. Beyond that point opinions were divided, but all of these writers of the 1940s restated their support for a new form of democracy, one whose spirit and institutions were infused with a robust commitment to rooting out the devils of arbitrary, publicly unaccountable power. The American theologian Niebuhr (1892–1971), who later won prominent admirers including Martin Luther King, Jr., provided one of weightiest cases for renewing and transforming democracy along these lines. "The perils of uncontrolled power are perennial reminders of the virtues of a democratic society," he wrote. "But modern democracy requires a more realistic philosophical and religious basis, not only in order to anticipate and understand the perils to which it is exposed, but also to give it a more persuasive justification." He concluded with words that became famous,

"Man's capacity for justice makes democracy possible; but man's inclination to injustice makes democracy necessary."[12]

This kind of thinking about the political dangers of injustice undoubtedly helped inspire one of the most remarkable features of monitory democracy: the marriage of democracy and human rights, and the subsequent worldwide growth of organizations, networks, and campaigns committed to the defense of human rights. The intermarriage had roots extending back to the French Revolution, certainly, but its immediate inspiration was two major political declarations inspired by the horrors of World War II: the United Nations Charter (1945) and the Universal Declaration of Human Rights (1948). The second was arguably the more remarkable candle in the gloom bred by the death of forty-five million people, terrible physical destruction and spiritual misery, and the mounting post-war tensions bound up with such political troubles as the bloody partition of Pakistan and India, the Berlin blockade, and the unresolved future of Palestine. Drafted in 1947 and 1948, the Universal Declaration of Human Rights seemed to many at the time a mere sideshow of questionable importance. Its preamble spoke of "the inherent dignity" and "the equal and inalienable rights of all members of the human family." It was, in effect, a call for civil societies and governments everywhere to speak and act as if human rights mattered; its practical effect was to help redefine democracy as monitory democracy. Today, networked organizations like Human Rights Watch, the Aga Khan Development Network, Amnesty International, and tens of thousands of other non-governmental human rights organizations routinely deal with a wide range of rights matters including torture, child soldiers, the abuse of women, and freedom of religious conviction. Their job is the advocacy of human rights through well-researched, skillfully publicized campaigns. They see themselves as goads to the conscience of governments and citizens, and they solve a basic problem that had dogged representative democracy: who decides who "the people" are? Most human rights organizations and networks answer: every human being is entitled to exercise their right to have rights.

Communicative Abundance

The fact that the intermarriage of human rights and democracy and that many monitory institutions sprang to life after 1945 proved that war is not always (as Percy *Bysshe Shelley* famously said in *Queen Mab*) the statesman's game, the priest's delight, the lawyer's jest, and the hired assassin's trade. Sometimes it is also an opportunity for citizens and institution builders to take things into their own hands. But if total war was the prime initial catalyst of the birth of monitory democracy, then, without doubt, communication media are among the principal drivers of its subsequent growth.

No explanation of monitory democracy would be credible without taking into account the way power and conflict are shaped by new media institutions. Think of it like this: every historical era of democracy is intertwined with a different mode of communication. Assembly-based democracy in the ancient Greek city-states belonged to an era dominated by the spoken word, backed up by laws written on papyrus and stone, and by messages dispatched by foot, donkey, and horse. 18th century representative democracy sprang up in the era of print culture—the book, pamphlet, and newspaper, and telegraphed and mailed messages—and fell into crisis during the advent of early mass communication media, especially radio, cinema, and (in its infancy) television. By contrast, monitory democracy is tied closely to the growth of multi-media saturated societies—societies whose structures of power are continuously questioned by monitory institutions operating within a new galaxy of media defined by the ethos of communicative abundance.

Compared with the era of representative democracy, when print culture and limited spectrum audio-visual media were much more closely aligned with political parties and governments, the age of monitory democracy witnesses constant public scrutiny and spats about power, to the point where it seems as if no organization or leader within the fields of government or social life is immune from political trouble.[13] The turbulence is being shaped by a variety of forces, including the decline of journalism proud of its commitment to fact-based "objectivity" (an ideal born of the age of representative democracy) and the rise of adversarial and "gotcha" styles of commercial journalism driven by ratings, sales, and hits. Technical factors, such as electronic memory, tighter channel spacing, new frequency allocation, direct satellite broadcasting, digital tuning, and advanced compression techniques have also been important. Chief among these technical factors is the advent of cable- and satellite-linked, computerized communications, which from the end of the 1960s triggered both product and process innovations in virtually every field of an increasingly commercialized media. This new galaxy of media has no historical precedent. Symbolized by one of its core components, the Internet, it is a whole new system of overlapping and interlinked media devices that integrate texts, sounds, and images and enable communication to take place through multiple user points, in chosen time, either real or delayed, within modularized and ultimately global networks that are affordable and accessible to many hundreds of millions of people scattered across the globe.

In the era of monitory democracy, all institutions in the business of scrutinizing power rely heavily on these media innovations; if the new galaxy of communicative abundance suddenly imploded, monitory democracy would not last long. Monitory democracy and computerized media networks behave as if they are conjoined twins. To say this is not to fall into the trap of supposing that computer-linked communications networks prefigure a brand new utopian world, a carnival of "virtual communities" homesteading on the electronic frontier, a "cyber-revolution" that yields equal access of all citizens to all media, anywhere, and at any time. The new age of communicative abundance in fact produces many symptoms of media decadence: disappointments, instability, and self-contradictions, for instance in the widening power gaps between communication rich and poor, who themselves seem almost unneeded as communicators, or as consumers of media products, simply because they have no market buying power. The majority of the world's people are too poor to make a telephone call; only a tiny minority has access to the Internet. The divide between media rich and media poor citizens blights all monitory democracies; it contradicts their basic principle that all citizens equally are entitled to communicate their opinions and periodically to give elected and unelected representatives a rough ride.

Yet despite such contradictions and disappointments, there are new and important things happening inside the swirling galaxy of communicative abundance. A striking example is the way "private life" and "privacy," and the wheeling and dealing of power that used to take place "in private," have been put on the defensive. Past generations would find the whole process astonishing in its global scale and democratic intensity. With the click of a camera, or the flick of a switch, the world of the private can suddenly be made public. Everything from the bedroom to the boardroom, the bureaucracy and the battlefield, seems to be up for media grabs. Thanks to stories told by citizens and professional journalists, themselves unelected representatives of publics, this is an age in which private text messages and video footage rebound publicly, to reveal sexual infidelity or alleged rape and force the resignation of a leading government official. It is an era in which Sony hand-held cameras are used by off-air reporters, known as "embeds," to file ongoing videos and blogs featuring election candidates live, unplugged, and unscripted; this is the age in which video footage proves that soldiers in war zones raped women, terrorized children, and tortured innocent civilians. In the age of communicative abundance, the private lives of politicians, unelected representatives, and celebrities and their romances, parties, health, drug habits, quarrels, and divorces are the interest and fantasy objects of millions of people. And thanks to talk shows, blogs, social networking sites, and other media acts, there is an endless procession of "ordinary people" talking publicly about their private fears, fantasies, hopes, and expectations. There are even simulated elections, in which audiences granted a "vote" by media companies are urged to lodge their preference for the star of their choice, by acclamation, cell phone, or the Internet.

Helped along by red-blooded journalism that relies on styles of reporting concerned less with veracity than with "breaking news" and blockbusting scoops, communicative abundance sometimes cuts like a knife into the power relations of government and civil society. It is easy to complain about the methods of the new journalism. It hunts in packs, its eyes on bad news, egged on by the newsroom saying that facts must never be allowed to get in the way of stories. It loves titillation, draws upon unattributed sources, fills news holes—in the era of monitory democracy news never sleeps—spins sensations, and concentrates too much on personalities, rather than time-bound contexts. The new journalism is formulaic and gets bored too quickly, and it likes to bow down to corporate power and government press briefings. It produces flat earth news and it serves as a vehicle for the public circulation of organized lies. These and other objections to media decadence must be taken seriously, but they are only half the story. For in spite of many worrying trends, red-blooded journalism, evident for instance in the controversial cablegrams released by WikiLeaks, helps keep alive the old utopias of shedding light on power, of "freedom of information," "government in the sunshine," and greater "transparency" in the making of decisions. Given that unchecked power still weighs down hard on the heads of citizens, it is not surprising, thanks to the new journalism and the new monitory inventions, that public objections to wrongdoing and corruption are commonplace in the era of monitory democracy. Scandals become commonplace. They seem to be never-ending; there are even times when scandalous revelations, like earthquakes, rumble the foundations of even the most publicly respected and powerful institutions.

In the age of monitory democracy, some scandals become legendary, like the public uproar caused by the inadvertent discovery of evidence of secret burglaries of the Democratic Party National Committee headquarters in the Watergate Hotel in Washington D.C., and by the subsequent snowballing of events that became the Watergate affair that resulted in threats of impeachment and the eventual resignation in August 1974 of President Nixon in the United States. On the other side of the Atlantic, major scandals have included the rumpus in the early 1990s within Spanish politics triggered by a government auditor's report that confirmed that senior Socialist Party officials had operated front companies known as Filesa and Time Export, and that they had been paid some 1 billion pesetas for consultancy services that were never rendered in what was known as the Filesa Affair. Then there was the nation-wide investigation by Italian police and judges of the extensive system of political corruption dubbed "Bribesville" (*Tangentopoli*), the so-called *mani pulite* (Italian for "clean hands") campaign that led to the disappearance of many political parties and the suicide of some politicians and industry leaders after their crimes were exposed. There was also the resignation of the French foreign minister and the admission by the French president on television that agents of the French secret service (DGSE) were responsible for the murder, in July 1985, of a Greenpeace activist and the bombing of their support vessel, the Rainbow Warrior, a boat that had been due to lead a flotilla of yachts to protest against French nuclear testing at Mururoa Atoll in the Pacific Ocean. Also, not to be forgotten, is the bitter global controversy triggered by the whopping lies about "weapons of mass destruction" spun by the defenders of the disastrous military invasion of Iraq in the early years of the twenty-first century—an invasion, according to the most reliable estimates, that resulted in many hundreds of thousands of deaths, produced several million refugees, and left behind many more traumatized children and orphans.

Viral Politics

These and other "-gate" scandals remind us of a perennial problem facing monitory democracy: there is no shortage of organized efforts by the powerful to manipulate people beneath them; and, hence, the political dirty business of dragging power from the shadows and flinging it into the blazing halogen of publicity remains fundamentally important. Nobody should be kidded into thinking that the world of monitory democracy, with its many power-scrutinizing institutions, is a level playing field—a paradise of equality of opportunity among all its citizens and their elected and unelected representatives. The combination of monitory democracy and communicative abundance nevertheless produces permanent flux, an unending restlessness driven by complex combinations of different interacting players and institutions, permanently pushing and pulling, heaving and straining, sometimes working together, and at other times in opposition to one another. Elected and unelected representatives routinely strive to define and to determine who gets what, when, and how, but the represented, taking advantage of various power-scrutinizing devices, keep tabs on their representatives—sometimes to great effect. The dynamics of monitory democracy are thus not describable using the simple spatial metaphors inherited from the age of representative democracy. Talk of the "sovereignty" of parliament; of "local" versus "central" government; or of tussles between "pressure groups," political parties, and governments is just too simple. In terms of political geometry, the system of monitory democracy is something other and different: a complex web of differently-sized and more or less interdependent monitory bodies that have the effect, thanks to communicative abundance, of continuously stirring up questions about who gets what, when, and how, as well as holding publicly responsible those who exercise power, wherever they are situated. Monitory democracies are richly conflicted. Politics does not wither away. Nothing is ever settled. Everything is never straightforwardly okay.

There is something utterly novel about the whole trend. From its origins in the ancient assemblies of Syria-Mesopotamia, democracy has always cut through and "denatured" the habit, prejudice, and hierarchies of power. It has stirred up the sense that people can shape and re-shape their lives as equals, and, not surprisingly, it has often brought commotion into the world. In the era of monitory democracy, the constant public scrutiny of power by hosts of differently sized monitory bodies with footprints large and small makes it the most energetic, most dynamic form of democracy ever. It even contains bodies (such as the Democratic Audit network and the Democracy Barometer and Transparency International) that specialize in providing public assessments of the quality of existing power-scrutinizing mechanisms and the degree to which they fairly represent citizens' interests. Other bodies specialize in directing questions at governments on a wide range of matters, extending from their human rights records, their energy production plans, and to the quality of the drinking water of their cities. Private companies are grilled about their services and products, their investment plans, how they treat their employees, and the size of their impact upon the biosphere. Various watchdogs, guide dogs, and barking dogs are constantly on the job, pressing for greater public accountability of those who exercise power. The powerful consequently come to feel the constant pinch of the powerless.

When they do their job well, monitory mechanisms have many positive effects, ranging from greater openness and justice within markets and blowing the whistle on foolish government decisions and corporate "mega-projects" to the general enrichment of public deliberation and the empowerment of citizens and their chosen representatives through meaningful schemes of participation. Power monitoring can be ineffective, or counterproductive, of course. It has no guarantees. Campaigns misfire or are poorly targeted; power wielders cleverly find loopholes and ways of rebutting or simply ignoring their opponents. Also large numbers of citizens sometimes find the monitory strategies of organizations too timid, or confused, or simply irrelevant to their lives as consumers, work-ers, parents, community residents, and young and elderly citizens.

Despite such weaknesses, which need urgently to be addressed both in theory and practice, the political dynamics and overall "feel" of monitory democracies are very different from the era of representative democracy. Politics in the age of monitory democracy has a definite "viral" quality about it. The power controversies stirred up by monitory mechanisms follow unexpected paths and reach surprising destinations. Groups using mobile phones, bulletin boards, news groups, wikis, and blogs sometimes manage, against considerable odds, to embarrass publicly politicians, par-ties, and parliaments, or even whole governments. Power-monitoring bodies like Human Rights Watch or Amnesty International regularly do the same, usually with help from networks of supporters. Think for a moment about any current public controversy that attracts widespread attention: news about its contours and commentaries and disputes about its significance are typically relayed by many power-monitoring organi-zations, large, medium, and small. In the world of monitory democracy, that kind of latticed pattern—viral, networked—is typical, not excep-tional. It has profound implications for the state-framed institutions of the old representative democracy, which find themselves more and more enmeshed in sticky webs of power-scrutinizing institutions that often hit their target, sometimes from long distances, often by means of the boomerang effect.

In the age of monitory democracy, bossy power can no longer hide comfortably behind private masks; in principle, and often in practice, power relations everywhere are subjected to organized efforts by some, with the help of media, to tell others publicly about matters that previ-ously had been hidden away, "in private." This public denaturing of power is usually messy business, and it often comes wrapped in hype. But the unmasking of power resonates strongly with the power-scrutinizing spirit of monitory democracy. Some people complain about its negative effects, like "information overload" and the tendency of media scrutiny to drag down the reputations of politicians and "politics." But, from the point of view of monitory democracy, it is at least arguable that communicative abundance on balance has positive consequences. In spite of all its hype and spin and other decadent features, the new media galaxy nudges and broadens people's horizons. It tutors their sense of pluralism; reminds them that "truth" depends on context and perspective; and even prods them into taking greater responsibility for how, when, and why they communicate. The days when children were compulsorily bathed and scrubbed behind the ears, sat down in their dressing gowns prior to going to bed, and required to listen to radio or television programs with their families—these days of representative democracy and spectrum-scarcity broadcasting and mass entertainment are over. So, too, are the days when millions of people, huddled together as masses in the shadows of totalitarian power, found the skillfully orchestrated radio and film performances of demagogues fascinating and existentially reassuring.

Message-saturated democracies, by contrast, encourage people's suspicions of unaccountable power. Although (to repeat) there are more than a few threats on the horizon, including Chinese government-style efforts to manipulate the mechanisms of communicative abundance to reduce democratic openness, all of the king's horses, and all the king's men are unlikely to reverse the tendency to regard arbitrary power with suspicion. Within the world of monitory democracies, there is a long-term mood swing happening. People are coming to learn that they must keep an eye on power and its representatives, that they must make judgments and choose their own courses of action. Citizens are being tempted to think for themselves; to see the same world in different ways, from different angles, and to sharpen their overall sense that prevailing power relationships are not "natural," but contingent. In this sense, communicative abundance and monitory institutions combine to promote something of a "Gestalt switch" in the popular perception of power. The metaphysical idea of an objective, out-there-at-a-distance "reality" is weakened; so too is the presumption that stubborn "factual truth" is superior to power. The fabled distinction between what people can see with their eyes and what they are told about the emperor's new clothes breaks down. "Reality," including the "reality" of the powerful, comes to be understood as always "produced reality," a matter of interpretation—but also the power to arbitrarily force particular interpretations of the world down others' throats.[14]

There is admittedly nothing automatic or magical about any of this chastening of power. In the era of monitory democracy, communication is constantly the subject of dissembling, negotiation, compromise, and power conflicts. In short, it is a matter of politics. Communicative abundance for that reason does not somehow automatically ensure the triumph of either the spirit or institutions of monitory democracy. Message-saturated societies can and do have effects that are harmful for democracy. In some quarters, for instance, media saturation triggers citizens' inattention to events. While they are expected as good citizens to keep their eyes on public affairs, to take an interest in the world beyond their immediate household and neighborhood, more than a few people find it ever harder to pay attention to the media's vast outpourings. Profusion breeds confusion. There are times, for instance, when voters are so pelted with a hail of election advertisements on prime-time television that they react frostily. Disaffected, they get up from their sofas, leave their living rooms, change channels, or mute concluding with a heavy sigh that the less you know, the better off you are. It is only a few steps from there to something more worrying: the unwitting spread of a culture of unthinking indifference. Monitory democracy certainly feeds upon communicative abundance, but one of its more perversely decadent effects may be to encourage individuals to escape the great complexity of the world by sticking their heads, like ostriches, into the sands of willful ignorance, or to float cynically upon the swirling tides, waves, and eddies of fashion—to change their minds, to speak and act flippantly, to embrace or even celebrate opposites, to bid farewell to veracity, to slip into the arms of what some carefully call "bullshit."[15]

Foolish illusions, cynicism, and disaffection are just several of the many temptations and difficulties confronting citizens and their elected and unelected representatives in our times. Can monitory democracy survive their toxic effects? Or will folly, negativism, and disaffection, among other forces, serve to dampen and undo enthusiasm for monitory democracy? It is too early to tell—not just because the whole political business of keeping reins on those who exercise power is by definition always unfinished but also, and above all, because a strong normative case for the superiority of monitory democracy as a new method of controlling the risks and dangers of arbitrary power has yet to be made.

Notes

1. The adjective "monitory" derives from the medieval *monitoria*, from *monere*, to warn. It entered Middle English in the shape of *monitorie* and from there it wended its way into the modern English language in the mid-fifteenth century to refer to the process of giving or conveying a warning of an impending danger, or an admonition to someone to refrain from a specified course of action considered offensive. It was first used within the Church to refer to a letter or letters (known as "monitories") sent by a bishop, a pope, or an ecclesiastical court who acted in the capacity of a "monitor." The family of words "monitor," "monition," and "monitory" was soon used for more secular or this-worldly purposes. The monitor was one or that which admonishes others about their conduct. The word "monitor" was also used in school settings to refer to a senior pupil expected to perform special duties, such as that of keeping order, or (if the pupil was particularly bright or gifted) acting as a teacher to a junior class. A monitor also came to mean an early warning device; it was said as well to be a species of African, Australian, and New Guinean lizard that was friendly to humans because it gave warning of the whereabouts of crocodiles. Still later, the word "monitor" came to be associated with communication devices. It referred to a receiver, such as a speaker or a television screen, that is used to check the quality or content of an electronic

transmission; and in the world of computing and computer science, a "monitor" either refers to a video display or to a program that observes, supervises, or controls the activities of other programs. In more recent years, not unconnected with the emergence of monitory democracy, "to monitor" became a commonplace verb to describe the process of systematically checking the content or quality of something, as when a city authority monitors the local drinking water for impurities, or a group of scientific experts monitors the population of an endangered species. Such usages seem to have inspired the theory of "monitorial democracy" developed by the American scholar, Michael Schudson (interview, New York City, 4 December 2006). See the following two sources, for respectively, a brief and a fuller version of the work to which my use of the term monitory democracy is indebted: Michael Schudson "Changing Concepts of Democracy," *MIT Communications Forum* (8 May 1998); Michael Schudson, *The Good Citizen: A History of American Public Life* (New York: The Free Press, 1998).

2. The subject of countertrends and dysfunctions of monitory democracy is taken up in John Keane, *The Life and Death of Democracy* (London and New York: Simon and Schuster, 2009); a full range of related materials is to be found at *www.thelifeanddeathofdemocracy.org*

3. Examples include Adam Przeworski, Susan C. Stokes, and Bernard Manin, ed., *Democracy, Accountability, and Representation* (New York: Cambridge University Press, 1999); Adam Przeworski, *Democracy and the Limits of Self-Government* (New York: Cambridge University Press, 2010); and the review essay by Gerardo L. Munck, "Democratic Theory after Transitions from Authoritarian Rule," *Perspectives on Politics*, vol. 9, no. 2 (2011): 333–343.

4. Friedrich von Hayek, *Law, Legislation and Liberty: The Political Order of a Free People* (London: Routledge & Kegan Paul, 1979).

5. John Keane, "A Productive Challenge: Unelected Representatives Can Enrich Democracy," *WZB Mitteilungen*, vol. 131 (2011): 14–16.

6. George Eliot, *Felix Holt: The Radical* (Edinburgh and London: Blackwood and Sons, 1866), Chapter 5, 127; Walt Whitman, "Election Day, November 1884."

7. Archon Fung and Erik Olin Wright, "Thinking about Empowered Participatory Governance," in *Deepening Democracy. Institutional Innovations in Empowered Participatory Governance*, ed. A. Fung and E. O. Wright (London and New York: Verso, 2003): 5.

8. To rephrase this idea, if the principles of representative democracy turned "the people" of assembly democracy into a more distant judge of how well representatives performed, then monitory democracy exposes the fiction of a unified "sovereign people." The dynamic structures of monitory democracy serve as barriers against the uncontrolled worship of "the people," or what might be dubbed demolatry. Monitory democracy demonstrates that the world is made up of many *demoi*, and that particular societies are made up of flesh-and-blood people who have different interests, and who therefore do not necessarily see eye to eye. It could be said that monitory democracy democratises—publicly exposes—the whole principle of "the sovereign people" as a pompous fiction; at best, it turns it into a handy reference device that most people know to be just that: a useful political fiction. There are indeed times when the fiction of "the people" serves as a monitoring principle, as a former Justice of the Federal Constitutional Court in Germany, Dieter Grimm, has explained: "The circumstances are rare in which

the fiction of "the demos" is needed as a reminder that those who make the laws are not the source of their ultimate legitimacy. Democracies need public power; but they need as well to place limits on the exercise of public power by invoking "the people" as a fictional subject to whom collectively binding powers are attributed, a *Zurechnungssubjekt* that is not itself capable of acting, but which serves as a democratic necessity because it makes accountability meaningful" (interview, Berlin, 23 November 2006).

9. President Roosevelt, Address to the White House Correspondents' Association, Washington (15 March 1941).

10. The surviving electoral democracies included Australia, Canada, Chile, Costa Rica, New Zealand, Sweden, Switzerland, the United Kingdom, the United States, and Uruguay. Despite its use of an electoral college to choose a president under high-security, wartime conditions, Finland might also be included.

11. The early years after World War II witnessed many new lines of thinking about the future of democracy within a global context. See, for instance, Thomas Mann, *Goethe and Democracy* (Washington, D.C.: Library of Congress, 1949); Jacques Maritain, "Christianity and Democracy," a typewritten manuscript prepared as an address at the annual meeting of the American Political Science Association (New York, 29 December 1949); Harold Laski et.al., *The Future of Democracy* (London, 1946); Albert Camus, *Neither Victims nor Executioners* (Chicago: World Without War Publications, 1972 [first published in the autumn 1946 issues of *Combat*]); Reinhold Niebuhr, *The Children of Light and the Children of Darkness. A Vindication of Democracy and a Critique of its Traditional Defenders* (London: Nisbet & Co., 1945); Pope Pius XII, *Democracy and Peace* (London, 1945); Sidney Hook, "What Exactly Do We Mean By 'Democracy'?," *The New York Times*, 16 March 1947: 10ff; and A.D. Lindsay, *Democracy in the World Today: A Lecture* (London, 1947).

12. Niebuhr, *The Children of Light and the Children of Darkness*. vi.

13. An extended account of the following trends is developed in my forthcoming book, *Democracy in the Age of Media Decadence* (London and New York, 2012).

14. See Gianni Vattimo, *A Farewell to Truth* (New York: Columbia University Press, 2011).

15. Harry G. Frankfurt, *On Bullshit* (Princeton and Oxford: Princeton University Press, 2005).

Chapter 2

CIVIL SOCIETY IN THE AGE OF CRISIS

John Clark

Introduction

Today's political topography is dominated by mountain ranges of global crises—actual and emerging. While other issues are extremely important, three peaks dominate: the global financial crisis and attendant unemployment, widening socio-cultural schisms emanating from the so-called "war on terror, " and climate change and the collapse of ecological systems. A 2005 global survey of citizens' concerns[1] confirms these are the top worries of 62 percent of the world's public. Myriad actors in civil society respond energetically to them and have significantly influenced public opinion and policy-makers; however, this chapter looks at the opposite direction of causality, asking how have these global crises molded the contours of civil society itself?

The conclusions are that—while some NGOs demonstrate prescient analysis and various social movements are leaders of public opinion— these global crises have largely been tough on civil society. Together they have forged divisions, weakened its political influence and effectiveness, reduced citizen support for many civil society organizations (CSOs), led the public to see states (not CSOs) as the "savior," and exacerbated tensions between state and civil society. Moreover, opponents of values-driven CSOs often adopt similar tactics, confusing the public about what civil society stands for.

While to date these have been warning tremors rather than major earthquakes, they are trends civil society must ponder. Do they warrant some shifts in tactics? Is there a case for forging alliances with allies in governments and official bodies, or for focusing less on the substance of policy-making and more on its processes (i.e. governance, and specifically the institutional links between CSOs and the state, at local, national, and global levels)? This resonates with John Keane's analysis in this book.[2] He views the critical contribution of CSOs and citizens as monitoring the use and abuse of state power. Conversely, is it the time for greater stridency, to shake societies out of the apathy that permits policy-makers to leave the crises unresolved?

This chapter looks in turn at the three main crises and how they affect civil society. Many factors emerge, but a common one is that civil society has been more effective and united during the identification and formation stage of a crisis—when its task is getting the issue onto the agenda—than the resolution stage. At the latter point, civil society tends to fragment. Variety in tactics for alerting public concern on a topic is strength, but advocacy of wildly different, often contradictory, policy responses is divisive. Furthermore, the tactics required to convince politicians to change policy tend to be at odds with those for awakening interest within the broad public. The media-grabbing and colorful tactics of mass demonstrations and direct action tend to turn off policy-makers.

Keane describes the diverse ways in which citizens today can participate directly in democracy but he doesn't attempt to predict the future of the phenomenon. This chapter, in contrast, looks at one of the most powerful instruments of "monitory democracy"—namely civil society—and assesses how it is influenced by contemporary crises. The conclusion is that in the immediate future the prospects are rocky, but addressable.

All the crises are global in nature, require globally concerted responses, and can only be addressed meaningfully by governments, especially the most powerful ones. Hence the fashion in the 1980s and 90s for seeking "less government" and more citizens' action has manifestly turned round. Ronald Reagan, in his first inaugural address as President of the U.S. in 1981 famously said, "Government is not the solution to our problem; government *is* the problem." This emphasis on rolling back the state provided additional space for civil society to grow. Today, however, the Organization for Economic Co-operation and Development (OECD) governments are mostly criticized for doing too little, not too much—for not enforcing stronger greenhouse gas restrictions, regulating banks, or building international consensus in fighting terrorism.

This new trend puts civil society relatively into the shade. There are signs that this may lead to reduced financial and membership support, less traction with regard to influencing policy, and a more hostile environment for the sector. This chapter explores these trends as it looks in turn at each of the major global crises, and concludes with some tentative thoughts on future civil society strategies that might provide some protection.

Impact of the Global Economic Crisis

The global economic crisis has impacted civil society in three principal ways. First, it has eroded the finances of CSOs (especially NGOs and trade unions). Second, the sector has been somewhat marginalized since it is not widely credited either for having foreseen the crisis, or for presenting credible solutions. Third, the financial meltdown and international economic precursors to it have revealed deepening divisions within the sector; while diversity is often a strength, for this issue it manifests as confusion and lack of confidence. These factors are now examined in detail.

The Financial Hit

Public contributions to CSOs have generally dwindled as household budgets are squeezed, more people have become unemployed (or fear becoming so), and there is increased anxiety about the security of mortgages and savings accounts. Although 2008 figures showed only modest decreases, it appears that the downturn steepened in 2009.

The American Red Cross, for example, experienced a 30 percent drop in responses and contributions from new donors, as well as a fall in corporate donations (in spite of heightened public concerns about disasters brought about by 2008's hurricanes, tornadoes, and floods).[3] Across the U.S., philanthropic organizations report similar trends and attribute them, at least in part, to the credit crisis and plunge of financial markets. An October 2008 survey of more than 2,700 nonprofit groups in the U.S. found that in the first nine months of 2008, more than a third saw contributions decrease, and donations were stagnant for another 25 percent. The equivalent survey in 2009 showed that the situation had deteriorated, with 51 percent of nonprofits reporting decreased contributions in the first 9 months of 2009. The situation did not recover in 2010; when 37 percent of nonprofits surveyed reported decreased contributions and 26 percent reported that total giving remained the same.[4] Other sources tell a similar story. One analyst of the nonprofit sector estimates that charitable giving from individuals, corporations, and foundations fell 3.9 percent in 2009.[5] In response, while there has been an increased demand for the services provided by nonprofits during the recession, most U.S.

nonprofits have had to make cuts or borrow to retain their programs. In one survey of human service groups, 82 percent reported that they have scaled back their operations, typically by cutting programs or services (21 percent), or by freezing or reducing staff salaries (50 percent). Others responded by drawing on their reserves (39 percent), or by borrowing money (22 percent).[6]

In Europe, the drop in public giving does not seem to be as great, but is nevertheless real and could deepen. In the U.K., a survey of large charities shows a 13 percent drop in contributions but an 18 percent increase in demand for their services. 29 percent of charities laid off staff and 56 percent curbed salary increases.[7] For U.K. development NGOs, whose public contributions have grown continuously and steeply over the last 20 years, the concern is more that incomes have stagnated.[8]

The bigger concern for NGOs and foundations in many countries (such as the U.K. and Australia), and for CSOs in poorer countries that derive funding from them, has been the change in exchange rates. This has devalued their grants in countries where prices are linked to the dollar or other stronger currencies. From May 2008 to 2009, the U.K. pound lost 25 percent of its value against the dollar, and since much of the NGOs' expenditures are linked to the dollar, this represents a major fall in the buying power of British philanthropy.

In a few cases, poor governance has compounded the financial squeeze, sometimes even fatally damaging NGOs who were thought to be "too big to fail," as it has with some banks and large corporations. The most widely known case is UNICEF Germany (a very well connected NGO addressing child poverty and education at home and overseas). Bad management of its funds led to economic difficulties and an ensuing scandal, causing the resignation of its CEO and entire board in February 2008. This not only had a severe impact on the charity (with a loss of 30,000 supporters), but it had a severe contagion effect on about half of all German charities.[9] Such experiences have alerted larger NGOs about the need for careful NGO governance and have reminded them about their vulnerability to turmoil in financial markets.

The situation is considerably worse for CSOs in developing countries for three reasons: the economic impact of the crisis has often been deeper; citizens with little spare money (on average) are likely to cut their CSO contributions first; and about one-sixth of CSO income in developing countries comes from overseas funders who, as we have seen, are cutting their grant-making. In South Africa, for example, a major network of NGOs and community organizations reports that their members are feeling an acute pinch, and many NGOs and charities are closing down.[10] In Russia, 50 percent of NGOs experienced a considerable funding drop (especially in corporate giving); hence 18 percent are cutting staff, 26 percent are cutting salaries, and 18 percent are delaying salaries.

More direct evidence points to the funding decline from foundations.[11] While the assets of foundations in the U.S. had doubled to $682 billion from 1997 to 2007, they shrunk to $533 billion in the following year—i.e., $150 billion in charitable resources were lost in a single year.[12] A further $50 billion was lost in 2009 and 48 percent of foundations reported budget cuts of 10 percent or more in 2009.[13] European foundations may use more conservative investment strategies and so may not have had to reduce grants to the same degree.[14] All, however, are experiencing a decline in revenues while interest rates remain extremely low and grant making is tied to foundation earnings.

The one source of civil society funding that has not as yet been cut, and is indeed expanding, is OECD governments. Partly due to fiscal stimulus packages that seek to address social needs, amongst other goals, and partly due to social service and aid ministries, considering that they get better value-for-money by outsourcing to NGOs, there is an increase in governmental funding for many CSO categories, especially those providing public services (whether in health care or fighting corruption). A related concern that grows with state funding, however, is that of state co-optation. The CSO programs are often designed by the government agencies that fund them, rendering the CSOs barely distinguishable from consulting companies.

To summarize: there has been a substantial fall in public donations for domestic and international civil society activities; there is likely to be a drop in funding from foundations and other private sector linked funding sources; and the increased reliance on governmental funding leads to reduced independence of CSOs and an increase in their welfare and service delivery roles.

The Challenge of Relevance

After many years of retreat for the political left, the last decade has witnessed its resurgence. Most prominent has been the amorphous "anti-globalization" or "alter-globalization" movement (henceforth called the Movement[15]), characterized by its protest activities at large global events (such as G8, IMF, or WTO meetings), and its annual World Social Forum (WSF). Paradoxically, while the Movement called for systemic change before the financial crisis demonstrated the need for it, in the face of the crisis it has somewhat withered, rather than grown in strength and stature.[16] Why?

The main reason is that while the Movement[17] harshly attacks capitalism, it offers no convincing alternative. The reflective CSOs that provided its intellectual leadership did not pinpoint specific threats posed by the sub-prime mortgage market, debt swaps, derivative trading, and the other ingredients of what became the perfect financial storm. (To be fair, mainstream financial analysts and journalists failed similarly.) The lacuna is due partly to the strong divisions that have become manifest within the Movement (discussed presently), and partly to the attention of civil society being diverted elsewhere.

The crisis has revealed, specifically, the degree to which most CSOs had ignored financial regulation, the banking sector, and governance of the private sector. Over the last 20 years, plenty of CSOs have become exceedingly skilled in matters relating to the governance of national and sub-national governments and international organizations. The author has been involved in both sides of civil society efforts to effect change in inter-governmental institutions.[18] While there are many anti-capitalist groups and business-focused campaigns,[19] until recently there have been few effective CSO endeavors to reform the governance of the private sector in general, or fix today's economic crisis.[20]

Organizations like the IMF and the World Bank have proved more popular targets than commercial banks and more likely to divulge the information necessary for an effective campaign. Whatever the reasons, while mass protests abound about governments' response to the financial crisis (such as the riots against raising student fees in the U.K. or the retirement age in France), there has been a relative dearth of civic activism on the current credit crunch itself,[21] just when public fury with the finance sector is at its peak.

While bankers' bonuses, the fragility of the global economic system, the ethics of speculation, etc. have been roundly decried by CSO activists, no coherent and common set of prescriptions is presented as an alternative to the current laissez-faire global economic management. The Movement easily identifies systemic faults, but its mode of operation (largely web-based, meeting occasionally in large and amorphous gatherings, eschewing strong leadership) prevents clear messages about the alternatives advocated—other than the vague sentiment that "another world is possible."[22]

Geoffrey Pleyers offers the most insightful analysis of the decline of the Movement.[23] He suggests that the clearest sign of this was its failure to mobilize a significant presence at the WTO meeting in Geneva in July 2008—given that this was in many ways a make-or-break meeting for the WTO. Nate Cull, a WSF participant from New Zealand, similarly notes that the 2009 forum was less well attended than previous ones and "more

chaotic and less well-organized than Porto Alegré 2005."[24] It has also become much more dominated by Latin American participants.

Overall, therefore, the economic crisis has paradoxically not helped
the CSOs who most vociferously condemn international finance and
neoliberalism. Pleyers describes this as the "failure of success" and that
the Movement has achieved a victory, since even the defenders of the old
order are now also calling for systemic change to curb "casino capitalism."
While true in part, the Movement's inherent weaknesses and contradictions have become more evident, in particular internal divisions have
spurred its withering.

Divisions in Activism

The Movement's zenith was the "Battle of Seattle" of 30 November 1999,
triggered by the protests at the WTO meeting, and the subsequent six
years in which the WSF grew in strength.[25] But its diversity and dependence on information technology were weaknesses as well as strengths.
In being a collection of only loosely-related causes (in effect a "Protest
Mall," not a campaign), being mediated mostly via web-based communication, and being culturally hostile to strong leadership, it has been
united more by what it is against rather than what it stands for, resulting
inevitably in tensions and divisions.[26]

These divisions have been widened by the current economic crisis.
Some observers of the WSF have written of its bifurcation into a periodic
mass encounter for social movement activists on the one hand, and an
"organized network of experts, academics, and NGO practitioners" on the
other who seek to "re-establish the role of professional revolutionaries."[27]

Pleyers (2009) laments the Movement's weakness just as the opportunity presents itself for "building a new and fair global order." Drawing on
his analysis it appears that three incompatible currents are discernible:

- The Localists who want a global network to share experiences on
building communities' local autonomy via participatory self-government as the true alternative to corporate globalization—such as
through "collective purchase groups" and even creating alternative,
local currencies;
- The Advocates who promote specific-issue campaigns and who regard the WSF and the broader movement both as vehicles for their
causes and a meeting point to share experience, give mutual support, and perhaps raise broader questions that are common to the
multitude of campaigns;

- The Statists who see populist, leftist governments, such as Venezuela's Hugo Chávez and Bolivia's Evo Morales, as beacons for a new way.

One can add a fourth group—The Anarchists—who are cynical of the advocates and statists but who are keener to attack the current global system than to work for local alternatives.

The incompatibility of these groupings weakens the Movement's body politic, but it is the nature of the current crisis that has so starkly exposed this weakness. The perfidious universality of the credit crunch's impact renders dependence on local solutions implausible and makes the piecemeal prescriptions of the advocates seem inadequate. It is not the populist governments that are spearheading solutions to the crisis, but centrist governments of rich countries, and the solutions that are supported by most citizens (except the most conservative) require stronger governments, not anarchy.

Economic crisis—a triple blow for civil society

As we have seen, the credit crunch has been difficult for civil society and has impacted its agency in three ways. It has made a financial hit—significantly denting CSOs' income, especially in developing countries. It has posed a challenge of relevance—paradoxically contributing to a weakening of the very social movement that most vociferously criticized the ailing global financial system since it has been unable to galvanize unity around solutions to the crisis. And it has led to divisions in activism—as current events have exposed and deepened the tensions and divisions in the leadership of the Movement.

Impact of the "war on terror"

As President Bush and his allies prepared for war in Iraq, CSOs and social movements mobilized record-breaking numbers onto the streets. The protests of 15 February 2003, involving tens of millions of people in about 800 cities around the world, is listed in Guinness World Records as the largest protest ever.[28] *New York Times* writer, Patrick Tyler, stated that the protests showed that there were two superpowers on the planet: the United States and worldwide public opinion.[29]

For a while, this reinvigorated radical elements in civil society, but as the war effort moved forward undaunted, the demonstrations grew thinner—even though public opinion against the Iraq War hardened. Paradoxically, as the public thirst for ending the war grew, mass activism shifted back to other focuses, such as (in the U.S.) opposing tax increases. Why? It might be that once the war started it appeared unpatriotic to campaign against it, or that this would appear disrespectful to the families of fallen soldiers. Or it might be that objectors felt powerless to oppose the war. Those against the war were also deeply divided about the strategies both for ending it and fighting terrorism. These and other factors eroded the public appeal of the antiwar cause.

The "war on terror," then, has been a roller coaster for social movements and radical CSOs and has had two other major impacts. It has increased public skepticism of faith-based CSOs, and authorities have intervened more intrusively in the affairs of CSOs in their antiterrorism strategies or in copycat measures on the part of regimes hostile to civil society. Both these phenomena represent serious detriments to civil society.

Losing Faith in Faiths

During the Cold War, faith was a significant factor in framing the ideological debate, especially in America where Christians projected a sense of moral superiority towards the "godless atheism" of Marxism. This religious factor was unidirectional in strengthening anticommunist sentiments. Within the Soviet Union, adherence to atheism was not itself a rallying point, and, hence, the religious divide did not add directly to the flash points.

Today, the ideological fault-lines are different, and religion is a primary source of tension. For both sets of protagonists, the religion and culture of the other is a (if not the) source of tension, and many have become mistrustful of religion itself, viewing it as a perennial source of social conflict, repression, and violence. Militant Islam has replaced the Soviet Union in the eyes of most Westerners (especially Americans) as the chief threat to their values and ways of life, and militant extremism is widely seen as inherent in the Muslim faith. Evangelicals (46 percent), Mainline Protestants (45 percent), and Jews (43 percent) are the most likely Americans to assert that Islam encourages violence more than other religions.[30] These same groups (except the Jewish community and black Protestants) formed parts of the support base for the U.S. invasion of Iraq. This distrust of Islam is not restricted to the U.S.. A multi-country survey for the BBC (British Broadcast Corporation)[31] showed that about 60 percent people in Spain, 52 percent in Germany, 41 percent in France, and 32 percent in Britain associate Islam with violence.

Unlike in the Cold War, religion has become the pivotal contested area. Citizens of the developing countries (especially in the U.S.) regard Islam in general—not just militant Islam—as a major threat. This has been powerfully illustrated by the vehement and widespread opposition mounted against plans by a group of leading Muslims to build a mosque and inter-faith community center (the Cordoba House project[32]) close to Ground Zero in New York.[33] Similar protests have sought to block the building of mosques elsewhere in the U.S. (including Staten Island, New York; Temecula Valley, California; and Sheboygan, Wisconsin).[34] In parallel, attitudes of Muslims have become very negative towards the West. Hence, in Muslim countries, some 68 percent of respondents to the BBC poll regarded Westerners as violent, 77 percent as selfish, and 52 percent as fanatic.

Such findings give credence to pundits who claim that today's schism reflects a "clash of civilizations" rooted in different value systems.[35] Religion is increasingly a source of conflict and divisions, not harmony and understanding. A 2005 survey concluded that three-quarters of the U.S. public consider that religion either has a great deal (40 percent) or a fair amount (35 percent) to do with most wars and conflicts in the world today.[36] Similarly, an Ipsos MORI poll revealed that 60 percent of British people consider religion now to be a more significant source of division than race. This helps explain the decline in religious affiliation in much of the world. While the majority still describes themselves as believers in the U.K., 83 percent of the population is now not involved in any regular religious practice.[37] Faith-based groups in many countries are, consequently, losing their power to contribute to social cohesion and conflict resolution.

Tightening the Reins

Potentially the most damaging indirect impact of the "war on terror" on civil society stems from the heightened governmental scrutiny and restrictions CSOs are subjected to. This started soon after the 9/11 attacks when senior officials from mostly OECD countries came together to discuss concerted action to fight terrorist cells by identifying and cutting off their funding. The Financial Action Task Force on Money-Laundering and Counter-Terrorism (FATF) was set up in 1989 and comprises officials from 34 countries representing finance ministries, central banks, intelligence agencies, police, and other departments. In October 2001, the FATF's original money-laundering mandate was expanded to "incorporate efforts to combat terrorist financing."[38]

At its first meeting with this wider mandate, FATF drew up "8 Special Recommendations ... on Terrorist Financing."[39] The first seven of these were unexceptional and largely restated and nuanced existing measures against money laundering. Special Recommendation 8 (SR8) was new, however, and related to "non-profit organizations" (NPOs). Though illegal causes have long been financed through philanthropies[40] (e.g. Irish-American groups funding the Irish Republican Army to fight British forces in Northern Ireland, finance for ETA—the Basque-separatist movement, and President Suharto's use of family foundations to extract large amounts of money from Indonesia), internationally coordinated action related to CSOs had never been agreed before. In the face of Al Qaeda, however, all that was to change.

FATF asserted that there was considerable proof that NPOs had on many occasions supported terrorism in one of four ways: by raising funds, illegal transfers, direct logistical support, or serving as a cover for terrorist operations.[41] In practice, most of the evidence made public was either too vague to be scrutinized or consisted of hearsay. Nevertheless, FATF alleges that the problem is so great that misuse of NPOs by terrorists "not only facilitates terrorist activity but also undermines donor confidence and jeopardizes the very integrity of NPOs." (A sweeping statement given that it relates to the whole sector.) In SR8 it, therefore, called on all governments to "review the adequacy of laws and regulations that relate to entities that can be abused for the financing of terrorism" and complained that "NPOs may often be subject to little or no governmental oversight (for example, registration, record keeping, reporting, and monitoring), or few formalities may be required for their creation"[42]—implying that this is a matter of grave concern, even though no evidence is given to suggest that NPOs are more prone to terrorist links than businesses.

Scrutinizing SR8 reveals FATF's meager understanding of civil society. It defines an NPO as "a legal entity or organization that primarily engages in raising or disbursing funds for purposes such as charitable, religious, cultural, educational, social, or fraternal purposes, or for the carrying out of other types of 'good works.'"[43] This limits the focus to legally registered NPOs. In many countries, it is common for NPOs not to be legal entities (even if they do have a bank account); indeed it is often only required in the case of organizations that seek tax relief or other state benefits.

The lack of analysis behind FATF recommendations is further illustrated by its advice regarding government scrutiny of NPO overseas funding. It argues for particular scrutiny of: "NPOs which account for (1) a significant portion of the financial resources under control of the sector; and (2) a substantial share of the sector's international activities." The implication is that the largest charities are the greatest threat, and that the smallest ones can be ignored. The reverse is more likely; in the U.K., terrorism is more likely to be financed by small outfits—who are not registered charities but who are linked to radical Islamic groups—than by the National Trust or Red Cross.

FATF goes on to prescribe a series of actions[44] that have proved extremely burdensome to CSOs. It calls on governments to: (a) require all NPOs to thoroughly know their partners and those they fund overseas; (b) review the legal and reporting requirements of NPOs; and (c) strengthen government supervision and monitoring of NPOs. It advises governments to consider "reversing the burden of proof" by requiring NPOs to prove that "their overseas operations ... are conducted in accordance with their stated purpose and by-laws."

In the U.S., the requirement of NGOs and Foundations to know their partners and funders has been made a legal requirement that renders the trustees (or board members) criminally liable for any misuse of the organizations' funds in activities that could be construed as linked to terrorists.[45] A seasoned expert on NGO legislation, Barnett F. Baron, described these new provisions as risking "setting potentially unachievable due diligence requirements for international grant-making, [and] subjecting international grant-makers to high but largely undefined levels of legal risk."[46] These actions have deterred many organizations from making any overseas grants (especially those for which this was not a major purpose of their organization).[47] U.S. NGOs have campaigned against the government's approach not only because it implies that the non-profit sector is a problem, rather than an important bulwark against terrorism, but also because it implies "that charitable organizations are agents of the government."[48]

Such problems are not restricted to the U.S. In Canada, legislation introduced in 2004 renders a charity susceptible to criminal charges if it even unwittingly facilitates or supports terrorist activities. This could result in the charity losing its charitable status and the corresponding exposure of its directors to personal, criminal liability.[49] In the U.K., the main umbrella of philanthropies, the National Council of Voluntary Organisations (NCVO), considers that U.K. counter-terrorism measures have deterred legitimate NGO activities in ways that "have had a negative impact on CSOs, particularly those working with Muslim communities and/or in areas where the threat of terrorism is high."[50] NCVO calls these measures "heavy handed ... they have tended to assume that because a small number of charities have been implicated in investigations into terrorist activity, all charitable organizations are at risk."

In light of concerns about NGOs being used to finance terrorist activities, reporting requirements have been made much stiffer and onerous for NGOs in a number of countries. In the U.S. the 990 form that the IRS (Internal Revenue Service) requires all registered NPOs to submit each year now requires much more detailed submissions. For a typical medium to large NGO that operates internationally, the 990 submission has expanded from six pages of information in 2000 to about 35 pages at present. This amounts to a severe burden for NGOs and the additional scrutiny required is a deterrent to overseas activities and grants in particular for all but the large NGOs.[51]

Given that support for Islamic organizations and causes in Muslim countries are particularly scrutinized, these measures have had severe consequences. While Muslim anger generated by the "war on terror" has fueled international "solidarity" funding for mosque-based and anti-Western movements, the increased difficulties philanthropies in rich countries experience in financing activities in Muslim countries has resulted in a significant decrease in support.[52] Given that the latter typically supports social, charitable, and inter-faith activities, CSO funding from rich countries to Muslim civil society has in effect gravitated from secular to Islamic causes, so heightening religious divisions.

Paradoxically, just when world security demands greater harmony between people of different faiths and cultures and when the West needs to improve its image in Muslim countries, the over-reaction of rich countries in the name of counter-terrorism risks the opposite.[53] Though efforts to track the financing of terrorism are very important (whether via CSOs, businesses, or states), by stigmatizing charities as part of the terrorist problem, many people of goodwill throughout the world have become alienated. Nationalists also increasingly criticize western-funded groups as suspect.

According to Peter Weber,[54] many American foundations, in particular, now avoid direct funding of local Muslim nonprofit organizations by supporting "Friends of" organizations, and big international humanitarian organizations. Weber suggests a "double negative outcome of this approach," namely less efficient philanthropy due to the suspicions of Muslim populations toward Western organizations, plus "holding back the development of a strong and pluralist third sector in countries where it is more likely needed, in particular in those countries where there are located Western military bases," as the new funding modality polarizes support to a few local groups that are trusted in the West.[55]

FATF alleges, without providing any evidence, that "NPOs may often be subject to little or no governmental oversight (for example, registration, record keeping, reporting, and monitoring), or few formalities may be required for their creation." This gap is seen by FATF as a major weakness, but it assumes that NPOs ought to report to and be monitored by governments, which runs counter to the notion that civil society should be independent of the state (excepting, to some degree, those CSOs that receive funding or important concessions from the state). The deepening concern of CSOs around the world is the degree to which FATF-inspired actions conflict with one of the basic and internationally-certified human rights, namely the right of association, as defined in Article 22 of the International Covenant on Civil and Political Rights. This article makes clear that the only government interference with the right of association should stem from matters of national security or other overwhelming imperative. There appears to have been no discussion within FATF about how to safeguard this. Hence, we find that the actions taken in practice result in a major compromise of associational rights.

The commonest restrictions on CSOs that have been introduced by governments in recent years are:

- Restrictions on the right of independent CSOs to exist at all in a meaningful way: e.g. Saudi Arabia, Libya, Cuba, China, Vietnam;
- Restrictions on the right to register or form CSOs: e.g. Azerbaijan, Ethiopia, Algeria;
- Restrictions on the right to hold gatherings: e.g. Belarus;
- Restrictions on the right to receive foreign funding without prior approval: e.g. Eritrea, Uzbekistan, Zimbabwe;
- Arbitrary termination/dissolution of CSOs: e.g. Belarus, Egypt;
- Arbitrary and stringent oversight and control of CSOs: e.g. Turkey, Belarus; and
- Imposing criminal penalties against individual officers: e.g. Egypt.

While few of these restrictions directly stem from antiterrorism, this context has been used by many governments to outlaw and establish a stricter control over both national and international NPOs for political rather than security reasons.[56] Some governments have always been suspicious of independent civil society, even if they warily permit its continued existence (perhaps only as a sop to rich countries whose aid they want). They now see greater common ground with Western governments in their suspicion of CSOs and are taking advantage of this current climate to increase restrictions on civil society.[57]

In the decades up to 2001, there was a gradual expansion of associational freedom and other civil and political rights, but there has been a reversal since then. According to Mark Sidel, in the first five years after 9/11, various forms of antiterrorism regulations have affected or threatened to affect the third sector in a wide range of nations including Australia, Cambodia, Canada, Central Asia, China, India, The Netherlands,

Pakistan, U.K., U.S. and Zimbabwe.[58] This pattern continues. A specialized NGO that monitors and provides advice on association law (the
International Center for Not-for-Profit Law, ICNL) identifies more than
24 laws that have been introduced or enacted from 2008 until mid-2009
that restrict the legal space for civil society.[59]

One increasingly common measure is to require NGOs to channel
their funding "through explicitly authorized and monitored local organizations."[60] This is usually interpreted to mean a quasi-autonomous
non-governmental organization (QUANGO) or state-authorized NGO
umbrella that ensures that foreign funding is only made available to gov-
ernment-approved activities.

The increased state interference with CSO freedoms led the United
Nations Human Rights Council to agree, in 2010, to appoint a new Special Rapporteur for Freedom of Peaceful Assembly and Association.

Impact of the Climate Change Debate on Civil Society

No field has historically been more influenced by civil society than the
environment. Until recently, the major environmental groups, rather
than governments, have shaped public opinion, dominated the media,
and provided leadership in policy-making, while governments and the
scientific establishment lagged behind. There are signs that this is now
changing for three reasons. First, governments (especially in the U.S. and
Europe) are keen to seize issue leadership; second, a new breed of climate-skeptic CSO has emerged—comprising largely of right-wing politicians, business interests, and conspiracy theorists—which has muddied
the public debate; and third, CSOs have often been linked to exaggerated
claims and polarized positions from which policy-makers and climate
scientists are increasingly keen to distance themselves. These factors are
discussed in turn before asking how long the present loss of favor might
last, and what strategies CSOs might adopt to counter them.

The Problem of Success

When it was a relatively new subject in the public eye,[61] the media would
draw on the best-known environment groups—such as Greenpeace,
Friends of the Earth (FoE), or Worldwide Fund for Nature (WWF)—for
evidence and policy sound bites. As climate change became more widely
accepted, leading politicians tended to claim the limelight. Hence, when
the media carries a climate change story now, its interviewee is likely to

be governmental rather than non-governmental unless the story concerns a particularly strident or eye-catching piece of action. Having succeeded in getting politicians to take the issue seriously, NGOs are now marginalized on the issue.

Pressure groups can flag a new concern, educate citizens, mobilize people to demonstrate public interest, and lobby legislators, but once an issue becomes a priority, politicians and the media look to other sources for their ammunition. In this case, the main source of policy expertise is the Intergovernmental Panel on Climate Change (IPCC) and its various Working Groups.[62] Many governments (especially of richer countries) have also appointed their own expert advisory groups. The more articulate scientists are also most likely to be the media's interviewees of choice. NGO leaders who continue to be prominent in the public debate are often those (such as Jonathan Porritt in U.K., former director of Friends of the Earth) who have been appointed as government advisors.

Out of the first 120 entries in a Google search on "climate change," 49 were government or intergovernmental sources, 21 were civil society (including 2 climate change skeptics), 23 were media sources, 20 were scientific or educational, 3 were business, and 4 were private blogs. Though this is purely illustrative, it suggests that fewer web users are drawing on CSO sources than would have been the case in the 90s. Moreover, less than half of these 21 CSO entries belonged to mainstream groups (such as Worldwide Fund for Nature, Greenpeace, Friends of the Earth, Nature Conservancy, Oxfam, the Catholic Church) who played a crucial role in bringing the issue to global prominence. The majority are groups that may have little history on the issue, but who adopt much higher profile, or controversial campaigning, or are well connected with the media, including Climate Change Camp, Climate Ark, Campaign against Climate Change, the Al Gore Foundation, and the David Suzuki Foundation.

The fight-back by climate change skeptics

At the same time, business interests have retaliated against the mounting consensus for emissions regulation. One strategy of the "climate skeptic" lobby has been to adopt civil society campaigning tactics itself. Several groups, whose names often suggest they are academic centers (such as Global Warming Policy Foundation, Nongovernmental International Panel on Climate Change, and International Climate Conference) have emerged in the last two years specifically to reduce the momentum towards action on climate change. Their strategies are to publicize any evidence or authority that appears to run counter to the scientific consensus, to impugn the motives or integrity of those who call for reducing emissions, and to claim that the measures so advocated would be ruinously expensive. Some who speak against major action to reduce emissions (such as the Copenhagen Consensus Center) accept that there is a greenhouse effect, but argue that it is too costly to address today and that the immediate priority should be on helping vulnerable communities adapt to a hotter climate and higher sea-levels, postponing for decades or centuries policies to reduce emissions.[63]

The most prominent climate-skeptic groups who are registered as NGOs or think tanks are generally reticent about their funding sources. Those who have researched this issue have found that much, if not most, funding derives from the energy industry.[64] The oil and gas industry has greatly increased its budget for lobbying overall as the climate debate becomes more prominent, dwarfing the equivalent expenditures of environmentalists.[65]

A key strategy of climate-skeptic CSOs is to argue that scientists are deeply divided over the evidence for climate change. While there is indeed an active debate, this tends to focus on the rate of acceleration of climate change, the role of water vapor, the sink-effect of oceans, and other environmental variables and technical issues. Most climate scientists (84 percent in the U.S.) now agree that human activities are causing climate changes that are extremely serious and demand urgent action, and only 5 percent believe that human activity does not contribute to greenhouse warming.[66]

Climate change skeptics, however, continue to proclaim that scientists are deeply divided. Hence, the International Climate Conference says: "the real science and economics of climate change support the view that global warming is not a crisis and that immediate action to reduce emissions is not necessary. This is, in fact, the emerging consensus view of scientists outside the IPCC and most economists outside environmental advocacy groups." The Heartland Institute makes similar claims and has erroneously listed scientists who support such views, refusing to delete these names when the scientists concerned protested.[67]

Conservative think tanks are constantly on the lookout for scientists who express doubts about climate change, sometimes offering them financial incentives to do so.[68] When they do find academics that are climate change skeptics, they widely publicize their views and provide them with public platforms. While most are economists and non-scientists, some are scientists and some (very few) are even climate scientists who buck the strong consensus in their community to recognize anthropogenic climate change.[69] Such sources are used by these groups to contradict and pour confusion over global warming.[70]

More unethically, some activists have obtained documents by hacking into private email accounts of climate scientists and scientific units to search for any illustration of practices that are less than perfect or conclusions that are dented. In particular, hacked emails from Professor Phil Jones of the Climate Research Unit, a think tank housed at the University of East Anglia, have been used in a campaign to imply that IPPC climate scientists are routinely exaggerating the climate change issue.[71]

Helped by the right-wing press, such efforts have been chillingly successful. Public opinion surveys in the U.S. and elsewhere demonstrate a dwindling public conviction about the science of climate change while scientists have become more convinced.[72]

The Environment Lobby—Shadows of Doubt

In the face of this increasingly aggressive counter attack and mounting public confusion over the issue, CSOs who are concerned about climate change face a dilemma. On the one hand, policy action costing huge sums of money and globally concerted responses require both confidence that there are no cheaper alternatives and massive public support for that action. On the other hand, the case that the emissions of CO_2 and other gasses cause anthropogenic climate change is based on climate science that depends on a large number of variables and can only approximate probabilities that certain levels of emission will result in particular increases in mean global temperature.

Cautious language about the percentage probability that global temperatures will rise by 3°C rather than 2° in timescales of several decades does not motivate public opinion. Most campaigning environmental groups therefore make statements that are bolder, relegating the detailed analysis to footnotes—resulting in a tone of precision and certainty that climate scientists eschew. Greenpeace, for example, says that, because the Copenhagen conference failed to agree to a 40 percent cut in emissions, "We are on track for more than 3°C temperature rise." Friends of the Earth predicts that, without abating emissions, there will be: "much greater temperature rises—even up to 7°C... Mountain glaciers may almost entirely vanish this century." Oxfam argues that the failure of Copenhagen might have put "the world on track for a catastrophic temperature rise of almost 4°C." Even the more cautious WWF says that: "Global emissions need to be at 44 giga-tons of CO_2 equivalent [i.e. 2005 levels] or lower, by 2020 if the world is to have a better than 50 percent chance of staying below 2°C warming... [the world could] be locked in to warming of 3 or 4°C or more. The consequences for people and nature on Planet Earth would be catastrophic."[73]

While these statements may well be proved true, and there is science behind them, they are couched in more alarmist and confident language than climate scientists typically use—especially as the climate skeptics have so successfully used advocacy and media strategies to magnify doubts about every scintilla of evidence.

Hence, while scientists and policy-makers once had much closer links with environment groups, now there is a cautious distance. The recent controversy about the melting of Himalayan glaciers has deepened this divide. A 938 page IPCC report, released in 2007, carelessly included a short statement warning of the likelihood of these glaciers "disappearing by the year 2035 and perhaps sooner." This passage was not based on the IPCC's peer review process, but on a scientific paper included in an annex. This has damaged the credibility of the IPCC. Embarrassingly, the author of the paper and this wild claim was WWF-Nepal. IPCC and climate scientists will inevitably be more cautious with evidence from NGOs in the future.[74]

Conclusions on the Climate Debate

As we have discussed, although the consensus amongst scientists of anthropogenic climate change and the need to take action to reduce greenhouse gas emissions is stronger than ever, and although civil society can be credited with awakening the world to the urgency of this issue, the current juncture is more hostile to the very organizations that elevated the issue. Politicians now want to make the running, not NGOs, and aggressive tactics by oil industry lobbyists and conservative pressure groups have poured doubt on the case and raised doubt amongst the general public.

It is unfortunate that the two most prominent incidences clouding the reputation of climate science are linked to CSOs. IPCC's erroneous reference to the rapid melting of Himalayan glaciers comes from the WWF and the "climate-gate scandal," alleging bias and distortion in the use of scientific data, originates in hacked emails from the U.K. think tank the Climate Research Unit. Scientists, with their reputation having been damaged as a result of a few careless statements, are asserting their objectivity by distancing themselves from CSOs.

While even most oil companies recognize that there is a problem, and indeed that there is a need to act, the debate has turned to one of how to act. The skeptics call for very limited measures (in particular adapting to climate change, rather than trying to avoid it) while the environment lobby urges sweeping and global measures. NGOs typically are better at the headlines than the detail. This isn't to say that leading environment groups don't have rigorous analysis and sound recommendations. Indeed they do. However, they face a dilemma. If they make bold claims and call for dramatic action their supporters are moved, and the media report their case—but they risk being labeled "alarmist," which tarnishes their image amongst policy makers and scientists. On the other hand, if they draw fully on the research and set out a rigorous case, they quickly lose their audience and lose ground to the newer, smaller pressure groups that have fewer scruples.

Further civil society divisions relate to policy prescriptions. Some CSOs call for reducing CO_2 emissions by reducing energy consumption, such as by high taxes on air travel and petroleum products. Others see this as unrealistic and call for increasing renewable energy production, but "green energy" initiatives (such as wind farms, hydro-electric dams, and wave barrages) are often criticized by local civic groups. Some NGO leaders (even those who were previously vocally opposed) have become advocates for returning to nuclear fuel, but this remains deeply divisive. Some NGOs recognize that, in reality, fossil fuels will continue to predominate for many years to come and so argue for carbon sequestration and other technological fixes that reduce or delay the greenhouse effect.[75] These, in turn, are condemned by other NGOs to whom coal and oil are anathemas. Likewise, some organizations have pressed for climate change mitigation measures (especially for island and low-lying states), while others consider this defeatist, since it assumes that global warming will continue. Also civil society voices on the environment are far from limited to environment groups. In many countries (particularly the U.S. and the U.K.) some of the largest public protests in recent years have been organized by the drivers' lobbies against taxes on fuels. While civil society has put this issue on the agenda, it is difficult to think of another topic that has been more divisive.

Finally, it is important to stress that, while this section has stressed the difficulties, not all is gloomy in the civil society camp. TckTckTck is a widely supported campaign launched by a coalition of development, environment, human rights, religious, and other groups, including household names such as Oxfam, Amnesty, and WWF. Its petition for a fair, ambitious, and binding climate change agreement, launched 100 days before the Copenhagen summit, mustered 15 million signatures. Also the largely web-mediated 350 Organization (which presses for a global commitment to reduce CO_2 emissions to 350ppm) organized a "planetary day of action" on 24 October 2009 that comprised 5,281 actions in iconic places in 181 countries around the world; this was described by CNN (Cable News Network) as the "most widespread day of political action in history."[76]

There are also a myriad of scattered actions that emphasize personal responsibility and community-level action. Hence, a Friends of the Earth survey in the U.K. concluded that there are some two to four thousand community-based groups working on climate change in the U.K., and that this number is growing rapidly (indeed some 40 percent of these groups were set up since 2005), but the survey also showed that 59 percent of these are independent, not affiliated to any national group, and a further 8 percent are affiliated to faith organizations. Hence, relatively few are part of a national environmental campaigning movement.

Conclusions

As we have demonstrated, the major 21st century crises have reduced citizen support for CSOs, reduced the influence of civil society as a corrective force, triggered a renaissance of the "state as savior" (as opposed to civil society solutions), and exacerbated tensions both between the state and civil society and within civil society.

While the 1980s and 1990s were periods in which governments were in ideological retreat (with the private sector and, to some extent, civil society enjoying a parallel ascendancy), today's nexus of larger crises is perfect territory for governments, since only they are able to tackle them. While civil society remains important, it finds itself overshadowed today by state actors. As a consequence, public support for transformational CSOs has dropped steeply in recent years (as evidenced, for example, by the declining membership of the major environment NGOs, or participation in the World Social Forum, or large numbers of protesters at the main meetings of global leaders).

Many governments have become more hostile to civil society in response to protests against the Iraq War and governmental negligence in addressing the social impact of the financial crisis. As a consequence, they have become less receptive to CSOs. Governments elsewhere in the world have often latched onto this changed mood as a pretext for reverting to more repressive measures against domestic civil society.

CSOs have often responded either by remaining silent or by becoming shriller in their criticism of governments. This spiral of mistrust and antagonism is counterproductive for both sides. It leads to the further marginalization of civil society, but more importantly, it distracts and deters governments from the path the world needs them to follow.

Today's crises can only be effectively tackled by governments and, moreover, by governments acting collectively. This requires governments that are both strong and confident. Governments that feel vulnerable look inwards; they look to measures that give them the most chance of clinging to power—i.e., matters that are short-term and local, whereas the critical fixes that are needed are long-term and global. Only governments that feel strong and relatively safe on their home front are prepared to make the compromises needed for international cooperation. Strong opposition, whether from political adversaries or social movements, is likely to make them feel vulnerable.

Herein lies the dilemma for civil society. Public pressure on issues of global public concern needs to be strong enough to ensure that governments are resolute in addressing them. But CSOs also need to assure governments that they can provide practical help and deliver public support for the necessary government action—i.e., that they are not anti-government per se. The challenge for CSOs is how to press for resolute action without further eroding public trust in governments, indeed how to foster government leadership tomorrow on the very issues that governments are castigated for ignoring today. This requires different strategies to those normally deployed—namely the exaggeration of official errors and demonstrating overwhelming public disgust for these sins.

What this means in practice is more civil society attention to matters of governance and accountability. CSOs can help elected representatives in their oversight of government practices relating to global challenges and can respond to, and even create, opportunities for direct citizen participation in the affairs of governments at local, national, and global levels. Such measures will encourage governments to put into practice the rhetoric of their stated policies, will provide feedback on the degree to which this is achieved, and the efficacy of those measures.[77]

Civic engagement is particularly pertinent to today's global crises. These require much greater participation by citizens and non-governmental experts in the making and execution of policy and in rigorous oversight of government performance—what Keane, in this book, calls "monitory democracy." Many CSO networks are now cooperating internationally to promote such participation. They have often seen the need to get out of their "issue silos" (whether relating to the environment, gender, arms trade, third world debt, or whatever) to focus on broader concerns of global governance. Examples include the International Association of NGOs (bringing together the major development, human rights, and environment NGOs on trans-sectoral campaigns) or the "TckTckTck" alliance on climate change and social development.

What such networks have in common is the view that the necessary measures to address global crises are often relatively clear, but there is little action throughout the world on that agenda, and that, therefore, what is needed is civic action to change the zeitgeist from "political won't" to "political will."[78]

While the single-issue focus has clearly been effective, it also has increasingly clear pitfalls: (a) it tends to atomize politics into countless causes that politicians find difficult to reconcile; (b) activists tend to concentrate on international and perhaps U.S. decision-makers in ways that ignore national governments and parliamentarians; and (c) the causes tend to be somewhat elitist (just a few faces keep surfacing and only the elite media follow them). An unfortunate side effect is that it often makes people more cynical about their national democratic processes—which can be counter-productive. Connecting citizens and the state in ways that are productive and constructive while safeguarding CSO autonomy is not easy to achieve at a time when civil society itself is under threat. But at present the sector feels squeezed by "managed democracies" and authoritarian regimes alike as they impose increasingly tough restrictions on CSOs. As an added challenge, limited examples of NGO errors or exaggerations are widely cited to impugn the integrity and competence of NGOs in general.

Historically civil society, like democracy, has been built from the local level upwards. Citizens form local action groups and share experiences with counterparts in neighboring communities, perhaps networking at the regional or national level. Modern technology is changing the geography of politics. It is no longer necessary to be grouped together only according to the communities where we live. Through participatory democracy, we can aggregate communities of interest that can be global as readily as local. The resulting global policy networks have engaged effectively with the institutions of global governance (the UN, World Bank, WTO, G8, etc.) and with journalists in their coverage of world affairs. Policy shifts and "monitory democracy" may be easier to attain at the local or national level (where political power resides and most decisions are made), but through such networking, civil society has achieved a role in governance at the international level—where traditional instruments of oversight (such as the monitoring departments of governments and elected representatives) are very weak, but where critical agreements are forged on environmental and economic matters.

Indeed, in order to remain relevant in today's policy arena, civil society must demonstrate its ability to contribute effective responses to today's major crises, rather than just putting issues on the public agenda. In other words, it must point to solutions, not just identify problems. The trends discussed in this chapter make it difficult to do this. While these difficulties are not as yet insurmountable for the sector, they are ones that civil society leaders should reflect on carefully because they may become more troublesome in the future and because they warrant significant shifts in tactics. In particular, there is a case for more strenuously seeking influential allies in governments and official bodies; for focusing more on the process of policy-making (i.e. governance) rather than its substance; for searching out non-traditional allies, such as activist shareholders or scientists; for forging new allies within civil society (such as NGOs partnering with professional associations or faith leaders); and for looking for good models of "co-governance" involving both state and civic actors, as illustrated most effectively in Nordic countries.[79]

Given the relatively high degree of consensus today about what crises need to be addressed, and the approximate direction policy needs to take, the key areas of contention concern the exact strategies to take, as well as the sequence and burden-sharing of these actions. This territory hasn't traditionally been the comparative advantage of CSOs, but must become so if civil society is to pull its weight. The key challenge for CSOs is to demonstrate that they can indeed contribute in such areas while at the same time not losing the interest and support of their adherents.

To adapt in this way would prove most difficult, especially for the many activists who provide the ideas for, and the shape of, the anti-globalization movement. For them, the modus operandi has been to scorn Western governments and caricature them as offering undiluted capitalist dogma as the solution to all problems. At the same time, the diverse groups focus on a myriad set of issues—social, cultural, environmental, and economic—presenting even more diverse and often idiosyncratic solutions to the problems highlighted. They present a semblance of unity in rejecting this type of globalization and seeking an alternative.

Their slogan has been: "One big 'NO!' and many small 'YESES.'"[80] This was appealing for a while, but in the face of the three major global crises discussed it has evidently palled, as revealed by the diminishing scale of the Movement's events and protests. Mass movements may be effective at registering concerns (the concerted "NO"), but once on the political agenda the contest of ideas and leadership requires convincing alternatives to policies being pursued. A multitude of small "YESES" is neither convincing to policy-makers, nor sustainable for public motivation, especially as these solutions are often untested or poorly thought through, making them instead appear as a handful of "MAYBES."

The challenge for civil society today is to demonstrate not that it can see more clearly the problems of today's globalization, but that it can pinpoint most compellingly the fairest and most effective solutions to those problems. To have any prospects of winning reforms by persuading governments at all levels of those solutions, the YESES promoted by civil society need to be at least as compelling as the NOs.

Notes

1. A global survey of citizen concerns confirms these to be the three highest public concerns. The 2005 GlobeSpan "Global Issues Monitor" survey in 22 countries asked respondents to rank what they regard as "the most important problem facing the world today." 30 percent of respondents ranked economic crisis, poverty, and unemployment as their top concern; 24 percent selected war, conflict, or terrorism; 8 percent opted for environment or climate change, while the remainder were scattered thinly over a number of other concerns such as HIV/AIDS, moral/spiritual decay, corruption, crime, the gap between rich and poor, etc.
2. Reference to John Keane's chapter in this volume.
3. Chief development officer for the American Red Cross, quoted in "It's a Hard time to be a Charity," *USA Today*, 27 September 2008. He commented that this: "is the worst fundraising environment I've ever worked in."
4. Guidestar annual economic surveys of 2008, 2009, and 2010, published by Guidestar—the leading research organization about philanthropy and the voluntary sector.
5. GivingUSA Foundation. Executive Summary. *Giving USA 2010*.
6. Grant Williams, "As Government Money Dwindles, Many Human-Service Groups Cut Back Assistance to the Needy," *Chronicle of Philanthropy*, 6 October 2010.
7. Charities Aid Foundation, source: *http://www.cafonline.org/default.aspx?page=16118*.
8. John Shaw, director of finance at Oxfam GB, stated that Oxfam reduced its 2009–10 forecasted growth from 5–6 percent to zero.
9. Martin Brookes, Chief Executive, New Philanthropy Capital, 11 August 2009
10. Report of the GreaterGood community networking website and Melanie Peters, "Charities, NGOs funds 'drying up'," *Weekend Argus*, 9 November 2008.
11. Foundations are trusts financed by corporate philanthropy, or endowed by donations, or legacies from wealthy individuals, or the proceeds from investing which are used to finance philanthropic activities. Some foundations support civil society activities at home or in poorer countries. Many developing countries (such as India, Philippines, and Brazil) have their own foundations, but these tend to be dwarfed by the large US and European foundations.
12. Foundation Center, *Foundation Growth and Giving Estimates: Current Outlook* (New York: Foundation Center, 2009).
13. Council on Foundations, "Foundations Respond to the Needs of Families Even as Their Assets Have Declined," 6 May 2009. Also, a survey of some of the largest US foundations, described by Noelle Barton and Ian Wilhelm, *Chronicle of Philanthropy*, 21 January 2009, showed endowments had declined by a median of 29 percent from 2007 to 2008 (i.e. before the worst impact of the crisis) and that two-thirds of foundations plan to reduce their giving as a result.

14. A survey conducted for the U.K. Charity Commission showed that most had experienced a small fall in income since the fall of 2008 but intended to hold funding levels steady for as long as possible due to the increased social needs (*Charity Commission*, U.K. Aug 2009).

15. A term commonly used by its own leading intellectuals, as described in John Clark and Nuno Themudo, "Linking the Web and the Street: Internet-Based 'Dot-causes' and the 'Anti-Globalization Movement'," *World Development*, vol. 34, no. 1 (2006): 50–74.

16. Geoffrey Pleyers, "World Social Forum 2009: A Generation's Challenge," Belgian Foundation for Scientific Research, University of Louvain, 28 January 2009.

17. This is shorthand for the anti-neoliberal activists who variously describe themselves as the anti-globalization, "alter-globalization," anti-corporate-globalization, or the global social justice movement.

18. Civil society campaigns relating to the World Bank are described in John Clark, "The World Bank and Civil Society: An Evolving Experience," in *Civil Society and Global Finance*, ed. J. Scholte and A. Schnabel, (London: Routledge, 2002): 111–127. There is a broader discussion of CSO activities relating to governance in John Clark, *Worlds Apart: Civil Society and the Battle for Ethical Globalization* (Bloomfield, C.T.: Kumarian Press, 2003).

19. Examples include campaigns on environmental damage caused by oil, mining, or logging companies; injustices related to the trade in specific commodities exported by developing countries; and the excesses of pharmaceutical or pesticide manufacturers.

20. There are numerous civil society activities that address corporate governance (e.g. Global Reporting Initiative, the Extractive Industry Transparency Initiative, Transparency International, Publish What You Pay, Global Justice, etc.) but these have little relevance to the current economic crisis. They mostly concern transparency in firms' relations with governments and few address the banking sector.

21. A number of CSOs have, however, campaigned for a "Tobin Tax" on international financial transactions which would both dampen speculation and mobilize considerable resources for international social and environmental needs. Most notable has been the campaigns of ATTAC, see *www.attac.org*, and Jubilee Debt Campaign and Jubilee Research—see *http://www.jubileeresearch.org/*

22. Clark and Themudo, "Linking the Web and the Street."

23. Op Cit.

24. Nate Cull writing in "The Observers," 2 February 2009 (an online news service of France 24), see: *http://observers.france24.com/en/content/20090202-anti-cap italist-world-social-forum-belem*. For data on participation by region see: *www .forumsocialmundial.org.br/noticias_01.php?cd*

25. Culminating in the 2005 Porto Alegre when the Forum had 200,000 participants and 2,500 workshops.

26. Clark and Themudo, "Linking the Web and the Street": 50–74, discusses both the inherent strengths and weaknesses of the Movement.

27. Franco Barchiesi, Heinrich Bohmke, Prishani Naidoo, Ahmed Veriava; "Does Bamako Appeal? The World Social Forum versus the Life Strategies of the Subaltern"; Contribution to the Workshop on the World Social Forum, Durban Centre for Civil Society, 22–23 July 2006.

28. Claire Folkard (ed.) *Guinness World Records* (New York: Guinness World Records, 2004).

29. Patrick Tyler, "A New Power in the Streets," *New York Times*, 17 February 2003.

30. Corwin Smidt, "Religion and American Attitudes toward Islam and an Invasion of Iraq," *Sociology of Religion*, 22 September 2005.

31. Pew Global Attitudes Survey (for the BBC), "The Great Divide: How Westerners and Muslims View Each Other," 22 June 2006.

32. For a description of the project's intentions, see: *http://www.cordobainitiative.org.*

33. In contrast, there were no objections to Roman Catholic centers or National Rifle Association offices in Oklahoma stemming from the faith and political pursuit of that city's bomber, Timothy McVeigh.

34. See *http://www.bbc.co.uk/news/world-us-canada-11076846.*

35. The author most famously associated with this position is Samuel Huntington, whose book *The Clash of Civilizations and the Remaking of World Order* (New York: Simon and Schuster, 1996) was extremely popular, especially with U.S. conservatives. However, the first to write on the "clash of civilizations" was Bernard Lewis whose article: "The Roots of Muslim Rage," *Atlantic Journal*, September 1990, is a well-argued and prophetic analysis of growing Muslim-Christian resentment.

36. Pew Research Center poll of the U.S. public, quoted in B. Grim and R. Finke, "Documenting Religion Worldwide: Decreasing the Data Deficit," *IASSIST Quarterly* (2005): 11–15.

37. Ipsos MORI survey for the Equalities and Human Rights Commission (EHRC), 20 January 2009.

38. See the Financial Action Task Force website: *www.fatfgafi.org/pages/0,3417,en_ 32250379_32236846_1_1_1_1_1,00.html*

39. See FATF website. The 8 Special Recommendations were expanded to 9 in October 2004 with the addition of one concerning "cash couriers."

40. Michael Jonsson and Svante Cornell, "Countering Terrorist Financing: Lessons from Europe," *Georgetown Journal of International Affairs* vol. 8, no. 69 (2007): 10.

41. Financial Action Task Force, Typologies Report 2003–2004. Paris: FATF 2004

42. FATF Interpretative Note to Special Recommendation VIII: Non-Profit Organisations; see: *http://www.fatf-gafi.org/dataoecd/43/5/38816530.pdf*

43. FATF, Interpretive Note.

44. These prescriptions comprise "Voluntary Guidelines," rather than international law, but each FATF member government must report on its actions with respect to them, and hence they carry considerable weight. Some commentators are worried that they may be used as the basis for future legal requirements.

45. These new US requirements for NGOs and foundations were set out by the US Treasury in late 2002 in *Anti-Terrorist Financing Guidelines: Voluntary Best Practices for U.S.-Based Charities.* These guidelines were revised in December 2005.

46. Barnett F. Baron, "Deterring Donors: Anti-terrorist Financing Rules and American Philanthropy," *International Journal of Not-for-Profit Law* 6, no. 2 (2004): 1–32.

47. Mark Sidel, "The Third Sector, Human Security, and Anti-Terrorism: The United States and Beyond," *Voluntas: International Journal of Voluntary and Nonprofit Organizations* 17, no. 3 (2006): 199–210.

48. Council on Foundations, *Letter to the U.S. Treasury Department on the Revised Anti-Terrorist Financing Guidelines* (Washington D.C.: United States International Grantmaking, 2006), available at *www.usig.org/PDFs/CommentstoTreasury.pdf*

49. Peter Christian Weber, "Terrorism and Philanthropy: Counter Terrorism Financing Regimes, International Civil Society, and Religious Fundamentalisms," paper presented at the 8th International Conference of the International Society for Third Sector Research (ISTR), Barcelona 9–12 July 2008.

50. Nolan Quigley and Belinda Pratten, "Security and Civil Society: The Impact of Counter-terrorism Measures on Civil Society Organizations," National Council for Voluntary Organizations (London: National Council for Voluntary Organizations, 11 January 2007): *http://www.ncvo-vol.org.uk/*.

51. When ICNL and other NGOs pointed out that an earlier 990 requirement to name all foreign grantees jeopardized the safety of individuals associated with some organizations, the Internal Revenue Service agreed that names of organizations could be withheld if disclosure would likely result in bodily injury.

52. See note before concerning IRS form 990.

53. President Obama touched on this issue in his Cairo speech on 4 June 2009. He said: "Freedom of religion is central to the ability of peoples to live together. We must always examine the ways in which we protect it. For instance, in the United States, rules on charitable giving have made it harder for Muslims to fulfill their religious obligation. That's why I'm committed to working with American Muslims to ensure that they can fulfill zakat."

54. Op Cit.

55. Op Cit.

56. Op Cit.

57. Jude Howell, Armine Ishkanian, Ebenezer Obadare, Hakan Seckinelgin, and Marlies Glasius. "The Backlash against Civil Society in the Wake of the Long War on Terror," *Civil Society Working Papers* No. 26 (Center for Civil Society, London School of Economics and Political Science, 2006).

58. Op Cit.

59. Personal Communication with ICNL's President, Doug Rutzen. See also ICNL's series, Global Trends in NGO Law reports.

60. FATF, *Money Laundering and Terrorist Financing Typologies*, 2003–4.

61. The contribution of man-made emissions to a greenhouse effect is not a new subject; it was first described by the Swedish chemist, Svante Arrhenius in 1895.

62. IPCC comprises 194 governments each of which appoints representatives to the panel and its affiliate bodies (usually top national scientists).

63. Bjørn Lomborg, *Cool It: The Skeptical Environmentalist's Guide to Global Warming* (London: Knopf, 2007); Copenhagen Consensus Center, "Copenhagen Consensus on Climate: Advice for Policymakers," (2009).

64. James McCarthy, President-elect of the American Association for the Advancement of Science, informed the US Subcommittee on Investigations and Oversight, House Science Committee on 28 March 2007 that Exxon-Mobil alone provided almost $16 million to a network of 43 such groups between 1998 and 2005. The U.K.'s Royal Society expressed concern (in a letter from Bob Ward to the company on 4 September 2005) that Exxon financed 39 organizations that "misrepresented the science of climate change" in 2005 alone, to the tune of at least $2.9 million.

65. In 2005, the oil and gas industry were 11th in the league of lobbying expenditures in Washington D.C., by 2009 they had risen to second place, after the pharmaceutical industry, spending $168 million in that year, see: *http://www.opensecrets .org/lobby/top.php?showYear=2009&indexType=i*. In the U.S., the industry devoted $168 million to lobbying in 2009, compared with $22 million by the environment lobby on all their causes (see: *http://www.opensecrets.org/lobby/index.php*).

66. A 2007 survey by Harris Interactive of scientists belonging to the American Geophysical Union and the American Meteorological Society (the two U.S. societies whose members are most likely to be involved in climate research) demonstrates scientists' confidence about anthropogenic climate change. 97 percent agreed that global temperatures have increased during the past 100 years, 84 percent say they believe human-induced warming is occurring, and 74 percent agree that "currently available scientific evidence" substantiates its occurrence. Only 5 percent believe that that human activity does not contribute to greenhouse warming and 84 percent believe global climate change poses a moderate to very great source (Robert S. Lichter, "Climate Scientists Agree on Warming, Disagree on Dangers, and Don't Trust the Media's Coverage of Climate Change," Statistical Assessment Service, George Mason University, 24 April 2008.

67. Sources: *http://www.desmogblog.com/500-scientists-with-documented-doubts-about-the-heartland-institute*, and *http://www.hearthlind.org/policybot/results*.

68. For example, the American Enterprise Institute wrote to climate scientists in 2006 offering large "honoraria" for "reviews and policy critiques" of a forthcoming IPCC report. Some recipients saw this as a crude attempt to fish for criticisms. See: *http://sciencepoliticsclimatechange.blogspot.com/2006/07/aei-and-ar4.html*. The full AEI letter is available at: *http://www.aei.org/article/25586*.

69. The most prominent such climate scientist is Professor Richard Lindzen, a meteorologist and former member of the Intergovernmental Panel on Climate Change (IPCC). Lindzen's arguments largely emphasize the complexity of factors making for climate change, and while recognizing that the average temperatures have risen since the industrial revolution began, argues that it isn't possible to assign all this to man-made emissions, that it is not possible to predict future trends, and therefore that the confidence of predictions of catastrophic climate change is unwarranted.

70. For example they disseminate graphs showing average global temperatures for a few carefully-selected recent years to suggest that there is cooling rather than warming and omitting that climate scientists are looking at trends over decades and centuries, rather than short-term patterns.

71. These emails dating from 1991 to 2009 were largely between Jones and fellow IPCC members. They were obtained by hacking into the CRU email system and first posted on a small web-server in the Siberian city of Tomsk (See: Quirin Schiermeier, Nature, 20 November 2009.). By taking sentences out of context, the leaks were used to promote a false impression that Jones' work deliberately cut out data that muddied the systemic rise in global temperatures and that he sought to remove from IPCC's literature database articles that ran counter to the field's orthodoxy. Further, by inference they promoted the idea that everyone involved in the IPCC is similarly biased and complicit in a grand deception.

72. Surveys by the Pew Research Center (*http://people-press.org/report/556/global-warming*) show that there has been a sharp decline in the percentage of Americans

who believe there is solid evidence that global temperatures are rising—from 77 percent in August 2006 to 57 percent in October 2009—while those recognizing global warming as a very serious problem has fallen from 44 percent in April 2008 to 35 percent in Oct. 2009.

73. All these statements come from the pages on climate change from the NGOs' respective websites.

74. The error was in IPCC's Working Group II report, Climate Change 2007: Working Group II: Impacts, Adaption, and Vulnerability, *http://www.ipcc.ch/publications_ and_data/ar4/wg2/en/ch10s10-6-2.html.* It derived from an annex to the report from WWF Nepal, dated 2005: "An overview of glaciers, glacier retreat, and subsequent impacts in Nepal, India, and China." Three other errors have been detected in the same report. Given the damage even one or two errors does to IPCC's credibility, it is under pressure to strengthen its review processes, see: *http://e360.yale.edu/ content/feature.msp?id=2245&utm_source=feedburner&utm_medium=feed&utm_ campaign=Feed percent3A+YaleEnvironment360+(Yale+Environment+360).*

75. One measure that is supported by some CSOs, but criticized by others, is the Reducing Emissions from Deforestation and Forest Degradation in Developing Countries scheme (REDD), in which carbon taxes and other resources from rich countries finance measures designed to increase CO_2 capture in poorer countries.

76. See the Afterword of this book by Bill McKibben for a detailed account of the 350 Campaign.

77. See "We the Peoples: Civil Society, the United Nations and Global Governance," UN General Assembly document, A/58/817, 11 June 2004 report; see also Lars Trägårdh, *State and Civil Society in Northern Europe: the Swedish Model Reconsidered* (Oxford and New York: Berghahn Books, 2007).

78. Carmen Malena, ed., "From Political Won't to Political Will: Building Support for Participatory Governance," CIVICUS (West Hartford, C.T.: Kumarian Press, 2010).

79. Op Cit.

80. The catch phrase of "Subcommandante Marcos," described in Paul Kingsnorth, "One No, Many Yeses: The Rise of the New Resistance Movement" (2003), available from: *http://www.signsofthetimes.org.uk/king.html*

Chapter 3

DIGITAL DEPRIVATION
NEW MEDIA, CIVIL SOCIETY, AND SUSTAINABILITY

Paddy Coulter and Cathy Baldwin

Introduction

The arrival of new digital media since the 1990s has offered unparalleled scope to civil society organizations to mobilize a supporter base, generate public concern, give citizens a voice, and promote social change. What challenges must be overcome to capitalize on these opportunities?

This chapter draws on academic assessments of development NGO activities and practitioner reports, together with interviews with senior figures in leading U.K.-based international non-governmental organizations, to explore the use of new media in development. We consider how NGOs can integrate new information and communications technologies (ICTs) into their work, and seek to assess what NGOs have achieved as a result of using new media. What is the potential of these technologies and what are their limitations? Where are the new media success stories? And what is the potential of the digital media to transform civil society?

We look particularly at non-governmental organizations (NGOs) which Manuel Castells has described as "the most innovative, dynamic, and representative forms of aggregation of social interests."[1] Our focus here is on the subset of NGOs that promote sustainable development in poorer countries, including international, national, and grassroots organizations.

By "sustainable development" we mean the Brundtland Commission concept, in other words, development that "meets the needs of the present without compromising the ability of future generations to meet their own needs."[2] One practical expression of this philosophy is the Millennium Development Goals (MDGs), adopted by world leaders in 2000 to tackle extreme poverty and ensure environmental sustainability.[3]

The contested analytical term "civil society" describes, among other things, a conceptual sphere as differentiated from family, state, and market, and a structured network of existent organizations at the levels of local and national societies. Today it arguably includes expanding transnational networks, which some theorists believe have formed a "global civil society." The traditional nationally-located civil society embraces a diverse array of different kinds of groups—in religious institutions, trades unions, cooperatives, and social movements among others; in Pippa Norris' phrase "multiple organizations buffering between citizens and the state." In an amalgamation of its conceptual and practical meanings, Michael Walzer stresses the essential voluntary character of civil society, defining it as "the space of uncoerced human association and also the set of relational networks formed for the sake of family, faith, interest, and ideology."[4] Contemporarily active development groups value the idealized autonomy of civil society which the International NGO Training and Research Center (INTRAC), the leading NGO training and research body in the U.K., defines as "organizations that self-organize to advance collective goals."[5]

Development groups often present themselves as being independent and innovatory agents of change, equipping people from the bottom up to participate as citizens by enhancing their power and agency. Although some NGOs espouse a rhetoric of bypassing the state altogether, it is obvious that state power cannot be simply willed away.[6] There can be a serious tension between their role in social mobilization (for example, when NGOs lobby the state on a human rights agenda) and their role in the delivery of services. For the latter, NGOs are required to engage with the state in its different aspects—as regulator, financial resource, development partner, or indeed as bureaucratic obstacle and political threat to new initiatives. The development groups we discuss in this chapter have a range of different structural relationships to the state, but as our goal is to be illustrative of the breadth of work being carried out on the ground, the most important factor here is that they all harness new media to deliver socio-economic development assistance to poor communities.

Theorists have pointed out how difficult the concept of "global civil society" is to define.[7] As Marlies Glasius writes, "counting the number of international NGOs in the world does not provide insightful conclusions about who the significant civil society actors are from a power perspective or a value one."[8] There are highly contested parameters around the kinds of organizations and actors that are included and excluded (e.g. NGOs versus Al Qaida), whether it is good or bad, global or Western, and how effective organizations flying the global civil society banner are, as compared to, say, governments, international organizations, and the private sector. However, the somewhat cynical "post modern account" offered by Glasius that "the arena or collection of actors in (uneven) contestation from a plurality of normative perspectives, not engaged in any one single master project" paints an accurate picture of the global arena in which NGOs in our examination operate, ranging from international organizations with household names and extensive funding, to small-scale groups on the margins of transnational activity based in developing countries.

Moving to the technologies themselves, the term "new media" includes the full range of digital information and communications technologies (ICTs), in particular the Internet, mobile telephony, and associated social networking and online applications.[9] In *The Rise of the Network Society*, Manuel Castells, the influential theorist of the impact of the Internet and digital technologies on economies and societies around the world, wrote, "The internet offers a great potential for the expression of citizen rights and the communication of human values."[10] A decade later, in the mission statement of the Facebook social networking site, chief executive Mark Zuckerberg set out a similarly ambitious aim for his company, "to give people the power to share, in order to make the world more open and connected."[11] This confidence in the power of new media was shared by ex-British Prime Minister, Gordon Brown, in his 2010 speech in Kampala to African leaders, "Africa's best hope for diversification is not just in improving agricultural productivity, which is a priority, but also creating jobs in the high-value sectors with a massive acceleration in the use of IT."[12]

But are such claims, as some have argued, a case of "Californian cyber-hyperbole"?[13] Some authors have challenged what is perceived as industrialized countries "techno-deterministic optimism"[14]—the faith that new media expansion necessarily leads to social and economic inclusion.[15] Others have signaled caution about hopes that new media can automatically increase democratic participation in the developing world.[16] An Nguyen, for example, writing about citizen journalism in Vietnam, criticizes the naivety of optimistic Western analysts celebrating the new information technologies as a pure democratizing force for the public good.[17] Evgeny Morozov, giving the subtitle "How Not to Liberate the World" to the British edition of his recent book *The Net Delusion*, appeals to westerners to, "ditch cyber-utopian assumptions and begin to think more critically about the role the internet can play in promoting democracy worldwide."[18] He gives numerous examples of repressive states using the power of the new media, for example in Belarus and Iran to track down social networking dissidents.[19]

John Keane takes a stance that is mainly optimistic, arguing that the new "communicative abundance" has brought media to many millions around the world, while acknowledging the gap between the communication rich and poor which "blights all monitory democracies." Norris shares the latter concern, pointing to the fact that it is the poor, the illiterate, ethnic minorities, and women who lack access to the new media and are therefore excluded from participation in the public sphere.[20]

Keane sees the digital media as facilitating the emergence of new, networked forms of civic participation, democratizing forces that are breaking down the distinctions between the local, the national, and the global. He credits "power-monitoring networks" with generating the major public issues of our time through their targeting of "the state-framed institutions of the old representative democracy." But this argument ignores the issues of state control over the telecommunications spectrum, the allocation of licenses, and the state's capacity in nations across the globe, as deployed recently by the Syrian government, to suppress unrest by disabling or shutting down Internet or telephony networks. To what extent are digital media democratizing forces if the state controls the infrastructure and therefore sets the terms of access and engagement with these new technologies?

The enthusiasts can also overstate the impact of "power-monitoring networks." For example, Keane describes the Make Poverty History lobby of the 2005 G8 (the Group of Eight) summit at Gleneagles as "the most spectacular attempt to transform top-down government summits into new channels." The scale of mobilization around the summit was indeed huge with civil society campaigns in some seventy countries but, for all the media extravaganza and involvement of celebrity rock musicians, three of Europe's leading countries—Germany, France, and Italy—have since reneged on their public pledges to increase aid. According to recent figures from the Organization for Economic Cooperation and Development (OECD), on current trajectories, G8 countries will supply less than half the $25 billion promised at the time to Africa. In the U.K., where 440,000 people emailed the Prime Minister about global poverty, the aid commitments have survived a change of government, but the effect of the Make Poverty History campaign on public opinion has proved very short-lived. The proportion of people saying that they are "very concerned" about global poverty—which in the U.K. tends to hover stubbornly around the 25 percent mark—went up to 32 percent in the run-up to Gleneagles but has since fallen back to around 24 percent at present.

The enthusiasts claim that new media offer developing countries the chance to make great leaps forward in educating and skilling their workforces, economic opportunity and prosperity, and civic equality, while skeptics argue that it reinforces, and indeed widens, inequalities because the benefits largely flow to elites. The skeptics point out that the same new media facilitate the global spread of jihadist propaganda and other "hate messages," and have been used by repressive regimes to target and harass activists, for example by hacking into the email accounts of dissident bloggers. How should civil society groups concerned with development respond? Should they encourage investment in these new technologies and, if so, would improving access in itself be sufficient to transform social, economic, and civic opportunities for the poorest?

There are conceptual and definitional issues at stake with regard to the technologies themselves. Some commentators reject a sharp dichotomy between these new media and the older media of newspapers, radio, and television broadcasting. For instance, James Deane, Head of Policy for the BBC World Service Trust, holds that it is a mistake to compare the newness of ICTs with "traditional" mass media when broadcasters and newspapers have also changed and become more interactive.[21] Gerry Power, Managing Director of Intermedia U.K., argues that the term ICTs itself needs to be unbundled, making a distinction between the Internet and telephony, as the technologies have a wide variety of social and economic impacts in different countries.[22]

While accepting the thrust of these contentions, we believe, nevertheless, that it is useful to retain the lumped category of ICTs as distinct from the older media because ICTs present new issues in policy terms. They are also treated differently by development donors who see the new media as offering greater potential than traditional media in terms of income generation, improved livelihoods, and economic growth. The important point to note is that NGOs' use of new media is not simply a means of communicating with their supporters and partner agencies, but can also make a direct contribution to local economic and social development.

In the sections that follow, we examine the early involvement of civil society activists with new media and the potential that this has offered NGOs thus far, before discussing the economic, socio-political, technical, and logistical obstacles thrown up by the uptake of ICTs in developing countries. In the context of these challenges, we discuss prominent examples of NGO projects using ICTs to review their successes and pitfalls and provide some conclusions on their impact.

Emergence of global interactive media

The explosion of new developments in ICTs over the past decade or so—in particular the diffusion of the Internet and email and the rapid advance of mobile telephony—has opened up a vast terrain of new communications possibilities for groups and individuals across great geographical distances. Activists around the world were quick to utilize these technologies. Prominent early examples of "Internet activism" from the 1990s include the EZLN Zapatista (Ejercito Zapatista Liberacion Nacional) movement in the Chiapas region of Mexico, the Falung Gong spiritual movement in China, and anti-globalization networks concentrated in industrialized countries that instigated, for example, the protest against the World Trade Organization (WTO) in Seattle in 1999. They assembled expansive online networks, hosted online debates, disseminated information, communicated with the mass media, and mobilized protests against state and international institutional policies.

ICTs were lauded as cheap, accessible, and ubiquitous, with the capacity to enable a two-way dialogue between groups and their audiences, meaning that the voices of marginalized communities could appear in an expanded range of public forums. In the case of Seattle, months of online debate prompted individual and collective decisions to protest. These networks appeared to override state and international bodies, unleashing the power of networked actions to make an impact through protest and media coverage,[23] and allowing civil society groups with global supporter bases to challenge the state.[24]

At about the same time, public audiences around the world began to communicate en masse with mainstream media corporations via ICTs. Britain's BBC, for example, began inviting viewers to email and text its television programs in 1999, starting with its flagship investigative current affairs show *Panorama*.[25] As technologies improved, these requests were extended to video clips and digital photographs sent via the Internet or mobile phones. Invitations to post videos, photographs, and comments have now become a standard item of the international and regional 24/7 television news channels, such as Al Jazeera and the Hindi channel Aaj-Tak, which have proliferated around the world since the success of the first such channel, CNN.[26] The volume of audience material generated has risen rapidly. The BBC News Interactive website[27] received 300 emails per day prior to the 7/7 London Underground attacks in 2005, rising to around 12,000 emails per day by 2008.[28]

Perhaps the most celebrated example of the new citizen journalism has been South Korea's dynamic online newspaper, *OhmyNews*, whose motto is "Every Citizen is a Reporter." From its launch in 2000 to its current network of over 30,000 citizen reporters supported by a small core staff of professional journalists and editors, *OhmyNews* has built a very substantial online readership and become a household name in Korea.[29]

The Asian tsunami of 2004 is well documented as the coming of age for citizen journalist interventions in a humanitarian crisis of global proportions.[30] Private individuals wishing to assist in the relief effort by documenting the scale of the catastrophe supplied media organizations and blog sites with hundreds of thousands of photographs, videos, and messages. Four years later, the Ushahidi website was launched in Kenya to track post-election violence, allowing volunteer monitors to submit eyewitness material on an open-source platform.[31] This East African initiative has since been involved in humanitarian response around the world, notably helping survivors in the early stages of the Haiti earthquake catastrophe in 2010 through the production of a crisis map.

These examples show the epic scale on which the convergence of ICTs with mainstream mass media can have an impact for civil society players.[32] Our focus here, however, is on uses of ICTs by NGOs engaged in longer-term sustainable development activity, rather than on humanitarian emergency warning systems or crisis management.

NGOs and digital media

Development NGOs operating at international, national, and local levels have incorporated new media into their work. These NGOs include innovative organizations that have dispensed with a geographical pitch and operate exclusively online. In the following, we show the range and potential at the different levels.

International NGOs

The largely northern hemisphere-based international NGOs, such as Oxfam, Friends of the Earth (FoEI), and the World Wide Fund for Nature (WWF), which have global networks of overseas branches and regularly work with both national and grassroots local partner organizations, have had a long history of constructive interaction with the mass media. Over decades, but particularly since the 1960s, they have drawn on relationships with broadcast and print media for campaigning and advocacy, for mobilizing networks of partners and individual supporters, and for reaching out to target communities.

Since the widespread diffusion of ICTs, international NGOs have embraced the full benefits of the Internet, email, and SMS messaging, including social networking sites such as Facebook; content sharing sites such as YouTube, Twitter, and blogs; and online e-petitions for communicating with their supporters and partner organizations. For instance, the London-based Christian Aid, with some six hundred partner organizations around the world, has made beneficial use of Skype, the broadband

Internet software that allows users to make low-cost or free-of-charge video and voice calls.[33] With around half of Christian Aid's staff overseas, the London HQ staff can track developments overseas and decision-making on grants can be devolved closer to projects on the ground. Local staff in developing countries are likewise brought closer to decision-making processes in London and can have greater input by strengthening the viewpoint of those in developing countries. Christian Aid has also been making extensive use of social networking to communicate with its supporters and wider audiences and now has a presence on Facebook, MySpace, Bebo, YouTube, Twitter, and podcasts.[34]

Nationally based NGOs

Nationally based NGOs, such as the Treatment Action Campaign (TAC) in South Africa, also use the Internet and other new media for a variety of purposes. TAC has a primary goal of raising awareness of HIV/AIDS and supporting sufferers of the illness. From its base in Cape Town, TAC has made effective use of website and email to communicate internationally and publicize its cause and local protest actions, for example, against excessive pricing of antiretroviral medicines by pharmaceutical companies, via news releases to influential supporters. These include World Health Organization (WHO); UNAIDS (Joint United Nations Programme on HIV/AIDS); foreign governments; international NGOs such as Médecins Sans Frontières (MSF); and others in South Africa, North America, and Europe.

These networks have also been used to co-ordinate local and overseas protests, particularly in the U.S. where large numbers of supporters also donate online. Significantly, however, there has been a failure to engage Internet users in other African states where, as in many countries of the developing world, the much-heralded ubiquity, accessibility, cheapness, and genuinely two-way nature of the new media is often very far from realization.

International partnerships and local interventions

National NGOs facilitating participatory "communication for development" (or C4D) projects[35] in developing countries themselves—Africa, the Indian sub-continent, Latin America, Asia Pacific, and elsewhere—have likewise extended their existing engagements with community radio and collaborative video to incorporate new media (ICT4D). This is often done in partnership or coalition with outside bodies.

Both UNESCO (United Nations Educational, Scientific, and Cultural Organization) and the Canadian-based International Development and Research Center (IDRC), for example, have a history of having supported a range of ICTs for poverty reduction initiatives in impoverished areas of the developing world. Evidence suggests that the more effective interventions have been where ICTs are introduced to tried-and-tested community radio or cable television stations or linked to established local information networks.[36]

A pertinent example is The Datamation Foundation. This Indian charitable trust, which endorses UNESCO's aim of increasing ICT penetration to reach "the unreached," runs one of its ICT projects in a community center (space donated by a local *madrasa*) in Seelampur, a poor area of northeast Delhi with high levels of illiteracy. The beneficiaries of the project are Muslim women with restricted opportunities for learning and social interaction, usually only mixing with their wider community at religious events. Thanks to special software developed by UNESCO—and a squad of volunteer intermediaries trained to help identify local information needs—the women of Seelampur have shared information on topics such as health services, education, livelihood opportunities, government welfare schemes, and available grants.[37]

Online NGOs and international digital campaigns

Further innovative uses of new media in campaigning and advocacy work have occurred entirely online. Digital technology has enabled a radically new type of NGO to emerge: the "dotcause." This is a civil society campaign group with little or no physical infrastructure operating almost entirely in cyberspace in contrast to traditional NGOs that use the Internet to complement their physical presence.[38] Dotcauses include international NGOs such as the International Campaign to Ban Landmines (ICBL), which has a network in over ninety countries, and national NGOs, such as Green-Web in China, with their volunteer organizers attracted by the low operational costs.

The Chinese environmental NGO sector has seen a huge increase in web-based organizations that dispense with formal office premises. They are not usually registered with official NGO status by the Chinese state whose policies tend to discourage the growth of NGOs, with restrictions frequently placed on their registration. However, unregistered voluntary organizations working on environmental issues are tolerated because they tend to be supportive of the state's policy on sustainable development.

Green-Web is one such independent environmental protection group with several thousand registered users.[39] It publicizes information, instigates online debates, enables users to develop face-to-face activities online, maintains an email list used to mobilize volunteers, distributes electronic newsletters, and hosts a bulletin board. Its successes include an online discussion about recycling that resulted in offline activity by students in Xiamen City who organized a community battery-recycling program and campaigned to stop the building of an entertainment complex on neighboring wetland in suburban Beijing. The building plan was suspended following an online petition and dispatch of letters to government agencies, together with publicity in the mainstream media.

New "clicks only" international advocacy campaigns such as People's Global Action (PGA) and the Free Burma Coalition have similarly been able to dispense with heavy office administration costs yet reach large numbers of people around the world.[40] The emergence of this entirely new type of civil society group, and the link with the anti-globalization movement, gave rise to much talk at the beginning of the twenty-first century about this one manifestation of a new global civil society. The new media allowed such groups the freedom to express their concerns in their own words, if necessary bypassing the traditional mass media. As a representative of McSpotlight, the anti-McDonalds dotcause, explained, "The internet is a medium that doesn't require campaigners to jump through hoops doing publicity stunts, or depend on the goodwill of an editor, to get their message across."[41]

There is a consensus among commentators that ICTs have revolutionized civil society advocacy work and facilitated the formation of international coalitions,[42] but there is less certainty about how far these benefits have percolated beyond an elite class of activists. For example, the International Campaign to Ban Landmines is based in the U.S. and its founding members all came from northern hemisphere countries, none of which were directly mine-affected. Its dotcause insistence on communicating by email has effectively discriminated against many people in mine-affected developing countries who do not have ready Internet access.[43]

The potency of the anti-globalization protest movement hinged on the fusion of the new communications technologies with established civil society organizations operating at local and national levels, such as environmental NGOs, trades unions, and churches. However, ICT-supported networks do not guarantee effective communications or create communities where these do not already exist.[44] Leading spokespersons often rely on traditional media to get their message across. For example, as John Clark has observed, the figureheads of the anti-globalization movement, such as Naomi Klein, Vandana Shiva, George Monbiot, and Noreena Hertz, far from bypassing the mainstream media, all write for established major newspapers.[45]

Barriers to ICT access in developing countries

Our examples so far have shown how these innovatory technologies have been used to greatly enhance organizations' ability to communicate within their networks; begun democratizing the internal structures of northern hemisphere organizations working with local staff in southern countries; provided new methods for communicating, campaigning, and advocating to larger audiences; evolved locally appropriate software; and offered new opportunities for awareness raising and education within beneficiary communities. However, as our examination of the southern digital landscape will reveal, despite effective usages of these technologies in individual organizations' projects, they are underscored by much deeper systemic and structural problems that occur within many developing nations. These hinder the large-scale improvements to individuals' life chances that ICTs have the potential to offer, and that NGOs need to take an active role in facilitating.

The "digital divide" debates in the development sector have served to highlight the huge disparity in access to ICTs between industrialized and developing countries.[46] According to recent statistics from the International Telecommunications Union (the lead UN agency on ICT issues), roughly a quarter of the world's population is now using the Internet and the number of users doubled between 2005 and 2010. It is not often recognized that the majority of the world's Internet users are now in developing countries, where 80 percent of the world's population lives. However, the proportion of the developing world population with Internet access, at only 21 in every 100 people, is much lower than in the developed countries where 71 in 100 have access. Internet penetration in Africa currently lags far behind with less than 10 in 100. Mobile telephony has grown even more markedly, currently estimated at 5.3 billion subscribers—two-thirds of the world's population—and nearly three-quarters of these are in developing countries.[47]

But the UN has warned that the broadband gap between rich and poor countries is widening. Australia (with a total population of 21 million), for example, now has more broadband subscribers than the whole of Africa (population almost 900 million). According to UN Under-Secretary-General for Communications, Kayo Akasaka, "A person in a developed country is, on average, 200 times more likely than someone in a least developed country to enjoy high-speed access to the internet."[48]

Accurate statistics on levels of connectivity in the poorer regions of the world are hard to come by and even harder to interpret. Most developing countries are now connected to the Internet, albeit often in a limited way due to underinvestment. The Sarvodaya Shramadana Movement, the largest NGO in Sri Lanka specializing in sustainable development, has estimated that over 80 percent of the Sri Lankan population is not connected to the digital age. Less than 3 percent of African households have Internet access and even in India, Internet penetration is currently estimated to be at most 70 million users (out of a total population of around 1.15 billion).[49]

As well as an overall lack of basic access and high speed broadband, Internet access in developing countries is predominantly available to the governmental, business, and educational needs of elites in key urban centers. This has created internal digital divides within developing nations, with rural communities, minorities, and less powerful groups remaining poorly connected. Significant factors in differential access in Africa, for example, are gender, ethnicity, socio-economic status, and location.[50] A recent survey of participatory media in Africa by the Ethiopian researcher Abiye Megenta found that the Internet in Africa "is still the preserve of the continent's elite" and that most African users of social networking sites are to be found in just three countries: Egypt, South Africa, and Morocco.[51]

The costs of a computer and Internet connection are too high for many individuals and families,[52] and although the growth in mobile telephony has been phenomenal in developing countries such as India, China, Indonesia, Brazil, and parts of Africa, phone subscriptions are still not widespread in many poor rural communities, even in Nigeria, Africa's largest mobile market.[53]

Sharing mobile phones is commonplace in Africa. A revealing ethnographic survey by Skuse and Cousins of 50 poor households in a rural village in the Mount Frere district of South Africa's Eastern Cape found that, despite a widespread vogue for mobiles, only 28 percent of households included a member who owned one, 68 percent of all calls were made from public phones within a 30 minute walk, 32 percent of calls received were on neighbors' or relatives' mobile phones, and 12 percent on a public mobile.[54] These disparities can exacerbate pre-existing inequalities.[55] People without access to phones have unequal access to social welfare services, economic opportunities, health information, and mobile banking.[56]

Some national governments together with international donors have made attempts to bridge the divide. In Senegal, for example, where two-thirds of the population lives on less than U.S. $2 per day, the state telecommunications company, *Sonatel*, had abandoned the provision of public telephone services by 1997. In their place it adopted a policy of widening community access to ICTs. By the end of 2000, there were more than 9,000 licensed telecenters in Senegal. These communal centers provide poorer communities with telephone, fax, computer, and Internet access, in addition to the commercial network of profit-making cyber cafes.[57] With assistance from international donors, telecenters have been piloted in a number of other countries in Africa and South Asia since the mid-1990s—with varying levels of success.[58]

The South African government promoted wider access through a combination of measures, first by liberalizing the state telecommunications market, encouraging competition, and licensing three phone operators—*Vodacom, MTN,* and *Cell-C*—to supply networks in rural areas; and second, by encouraging small, medium, and micro enterprises. These included public container phone units equipped with five to six mobile handsets and stand alone mobiles, such as Adondo's *GSM Community Phone,* at private homes or *spaza*[59] shops. However, call charges were much higher from stand-alone mobiles in rural shops, priced at U.S.$0.32 per minute, than calls made from urban container phones, which were charged at U.S.$0.14. Out of an average monthly income of U.S.$32.00, poor households in rural areas were spending around $4.00 on phoning relatives to secure the remittances on which they depended.[60]

To demonstrate the strategies that poor individuals will adopt to access communications, Skuse and Cousins give the example of Siyabonga, a seventeen-year-old male head of household who runs the village home for his younger siblings while his mother works in Cape Town as a domestic to a white family and sends back money. He does not own a phone himself but uses his aunt's mobile phone, a short walk away, to receive calls every week from his mother. In this way they keep in touch about family matters and arrange the sending of remittances. Occasionally, Siyabonga calls on the privately run community phone at the shop, one hour's walk away, where he pays $3.20 to speak to his mother for ten minutes.

Other barriers to ICT access for the chronic poor include a lack of reliable electricity supply;[61] low levels of literacy and technical skills leading to lack of confidence in their ability to master ICTs;[62] lack of fluency in English with a majority of websites written in English;[63] lack of relevant content for rural workers and manual laborers even if they speak English;[64] and institutional obstacles such as state censorship of websites, as in China, Ethiopia, and other developing countries.

Local NGOs who are trying to tackle both international and in-country digital divides in practical ways are placed in a challenging position, having to navigate between the priorities of states, international bodies, and the needs of the poor. They often find that outside donors put ICT resources in the hands of country elites upon whom the local NGOs are reliant for funding, but the agendas of these organizations may not include promoting the use of digital media by poor communities.[65] Transnational networks of global civil society can help by finding ways of channeling funding and investment into reputable and well-managed local initiatives that bypass the controls of those gate-keeping governments who misuse funds.

Although the structural problems outlined here are usually the preserve of governments, commercial operators, and supra-national funding bodies, NGOs, in their "middleman" position between governments and communities in national civil societies and locations within transnational networks, can utilize their powers of influence, fundraising, and service delivery to address the key priorities. As our case studies will show, some already do so. Overall structural priorities are to improve access to ICTs, particularly for marginalized and underserved groups, and where essential information, services, and opportunities can be obtained through them, to supply education and training in using ICTs and understanding their value. It is also important to liaise with software developers to highlight user needs so that programs and interfaces are available in formats and languages that individuals in developing countries can understand.

Progress on the ground

Moving forward to a more detailed examination of the work that NGOs have carried out, we ask what can be done to realize the potential of the new media to contribute to economic development while avoiding the pitfall of exacerbating digital deprivation. What should NGOs working at grassroots level be doing to make effective use of these technologies for campaigning and advocacy, for mobilizing partners and supporters, and to strengthen their practical outreach work with local communities?

To answer these questions, we now examine some well-documented case studies from the developing world. Each of these projects sought to use ICTs in distinctive ways to benefit the disadvantaged in their own societies—South Africa, Bangladesh, and Sri Lanka. They illustrate the importance of tailoring interventions to the local context, especially working within the cultures and conditions of daily life in locations where projects are delivered. For example, physical gatherings of people play an important role in many civil society projects—such as church congregations, who have proved highly receptive to face-to-face communications from NGO staff in the work of the Treatment Action Campaign in South Africa.[66] Of equal importance are combining the use of old and new media to reach a wider audience, and exploiting their use to meet the economic needs of local people.

South Africa: Using new media alongside traditional media for people with HIV/AIDS

The Treatment Action Campaign (TAC) uses the whole gamut of old and new media. Launched in 1998, it is an activist organization with an affluent urban supporter base working to assist people with HIV/AIDS in poor rural areas as well as cities. TAC has used a combination of website content, email, and SMS messages to mobile phones to distribute general medical and health information, information about antiretroviral therapy, and key legal judgments to inform its educated urban audience. For the rural and lower literacy communities, it relies on traditional methods such as word of mouth, printed pamphlets, faxes, or home visits to mobilize calls to action, distributed via its regional offices, NGO partners, and networks of supporters.

New media are not directly effective at the grassroots level, as many of the TAC's target beneficiaries, people with HIV/AIDS, have little or no access to the Internet. So the organization relies on intermediaries to disseminate their health information at churches, taxi ranks, and railway stations. Those TAC supporters with online access obtain the organization's email address from printed material published in the mass media, and subsequently join its electronic mailing lists, demonstrating effective use of a communications chain.

TAC has maintained a good relationship with the country's mass media, receiving extensive favorable coverage due in part to the respected image of its leaders and the elite class concern about HIV/AIDS. During its "Civil Disobedience" campaign, for example, six key journalists were emailed by TAC staff and asked to publicize it globally. Traditional media remain important to social movements such as TAC.

TAC's experience suggests that NGOs need to make an assessment of existing media and information channels, current levels of access and trends in usage, and take a realistic view on what might be achieved by extending a community's access. The ultimate objective is to understand how communities and technologies interact, and, if ICTs are going to be incorporated into outreach work, how best to link social and technical networks.[67]

This case study and other African examples allow the key observation to emerge that ICTs complement, rather than replace, existing relationships between NGOs, the mass media, and traditional forms of communication used to reach poor target communities in sustainable development programs. Where ICTs are being considered, NGOs should also assess their impact and effectiveness as much by the degree of agency they provide participants with as by the scale on which they are used. In Senegal, for example, the large numbers of people communicating through messages relayed by one caller in a telecenter is more illustrative of communications trends than the number of individual mobile phones owned.[68]

New media should not be the automatic preference of NGOs, rather they need to value all poor people's communicative actions equally regardless of what forms of media technology they use.[69] In Kenya, for example, in spite of a dramatic growth in mobile telephony use with 48 mobile subscriptions per 100 people in 2009,[70] recent surveys[71] show radio—very much an "old" media—is the main information source for adult Kenyans, 89 percent of whom use this medium weekly for news and information.

NGOs should not, therefore, rule out any affordable communication methods. The need is to focus on social uses by the community and not get distracted by technologically determinist thinking.[72] A return to old media, in some cases, is a step forward not backward. For example, the African social justice network Fahamu, which has pioneered new media applications such as SMS text petitioning, is planning an expansion into print. Its influential online newsletter, *Pambazuka News*, has been very effective in bringing African voices, in particular those of civil society activists, to northern donors, governments, and publics where national and local media limit them in their own countries. However, within Africa, *Pambazuka News* circulates only to a relatively narrow audience of middle-class activists with Internet access. Fahamu calculates that *Pambazuka News* in print form would reach a much larger number of beneficiaries.[73]

Hybrid media, the combination of new and old media, can be effective in fostering democratic participation; the more media platforms, the greater the reach of the content.[74] Old and new media have also worked to transform each other in important ways. For example, the use of text-in and phone-in shows and the integration of Internet formats into community radio has revitalized community radio in Africa and other poor developing countries. Radio listening clubs have developed organically around radio shows for young people in countries as far apart as Cambodia and Angola where shared mobile phones are used to make calls into the show.[75] Myers reports a phenomenal boom in community radio in Africa—for instance, from 10 stations in the Democratic Republic of Congo in 2000 to more than 250 today—and a similar mushrooming in Latin America and Asia.[76] More than 40 percent of West African community radio stations surveyed by the Panos Institute in 2008 used mobile phones as a regular part of their programming. In Pakistan, a study of young radio listeners in 2008 found that 37 percent listened to radio on their mobile phone.

Taking strategic advantage of the mobile phone

The early impact of the Internet may have led some civil society groups to undervalue the other important digital application, mobile telephony. Many NGOs have not moved much beyond basic websites and email; few have taken full strategic advantage of mobiles which until recently had attracted far less attention.[77] Yet mobile use far exceeds landline and Internet use in developing countries.

The growth in mobile telephony has been explosive, although the rate of growth now appears to be slowing. Recent statistics from the International Telecommunications Union (ITU) show that while at the start of the new millennium the developing world accounted for about a quarter of the global total of mobile phone subscriptions, by 2010 their share had increased to virtually three-quarters of a global total of 5.3 billion.[78]

The Vodafone Foundation reported that South Africa's high mobile penetration rate of 41 percent and coverage rate of 90 percent was partly responsible for the success of a text-message based scheme for health-care workers run by the Cape Town-based NGO, Cell-Life.[79] Together with the University of Cape Town and the Cape Peninsula University of Technology, they created a mobile, technology-based program, *Aftercare*, to work with the public healthcare system and healthcare workers to provide home-based treatment for HIV/AIDS patients receiving anti-retroviral treatments. *Aftercare* workers captured vital patient data on their phones, which they sent by text message to a central server and database. A care manager used a web-based system to access and monitor the information, and advise the healthcare worker. The system facilitated patient care and provided an overview of the severity of the AIDS epidemic in the region. Early results from a monitoring and evaluation system showed that the quality of care for patients had improved.

The program and technology worked consistently and costs were kept low by using data collection software that functioned on low-cost phones. Achieving long-term financial sustainability would require the commitment of more healthcare partners and commercial telecoms operators in South Africa, as initially, the system could only be used on one network using prepaid accounts. Due to its success, Cell-Life considered improving the software and translating it into South Africa's eleven national languages in order to be able to scale up the project.

High mobile penetration rates also have consequences for Internet access. According to a report by the media development agency, Internews, "the three-quarters of the world who have yet to access the Internet or experience digital multimedia will mostly do both through mobiles."[80] Jeffrey Sachs of Columbia University's Earth Institute has described the mobile handset as "the single most transformative tool for development," but this perception has yet to shape many NGO policy priorities. It seems clear that the liberalization of the telecoms industry in developing countries could provide greatly expanded access to mobiles (and eventually even a low-cost mobile broadband service).[81] According to the BBC World Service Trust head of policy, getting the telecoms policy and regulatory side right is more important as a development intervention than individual projects.[82] This policy area is not one on which many NGOs are currently knowledgeable and engaged.

Bangladesh: The Grameen Village Phone Program and income generation

A pay phone project, established by the large Bangladeshi microfinance organization, Grameen Bank, in conjunction with the Norwegian telecoms company Telenor, is internationally regarded as a huge success.[83] Its village phone model is now being replicated by the Grameen Foundation (the non-profit trust set up by Grameen founder, Muhammad Yunis) in other developing countries as far afield as Uganda and Indonesia.

Village phone businesses are typically set up by a microfinance client (usually "a telephone lady") taking out a loan to purchase "a business in a box" consisting of a mobile handset, an antenna, and a battery. After receiving training, the village phone operator (or VPO) sets up her business in her rural village, renting the use of the phone on an affordable per-call basis, and in the process earning enough to repay the loan. There are now a quarter of a million VPOs in Bangladesh, each handling calls for many people.

Since its inception in 1997 when the company was awarded a national license for digital GSM (global systems for mobiles) phone services, Grameenphone has extended mobile telephony to tens of thousands of remote Bangladeshi villages which previously had little or no access to this technology. It now offers a range of vitally important services including electronic funds transfer, Internet access, market information, and mobile broadcasts of disaster alerts.[84]

This project demonstrates that mobile phone technology is more readily adaptable than the Internet (via personal computers) to the circumstances of the chronically poor. Mobile phones do not need a permanent electricity supply for recharging nor do they require literacy on the part of the user to operate them. They can easily be shared by people on very low incomes and indeed rented out.

The Grameen Village Phone scheme also shows that much more can be done to promote the diffusion of mobile phones to digitally deprived communities who would otherwise miss out on the social and economic

benefits. Its success hinges on the substantial involvement of the Grameen Bank with poor rural communities.[85] For instance, local knowledge
is helpful for the selection of village phone operators and the relationship between the VPO and the people in the community to whom she
is renting out phones. Also the success of the Grameen Village Phone
was due in large part to the fact that it combined substantially improved
communications access for the local population with valuable income
generation for the VPOs, giving them an incentive to provide the service
and thus ensuring its viability.

As the Cell-Life and Grameen cases exemplify, to operate at this scale
NGOs need to develop an understanding of macro-level ICT policy and
its potential impact on development sectors. This policy would typically
entail a national-level commitment to universal access through public
institutions such as telecenters and village phone centers. It would also
involve liberalization of the telecommunications market to ensure fair
competition for the provision of services and a commitment to locally
appropriate content creation. Partnerships would need to be forged between different interest groups, such as commercial service providers,
governments, public service providers, NGOs, and grassroots communities. By this means, economically viable ICT and other information-
providing initiatives could be progressively rolled out over a range of
development sectors such as health and education.

Returning to individual initiatives, NGOs need to become accustomed
to analyzing the local market for media and communications uses from
an economic perspective, examining where an intervention could be tied
into peoples' existing uses of commercial media and communications
services. Where people have to incur any cost to participate in an intervention, for instance to receive a text, NGOs need to assess willingness
to meet this expense. As the developing world now constitutes by far the
greater part of the global mobile phone market, major telecoms companies are now viewing the poor as value seeking consumers.[86]

The picture painted by the evidence from developing countries indicates that increased mobile phone penetration indeed has a significant
impact on economic development. A countrywide analysis of micro-
data on mobile phone coverage in South Africa discovered significant
effects of network rollout on rural labor markets, with women's employment showing a 12 percent improvement when a community gets
networked.[87] A study of poor Filipino households found that buying a
mobile phone increased household wealth by 11–17 percent, as farmers
were able to strike better deals with merchants and make more informed
choices about where to sell their crops.[88] Similarly, a study of fishing businesses in south India found that adopting mobiles led to an increase of
around 10 percent in fishermen's profits.[89] Another study from Lesotho

found a wide variety of benefits when they handed out mobile phones to women's farming co-ops—by selling mobile airtime at discounted prices, some women were able to branch out into cattle farming and tourism.[90]

Increasing access to digital technologies is insufficient on its own. Attention must also be paid to generation of reliable local content, for example local weather forecasts, crop protection, and seed information. For poor people to benefit from this, they also need access to credit, technical support, transportation to markets, irrigation, and safe storage.[91] NGOs should match their ICT interventions to other income-generation strategies to enable users to reap full economic benefits, including e-commerce and digital remittance transfers.

Investing in multi-media for grassroots development

To recap, international NGOs engaged with the sustainability agenda were very prompt to utilize ICTs for much improved communications between their (largely northern hemisphere-based) headquarters and their regional offices and partner organizations in developing countries.[92] ICTs have enabled them to produce their own media material more cheaply and easily. The range of new digital platforms—from the international NGOs' own websites to YouTube—allowed a more efficient distribution of this content to supporters and staff.[93]

However, there is concern that the international NGOs may be dominating national communications arenas in developing countries to the detriment of elevating voices from grassroots level to positions of prominence in their national media. They rarely strengthen local media either. According to Charlie Beckett, the director of the London School of Economics (LSE) policy think-tank, Polis, "they tend not to prioritize or resource local media work because it does not fulfill their traditional international fundraising and advocacy objectives."[94] However, the Kothmale Community Radio is an exception in that it was supported by international donor agencies and has evolved new formats in multimedia tools for development. This creative initiative fused the Internet with radio to provide community information and education for people living in a rural part of Sri Lanka.

Sri Lanka: Radio web browsing

Successful local media projects need to build on an in-depth understanding of pre-existing media uses and preferences in planning new initiatives. For example, in Sri Lanka, a radio Internet project has been running since 1999 from the local Kothmale community station, affiliated to the state-owned Sri Lankan Broadcasting Corporation. The project, funded by various donors including UNESCO and Dutch donor HIVOS, aims to bring ICTs to a poor rural area on the Mahaweli River and integrate Internet and radio in community communications. Kothmale Community Radio was an early pioneer of this format, which has since been replicated, with UNESCO funding, in other developing countries.

Television ownership is rare in the region and national newspapers are mistrusted as highly partisan and are also inaccessible to many because they are written in English, but radio ownership is near universal. The local Kothmale radio station is highly regarded for its sensitive programming. Phone use is limited and use of ICTs has been restricted to communicating with relatives abroad. Commercial cybercafés enable Internet access, but local people prefer face-to-face communications at meetings, for example in schools, temples, and teashops.[95] Kothmale Community Radio (KRC) has successfully tapped into the local preference through its broadcasts and website coverage of live face-to-face community events.

Listeners Request, a program format using radio web browsing, emerged from the radio station in 1999. This daily one-hour program, broadcast each weekday evening to around 250,000 local residents, comprises information obtained from the Internet (usually in English) read out in local languages, Singhalese and Tamil, in response to listeners' questions received by mobile phone, post, or in person. Studio guests are brought in to contextualize the information, for example a local doctor to explain medical data or an agriculturalist to advise on crop details.

This approach bypasses the literacy and skills requirements of individual Internet access and has met local information needs in the areas of health, agriculture, enterprise, and legalities. The Friday evening show involving a lawyer in the studio is particularly popular. The project provides free computer access at two local libraries, as well as the radio station, and listeners are encouraged to drop in to explore the Internet for themselves. The latest development is a mobile studio transported by an auto-rickshaw (or "e-tuktuk"), which takes its Internet-ready laptop, power supply unit, printer, and scanner to remote communities. Thus, the project has been innovative in introducing poor rural community members to ICTs and distributing valuable development information, marrying old and new media in the process.

Kothmale shows that even in a low-income area where Internet connectivity is limited, ingenious combinations of technology can be evolved with outside help to meet local needs. A UNESCO evaluation concluded that the local preference for entertainment uses of ICT was a more likely source of technical literacy and entrepreneurial skills development than formal instruction. However, while recognized and applauded by the international development sector for its convergence of Internet and radio, the format has not as yet been extended into other program slots. Critics have questioned Kothmale's editorial dependency on elite gate-keepers and challenged the authenticity of its community base as the station essentially belongs to the public broadcasting service of a repressive state.[96]

Conclusions

The intricacies of the Kothmale project illustrate the complexities of the use of new media by civil society in the developing world, in particular the ambivalent relationship between the state and civil society groups and impediments for the poor, especially the rural poor, in accessing Keane's "communicative abundance." The truth lies somewhere between the hype of "cyber-utopianism" and the pessimism of the skeptics. The Ethiopian commentator Abiye Megenta commented on the apparently endless see-sawing of the debate on the effects of the Internet, "Going through the stacks of literature, one cannot help but think that partisan scholars and analysts who simplistically categorized it into two contesting groups—techno-optimists and techno-pessimists—were sometimes talking past each other."[97]

In the immediate wake of the "Arab Spring" of 2011, where digital media have been seen to play a critical role in facilitating civil society organization, the current mood is swinging towards techno-optimism. Governments and international development agencies are paying renewed attention—for example World Bank President Robert Zoellick in a speech on a "New Social Contract for Development" in the Middle East and North Africa refers to the role of new technologies in creating "an empowered public" and a "robust civil society."[98]

How should NGOs respond? There is indeed much that international and national NGOs and aid donors more generally could and should be doing to improve the take-up of ICTs in developing countries. International NGOs in particular could do more to help create infrastructure in developing countries for local content development and engage more with the structural priorities we have outlined. They could also provide poor people with informal opportunities to experiment with ICT use on their own terms in centers such as libraries, community telecenters, and schools, as well as providing more formal technical skills courses.[99] A vital task is to create interventions that generate income so that they can become self-financing, either on their own or in partnership with a commercial service provider, beyond the initial funding cycle. The most successful initiatives in the long-term marry commercial interests with development gains. Civil society organizations and the private sector need to find common languages and ways of understanding each other's incentives. A senior representative of Vodafone U.K. told us in an interview that many projects simply evaporate beyond the initial pilot through lack of common ground.

The digital divide is real, and NGOs should be mindful of its impact on the lives of those who are excluded from the use of new communications technologies, even if it is only a minority of the population. As James Deane of the BBC World Service Trust says, "If access to information and communications means access to markets and power, then this is what is truly significant."[100] The case studies examined here underline the importance of careful adaptation of communication channels to the local context, striving to ensure that all sectors of the population can benefit.

But a key finding to emerge from our scrutiny of projects was that it is difficult to generalize about the best uses of ICTs in sustainable development in very different societies around the world. Understanding the local context is central to success in this as in all other areas of development. So NGOs, whether wanting to campaign and mobilize supporters, or planning ICTs for development, should not expect interventions suited to one country context automatically to be adapted successfully to another. Instead, they should take a local perspective and explore the "communicative ecology"[101] by carrying out a thorough media and communications audit[102] of each local context. This enables an understanding of what existing communications networks are in place.

While ICTs can open up vitally important new public spaces, they can also reinforce social hierarchies and create new ones. Just as the benefits of digital media can be over-hyped, so too can their more negative and divisive effects be downplayed (including downright sinister effects such as state surveillance). The "Arab Spring" of 2011 may have served to push new media up the international agenda but the development community is still very far from having a fully-fledged and evidence-based strategy in this area.

The new media do not of themselves create social movements, though they can help spread the word, amplify messages, and relay these to the mass media.[103] "Clicks only" campaigning appears to offer NGOs around the world unprecedented global reach for little more than the cost of creating a website. Transnational networks can offer cross-sectoral partnerships between civil society outfits, ICT companies, commercial operators, and others. But it is misleading to speak of a globally connected civil society when many hundreds of millions of people—rural populations, women, minorities, the chronically poor—are bypassed by the new media technology revolution and have digital deprivation added to their other social and economic disadvantages. For our purposes, acknowledging the close interrelation between the traditional civil society spaces and the agency located in transnational networks is enough. To confirm the existence of an all-encompassing global civil sphere might be going a step too far.

Increased ICT investment will come in large part from the opening up of competitive markets—with appropriate regulation—in developing countries. But the needs of the poorest people will require a greater focus by NGOs on closing the digital divide by working with local communications channels, ensuring that any innovation is economically viable and, where possible, investing in multi-media to promote grassroots development.

Notes

1. Manuel Castells, *The Internet Galaxy: Reflections on the Internet, Business, and Society*, (Oxford: Oxford University Press, 2001).
2. World Commission on Environment and Development, *Our Common Future* (*"The Brundtland Report"*), (Oxford: Oxford University Press, 1987).
3. *http://www.undp.org/mdg/*
4. *http://www.undp.org/mdg/*
5. INTRAC, "Civil Society and Aid in Theory and Practice" (conference paper) (Oxford, 2008) *http://www.intrac.org/data/files/resources/635/INTRAC-Confer ence-2008-Civil-society-and-aid-in-theory-and-practice-summary.*
6. Michael Walzer, "The Civil Society Argument," in *Dimensions of Radical Democracy: Pluralism, Citizenship, Community*, ed. C. Mouffe, (London and New York: Verso, 1992): 89–107; "civil society left to itself generates radically unequal power relationships which only state power can challenge."
7. Mary Kaldor, Helmut K. Anheier, and Marlies Glasius, *Global Civil Society 2003/4*, (London: Sage Publications, 2003).
8. Marlies Glasius, "Dissecting Global Civil Society: Values, Actors, Organisational Forms," in *Open Democracy*, (London: 50.50 Inclusive Democracy, 2010). *http:// www.opendemocracy.net/5050/marlies-glasius/dissecting-global-civil-society-values- actors-organisational-forms*
9. Jan Van Dijk, *The Network Society*, 2nd ed., (London: Sage, 2006). Van Dijk defines ICTs as "media which are integrated, interactive, and use digital code." Media industry convergence has meant older media becoming more integrated and interactive as radio makes use of mobile phones and mp3 recorders, newspapers broadcast real-time video, and television expands text services online.
10. Castells, *The Rise of The Network Society*.

11. Facebook, *2009 Mission Statement*, (Palo Alto, 2009).
12. Labour Party website (London, 2010). *http://www.gordonbrown.org.uk/gordon-brown-addresses-african-leaders*
13. Christian Fuchs, for example, criticizes Castells for his "technocratic language" which Fuchs likens to that surrounding the Californian dot.com boom of the 1990s, in "Reflections on Manuel Castells' 'Communication Power'" (Salzburg: Triple C Open Access Journal for a Global Sustainable Information Society, 2009) *http://triplec.at/index.php/tripleC/article/view/136/90*.
14. Christian Fuchs, "Reflections on Manuel Castells' *Communication Power* (Salzburg, 2009). *http://triplec.at/index.php/tripleC/article/view/136/90*
15. Jo A. Tacchi, "Supporting the Democratic Voice through Community Media Centres in South Asia?" in *3CMedia Journal of Community, Citizen's, and Third Sector Media*. Issue 1: 1–14 (Australia, 2005) *http://www.cbonline.org.au*; also Okoth Fred Mudhai, "Exploring the Potential for More Strategic Use of Mobile Phones," in *Reformatting Politics: Information Technology and Global Society*, eds. J. Dean, J. Anderson, and G. Lovinck (London: Routledge, 2006): 107–127.
16. Evegeny Morozov, *The Net Delusion*, (London: Allen Lane, 2011).
17. An Nguyen, "Globalisation, Citizen Journalism and the Nation-State: A View from Vietnam" in *E Citizen Journalism: Global Perspectives*, eds. S. Allan and E. Thorsen, (New York: Peter Lang, 2009).
18. Evgeny Morozov, *Financial Times*, London 17 June 2011.
19. Morozov quotes the boast of Iran's police chief, Ahmadi Moghaddam, that "the new technologies allow us to identify conspirators and those who violate the law, without having to control all people individually" (Morozov, *The Net Delusion*, 146).
20. Pippa Norris, *Public Sentinel: News Media and Governance Reform*, (Washington: World Bank, 2010).
21. James Deane, interview 2009.
22. Gerry Power, interview 2009.
23. Castells, *The Internet Galaxy*; Richard Kahn and Douglas Kellner, "New Media and Internet Activism: From the 'Battle of Seattle' to Blogging," in *New Media & Society*, vol. 6, no. 1: 87–95 (London: Sage Publications, 2004).
24. Walzer, "The Civil Society Argument," 89–107; Mudhai in *Reformatting Politics*, 107–127. Queries the extent to which this activity can legitimately be described as "global," pointing out that virtually all the international NGOs accredited to major international meetings are based in rich countries.
25. Peter Horrocks, "Finding TV News' Lost Audience," lecture delivered to Reuters Institute for the Study of Journalism, University of Oxford in November 2006. *www.bbc.co.uk/blogs/theeditors/2006/11/the_future_of_news.html*
26. The invitation of the CNN iReport claims "Your voice, together with other iReporters, helps shape how and what CNN covers everyday." *http://ireport.cnn.com/*
27. *http://news.bbc.co.uk/aboutbbcnews/hi/this_is_bbc_news/newsid_3280000/3280 463.stm*
28. Claire Wardle and Andrew Williams, "UGC at the BBC: Understanding Its Impact Upon Contributors, Non-contributors, and BBC News," (Cardiff School of Journalism, 2008). *http://www.bbc.co.uk/blogs/knowledgeexchange/cardiffone.pdf*
29. Stuart Allan, *Online News: Journalism and the Internet* (Maidenhead: Open University Press, 2006). Oh is the family name of the founder of the news site, Oh Yean-ho.

30. Glenda Cooper, "Anyone Here Survived a Wave, Speak English, and Got a Mobile? Aid Agencies, the Media, and Reporting Disasters since the Tsunami," 14th Guardian Lecture (Oxford: Nuffield College, 2007); Horrocks, "Finding TV News' Lost Audience"; *Kalinga* Seneviratne, "Citizen Journalism Need Not Be Anti-Governmental," (Queensland: University of Queenland, 2008). *www .uq.edu.au/sjc/docs/AMIC/Kalinga_Seneviratne.pdf*
31. *http://www.ushahidi.com/*
32. Virginia Nightingale and Tim Dwyer, *New Media Worlds, Challenges for Convergence*, (Oxford: Oxford University Press, 2007).
33. Steven Buckley, interview 2009.
34. Steven Buckley, interview 2009.
35. Alfonso Gumucio Dagron, *Making Waves: Stories of Participatory Communication for Social Change* (New York: Rockefeller Foundation, 2001).
36. Don Slater and Janet Kwami, "Embeddedness and Escape: Internet and Mobile Use as Poverty Reduction Strategies in Ghana," *Information Society Research Group (ISRG) Working Paper Series*, (2005): 1–16, *www.isrg.info*; Ian Pringle, Utpal Bajracharya, and Anuradha Bajracharya, "Innovating Multimedia to Increase Accessibility in the Hills of Nepal," in *Multimedia Research and Development* vol. 24, no 4, (2004): 292–297; Sarita Sharma, "eNRICH: Archiving and Accessing Local Information," in *International Journal of Education and Development using Information and Communications Technology* (IJEDICT) vol. 2, no. 1 (2006): 34–48; Tacchi, "Supporting the Democratic Voice through Community Media Centres in South Asia?" 1–14.
37. Sharma, "eNRICH: Archiving and Accessing Local Information," 34–48.
38. John Clark and Nuno Themudo, "Linking the Web and the Street: Internet-Based 'Dotcauses' and the 'Antiglobalization' Movement," *World Development*, vol. 34, no. 1 (2006): 50–74.
39. Guobin Yang, "Weaving a Green Web: The Internet and Environmental Activism in China," in China Environment Series, Barnard College, Columbia University (New York, 2003).
40. Clark and Themudo, "Linking the Web and the Street: Internet-Based 'Dotcauses' and the 'Antiglobalization' Movement," 50–74.
41. Naomi Klein, *No Logo: Taking Aim at the Brand Name Bullies*, (Toronto: Vintage Canada, 2000).
42. Margaret Keck and Kathryn Sikkink, *Activists beyond Borders: Advocacy Networks in International Politics* (Ithaca, N.Y.: Cornell University Press, 1998).
43. Mudhai in *Reformatting Politics*.
44. Susana Finquelievich, "Community Networks Go Virtual: Tracing the Evolution of ICT in Buenos Aires and Montevideo" in *Shaping the Network Society: The New Role of Civil Society in Cyberspace*, eds. D. Schuler and P. Day, (Cambridge, Massachusetts: MIT Press, 2004): 137–158.
45. John Clark and Nuno Themuda, "The Age of Protest: Internet-Based 'Dot Causes' and the 'Anti Globalization' Movement," in *Globalizing Civic Engagement: Civil Society and Transnational Action*, ed. J. Clark, (London: Earthscan, 2003).
46. Ming-Te Lu, "Digital Divide in Developing Countries," *Journal of Global Information Technology Management* vol. 4, no. 3 (2001): 1–4; Faye Ginsburg, "Re-Thinking the Digital Age," E-Seminar in 2007 for the European Association of Social Anthropologists Media Anthropology Network (EASA). *http://www.media-anthropology.net/ginsburg_digital_age.pdf*

47. International Telecommunications Union, *The World in 2010: ICT Facts and Figures*, (Geneva: ITU, 2010).
48. UN News Center, "High-speed Internet Gap between Rich and Poor Widening, UN Official Warns" 12 November 2009. *http://www.un.org/apps/news/story .asp?NewsID=32942&Cr=information+technology&Cr1=*
49. Anjli Raval, "Digital India: Less Talk More Action," *Financial Times*, 12 November 2010.
50. Herman Wasserman, "Renaissance and Resistance: Using ICTs for Social Change in South Africa," *African Studies* vol. 64, no. 2 (2005a): 177–199.
51. Abiye Megenta, "Can It Tweet Its Way to Democracy? The Promise of Participatory Media in Africa," Reuters Institute Report (Oxford, 2011).
52. Lu, "Digital Divide in Developing Countries," 1–4.
53. Osaro Odemwingie, Oxfam Abuja, interview 2009.
54. Andrew Skuse and Thomas Cousins, "Managing Distance: the Social Dynamics of Rural Telecommunications Access and Use in the Eastern Cape, South Africa," in *Journal of Asian and African Studies*, vol. 42, no. 2, (2007): 185–207.
55. Castells, *The Internet Galaxy.*
56. Francisco Rodriguez and Ernest J. Wilson, *Are Poor Countries Losing the Information Revolution?* (College Park: University of Maryland, 1999).
57. U. Afeman, "Internet in Senegal," in *African Media Cultures: Transdisciplinary Perspectives / Cultures de Médias en Afrique*, eds. R.M. Beck and F. Wittmann, (Cologne: Ruediger Koeppe Verlag, 2004): 287–310.
58. Pilots have been conducted by the International Development Research Center (IDRC) and UNESCO—see for example the UNESCO report "The Experience with Community Telecenters," (UNESCO, 2002).
59. *Spaza* is a South African term for a small family shop run from home.
60. Skuse and Cousins, "Managing Distance: the Social Dynamics of Rural Telecommunications Access and Use in the Eastern Cape, South Africa," 185–207.
61. Ginsburg, "Re-Thinking the Digital Age."
62. Castells, *The Internet Galaxy.*
63. Castells, *The Internet Galaxy.*
64. Dagron, *Making Waves: Stories of Participatory Communication for Social Change.*
65. Michael Wilmore, "The Digital Divide and the Social Divide in New Media Access and Their Implications for the Development of Civil Society in Nepal," in *Asia Rights* vol. 8 (2007). Available at: *http://rspas.anu.edu.au/asiarightsjournal/ Issuepercent20Eight_Wilmore.htm*
66. Wasserman, "Renaissance and Resistance," 177–199; also Robert Cornford, Oxfam Oxford, interview 2009.
67. Wasserman, "Renaissance and Resistance," 177–199; Tacchi, "Supporting the Democratic Voice through Community Media Centres in South Asia?" 1–14. *http://www.cbonline.org.au*
68. Wasserman, "Renaissance and Resistance," 177–199.
69. Wilmore, "The Digital Divide and the Social Divide in New Media Access and Their Implications for the Development of Civil Society in Nepal."
70. International Telecommunications Union, *The World in 2010: ICT Facts and Figures*, (Geneva: ITU, 2010).
71. AudienceScapes, "National Survey of Kenya," 2009. *http://audiencescapes.org/ country-profiles/kenya/media-and-communication-overview/media-and-communica tion-overview-153*

72. Deane, interview 2009.
73. Firoze Manji, interview 2009.
74. Tacchi, "Supporting the Democratic Voice through Community Media Centres in South Asia?" 1–14. *http://www.cbonline.org.au*
75. Correspondence with BBC World Service Trust, 2009.
76. Mary Myers, "Voices from Villages: Community Radio in the Developing World," CIMA Report (Washington, 2011).
77. Mudhai in *Reformatting Politics: Information Technology and Global Society.*
78. International Telecommunications Union, *The World in 2010: ICT Facts and Figures,* (Geneva: ITU, 2010).
79. Shelia Kinkade and Katrin Verclas, "Mobile Phones for Social Change: Trends in Mobile Use by NGOs," report for The Vodafone Group Foundation and the UN Foundation Partnership, 2008. *http://www.mobileactive.org/files/MobilizingSocial Change_full.pdf*
80. John West, "The Promise of Global Ubiquity—Mobile as Media Platform in the Global South," report for Internews Europe, 2008. *http://www.internews .org/pubs/ict/Promise_of_Ubiquity_Full_Version.pdf*
81. Rohit Singh, "Mobile Phones for Development and Profit: A Win-Win Scenario," Opinion report for the Overseas Development Institute (London: ODI, 2009). *http://www.odi.org.uk/resources/download/2846.pdf*
82. Deane, interview 2009.
83. Mudhai in *Reformatting Politics: Information Technology and Global Society.*
84. Mudhai in *Reformatting Politics: Information Technology and Global Society.*
85. M.J. James, "Information Technology and Mass Poverty," *International Journal of Development Issues* vol. 5, no. 1 (2006): 85–107.
86. Deane, interview 2009.
87. Stefan Klonner and Patrick Nolen, "Cell Phones and Rural Labour Markets: Evidence from South Africa," Proceedings of the German Economics Conference No. 56, (Hannover, 2010).
88. Julien Labonne and Robert Chase, "The Power of Information: The Impact of Mobile Phones on Farmers' Welfare in the Philippines," World Bank Impact Evaluation series IE 33 Policy Research working paper no. WPS 4996 (World Bank, 2009).
89. Robert Jensen, 'The Digital Provide: (Technology), Market Performance and Welfare in the South Indian Fisheries Sector' in *The Quarterly Journal of Economics* vol. 122, no 3: 879–924. (Oxford University Press: 2007)
90. Katharine Vincent, Tracy Cull and Nicholas Freeland 'Ever Upwardly Mobile: How do Cell Phones Benefit Vulnerable People? - Lessons From Farming Cooperatives in Lesotho', *Wahenga Brief no. 16*, Regional Hunger and Vulnerability Programme (RHVP). (South Africa, 2009) *http://www.wahenga.org/sites/default/ files/briefs/Brief_16_-_Ever_upwardly_mobile.pdf*
91. Vodafone, "India: The Impact of Mobile Phones," Policy Paper Series no. 9, 2009. *www.vodafone.com/publicpolicyseries*
92. Mudhai in *Reformatting Politics: Information Technology and Global Society;* Steven Buckley, interview 2009.
93. Charlie Beckett, *Supermedia: Saving Journalism So It Can Save the World,* (Oxford: Blackwell, 2009).
94. Beckett, *Supermedia.*
95. Slater and Kwami, "Embeddedness and Escape" 1–16.

96. Liz Harvey-Carter, "Kothmale Community Radio Interorg Project: True Community Radio or Feel-Good Propaganda?" *The International Review of Research in Open and Distance Learning* vol. 10, no. 1 (2009).

97. Megenta, "Can It Tweet Its Way to Democracy?"

98. *http://web.worldbank.org/WBSITE/EXTERNAL/NEWS/0,contentMDK:228 80264~menuPK:34473~pagePK:34370~piPK:42770~theSitePK:4607,00.html*

99. Tacchi, "Supporting the Democratic Voice through Community Media Centres in South Asia?" 1–14; Wilmore, "The Digital Divide and the Social Divide in New Media Access and Their Implications for the Development of Civil Society in Nepal."

100. Deane, interview 2009.

101. Wasserman, "Renaissance and Resistance" 177–199; Tacchi, "Supporting the Democratic Voice through Community Media Centres in South Asia?" 1–14.

102. The term *media audit* comes from BBC World Service Trust practitioners. We have added *communications* to indicate the need to analyse the whole gamut of face-to-face as well as mediated communications engaged in by the community in a locality before planning any ICT or multimedia intervention.

103. A post from the Ushahidi platform quotes advice from their co-founder Ory Okolloh, "Don't get too jazzed up! Ushahidi is only 10 percent of the solution," the other 90 percent is up to the organization. *http://blog.ushahidi.com/index .php/2010/05/19/allocation-of-time-deploying-ushahidi/*

Chapter 4

MONITORY VERSUS MANAGED DEMOCRACY
DOES CIVIL SOCIETY MATTER
IN CONTEMPORARY RUSSIA?

Kathryn Stoner-Weiss

Introduction

John Keane uses the term "monitory democracy" to describe the growing oversight role of civic groups—both local and international—in calling democratic governments to account. By Keane's reckoning, "democracy is no longer simply a way of handling the power of elected governments by electoral and parliamentary and constitutional means... people and organizations that exercise power are now routinely subject to public monitoring and public contestation by an assortment of extra-parliamentary bodies."[1]

In the struggle between state and society, informal social organizations, rather than formal checks and balances on state actors, are allegedly winning epic battles. Moreover, for Keane, civil society in this new form is back and bigger than ever. Non-state actors, he maintains, not formal electoral and state institutions, are paramount in enhancing the quality of democracy in the West and the South.

But is this really true in the East? In this chapter, I endeavor to address this question, in examining the existence, role, and efficacy of contemporary Russian civil society in monitoring state actors and institutions.

To some degree, there is a straw man aspect to Keane's argument when it comes to Russia. His observation regarding the newly enhanced powers of monitoring organizations surely is meant to apply to developed democracies—and most of us can agree that Russia today is not really a democracy at all. Despite this, Russia has come a long way since the collapse of the Soviet Union in 1991. Undeniably, most Russians enjoy far more political, economic, and social freedoms than under the Soviet regime. Regardless, since about 2004, few analysts or international organizations inside or outside of Russia consider the country a liberal democracy by almost any metric. Although elections at the national level do take place on a regular schedule, they are far from free or fair. Electoral outcomes are known in advance of most elections. The ruling party, United Russia, dominates the electoral process.

There has also been an electoral "recession" in Russia: elections for governors of Russia's 89 regions were cancelled in 2005 (governors are now appointed by legislatures and the presidential administration). Candidates from opposing parties are prevented from contesting elections by what frequently appears to be administrative fiat. Instead, those loyal to the ruling tandem of Dmitri Medvedev (Putin's protégé and successor as President as of 2008) and his mentor and all-powerful boss, Vladimir Putin, have decided who can run for office and who can win. In sum, early 21st century Russia cannot meet even a "procedural" or minimalist definition of democracy a la Robert Dahl.[2]

Beyond the procedural, however, Russian democracy is much more deeply flawed. The Russian constitution guarantees freedoms of speech and assembly, for example, yet the media is largely state run and non-sanctioned protests often end in the arrest of many of the protesters. Despite significant improvements in training of Russian judges and lawyers, few observers would consider Russia to have the "rule of law," if we understand this to mean the equal and impartial treatment of private citizens and public office holders by law enforcement or courts. Judges are sometimes dictated the outcome of their cases before the trial begins.

Putin himself has described Russia as a "managed" democracy. By this, he means a system where the president, his administration, and the government must carefully oversee society so that stability of the political and social spheres can be maintained. Granted, social forces can participate in certain areas of the polity, and while their input into policy is not completely dismissed, it is carefully monitored and not infrequently controlled. Other analysts have referred to the Russian system as "illiberal" democracy, or "over-managed" democracy, but if we think of the classification of political systems as a spectrum, there is little difference between these descriptions and a "liberal" or "soft" autocracy.

To be sure, Russia today is not the Soviet Union. There has been significant liberalization politically and economically, but the relative ranking of Russia, on various scales of democracy, has oscillated over time. The ideal of democracy is not necessarily dead, even if the practice (as many understand it) is on life support.

Given this background, and the difficulty in identifying the most accurate classification of the contemporary Russian political system, what is the role of civil society in "monitoring" the state? If we assume that meaningful democratic practice requires that state actors and organizations be held accountable to the citizenry, and given that formal democratic institutions are weak in Russia, what role, if any, do non-state actors play in performing this "monitory" function? Is it even appropriate to speak of "civil society" in Russia today, if what we mean by the term is a·,y activity outside the purview of the state? My answer to this, despite the fact that Russia is clearly not a democracy, is an unqualified "yes." Groups exist independently of the state in contemporary Russia, and often, they successfully provide public goods and services. They fall short, however, of the "monitory" ideal that Keane envisions in European democracies. This is largely a result of the fact that in Russia, the assumption on the part of state actors in particular (but also, much of society as well) is that the state must monitor and restrain society (and not the other way around as found in many established democracies). As a result, the Russian state assumes a strong monitoring and managerial role over society. Suspicion of non-state political monitoring activity is pervasive long after the fall of communism, and such activity is severely circumscribed, although certainly not absent.

This chapter is organized as follows: I begin by first defining civil society as I use it in the analysis to come. I then describe the rapid rise of civic activity between 1987 and 1991 in advance of the collapse of the Soviet Union, and the more liberal relationship between the post-Soviet Russian state and emerging social forces in the tumultuous 1990s. Subsequently I analyze the reversion to state management of society under Russia's former president, and current Prime Minister, Vladimir Putin between 1999 and the present. Then I argue, however, that some forms of civil society are very active in Russia today, although some activities are more welcomed by the state than others. Taking on a local government for not providing a playground, for example, is permissible, but demonstrating in support of the freedom to assemble as guaranteed by the Russian constitution is not. Indeed, despite a few recent victories of civil society organizations in monitoring state behavior, serious challenges or attempts to "monitor" the political system by any opposition are limited.

Moreover, I argue that the central difference between Keane's "monitory" democracy and the Russian system is a fundamentally divergent understanding of state and society relations. In contemporary Russia, political elites and much of the Russian public view the state, not society, to be the natural source of both stability and innovation. Society is a potential threat to the state's mission and interests—and particularly the current interest in stability—and so state actors and institutions view it as crucial to monitor and constrain social forces when necessary, and not the other way around.

Defining Civil Society

In order to discern any inkling of a monitory function for non-governmental organizations and institutions, I take a relatively broad view of civil society. I understand Russian civil society to include groups formed outside of the state or government at the initiative of private citizens of a given country, or citizens of another country resident in a given country (domestic and international non-governmental organizations, for example). Thus, my definition and subsequent analysis of Russia includes the more traditional set of organizations that one would normally refer to as "non-governmental organizations" like charities, opposition political parties, social movements, human rights monitoring organizations, sports clubs, and the like. While I also include the traditional print and broadcast private media, I move beyond this, following Keane, to include the new media (the Russian blogosphere, etc.) and their potential monitoring role vis-à-vis the Russian state.

My definition of civil society includes what some other analysts might not allow. Unlike, for example, Larry Diamond, I include both violent and peaceful organizations, be they political or social.[3] Diamond construes these groups as "uncivil" society in that they use violence to promote political or social causes, and therefore should not be considered part of "civil" society in the sense of working within the established political and legal system. In the Russian context, however, because other avenues of protest are closed to citizens, some interests (such as the Chechen widows) might resort to violence to promote their social or political agenda. Their violent actions could potentially affect policy or state behavior, and so I include them here. I also include violent informal organizations such as suicide bombers, for example, since they represent a public interest despite the fact that they use violence to draw attention to their cause. I exclude the mafia, however, from my definition and analysis because their members are acting for the sake of private gain and not a discernible public interest.

Finally, although my definition of civil society includes business associations (trade groups, etc.), I exclude for-profit corporations in my analysis for two reasons. First, they are devoted to private gain exclusively, rather than public activity. Second, and perhaps of greater consequence is the fact that in the contemporary Russian context it is often difficult to discern the line between business and government, and this would muddy any assessment of the monitory capacity of individual business groups over the Russian state.

In sum, my conceptualization of civil society is broad enough to enable a thorough search in the Russian context for the monitory elements that Keane describes in Western Europe. As noted above, some elements of this broad definition of civil society are alive and very well, but others—particularly those that Keane would include as the crux of his concept of monitory democracy—are as yet largely ineffectual in reliably calling the Russian state to account.

The Re-emergence (and Reinvention) of Civil Society in Post-Soviet Russia

Even in the Soviet period—when the state endeavored to control virtually all aspects of the private lives of its citizenry through the Communist Party of the Soviet Union (CPSU) and its institutional tentacles, the command economy, state owned media, or social institutions—historians still were able to identify independent civic organizations and groups. The idea that totalitarianism meant "total" control was put to rest decades ago. Despite the highly controlled, statist system, there was a small "private" sphere. In the 1970s, some analysts argued that within the Soviet system itself, there was some modest plurality of interests that they deemed "institutional pluralism." This though, could hardly meet even the broadest definition of civil society, since the term really described divergent policy views and institutional interests (e.g., the Ministry of Agriculture versus the Ministry of Defense) within Soviet state or party institutions themselves rather than society in broad terms.[4] Other faint signs of oppositional activity in the Soviet system appeared in the 1960s with Khrushchev's thaw and the stirrings of dissent, particularly from the intelligentsia, and with the urbanization that took place in the late 1960s through early 1970s.[5]

The late Soviet period was clearly a time of considerable social change and in a sense might have foreshadowed the growth of civil society that we eventually see in the period beginning in 1985 with the ascendancy of Mikhail Gorbachev to the post of General Secretary of the CPSU. It is hard though, to draw a straight line between these early indications of social change and oppositional activity and the tremendous (and retrospectively, rather brief) burst of activity we witness at the end of the

1980s in particular. Moreover, if one believes that social liberalization and the growth of civil society activity that calls a state to account for its decisions comes about as a result of economic modernization, then the Soviet system is an anomaly. As Alfred Evans notes, "social and economic modernization [that took place under Soviet rule] were not sufficient to create the attitudes and behavior that are essential for the operation of secondary associations that are expected of civil society."[6]

Nevertheless it is important to bear in mind that the social project of communism—in terms of both its intent and its execution—was most certainly not liberal democracy. The Soviet party-state emphasized collective over individual interest and the state over society in its quest to build the "perfect" society that would end the economic exploitation of man by man, as described by Marx. Indeed, the system—which Lenin founded, Stalin ultimately perfected, and Gorbachev unwittingly dismantled—was reliant on the repression of social opposition to the party and the state it controlled.

By the time Gorbachev rose to power in 1985, the system Lenin had envisioned as being a dictatorship of the proletariat had become a dictatorship of the communist party. It bloated state over the proletariat and indeed over almost all aspects of Soviet society. Since the CPSU was the leading and guiding force of the Soviet system (enshrined in Article 6 of the Soviet Constitution), primary party organizations permeated virtually every social organization outside of the government. Perhaps most significantly for the conceptualization of state-society relations in post-communist Russia was that, during the Soviet era, "social organizations were to be founded by the initiative of the political regime."[7] Trade unions, therefore, were arms of the party-state rather than representatives of workers to their employers. Even sports clubs were effectively arms of the party and state. The print and broadcast media were state owned and closely censored to maintain control over popular perceptions of the Soviet state. The state security apparatus also played a key institutional role in controlling the population through continuous surveillance. Other mechanisms of social control were less overt, however, including the system of internal passports and housing permits limiting social mobility. By means of these various instruments of control, dissent was severely circumscribed. The most stubborn dissidents were thrown in jail or sent into exile abroad. Political discussions that led to any criticism of the regime took place in the privacy of people's kitchens, not on the streets.

Still, state control over society in the Soviet period, although tight, was not total. Word of Khrushchev's Secret Speech in 1956 exposing the crimes of his predecessor, Joseph Stalin, leaked out to the broader Soviet population, and even Gorbachev himself notes the impact this had on his generation, and their belief in the legitimacy of the Soviet system.

The official myth of the perfection of the system Stalin built was clearly eroding by the 1970s. The command economy functioned, although it resulted in a chronic scarcity of consumer goods leading to an active black market to grease the wheels of supply. Indeed, to some degree, the system was a victim of its own developmental successes. A country that had been largely agrarian and illiterate in 1917 had grown to a nuclear superpower with a 99 percent literacy rate by 1985. These accomplishments came at tremendous human cost, which undoubtedly brought the system's legitimacy into question among the wider population over time.

As the population had become increasingly sophisticated, the Soviet "social contract"—whereby the party-state provided cradle to grave social services (of questionable quality) in return for limited accountability to Soviet society—began to erode. Many observers, in explaining the rise of Gorbachev following the long tenure of his predecessor, Leonid Brezhnev, noted that, "Soviet society changed while Brezhnev slept."[8] The system faced a crisis of legitimacy that stretched from top to bottom.

That said, in 1985, when Mikhail Gorbachev ascended to the role of General Secretary, the system was not in danger of imminent collapse. Few predicted its spectacular fall only six years later. As Michael McFaul noted, "In fact, in 1985, ... there were few signs that this system would collapse. On the contrary, the Soviet regime seemed insulated from societal pressures for change, immune from exogenous shocks, and supported by those within the system capable of undermining [it]."[9]

Recognizing its legitimacy crisis and growing economic woes, Gorbachev planned to rejuvenate and revive the system, although he did not intend to turn it into a liberal democracy with a market economy. In reflecting upon this period, Gorbachev himself has noted: "*Perestroika*—the process of change in our country—started from above. It could not have been otherwise in a totalitarian state."[10]

Early in his tenure as General Secretary, and following his initial failures in "top down" reform attempts, Gorbachev introduced some decentralization of the party's tight grip on society and the economy. As part of his *glasnost* and *demokratizatsiya*, Gorbachev allowed the establishment of informal social organizations founded by individual citizens rather than by the state. This was the introduction of a new model of state-society relations where society was permitted (and even encouraged) to provide some degree of monitoring activity of state policy. As part of this initiative, in June of 1986 Gorbachev permitted the media greater freedom (*glasnost*); archives were opened (even those of the KGB, the infamous Soviet security apparatus); and the state allowed spontaneous public political demonstrations whether in support of or against *perestroika*, Gorbachev, and the Party.

Reports on the number of informal groups active at this time vary widely, but their areas of social activity ranged broadly from music, to politics, to exposing the secrets of Soviet history (including the bloody purges under Stalin).[11] Environmental movements were also founded in this period, often succeeding in drawing attention to the shoddy construction of Soviet nuclear power plants, as well as the rampant destruction of natural wonders such as Siberia's Lake Baikal. Informal labor organizations emerged in this period as well. Workers in the coal industry, for example, organized strike actions aimed directly at holding the state accountable for improving their difficult working conditions. Gorbachev enabled the reopening of Russian Orthodox churches and some synagogues and mosques throughout the Soviet Union, with the 1990 Freedom of Conscience Act, which guaranteed religious freedom.[12]

Dissidents such as Andrei Sakharov, the father of the Soviet nuclear program, were called back from exile in 1986 and even invited to participate in the emerging electoral process Gorbachev had created. By the late 1980s, ethnic movements had emerged as potent political forces advocating independence from the Soviet Union. Factions within the Communist Party itself also developed, with Gorbachev battling not only Boris Yeltsin in the newly sovereign Russian Federation, but members of his own Politburo who lead a coup attempt against him in August 1991. As a result of the electoral process (at first limited, and then more open by 1990), political organizations and parties arose in this period and candidates from these organizations or running as independents provided meaningful alternatives to the rule of the CPSU.[13]

Despite this dramatic increase in civil society and oppositional activity, it would be a mistake to conclude that social forces were primary in bringing about the collapse of the Soviet Union. In fact, despite significant social mobilization and a resulting increase in the monitoring of many spheres of state activity, the collapse was caused not by popular protest, but by elite infighting.

Indeed in the spring of 1991, Soviet citizens freely (and fairly) voted in favor of the preservation of the Soviet Union, while at the same time advocating the establishment of a presidency within the Russian Republic. Even during the August coup, which was expressly directed against the results of Gorbachev's *perestroika* and his loosening of social and political restrictions, these newly emergent social forces were relatively passive. M. Steven Fish notes that often the new civil society organizations created in this period were disorganized and were unable to reliably and consistently articulate their interests to state actors.[14] Few supporters of Gorbachev, Yeltsin, or the coup plotters came out onto the streets in Moscow or any other major Soviet city. Perhaps because of this, the collapse of the Soviet Union was sudden and largely bloodless.[15]

With the collapse of the Soviet Union in 1991, Boris Yeltsin, Russia's first democratically elected President, took the helm of the Russian political system, but without the institutional bulwarks of the Soviet state—the CPSU, the command economy, or the state security apparatus. The halting economic reforms that he initiated between 1992 and his resignation as president in December 1999, coupled with the lingering effects of Gorbachev's failed reforms and the collapse of the Soviet system, brought about tremendous economic hardship and continued social dislocation. While Yeltsin achieved the destruction of the Soviet system, he did not manage to create institutions to effectively govern Russia. Still, he created the framework for an electoral, if not fully liberal, democracy. Competitive elections began in 1990 with the election of a Russian parliament, and then in 1991 for the President of Russia himself. In October of 1993, Boris Yeltsin and the Russian parliament, the Congress of People's Deputies, came into armed conflict over their relative power. Yeltsin ultimately used force to crush the parliament and usher in a new constitution, and new electoral and legislative system by December 1993. A party system was in place by 1996, although the Communist Party of Russia held the peculiar distinction of being the most popular "postcommunist" party in Russia.

Despite the unpopularity of Yeltsin's economic policies, he resisted the temptation to crack down on opposition after 1993. The print and state media remained largely free of systematic state control. During the privatization process of the 1990s, former state television stations and newspapers were purchased by so called "oligarchs" including Boris Berezovsky and Vladimir Gusinsky. These men certainly had their own interests at heart in taking over these assets, but they did not completely dictate editorial lines to journalists either. Television shows, such as Kukuly, freely satirized Yeltsin and his entourage (known as "the family") in their national broadcasts. Russian journalists also actively covered the First Chechen War from 1994–1996, exposing some of the atrocities committed by the Russian military against Chechen civilians, as well as the hardships of the under-equipped Russian conscript army. The revelations in some of this media coverage contributed to the formation of the "Soldiers' Mothers" group that mobilized women to confront Russian commanders in Chechnya and demand the release from duty of their conscripted soldier-sons. Both the movement and the media contributed to the unpopularity of the war and moved Yeltsin to seek a peace deal to end the Chechen conflict in 1996.

Between 1992 and 1999, civil society became more complex, and performed some of the monitory functions of the state that Keane notes in developed democracies. Both domestic and international NGOs developed inside of Russia, largely unregulated by the state. The United States government, the World Bank, the United Nations Development Program, and various private foundations (including the Mott Foundation, Soros Foundation, the Ford Foundation, and the McArthur Foundation) provided money and often helped to train and promote civic organizations, believing that there was a firm connection between better governance in Russia and a strong civil society. The National Democratic Institute, a quasi-governmental agency, held training seminars on running campaigns for rapidly emerging political parties, as well as training programs for human rights groups and environmental organizations on how to build coalitions and run national campaigns to influence state policy.[16] Between 1992 and 1998, the United States Agency for International Development (USAID) reportedly spent $92 million on civil society organizations. Sarah Henderson (2003) reports that, "in 2000 alone, the Russian branch of George Soros' Open Society Institute funneled more than $56 million to NGO's, universities, and other civic minded organizations in order to create a lasting civil society."[17] Henderson notes that civil society organizations grew quickly from 1990 to 2001, with about 450,000 estimated to have existed in 2000. At this point, the focus was primarily on human rights, the environment, and the women's movement.

Despite considerable financial and technical support, one of the challenges Russia's new "civil" sector faced was the general wariness of post-Soviet Russian society of voluntary organizations in general. The concept of private citizens forming public interest groups to influence or monitor the state was alien, and had, of course, been dangerous in the communist period. In addition, the connection was sometimes tenuous between these organizations and Russian society or the constituencies they hoped to represent to the state. This was not, however, only due to lack of public recognition. Henderson, for example, argues that often those organizations that received the most money from international donors made the mistake of seeing the donors, and not the community interest they had been formed to represent, as their most important constituency.

Even in the face of these considerable organizational challenges, Russian civil society grew rapidly in the first ten years following the collapse of the Soviet Union. Different sectors were modestly effective in monitoring the state as in the case of the Soldiers' Mothers. But if this was the "golden age" of Russian civil society, then the period that followed can only be classified as the "dark ages" when Russia became an overly state-managed democracy.[18]

Russian "Managed," not "Monitory" Democracy

Since the mid-2000s, the decline in civil society's monitory capabilities over the state was caused mostly by deficiencies within Russia's electoral process. In addition, the dominance of the office of President in the Russian political system, and the corresponding unimportance of parliament and political parties, made the task of organizing interest groups more difficult.[19] Yeltsin's presidential authority had been checked by a noncompliant Duma (elective legislative assembly) controlled by the Communist Party of Russia (KPRF). His successor, Vladimir Putin, did not have to reckon with these challenges, in part because he created a new party, the United Russia, which displaced the KPRF in the parliamentary elections of 1999. Putin then used successive changes to Russian electoral law to marginalize the KPRF and other opposition parties, which increased United Russia's dominance in parliament and his uncontested control of state policy as President. In explaining the weakness of civil society in Russia under Putin, some have argued that, "the only way to achieve significant influence on politics was by cultivating personal connections with insiders in the executive leadership."[20]

In this section, I track the formal changes Putin made to the Russian electoral system, regional governments, and the upper house of the Russian parliament to maximize the authority of the already powerful Russian presidency. I then examine his establishment of control over the Russian media, further extending his personal authority over the system, generating social support for his regime, and securing the electoral success of United Russia in successive parliamentary elections. I then turn to the administrative oversight he instituted on Russian civil society organizations beginning in 2004, and his resurrection of the importance of the state security apparatus in ensuring social compliance to the state policy. Finally, I examine the state sponsored social organizations that were created under Putin's presidency with the intention of channeling and, at times co-opting, social criticism of the regime so that it would not be able to destabilize the system as a whole.

Formal institutional changes to elections, regional government, and parliament

The Kremlin's dominance over the electoral process at the national level began in 1999 with the parliamentary victory of Unity (which later became United Russia), the president's "preferred" party. On the United Russia official party website, Putin was featured as the moral leader of the party, although he was technically, at the time, not a member.[21] The party continued to dominate in the next parliamentary elections in 2003, winning 37 percent of the popular vote and thrashing the second and third place finishers, respectively the Communist Party of Russia with 12.7 percent and the Liberal Democratic Party under extremist politician Vladimir Zhirinovsky with 11.6 percent.

Since 2003, United Russia generally has maintained over 300 representatives in Russia's 450-seat parliament and, as a result, the Duma (the Russian lower house) is popularly viewed as a rubber stamp for the policies of the President, rather than a vehicle for monitoring or debating state policy. It can in no way be considered an effective check on executive power and meaningful opposition parties have largely ceased to exist.[22] This came about largely as a result of a series of reforms to electoral law and laws on political parties.

The Russian Federal Law on Political Parties first came into effect on 14 July 2001. It was later revised and tightened making it more difficult for political organizations to be officially registered as parties and able to field candidates for national elections. According to the law, by January of 2006 each political party had to demonstrate that it had a minimum membership of 50,000, as well as more than 45 regional branches, with at least 500 members in each regional branch.[23] Although multiple parties are permitted to run in Russian elections, the field narrowed in anticipation of the 2007 Duma elections. In part, this is perhaps a natural process of attrition and focusing of what was a very broad and irrational spectrum of parties in the 1990s, but it is also due to other administrative and legal challenges to the maintenance of a truly competitive electoral system. First, in local elections, non-approved candidates for local parliaments routinely are denied registration on questionable grounds (either being accused of having falsified signatures or of improperly filing the paperwork necessary to register for the elections). Second, in advance of the Duma elections in December 2007, further legal changes led to the minimum threshold for parties to gain representation in parliament being increased from 5 percent of the vote to 7 percent. This had the effect of completely eliminating the smaller parties that had hovered at around the 5 percent level in previous Duma elections (parties that were liberal and not backed by the Kremlin). Finally, and perhaps most dramatically, in 2007, the Russian Duma was elected according to party lists through an exclusively proportional representation system.

This is not necessarily a less democratic system of electing representatives to parliament. However, in the current Russian political context, given that the regime controls party registration, and that pro-Kremlin parties have historically always done best in proportional representation as opposed to single mandate majoritarian races, the change from a mixed electoral system to a system based only on proportional representation worked to increase the number of seats for United Russia in the Duma.

Furthermore, the changes to campaign laws in late 2006 included restrictions on political parties' use of airtime on television to campaign against other candidates and political parties. This did not include television coverage of members of the government (especially the president and prime minister) on the nightly news to the exclusion of almost any other news. The law also eliminated the minimum voter turnout requirement for elections at national, local, and regional levels, such that even elections with turnout of 10 percent or less would be counted as valid.[24]

Taming Regional Critics

Regional governors and presidents of Russia's ethnic republics had been constant sources of trouble for Boris Yeltsin. With the introduction of gubernatorial elections in the mid-1990s in Russia's provinces, they had demanded more policy authority relative to the federal state. Many had even signed bilateral agreements with Moscow enabling them to codify the economic and tax concessions they had forced Yeltsin to make. Some had even sought sovereignty over their own affairs. The most striking example of this, of course, is Chechnya. Putin reignited the Chechen conflict in 1999, but this time he was savvy enough to curtail media access to the front lines, while capitalizing on growing negative public opinion within Russia of non-ethnically Russian citizens. Hence Russian military action there enjoyed strong popular support in contrast to the first phase of the conflict from 1994 to 1996 under Yeltsin.

Using crisis as opportunity in the wake of the tragic killing by Chechen militants of several hundred school children and their parents in Beslan in September 2004, President Putin abolished direct elections for all governors of provinces (oblasts) and presidents of republics throughout the country. Since then they have been appointed by the presidential administration in Moscow on the recommendation of elected regional legislatures. This change succeeded in reigning in the regional authorities that were overly independent in the 1990s. It also effectively ended democratic governance in Russia's regions since the heads of regional executives are the dominant political figures and exercise sweeping control over policy relative to the weak, but popularly elected, regional Dumas.

To further increase his control over Russia's sprawling provinces, Putin changed the system by which the Federation Council, Russia's upper house of parliament, would be formed. Rather than electing, or having elected Russian governors to serve in the Federation Council, as it was done under Yeltsin, "senators" are nominated by appointed regional executives and legislative branches of government with the approval of the presidential administration in Moscow. Many of the holders of seats in the Federation Council, therefore, are patronage appointees; sometimes natives of Moscow who may well have never even visited the regions that they ostensibly represent. Since their appointment depends also on the continuing approval of the presidential administration, there is little incentive for Russian senators to oppose, or even question, presidential decrees or the legislation coming out of the presidentially controlled State Duma.

Reigning in the Russian Media

Paralleling these formal changes that significantly weakened Russian electoral processes and legislative institutions, President Putin began to curb the monitory capacity of the Russian media early in his first term at Russia's helm. His tight control of the political system was supported by a reinstatement of centralized state control of the media. There remained, however, some degree of freedom of speech. There have certainly been journalists in Russia who have criticized the state, and a few brave souls who have gone so far as to expose official corruption in exchange for their lives. The murder of 48-year-old Anna Politkovskaya in her apartment building on 7 October 2006 was among the most notable of these deaths.

Politkovskaya was a special correspondent for the Russian journal, *Novaya Gazeta*, which has maintained its independence from the state. For seven years she fought tirelessly—to the irritation of Russian military and political officials—to bring the story of the Chechen conflict to light, despite the dangers involved in doing so. Politkovskaya was threatened and imprisoned for writing stories that told of the human rights abuses suffered by Chechen civilians at the hands of the Russian military and Chechen officials, especially its Russian backed president, Ramzan Kadyrov.

Days after the murder at a press conference in Germany, when asked about Politkovskaya's death, President Putin described her as an "insignificant" figure and dismissed the notion that there was any official involvement in her killing. Twelve months after her murder, the Russian Prosecutor arrested ten people thought to have perpetrated her abduction and killing. Russian journalist and political analyst Masha Lipman reported that the names and sources were leaked to the press gradually over the next few days, giving the key perpetrators of the crime the opportunity to flee: "the alleged killer fled Russia soon after the prosecutor general's news conference and the subsequent leak of the suspects' names. He was charged at the trial in absentia. Overall, the case of the prosecution was so weak that all the suspects were acquitted ... and Politkovskaya's killers remain undisclosed and at large."[25] In 2008 and 2009, other journalists were killed for writing stories critical of state policy at both national and regional levels.[26]

Other developments in the media have also been troubling in Russia in recent years. In 2006, in advance of the G-8 summit in St. Petersburg, the Russian Duma passed a bill, that President Putin signed into law, which broadened the definition of extremism to include criticism of public officials in the media. According to the Committee to Protect Journalists, several journalists have been charged under this new law, including Dmitry Tashlykov, a reporter for a regional paper, and Vladimirsky Krai, who allegedly "defamed" the governor of the Vladimirov region in an Internet chat room.[27]

Since the mid-2000s, the tendency of Russian print and television media to be consolidated into private hands close to the Kremlin (or even come under direct control of the Kremlin) continued with the purchase of *Kommersant* in the fall of 2006 by Alisher Usmanov, an "oligarch" with close ties to the Kremlin. He assured *Kommersant* journalists that he would not interfere with the paper's sometimes critical editorial line, but his purchase of the paper was generally seen as a further step along the path of fuller media control in the run up to the 2007 Duma elections and 2008 presidential elections. Indeed, IREX's Media Sustainability Index notes a steady decrease in freedom of the press since 2001. There is also a lack of fairness in the issuing of broadcast licenses such that competitive licensing bids depend on loyalty to particular national or local officials or groups. There is little transparency in broadcast licensing decisions.[28]

With the increasing closeness between the Kremlin and the news media, there is the tendency for journalistic self-censorship to become more prevalent for fear of attracting too much official attention. It would be a mistake, however, to assert that there is no freedom of press whatsoever. Ekho Moskvy (Echo of Moscow) radio station continues to run critical pieces. Similarly, REN-TV, has a relatively large audience and a considerable degree of editorial independence. In the print media, papers such as *Novaya Gazeta, New Times,* and *Russian Newsweek* often write critically of state policy. But, as Lipman notes: "most journalists working in these Moscow outlets are not crusaders akin to Anna Politkovskaya. If they are careful not to encroach on powerful interests, reporters working for prominent Moscow publications can get away with challenging specific government policies or high-ranking officials."[29]

Although Russia's current leadership puts up with some criticism in the press, it is careful to ensure that none of this has an impact on social action; "the Kremlin is highly committed to making sure that discontent does not spill over into political activism of any sort."[30] It does this through the manipulation of journalists, and also by overseeing ownership of national television stations, where most Russians get their information.

The national television market in Russia is dominated by three television channels that have come to serve as the state's main conduit of information, based on which the Russian public tends to form its opinions. For example, early in Putin's first term as president, he was able to divest Berezovsky and Gusinsky of their television holdings by threatening them with prosecution for theft and corruption related to the acquisition of virtually all their assets.[31] Media content changed dramatically after this on Russian television. Gone were the political satire programs that had lampooned Yeltsin and his top advisors. These were replaced by steady positive coverage of President Putin, and then Medvedev when Putin designated him his preferred successor as President. Henry Hale, Nicolai Petrov, and Masha Lipman contend that "the managers of the three major networks actually personally coordinate their content in weekly Friday meetings with the head of the Kremlin press service and in follow-up meetings during the week."[32]

This degree of Kremlin interference, and the emasculation of the political opposition through manipulation of electoral rules, have undoubtedly helped Putin and Medvedev to maintain unfailingly high approval ratings of over 70 percent—even during the global financial crisis—and boosted the prospects of United Russia over other parties in Duma elections. By focusing so much exclusively positive attention on the leadership tandem, the three main television channels render any alternative to them irrelevant. The message is clear: Russians can relax; the current leadership has everything under control. At times, some of these efforts are rather extreme. For example, in the summer of 2010, Putin was shown on Russian television personally taking charge over the devastating peat fires plaguing the country—at one point even shown pulling a lever in a plane in order to quench the flames. ("A perfect hit!" exclaims the pilot next to him after the water is discharged over a forest.) Opposition figures are not provided any coverage on the national television news, so Russian voters can be forgiven for thinking that there is simply no alternative to the current leadership in Russia, which seems to be doing a pretty good job. Why bother, many think, to get involved in politics?

Russian television is more competitive (and interesting) in the entertainment field, however, and this is why Russians tune in and stay in their seats to watch the news that precedes or follows entertainment programming. Given the domination of national television by the state, as well as the small space occupied by the critical press in Russia and the self-censorship of many Russian journalists, it is difficult to see how the traditional print and broadcast media could provide any true "monitoring" of the activities of the Russian state.

Keane makes much of the importance of the new media in other democracies, and their potential to monitor state action. The Russian blogosphere shares this attribute—at least in potential. There is no obvious censorship of the Russian Internet and some blogs are highly critical of the regime. The issue, however, is that although Internet penetration is increasing rapidly in Russia, people appear to be using it more for entertainment purposes, rather than for news. As a result, it does not (yet?) provide an effective or widespread means of social monitoring of the state.[33]

In Russia today, there is "no shortage of alternative sources [of media coverage of government], but a shortage of demand."[34] Public apathy supports state dominance of the media and vice versa. Polling data support this conclusion: a November 2007 Levada Center survey of Russian citizens indicated that 37 percent said that the population could not restrain state authorities.[35] In contemporary Russian circumstances: "the media can inform, but they do not have an impact. While there may be freedom of expression, there is hardly press freedom if the latter is understood to serve as a mechanism of public accountability."[36]

"Organizing" Civil Society Organizations

Beyond the electoral system and mass media, a third type of control of the state over society is the management of civil society organizations themselves by the state. In January 2006, President Putin signed a controversial law designed to bring foreign and domestic non-governmental organizations under tighter state oversight. Putin defended the law as a necessary step to prevent foreign incursion into Russia's politics. Critics, however, saw the law as a restriction on the previously vital civil society that had arisen in Russia after the collapse of the Soviet Union.

The Law required the reregistration of all groups with the Russian Ministry of Justice by mid-October 2006. Many groups in practice, however, failed to meet this deadline and fulfill the relatively onerous registration requirements and those that did had difficulties filing an annual "work plan" beginning in 2007. As a result, many were forced to close until they were able to supply the required documentation. Some ceased to function in Russia completely. Notable among over 90 international organizations forced to close their doors at least temporarily were Human Rights Watch, Amnesty International, the National Democratic Institute, and the International Republican Institute.

Most of these groups eventually reregistered with the Ministry of Justice, but virtually all reported the process to have been a cumbersome distraction from their actual goals.

The law on public organizations gives the Russian government unprecedented authority to regulate NGO activities, and to decide what projects are permitted and which are not. This authority has not been exercised evenly, however. Human rights organizations and political oppositional organizations get more attention from the Ministry of Justice and local branches of the FSB (the internal security service) than do, for example, sports organizations. Some organizations were also shut down completely by administrative means. These included the Moscow office of Internews, which protects journalists, and the Open Society Institute, funded by Hungarian billionaire, George Soros. In September 2010, presumably in preparation for elections in many of Russia's regions the following month, the Moscow offices of Human Rights Watch, Transparency International, an international organization that tracks and reports on corruption in government and in business world-wide, and Golos, Russia's only domestic electoral monitoring agency independent of the state, received faxed requests from the office of the prosecutor general to produce financial documents and records of their current activities within 12 hours of receiving the official request, or shutdown their operations.[37]

Perhaps not surprisingly, given the range of administrative and legal controls that have been imposed, freedom of association in Russia has become increasingly circumscribed over the last several years and this too has greatly decreased the monitoring capability of society over the state. By the spring of 2007, it had become increasingly dangerous to undertake any form of political activism on the streets in Russia. Licenses and permits for rallies have been increasingly difficult to obtain in major cities.

Real opposition though is only occasionally violently repressed. In 2010, opposition groups employed "Strategy 31" in order to protest legal and administrative restrictions on the rights of Russians to exercise the right to freedom of association guaranteed in Article 31 of the constitution. The groups are usually denied the legal permits they need to hold the protests where they want to in central Moscow. When they have organized their rallies regardless, they have been arrested, although they are usually quickly released. The police have become increasingly violent over time, however, as these monthly gatherings appear to irritate the regime. The police may have found encouragement in this more violent approach by the then Prime Minister Putin who, in an interview on 30 August 2010 with a national newspaper, warned that anyone caught protesting without a valid permit "should be hit upside the head with a truncheon."[38]

Still unsanctioned and even sanctioned protests do take place with some actually resulting in the state altering (or at least delaying) its planned policy. Among the most notable of these was a series of protests against changes in their social benefits by older and disabled Russians in January 2005. They became the first large rallies since Putin's assumption of the presidency that had not been organized by government authorities or United Russia.[39] The new law initiated a system whereby disabled citizens, pensioners, and war veterans would be given cash payments rather than in kind benefits like free transportation on buses and subway systems and free medications. In St. Petersburg on 15 January 2005, over 10,000 people reportedly attended a rally protesting the changes with some even calling for President Putin to resign.[40] Other demonstrations took place in Siberian regions and across Russia as far east as Sakhalin Island. The result of the protests was a change in policy at the national level.

Other important and effective challenges to government actors and policy have occurred in the first ten years of the 21st century. Among these was a meeting of a group of opposition political movements known collectively as The Other Russia held in July 2006 in Moscow in advance of the upcoming G-8 summit in St. Petersburg. The Other Russia is an amalgamation of organizations and civic activists from across the political spectrum led by former Prime Minister Mikhail Kasyanov and Garry Kasparov, a world chess champion. About 300 Russian civil society activists attended the meeting as well as about 40 foreign guests.

Some Russian participants reportedly had difficulty reaching the meeting and were arrested or detained en route. Despite this, the July 2006 meeting succeeded in bringing together a disparate group of activists concerned with the narrowing public space for Russian civic organizations. On 3 March 2007, The Other Russia staged a political rally on the streets of St. Petersburg with several thousand protesters.[41] Although they were formally denied permission to rally, and were initially blocked from the city center, the crowd broke through police barriers and marched down Nevsky Prospekt, the city's main street. A similar rally in December 2006 in Moscow was notably less successful as about 4,000 riot police blocked 2,000 protesters from marching into the center of the city. Both protests were against the circumscribing of civic and political rights in Russia.

Other citizen initiated political protests have succeeded in various parts of Russia. In the Kaliningrad province, for example, public protests against the unpopular appointed governor, Georgi Booz, resulted in his replacement by Moscow. In the early fall of 2010, a group of environmental protestors scored a victory in forcing the government to reexamine building a national highway that cut through the historic Khimki forest outside Moscow.

In general though, independent civic organizations face tremendous difficulty and resistance in trying to monitor or change government policy. Faced with virtually no political parties or leaders that provide realistic alternatives, a constrained media, and state monitored civil society organizations, Russian society has become politically apathetic. This means that the state only rarely reverts to the use of violence to keep errant social forces in line. Violence can be used strategically, but for the most part, social forces that might provide an alternative political narrative to the Russian public are rendered ineffective in this regard through the use of administrative fiat, a lack of critical news coverage of the state, and only occasionally, force.

Substituting State Sponsored Civil Society Institutions

Presumably in order to maintain stability, and to enable the regime to gather some information on social preferences where elections and civic organizations cannot, the Russian government has created substitute social institutions. These "government organized non-governmental institutions" (GONGOs) substitute pro-government messages for those that are more critical, and in some cases directly counter criticism of the state by independent civic organizations.

To better control and channel the kind of potentially destabilizing youth movements that arose in Serbia in 2000, as well as Georgia and Ukraine in 2003 and 2004 respectively, the Russian government has even built its own civic and political organizations in Nashi, the pro-government Russian youth organization, and United Russia, the political party of power that is now so dominant in Russian politics. Nashi has organized flash mob protests against social critics in Moscow, and at its annual summer retreat for youth, playfully (and sometimes viciously) criticizes the already isolated and ineffective political opposition that does exist.

Under Putin in 2004, the government created the Public Chamber, a group of civil society representatives selected by the Kremlin. The idea behind the Chamber was to gather information from social organizations regarding potential policy needs from constituencies these groups might represent. Since elections are not free and fair in Russia, as discussed earlier in this chapter, they do not transmit reliable information from society to the state, and the Duma and Federation Council are not reliable mechanisms of information about social preferences.[42] Public Chamber membership rotates according to Kremlin wishes, and although it has no constitutional status, President Putin gave it a role in drafting some legislation.

A variety of ad hoc commissions on issues of social concern such as corruption, human rights, and the environment were also formed under both Putin's and Medvedev's presidencies. The membership of these commissions is diverse—drawing from regime opponents and supporters alike—but like the Public Chamber, this is a tightly controlled form of societal input into state policy. The mandates of these commissions are uncertain, and their efficacy in contributing to policy change is uneven. The Corruption Commission, however, may have been responsible for the publication of the annual income of top Russian political office holders, including Putin and Medvedev. The discrepancies that turned up as a result of the publication of this information between official salaries and reported assets have not been prosecuted, however, and so it is not clear what effect the mere publication of incomes of state leaders will have on reducing corruption levels in practice.

These "substitute" institutions do not really play an independent monitoring role over the state, although they do at times, as I have noted, make some important inputs into policy. As Petrov, Lipman, and Hale conclude, these ad hoc substitute institutions help to tighten centralization of administrative levers of the state. These tools of "over-management" of democracy in Russia significantly reduce uncertainty in the political process. The problem, of course, is that "eliminating democracy's uncertainty … removes the very core of democracy."[43]

The regime's overarching interest in stability has meant that it does not take chances with opposition, the media, or social organizations overstepping the tight boundaries that have been imposed over the last ten years. Nor does it rely on substitute institutions alone to channel social discontent to productive purposes. The role of the security forces has also become stronger in monitoring Russian society. In July 2010, a new law on state security allowed for the FSB to convey an official warning to a person deemed by FSB agents to be moving toward committing a crime against the security of Russia.[44] That is, no crime has to be committed in order for the FSB to take action. The original version of the bill was more strongly worded, however, and allowed for jail time and fines for anyone who ignored a summons by the FSB, so here too we see a modest victory for social forces in moderating state action.

When and Where Does Russian Civil Society Succeed in Monitoring the State?

In the end, there are only very faint parallels between what Keane observes in Europe and the relations in contemporary Russia between the state and civil society. In Russia, as in the European democracies that Keane describes, political parties do not perform the main monitoring role of society over the state. But the reason why parties do not matter in this respect in Russia, as opposed to Europe, is radically different. In Russia, opposition parties and social organizations that might want to monitor state activity are effectively controlled or neutralized by the state. Therefore, they are not able to effectively and consistently represent and defend societal interests in the face of an overbearing state.

Nonetheless, as I noted in the section above, the situation in Russia cannot be described in terms of black and white. There have been significant controls on civil society's monitoring functions, but there also have been some important instances when civic action has changed state policy. Debra Javeline and Sarah Lindemann-Komarova make this argument in an attempt to provide a more "balanced" assessment of Russian state and society relations.[45] They insightfully note that too often generalizations about the state of Russian civil society are made in the absence of hard data. The number of NGOs indeed has decreased since the passage of the 2006 law regulating their activity more closely. In 2007, over 2,000 civic organizations were involuntarily shut down. But Javeline and Lindemann-Komarova also point out that according to a USAID survey, many NGOs in Russia have been shut down voluntarily or have been shuttered by state authorities due to genuine corruption or mismanagement.[46]

They also note that in many provincial areas, civic organizations have been successful in collectively providing goods and services that local governments are not able to provide, and that the Russian government even has well organized grant competitions for civil society organizations. They also indicated that the Duma approved a bill in early 2010 to support citizen-initiated projects for the environment, poverty and welfare assistance, and historical and cultural preservation.[47]

All of this is true. It is important to point out, however, that few of these groups can mount serious challenges to the regime's stability. They do, however, as I have noted, score occasional (and significant) victories.

The persistent problem, however, is that groups with overtly political interests—such as The Other Russia—are unlikely to receive equal treatment by the Russian state. In addition to denying state funding, state authorities have numerous ways of preventing citizen initiated political organizations from monitoring state activity or mobilizing against it when necessary. They can, as we have seen, deny them permits to hold public demonstrations, find administrative reasons as to why non-sanctioned opposition candidates cannot contest elections, invent financial irregularities in their accounting, accuse them of compromising state security, seize their computers on the pretext that these groups are using pirated software, or harass them with a blizzard of unreasonable requests for financial documentation.

Providing a public good to a community like a playground might be a welcome civic activity for many local governments. Protecting a historical or cultural treasure or gathering used clothing for poor families are undoubtedly citizen-initiated activities that are even encouraged by the national government in Russia. But these are not threatening to the state's obsession with social stability. When civic organizations venture too far into the realm of politics or protest, the state is quick to prevent civil society from troublesome social mobilization.[48]

Since serious, citizen initiated political protest does not have outlets for expression in opposition political parties, or independent media, the most serious conflicts over politics and policy in Russia occasionally come crashing out onto streets. We saw this in 2005 with the popular rallies against proposed social reforms, again in 2009 with the Dissenter's March, and in 2010 with protests against the destruction of the Khimki forest. Some forms of social protest of Russian state policy even become violent not because of a government led crackdown on protesters, but because some activists see no other way to express their frustration—as witnessed with the suicide bombings that have taken place in major Russian cities since 2007.[49]

Conclusions

The Russian case demonstrates that civil society plays an effective, monitory role when other institutions crucial to democratic practice are present or have an established record and work in tandem with civil society organizations, but even with the diffusion of new technologies, civil society falls short of monitoring the state when more formal institutions of democracy are weak or largely absent from the political system.

First, in order to develop, a monitory democracy requires some traditional institutional underpinnings. Most of all, civil society requires first a free and fair electoral framework where opposition parties and candidates can compete and win seats in a legislative assembly that is functionally independent of the executive branch of government. Without competitive and open elections, civil society groups aspiring to monitor the state cannot find a hook on which to hang. They cannot pass their collective interests reliably and constructively to representatives of the state. Second, in order to gain traction, citizen initiated organizations with a monitory function need some form of free media to report their activities and convey the public interest to politicians.

In post-communist Russia, civil society is only able to weakly and sporadically challenge the state due to the weaknesses of these formal institutions through which the type of monitory democracy Keane envisions might operate. In modern Russia it is, more often than not, the state that monitors society.

Notes

1. John Keane, Chapter 1 "Civil Society and Monitory Democracy?" (this volume): 3–4.
2. Robert Dahl, *Polyarchy: Participation and Opposition* (New Haven, C.T.: Yale University Press, 1971).
3. See for example, Sheri Berman, "Civil Society and the Collapse of the Weimar Republic," *World Politics* vol. 49, no. 3, (1997): 401–429; Simone Chambers and Jeffrey Kopstein, "Bad Civil Society," *Political Theory* vol. 29, no. 6, (2001): 837–865; and Larry Diamond, *Developing Democracy: Toward Consolidation* (Baltimore: Johns Hopkins University Press, 1999).
4. See, for example, H. Gordon Skilling and Franklyn Griffiths, *Interest Groups in Soviet Politics* (Princeton N.J.: Princeton University Press, 1973).
5. Moshe Lewin, *The Gorbachev Phenomenon: A Historical Interpretation* (Berkeley: University of California Press, 1988): 31–32.
6. Alfred B. Evans, Jr., "Civil Society in the Soviet Union?" in *Russian Civil Society: A Critical Assessment*, ed. Alfred B. Evans, Laura A. Henry, and Lisa McIntosh Sundstrom (New York: M.E. Sharpe, 2006): 29.
7. I. N. Il'ina, *Obshchestvennye Organizatsii Rossii v 1920-e gody* (Moscow: Russian Academy of Sciences, Institute of Russian History, 2000): 111, as cited in Evans, Jr., "Civil Society in the Soviet Union?" 28–56.
8. Martin Walker as quoted in Lewin, *The Gorbachev Phenomenon*, 2.
9. Michael McFaul, *Russia's Unfinished Revolution: Political Change from Gorbachev to Putin* (Ithaca: Cornell University Press, 2001): 36.
10. Mikhail Gorbachev, *Memoirs* (New York: Double Day Press, 1996): 175.
11. Anne White, *Democratization in Russia under Gorbachev, 1985–1991: The Birth of a Voluntary Sector* (New York: St. Martin's Press, 1999): 12; see also M. Steven Fish, *Democracy from Scratch: Opposition and Regime in the New Russian Revolution* (Princeton, N.J.: Princeton University Press, 1995).
12. Evans, "Civil Society in the Soviet Union?" 45.
13. For a full catalogue and description of these organizations, see for example McFaul, *Russia's Unfinished Revolution*, 63–69.
14. Fish, *Democracy from Scratch*, 56–57.

15. Two protesters were run over by a tank; see John Dunlop, *The Rise of Russia and the Fall of the Soviet Empire* (Princeton: Princeton University Press, 1993).
16. See Sarah L. Henderson, *Building Democracy in Contemporary Russia* (Ithaca: Cornell University Press, 2003): 2–5.
17. Spending numbers come from Henderson, *Building Democracy in Contemporary Russia*, 7.
18. The term "over-managed democracy" comes from Nikolai Petrov, Masha Lipman, and Henry E. Hale, "Overmanaged Democracy in Russia: Governance Impications of Hybrid Regimes," Carnegie Papers, Russia and Eurasia Program no. 106, February 2010 (Washington: Carnegie Endowment for International Peace).
19. M. Steven Fish, *Democracy Derailed in Russia: The Failure of Open Politics* (New York: Cambridge University Press, 2005).
20. Evans, "Civil Society in the Soviet Union?" 153.
21. See *www.ednorus.ru*
22. Vladmir Gel'man, "Political Opposition in Russia: A Dying Species? *Post-Soviet Affairs* vol. 21, no. 3, 2005.
23. Federal Law No175-FZ "On the Election of Deputies of the State Duma of the Federal Assembly of the Russian Federation" (11 December 2002).
24. *http://www.legislationonline.org*
25. Masha Lipman, "Freedom of Expression without Freedom of the Press," *Journal of International Affairs* vol. 63, no. 2, (Spring/Summer 2010): 155.
26. See Lipman, "Freedom of Expression without Freedom of the Press," 156.
27. "Russian Journalist on Trial for Defaming Local Governor in Internet Chat Room, Committee to Protect Journalists News Alert," 23 February 2007: *http://www.cpj.org/news/2007/europe/russia23feb07na.html*.
28. Russian Media Sustainability Index, (Washington, D.C.: International Research and Exchanges Board, 2005).
29. Lipman, "Freedom of Expression without Freedom of the Press," 158.
30. Lipman, "Freedom of Expression without Freedom of the Press," 160.
31. This is not to say they were innocent of any crimes, necessarily. The issue is the inequality of application of law to business people who owned assets deemed of state importance by the regime. Other "oligarchs" who may also have been eligible for theft and corruption charges at the time were left with their assets intact.
32. Petrov, Lipman, and Hale, "Overmanaged Democracy in Russia," 15.
33. Petrov, Lipman, and Hale, "Overmanaged Democracy in Russia," 18.
34. Lipman, "Freedom of Expression without Freedom of the Press," 160.
35. Cited in Petrov, Lipman, and Hale, "Overmanaged Democracy in Russia," 26.
36. Lipman, "Freedom of Expression without Freedom of the Press": 162.
37. "Rights Groups Undergo Surprise Checks" *Moscow Times*, 14 September 2010. Accessed on 15 September 2010 at *http://www.themoscowtimes.com/news/article/rights-groups-undergo-surprise-checks/416096.html*
38. Vladimir Putin, Interview in *Kommersant*, 30 August 2010.
39. Sergei Borisov, "Russia: The Pensioners' Revolt," *Transitions Online*, Week in Review, 11–17 January 2005 *www.tol.org*.
40. Valentinas Mite, "Russia's Pensioners' Protests Mount Growing Challenge to Putin" 17 January 2005, Radio Free Europe/Radio Liberty. *http://www.rferl.org/featuresarticle/2005/01*

41. Masha Lipman, "Breaking The Cordon," *The Moscow Times*, 12 March 2007: 10.
42. Petrov, Lipman, and Hale make this point in "Overmanaged Democracy in Russia," 2.
43. Petrov, Lipman, and Hale, "Overmanaged Democracy in Russia," 4.
44. Jim Heintz, "Russia's Duma OKs More Power for Security Service." *Associated Press*, 16 July 2010 as reported in *Johnson's Russia List*.
45. Debra Javeline and Sarah Lindemann-Komarova, "Rethinking Russia: A Balanced Assessment of Russian Civil Society." *Journal of International Affairs* (spring/summer 2010): 171–188.
46. Javeline and Lindemann-Komarova, "Rethinking Russia," 174.
47. Javeline and Lindemann-Komarova, "Rethinking Russia," 177.
48. Petrov, Lipman, and Hale make a similar point in "Overmanaged Democracy in Russia," 12–15.
49. Reports on the exact numbers of terrorist incidents vary among Russian sources. The trend, however, is undeniably up in the last several years. Opposition political leader Boris Nemtsov with his co-author, former Deputy Minister of Oil Vladimir Milov, claim a six-fold increase in terrorist incidents between 2000 (when there were a reported 134 incidents) and spring 2010 (when they claim there were 786 incidents) including for example, the attack by female suicide bombers from Chechnya of the metro station just outside the FSB headquarters in central Moscow. This was one of a string of attacks by Chechnya's so-called Black Widows, young women widowed by the deaths of their Chechen fighter husbands at the hands of Russian forces. See Vladimir Milov and Boris Nemtsov, *What 10 Years of Putin Have Brought: An Expert Evaluation* (Moscow: 2010): 15.

Chapter 5

MONITORY DEMOCRACY AND ECOLOGICAL CIVILIZATION IN THE PEOPLE'S REPUBLIC OF CHINA

James Miller

Introduction

In what sense can religious values and institutions in China be seen as elements of civil society that have the function of challenging and monitoring the interests, values, and actions of the state? To answer this question, this chapter considers both the ways in which religious issues have played a small role in containing—rather than enhancing—the ideological authority of the current Chinese state, and whether they may be regarded as functioning in a way similar to Keane's concept of monitory democracy. The first issue to be considered is the role Daoist values play in promoting awareness of environmental issues that support local efforts to resist centrally imposed economic agendas. This leads to a broader discussion of religious values, both national and transnational, and their ability to offer sustainable alternatives to the dominant ideology of state capitalism.

Monitory Democracy and Environmental Policy

John Keane's concept of monitory democracy is particularly salient as regards the relationship between civil society and ecological sustainability in China. China's unique political structure allows for a measure of indirect representative democracy, but this is always circumscribed by the political direction imposed upon the state by the Communist Party. In China's case, the formal measures that permit democratic representation may thus be less significant than the ways in which China's emerging civil society attempts to slow down the pace of environmental engineering and locally resist the imposition of central policies and plans.

There are valid historical reasons for thinking that these effects of monitory democracy are particularly important as regards environmental issues in China. Judith Shapiro has amply demonstrates how "utopian urgency" and "dogmatic formalism" contributed to a series of policy disasters regarding the natural environment in China in the twentieth century.[1] Shapiro's explanation for these mistakes lies, intriguingly, in the realm of values. While she acknowledges the difficulty of relating cultural values to policy decisions, she nonetheless articulates her basic thesis as "how Maoist values came to dominate and govern the human-nature relationship."[2]

In her analysis of the Great Leap Forward, for instance, Shapiro explains how the Maoist rhetoric of "compressed time" constituted the core value of this campaign to overtake the West in terms of industrial development.[3] She writes, "Its defining characteristic was speed: urgency in reorganizing society, urgency in catching up with Britain in industry, urgency in raising agricultural yields, urgency in building water conservancy projects, urgency in ridding China of pests, and so on."[4]

Political disputes leading up to the Great Leap Forward centered not on the basic goal of industrialization, but on the question of how fast the goal could be achieved. When the Maoist policy of "opposing opposing-rushing-ahead" won out and the Great Leap Forward was formally announced, the notion that there might be limits to the rate of development was considered heresy. Two consequences for the natural environment were evident. The first was that any attempt to reduce expectations as to what could be wrested from nature was regarded as ideologically suspicious. When, in the summer of 1958, Zeng Jia, a vice-Party secretary in Sichuan, objected to unreasonable expectations regarding grain production, he was admonished: "The Communist Party has made it possible for a field to produce 10,000 jin. If you do not believe it, where has your Party spirit gone?"[5] To suggest that nature might impose limits on the will of the Chinese people was to commit an ideological crime of the highest order. As the Great Leap Forward got underway, the masses were mobilized to set up backyard steel furnaces to provide the massive amounts of steel required for China's industrialization. The consequence was massive deforestation as trees were cut down to provide firewood for this failed experiment.

During the Great Leap Forward, the slogan "Man must conquer nature" made it clear that nature was the enemy. Mao's extreme humanism had no place for any notion of balance between humans and the natural world, nor could it conceive of an ecological understanding in which the flourishing of human life could be seen as dependent upon the flourishing of a range of ecosystems. Inflated expectations regarding grain production and massive deforestation to support steel making had dire consequences for the health of Chinese people and the Chinese environment. It is estimated that the tremendous famine that ensued from these policies led to the deaths of 35–50 million people between 1959 and 1961.

During the Cultural Revolution (1966–76) Mao developed another disastrous strategy, which Shapiro terms "dogmatic formalism." The case here revolves around Mao's slogan "Learn from Dazhai." In 1963, the Dazhai brigade of the Dazhai people's commune in Shanxi province overcame a natural disaster through a policy of extreme self-reliance. While this policy was clearly rooted in the earlier ideology of human voluntarism, this policy was taken in a new direction, as it was "applied mechanistically in scenarios where it could not possibly succeed because it was inappropriate for local conditions."[6] In particular, Shapiro documents how one specific environmental policy from Dazhai, namely, terracing hillsides to create arable land, was reproduced across China in environments for which it was not suited, "inappropriate terracing on steep slopes and areas with thin topsoil brought deforestation, erosion, and sedimentation, while encroachments on lakes and rivers led to ecosystem imbalance, microclimate changes, and increased flooding." [7]

In her conclusion, Shapiro briefly compares China's efforts to conquer nature with similar campaigns in socialist Cuba and the former USSR.[8] Although she argues that the uniqueness of China's situation makes it difficult to generalize conclusively regarding politics and the environment, she does highlight two lessons that can be learned from China's disastrous experiments in the Maoist era. The first is that a higher level of democratic participation would have made it easier to resist the urgency of Mao's utopian fantasies regarding the rate of industrial development. At the same time, a system of democratic representation would have enabled local areas to have greater power over their own environments, and this might have mitigated the effects of imposing the Dazhai model uniformly across China's varied topography.

These lessons are relevant for considering the ways that monitory democracy and the development of civil society in China can play a positive role in the transition to ecological sustainability as a core value of Chinese policymaking. In particular, is it possible to see how monitory activities play a role, whether positive or negative, in simply slowing down the implementation of policies? Second, can monitory democracy be seen in the ways that local regions resist the efforts of the state to impose its central vision upon the breadth of China's geography? Although China has only limited channels for formal democratic representation, the rise of environmental NGOs and specific environmental protests during the past thirty years of economic reform may go some way to indicate that a form of monitory democracy is functioning in contemporary China.

There are, however, four questions to be asked. First, does the sporadic scrutiny of and local protests against China's emergent economic plans have any substantial effect on environmental policies? Second, does this ultimately benefit China's environmental sustainability? Third, how are various non-state actors able to contribute to a higher-order debate about the basic values that underlie China's quest for economic development? And fourth, are environmental or other movements able to substantially engage with a broad range of publics in questioning the fundamental direction that China's development is taking?

In order to answer these questions, I would like to look at the case of Dujiangyan—a UNESCO world heritage site near Chengdu, Sichuan province—where a grassroots campaign succeeded in reversing governmental plans to build a hydropower dam. Dujiangyan has a good claim to be regarded as one of the wonders of the ancient world. Constructed between 267 and 256 B.C.E., Dujiangyan is an irrigation system that regulates the flow of the Min River during the spring floods, provides water for 50 cities, and irrigates 672,000 hectares of farmland. Remarkably, it is still in use today largely unchanged from its original design. It is regarded as a unique icon of Chinese cultural heritage not simply because it is an engineering marvel, but also because it concretely symbolizes an authentically Chinese philosophy of harmony between human beings and their natural environments. Li Bin, the project's architect, made use of a natural feature in the topography of the Min River to create a weir and irrigation channel that function together to divert floodwater in a controlled way throughout the Sichuan basin. In this way flooding is not only prevented, but rather channeled into an elaborate system of irrigation canals enabling Sichuan to be a rich and fertile agricultural land. To this day Li Bin is memorialized in a Daoist temple built on the site. In 2000, Dujiangyan, together with the neighboring Daoist temple complex on Mt. Qingcheng, received designation as a UNESCO World Heritage Site.

Plans to dam the Min river date back to the period of Sino-Soviet cooperation of the 1950s. A dam was partially built in 1958, but construction stopped in 1961. The unfinished structure is still visible to this day about half a kilometer from the Dujiangyan site. In 2001, however, engineers began construction of a massive hydropower dam at Zipingpu, some seven kilometers upstream from Dujiangyan. In contrast to the subtle and elegant engineering of Dujiangyan, Zipingpu is a 156 meter-high dam, the highest of a series of cascading dams designed to provide irrigation water, flood control, and hydropower. The dam was severely damaged during the Wenchuan earthquake of 2008, but a complete breach was thankfully avoided.

As Andrew Mertha reports, the construction of Zipingpu led to a series of environmental protests based at Dujiangyan that were successful in reversing the central government's decision to build a smaller dam at Yangliuhu close to Dujiangyan.[9] In 2003, opposition to Yangliuhu crystallized around the cultural argument that this new dam would irreversibly damage Dujiangyan's status as a key treasure of China's heritage. As one Dujiangyan official put it, "Should we sacrifice the heritage of the people and the world to the interests of some [political] departments?"[10]

It is worth considering this case in comparison to the failed attempt by many of China's leading intellectuals to oppose the construction of the Three Gorges Dam. Why did opposition to that project fail, and why was the Dujiangyan protest successful? One answer, provided in Mertha's analysis, is that rather than directly oppose the plans of the central government, local organizations made their views known to a broad circle of media organizations, thus espousing an indirect approach, rather than formal representations.[11] In this regard, the Dujiangyan case lends some support to Keane's theory of monitory democracy: that the scrutinizing function of the media is just as important for the democracy as a formal process of representation. As Premier Wen Jiabao declared in 2005, "for a project which has aroused such public concern, we need to devote more time and make assessments based on scientific considerations."[12]

A second reason for the success at Dujiangyan, however, is the broad set of cultural and even philosophical issues that were at stake. Not only was Dujiangyan widely regarded as a cultural heritage work as significant as the Great Wall, Dujiangyan also signified the concrete expression of Daoist philosophy. It thus embodied a uniquely Chinese vision of human relations with the natural world, a vision proudly claimed by Sichuan local authorities. A senior government official of Dujiangyan city explained to me that just as Daoist philosophy came to be expressed spiritually in the religion that emerged around Qingcheng Shan (second century C.E.), the same philosophy was also expressed materially in the Dujiangyan irrigation system.[13] That is to say, a significant local reason to oppose the development at Yangliuhu was its connection to the values and heritage of Daoist philosophy.

At the heart of this philosophy lies the concept of *wuwei*, variously translated as "non-action," "non-aggressive action," or "effortless action," which signifies a uniquely Daoist method of praxis in which the maximum effect is achieved by taking advantage as much as possible of the natural power inherent in things, rather than imposing one's will directly upon them. Dujiangyan is regarded as a model of "effortless action" because rather than damming the river completely, the site employs a weir and irrigation system to channel and regulate the water's natural power.

It is hard to underestimate the cultural significance of this metaphor within China. Not only does the vision of flood control go to the heart of China's origin myths—see, for example, the so-called "hydraulic state thesis" of Karl Wittfogel[14] —the concept of water-flow is a key metaphor of Chinese philosophy.[15] In Daoism, water is a frequent image for the Dao itself or for virtuous behavior: "Best to be like water, which benefits the ten thousand things and does not contend. It pools where humans disdain to dwell, close to the Tao."[16] In Chinese popular culture, water features are key elements of *fengshui* and are taken into consideration particularly in deciding upon the locations of tombs. In aesthetics, the sound of water flowing was deemed to be highly desirable.[17] In Chinese medical anthropology, moreover, human bodies are envisioned as porous beings in which fluids circulate providing health and long life.[18] To dam water is to obstruct the natural flow of things, and in the holistic systems approach of Chinese culture, the blockage of energy is a principal cause of disease and death.

The Dujiangyan case thus not only invokes analysis in terms of how local actors mobilized media channels to resist the imposition of central power, it also goes to the heart of what values underpin China's quest for modernization and development. Monitory democracy, such as it is in the People's Republic of China, is not only relevant for the way that it scrutinizes state power, but also for the way that it challenges the fundamental values upon which that power is based.

Civil Society and Alternative Religious Values

This "monitory" function is perhaps more relevant in China than in other states where the fundamental values of the state seem relatively well established by popular consensus. The first reason for this is that China's revolutionary history over the past century and more has produced a profound instability of the core values among its people. The massive migration of over one hundred million people from the countryside to the city is one of the great transformations of human-nature relationships in world history. A second remarkable story is the rapid explosion of Christian faith and Buddhist practice throughout the mainland. The net result of these profound social, cultural, and environmental shifts has been to occasion a public dialogue regarding the fundamental values that underlie China's modernization. Scrutiny, therefore, is one reason for the success of Dujiangyan: it caused the central government to rethink its exercise of power in this particular matter. But scrutiny also touched on deeper notions of Chinese identity, cultural heritage, and spiritual value.

Another example of how the process of scrutinizing state power raises fundamental questions of value can be seen in the public debate in 2005 over the concept of "revering nature" (*jingwei ziran*). He Zuoxiu, a noted theoretical physicist closely allied to the Communist Party, sparked this debate when he proposed the notion that "revering nature" was a superstitious, anti-science concept that would not help China to deal with its environmental problems. He wrote: "I want to challenge the contention that people ought to respect and hold nature in awe, advanced by one professor. He asserts that mankind should not use science and technology to transform nature, but maintain an attitude of respect and awe. Such an attitude is "anti-science," especially when we are confronting natural disasters like the tsunami or epidemic outbreaks. I hold the opposite view. We human beings should try our best to prevent and reduce losses incurred in natural disasters. Reverence and awe make no sense."[19]

In response, Liang Congjie, the head of Friends of Nature, China's leading environmental non-governmental organization, criticized He Zuoxiu's humanistic, anthropocentric values by invoking the value of nature in China's cultural heritage. He wrote, "Numerous Chinese classical works have shown that we have always placed great value on nature, far more than just being a tool."[20] Similarly, Pan Yue, vice-minister of the Ministry of Environmental Protection, has also extolled traditional Chinese ideals and values in regards to the natural environment.[21] Although he warns, "when we talk about the revival of the Chinese civilization, we do not mean to mechanically restore the traditional natural economy and cultural traditions of Confucianism, Buddhism, Daoism, and Legalism." He nonetheless sees the development of an "ecological civilization" as something that integrates traditional Chinese values into a new cultural whole[22]:

> The intrinsic spirit of traditional Chinese culture and the environmental culture gathering momentum in the contemporary world are strikingly compatible. It is well known that traditional Chinese culture has always pursued harmony between man and nature, presumed morals to follow nature, abided by the laws of nature, aspired to the unity of man and nature, embraced the idea of equality among all individuals, and highlighted the security of lives

and the continuity of civilization. Based on this spirit, traditional Chinese philosophies, religions, literature, art … all demonstrate harmonious relations between man and nature, profound and far-sighted ecological civilization, and harmonious aesthetics of heaven, earth, and humanity. If we make a comprehensive survey of the world, both ancient and modern, we may observe that in the past several thousand years, there have been many ancient civilizations with prosperous days and golden ages; but through the destruction of nature, these came to an end. The Chinese nation is the only exception, preserved integrally and unbroken, with the same roots, race, language, and culture.[23]

Although Pan Yue is writing as a government leader, it is easy to see that his language has important consequences for the emergence of a civil society in China that is explicitly construed around a distinctively Chinese understanding of what "civil" means. Far from wholeheartedly establishing "the environment" as a global issue to be solved by international consensus, the rise of environmentalist discourse in China has opened the door to the possibility of framing environmental issues in terms of an emergent nationalist rhetoric formed around "traditional Chinese values." This possibility lends weight to the notion articulated by Nina Witoszek in this volume that the emergence of civil society may also be linked to a re-tribalization of civil identities forged, in this case, around the values, ideals, and history of the Han people.

The case of Dujiangyan is just as instructive here as the media debate between Liang and He, or the arguments of Pan Yue. In the context of Dujiangyan, the public outcry regarding the possible negative effects of building dams was similarly couched in a nationalist language. Arguments for the preservation of Dujiangyan were not explicitly made in terms of the UNESCO world heritage designation, even though that may have been an important factor in the final decision. Rather, the arguments centered chiefly on Dujiangyan's status as a unique symbol of Chinese heritage whose meaning could not, ultimately, be separated from the uniquely Chinese philosophy and religion of Daoism. Indeed, this powerful nexus of national identity, spiritual value, and ecological relevance has not been lost on the Chinese Daoist Association, which has publicly allied itself with the issue of environmentalism.[24]

The role that may be played by religious cultures, including Confucianism, in any emergent Chinese civil society is not to be discounted, whether in terms of offering alternative aspirations (the question of ultimate values) or alternative identities (the question of tribalization). The attention paid to religious and ethnic issues by the Chinese state may indeed constitute evidence for their relevance in this matter. It is not simply that the state is opposed to the values of Daoism, Buddhism, or Christianity for purely idealistic reasons, but rather because it recognizes the real alternatives they pose to its own vision of civil belonging. This antagonism between the state and religious organizations goes back to the early twentieth century when nationalist reformers, both Republican and Communist, sought to establish the state as the sole object of Chinese people's devotion. Indeed, Prasenjit Duara has argued that the formation of the modern Chinese state in the early twentieth century was based in part on its ability to supplant local religious associations as networks of civil society, thereby replacing the patchwork of local affiliations with one focused on a single nation state.[25] As local religious associations and the veneration of local gods were attacked under the new ideological category of "superstition" (*mixin*), at the same time, national religious organizations were established and national gods (those venerated more or less uniformly throughout China) were brought under the umbrella of the state.[26]

The relationship between the state and religious organizations can thus be understood chiefly in terms of a "geography of power" in which the emergent nation state sought to exert its authority over the whole area of China, bringing all the various local factions, authorities, and associations under a single system of guidance and authority. This model of spatial authority was explicitly restrained with the reforms that began in 1978–79, in which religion was once again permitted to function, but only in specifically designated spaces. The fact that street evangelism or other forms of public religious activity are generally prohibited demonstrates the state's geographic concern that public space be purely secular space. However, inasmuch as religious activities do take place in authorized locations, they constitute a limited but tolerated alternative to the values and ideology of the Communist Party and its leadership of the nation.

In what sense, then, can such activities be said to constitute a form of emergent civil society that in some way monitors or challenges the functioning of the state? The fact that such organizations are restrained from physically encroaching upon China's purely secular public space might suggest that they have no real monitory power. But this would make the mistake of assuming a consistency between public and private discourse.[27] As Tam Wai Lun notes, "People display agnosticism or anti-religious stances in public as a strategy to avoid accusations of traditionalism and feudalism, and their public stance therefore cannot be taken at face value."[28] The discrepancy between public expression and private values means that any discussion of civil society in China must inevitably be more complex than what can be publicly gauged, and this makes it hard to calculate the effects of the rise of religious activity in China from conventional social science perspectives. Tam goes on to note that the resurgence of religious activity in China, "signals a search for alternatives or even a vague resistance to communist ideals," but it is naturally difficult to ascertain precisely what the consequences of such "vague resistance" might be.[29]

Anecdotal evidence can be found in the conflict between religious and secular authorities over the public meaning of sacred sites. On a recent field visit to the Daoist sacred mountain, Mt. Mao, in Jiangsu province, evidence of such conflict over fundamental values could be found in the signs that interpreted former sacred sites to the visitor in resolutely secular terms.[30] Conversely, signs on Mt. Qingcheng, the Daoist mountain jointly inscribed with the Dujiangyan irrigation system on the UNESCO world heritage list, proudly proclaim the beautifully preserved natural environment as a function of the environmental consciousness of Daoists in former ages. In both these cases, secular and religious authorities are vying to lay claim to the aspirational value and ultimate significance of China's iconic physical spaces.

Ian Johnson relates similar evidence in his report of a Daoist ceremony to consecrate a temple to the Jade Emperor on Mt. Yi.[31] In this case, the government officials, who viewed the religious dedication as a necessary but unwelcome element of their economic plan to boost tourism in the area, were obliged to compromise with the Daoist nun who insisted on a full four-hour ceremony. At the same time, the public was captivated by the intensity of her religious practice, which contrasted with the perfunctory performance of the officials, for whom the dedication ceremony was simply the culmination of their economic plan to boost local tourism. In this case, the performance by a respected ritual master stood not simply as an arcane curiosity, but as an authentic religious insistence on a set of values and longings that did not cohere with the narrow rational calculus of state capitalism. It is hard to imagine such a set of complex cultural and political interactions taking place in a European liberal democracy where the engagement of religion and the state is less frequently fraught with ideological subtexts.

In China, however, the unusual attention and significance given to religion by the state has the ironic function of endowing religious actors with the function of publicly challenging the values and ideals of the state itself, however much they may not wish to do so. The ideological monotheism of China's political system has the consequence that the mere performance of religious practices inherently challenges the values and goals of the state. It is doubtful whether religious actors would deliberately seek such ideological conflict with the state, but this unnecessary conflict is, of course, exploited by foreign governments who highlight China's religious policies as a means to exert leverage over the country in the international arena.

Finally, it is important to consider the ways in which religions have, for thousands of years, functioned as agents of globalization and transnational civil exchange. Operating both within and beyond the structures of military conflict, economic transaction, and cultural exchange, religious beliefs and practices continue to exert influence as non-government actors on the Chinese scene. Particularly salient in this regard are Buddhism, Islam, and Christianity, all of which are profoundly implicated in the basic question of the Chinese state's ability to maintain sovereignty over its geographic borders. Whether it is the Muslims in Xinjiang, Buddhists in Tibet, or Roman Catholics throughout China, these transnational religious movements are clearly seen by the state as inhibiting its ability to govern its own people. Religious movements act as a boundary, and thus a zone of conflict, between the individual religious practitioner and the apparatus of the state. The conflict between the Vatican and Beijing over who has the authority to appoint Roman Catholic Bishops, or the conflict between Dharamsala and Beijing over what procedures will be used to identify the next Dalai Lama, are in both cases seen by Beijing as a conflict over state sovereignty. They reflect, albeit on a much grander, geo-political level, the same issues that Johnson highlights in the story regarding the dedication ceremony to the Jade Emperor: whose values have authoritative meaning in this specific space?

This issue is of profound significance—not simply in terms of the centuries-old dream of the Han people to once again have the dominant, even the only, voice within the geographic space known as the Middle Kingdom, but it is also significant in terms of the issue of ecological sustainability. If China's environment is understood not simply as a blank space upon which competing secular and religious interests vie for authoritative dominance, but as an active participant in the complex ecology of interests in which 1.3 billion humans live, then there is a greater chance that the "ecological civilization" much vaunted by China's Communist Party will become a reality. From this perspective, the question of democracy is not simply about which group's voice will be heard the loudest, but about how to incorporate the interests of all the factors that constitute China's complex and precarious ecology.

Notes

1. Judith Shapiro, *Mao's War Against Nature: Politics and the Environment in Revolutionary China* (Cambridge: Cambridge University Press, 2004).
2. Shapiro, *Mao's War Against Nature*, 11
3. Shapiro, *Mao's War Against Nature*, 70

4. Shapiro, *Mao's War Against Nature*, 71
5. Shapiro, *Mao's War Against Nature*, 79
6. Shapiro, *Mao's War Against Nature*, 98
7. Shapiro, *Mao's War Against Nature*, 98
8. Shapiro, *Mao's War Against Nature*, 201
9. Andrew C. Mertha, *China's Water Warriors: Citizen Action and Policy Change* (Ithaca, N.Y.: Cornell University Press, 2011).
10. Mertha, *China's Water Warriors*, 102
11. Mertha, *China's Water Warriors*, 106
12. Mertha, *China's Water Warriors*, 108
13. Personal comment 2004
14. See Karl A. Wittfogel, *Oriental Despotism* (New Haven, C.T.: Yale University Press, 1957).
15. Sarah Allan, *The Way of Water and Sprouts of Virtue* (New York: State University of New York Press, 1997).
16. Stephen Addis and Stanley Lombardo, trans. Lao-Tzu, "The Daode jing" in *Tao Te Ching* (Indianapolis, I.N.: Hackett Publishers, 1993).
17. Edward H. Schafer, "The Conservation of Nature under the T'ang Dynasty," in *Journal of the Economic and Social History of the Orient* vol. 5 (1962): 279–308.
18. James Miller, "Daoism and Nature," in *The Oxford Handbook of Religion and Ecology*, ed. R. S. Gottlieb (New York: Oxford University Press 2006): 220–235.
19. He Zuoxiu, "Man Need Not Revere Nature." *Friends of Nature* vol. 2 (2005): 19–20.
20. Liang Congjie and Yang Dongping, eds., *The China Environment Yearbook (2005): Crisis and Breakthrough of China's Environment*, (China: Brill Academic Publishers 2007): 14.
21. Pan Yue, *Thoughts on Environmental Issues* (Beijing: China Environmental Culture Promotion Association, 2007).
22. Pan Yue, *Thoughts on Environmental Issues*, 31.
23. Pan Yue, *Thoughts on Environmental Issues*, 30–31.
24. See James Miller, "Is Green the New Red? The Role of Religion in Creating a Sustainable China," forthcoming 2013.
25. Prasenjit Duara, "Knowledge and Power in the Discourse of Modernity: The Campaigns against Popular Religion in Early Twentieth Century China and Campaigns against Popular Religion," *Journal of Asian Studies* vol. 50, no. 1, (1991): 67–83.
26. This policy has been reanimated in recent years in the exaltation of Confucius as a non-theistic spiritual icon of the Chinese people.
27. Goran Aijmer and Virgil K.Y. Ho, *Cantonese Society in a Time of Change*, (Hong Kong: Chinese University Press, 2000): 39.
28. Tam Wai Lun, "Local Religion in Contemporary China," in *Chinese Religions in Contemporary Societies*, ed. James Miller (Santa Barbara, CA: ABC-CLIO, 2006): 80.
29. Tam Wai Lun, "Local Religion in Contemporary China," 80.
30. See Miller, "Is Green the New Red?".
31. Ian Johnson, "The Rise of the Tao," *The New York Times Magazine*, 7 November 2011.

Chapter 6

TENUOUS SPACES
CIVIL SOCIETY IN BURMA/MYANMAR

David I. Steinberg

Introduction

Although Burma (Myanmar) is on the cusp of political change through the transformation of its formal mechanisms of authority, its political system has been based on the military dictatorship, which was legitimized by the constitution approved in a manipulated referendum in 2008. A new phase started—if only at the level of rhetorics—after the elections on 7 November 2010, which were swept by the military's surrogate party, the Union Solidarity and Development Party (USDP). As described in March 2009 by Senior General Than Shwe, then the head of state, governance was to be a "discipline-flourishing democracy," which would be like a new well that at first produces muddy water. By analogy, the military was to be the "muddy water" for some indefinite, probably prolonged, period. The very metaphor of "discipline-flourishing democracy" prompts reconsideration of the Burmese past, as well as rethinking of the potential role of civil society, its impact, and its perception by foreigners.

The popular and widespread negative delineation of Burma/Myanmar, not only in the Western media, but also in more policy-oriented circles, obscures the nuances that require deeper analyses if that complex society is to be understood, and if effective policies are to be instituted. Extreme characterizations of Burma as "obscure," "isolated," "xenophobic," "totalitarian," "authoritarian,"—let alone rogue, thuggish, and a pariah—transmogrify reality and subvert rational policy formulation. Furthermore, they effectively prevent any lessons, especially in regard to civil society, that might have been learned from the Myanmar experience and applied to other authoritarian contexts.

Focusing on Burma/Myanmar, in this chapter civil society organizations are defined as relatively permanent not-for-profit groups, operating in the space between the state and the extended family, while having a significant degree of autonomy in choice of leadership, programming foci, and funding. This definition excludes political parties, the private business sector, quasi-governmental institutions (QUONGOs), government organized but ostensibly private groups (GONGOs), and other institutions, the exploration of the roles of all of which could bear substantial fruit in analyzing the Burmese context, but must be excluded herein.

There is a series of issues that need to be addressed in order to illuminate not only the dynamics of civil society's potential impact in Burma, but its implications for the democracies in other corners of the world. These include:

1. Whether civil society *par excellence* can only exist in democratic states, or ironically, whether civil society is needed to form such states;
2. Whether civil society can exist and function effectively in totalitarian or authoritarian states;
3. Whether civil society can help democratize states through the development of social capital, leading to political trust;
4. Whether civil society can assist in the positive development of authoritarian states through the delivery of goods and services beyond the ken of governments;
5. What is or may be the relationship among international NGOs, authoritarian governments, and indigenous NGOs; and
6. Whether the complex relationships between donors, international NGOs, and indigenous NGOs are effective and produce the desired developmental and political results.

These issues are compounded by a number of other potential questions concerning civil society, including their relationships to political pluralism, economic development, poverty alleviation, social needs and promotion of social mobility, institution-strengthening, capacity enhancement, environmental protection, cultural continuity and, possibly, diversity.

Following the 2010 Myanmar elections—in early 2011—a bicameral national legislature, 14 regional legislatures, and six legislatures for selected, smaller, minority areas, were established. The questions remain how much this new Burmese political incarnation of a partly elected government (25 percent of all legislature seats will be appointed by active-duty military) will reflect traditional Burmese normative concepts of power, how much internationalized ideals, and to what degree an underlying substratum of power relationships have influenced civil society's identity and role.

Setting the Stage

Although the Burmese state[1] became a parliamentary democracy after gaining independence in 1948, it governed through a broad but loose civilian coalition known as the Anti-Fascist People's Freedom League (AFPFL). It failed on a number of accounts, most importantly because personalized loyalties resulted in the potential for civil war in 1958, which prompted a military "constitutional coup," one authorized by the legislature to rule for 18 months.[2] The civilian government was less than successful in attempting to forge a unified nation from a number of ethnic minorities and the majority Burmans, who make up some two-thirds of the population. Following a military-supervised civilian election in 1960, won by a party to which the military objected, this inept government failed, resulting in a military coup in 1962 that brought forth isolationist tendencies under direct military rule from 1962 to 1974 with a socialist ideology, and then under the military-dominated civilianized control of the Burma Socialist Programme Party (BSPP) from 1974 to 1988. From 1962 until 1988, Burma met the definition of a totalitarian state. Such states have "a monistic center of power, an exclusive or more or less elaborate ideology, which provides an ultimate interpretation of social reality, and they actively mobilize the population through a single party and the monopolistic groups deriving from it."[3] Since it was without the rigors or gulags of a North Korean regime, it is perhaps best considered as a "soft" totalitarian state.

The coup of 18 September 1988, which ended the BSPP period and was designed to shore up continued military control through alternative mechanisms, brought forth the formation of the State Law and Order Restoration Council (SLORC) and its 1997 continuing incarnation, the State Peace and Development Council (SPDC), both exclusively military. Although the military has continued to dominate since 1962, there have been substantial modifications within that context, allowing a description of governance in that society during the later period from 1988 to 2010 to be "soft authoritarian" rather than "soft totalitarian." Ruling by decree from 1988 to 2010, the junta eliminated the BSPP single party mobilization system by means of a rigid socialist ideology.

During this period, the private sector was theoretically encouraged, foreign investment was sought, and modest social space became apparent as types of civil society developed and as international NGOs increased operations. These changes did not in any sense diminish the hardships that have been placed on its population. Health and education deteriorated, as did standards of living with perhaps half the population of about 50 million at or below the World Bank-defined poverty line. The SLORC/SPDC military rule did allow for more, if still limited, social space and the new administration following the 2010 elections and the inauguration of the 2008 constitution should further define the extent of those openings.

Problems of Research and Definitions

The opaqueness of many non-democratic governments and administrations, including Myanmar, together with the lack of extensive academic access, inhibit the exploration and analysis of many aspects of authoritarian governance, including civil society. Certain types of civil society institutions have proliferated even in most of the non-democratic world, with the exception of North Korea. Their existence is widespread, virtually ubiquitous, even if researchers have limited access in many such societies, and even if the influence of such groups is severely circumscribed.

Civil society in the context of Myanmar has been defined above as a means to explore various policy issues. If, however, the term "civil society" is ambiguous, it is even more so in the Burmese context; the term has never existed in the Burmese lexicon. Varying definitions are prevalent due to societal organizations, political proclivities, foreign and domestic ideological considerations, and the research goals of various analysts at national, comparative, or theoretical levels. In some states, the term "civil society" has alternative connotations unlike the neutral designation it generally enjoys in the West. It has often been considered to refer to anti-state or potentially anti-state institutions, as in China. Very often, analysts place civil society in dichotomous contrast to state institutions, perhaps reflecting more the strong tradition of dualism in Western philosophical thought rather than the reality of social interaction, especially in parts of Asia.

Academic and policy studies of civil society have proliferated over the last decades. Interest in civil society in the West has been resuscitated by two factors: the recognition of the inadequacy of state-sponsored (bilateral or multilateral) foreign assistance that has failed positively to affect economic development and the lives of local peoples, and the liberalization of Eastern Europe, in which the NGOs played significant roles. Even more necessary are studies of their operations under authoritarian regimes because such societies have more opaque policy formulation and are often not subject to the rigors of intellectual interchange.

Globalization and rapid changes in technology affect civil societies as organizations and as social forces, as well as their host governments. These changes have both positive and negative implications. Civil society organizations are increasingly common throughout the world. The World Bank noted that while Cambodia had about 500 local organizations in 1995, China might have had a million (including community-based groups) in the same year.[4] And as civil societies become more influential in many states, governments sometimes respond with growing concern. Modern technology allows civil societies more freedom and international and national interconnections, and can reinforce the importance of their foci, but technology also provides the means for expanded state supervision and even suppression.

In many instances, civil society has become the monitor of state power, to allude to John Keane's concept.[5] More than legislatures and elections, civil society organizations continuously influence governance by questioning inadequacies in all fields. Monitory institutions extend far beyond the definition of civil society in this essay, and how this new movement will evolve and its sustainability is still uncertain. To what degree this monitoring capacity may occur in Myanmar under a new political configuration is exceptionally important, as elections and legislatures are likely to have modest social impact in the short term.

Globalization has linked discrete civil society organizations into worldwide networks with common problematic foci, thus increasing their potential influence by forcing unpleasant international scrutiny and comparisons in states ignoring or slacking in socio-economic, environmental, or political progress. These comparisons also cause many governments' anxiety. Crossing cultural boundaries creates pressures and focuses activities on generic issues—such as the environment, women's rights, labor, etc.—rather than culturally specific ones.

Some define civil society as those institutions that contend with the state for some aspect of power. Others see civil society as a third sector between public and private. Still others posit two versions: one is the innocuous civil society including associational forms of social life; the second is political—a "sphere of action that is independent of the state and that is capable—precisely for this reason—of energizing resistance to a tyrannical regime."[6] Even this dichotomy may, however, ignore the rapid development of the former into the latter, thus blurring and complicating their policy relevance. Some have equated the rise of civil society with the growth of the bourgeoisie or middle class, and others with market economies and economic development. Some have a romanticized view of civil society as expressing freedom, while characterizing the state as coercive. Civil society becomes the cavalry—coming to the rescue of beleaguered states, programs, or societies.[7] One specialist has commented, "The existence of an organized and effective civil society, including nongovernmental organizations (NGOs), is the greatest social phenomenon in the latter part of the twentieth century and, certainly, in this new millennium."[8] The argument that "real" civil society can only exist in relatively mature democratic and developed states is part of the tautological premise that one cannot have democratic and developed states without civil society, although civil society is commonly assumed to be a product of such states.

Most of the definitions and lessons are drawn from the Western experience, with a rich heritage from Greek philosophy through the Enlightenment. But civil society's modern influence begins perhaps with de Tocqueville, whose ideas could be misleading in terms of modern day policy. De Tocqueville considered community organizational relationships important and politically particularly American, but they operated at that time within a weak central governmental structure. In Asia today, most central governments have lengthened and embellished tentacles into society and should be considered "strong" in their attempts to control non-state actors, even if some governments are otherwise programmatically ineffective in delivering services to their people. Importantly, some scholars have considered that the focused trust or social capital illustrated by the formation of civil society groups may translate into political trust, and thus provides an important base for democracy. According to Kumi Naidoo and Rajesh Tandon, "Civil society is linked both conceptually and practically to the promotion of democracy, to good governance, to a hybrid of the two (democratic governance), and ultimately to sustainable development."[9] As Johan Saravanamuttu has noted: "It has become axiomatic that democratization cannot occur in the absence of civil society. The character of civil society in multicultural post-colonial political formations is especially becoming a subject of great interest as it pertains directly to the process of how democratization will unfold in a world "over determined" by ethnicity, and one in which political development is also ultimately tied to economic development."[10]

But if this statement is accurate, then is the reverse true? Can civil society in any of the multitude of Asian cultural contexts move authoritarian regimes along a more democratic or pluralistic track, and if so, how, how long, and under what conditions? And can international NGOs play a constructive role in this process? In other words, how great a role may "monitory" organizations play in positive change? This is a policy issue of singular importance to peoples, governments (both donor and recipient), as well as to international and indigenous NGOs, and of relevance in dealing with crises in the twenty-first century. Saravanamuttu continues:

> Is this too optimistic an approach? Do donors support civil society efforts that reflect their own donor values and visions—both democratic and specific interest group interests? Most donors ascribe fairly benign characteristics to civil society ... with common interest functions related to civil and political rights. This liberal condition often carries an assumption that strong civil society is conducive to, or even necessary for, democratization. However, this is meaningless unless one identifies the nature of the civil society in question. Not all civil society forms have an interest in democratization.... Nevertheless, the linkage between strong civil society and democratizations is often implicit and sometimes explicit in much donor thinking and consequently donor politics.[11]

Subtler, however, is the issue of whether, in authoritarian states, civil society organizations in the same cultures have alternative views of power, authority, and hierarchy than their governments. If indigenous NGOs reflect leadership patterns of their authorities, can they offer effective "monitory" functions?

In modern societies, the authority of the state extends horizontally to some defined, and often ethnically arbitrary, border, in contrast to state power in pre-colonial Southeast Asia. No institution is completely divorced from the state, its legal structure, and its interest in and capacity for surveillance, however benign or malignant. At some official administrative level, the state may ignore the operations of civil society, but in the present world their activities are noted. The degree to which governmental control impinges on civil society institutions is critical to their capacity for autonomous action, but that control is also usually defined in local and cultural terms. So the extent of state registration, funding, listing for or exclusion from taxation, influence, or surveillance will determine the autonomy of any non-governmental institution, but the results may well vary by society. Simple registration in one culture is benign, but in others it may lead to coercive control. Such registration and influence may also vary by the agency of the state, whether national, regional, or local; whether such agencies have potential or actual coercive power (e.g., ministries of home affairs, the military, etc.); whether they are functional ministries (health, education, etc.); whether registration takes place through intermediate or informal mechanisms subservient to the state; or any mixture of the above. The rigidity or laxity of registration requirements may also shift according to perceived internal political events.

This complexity—resulting from differing circumstances—creates problems for the abstraction of generic issues or comparative lessons, a frustrating matter to those academics who attempt to devise worldwide theories. It provides, however, solace to the practitioner, who not only searches for the potential programmatic space between state and society in any particular national setting, but also between localized institutional elements of control. According to He Baogang: "The notion of civil society being completely autonomous from the state is an ideological construct. The idea that state and society each carry on without getting in each other's way is a nostalgic, utopian illusion."[12]

Civil society is sometimes regarded as the panacea to governmental and bureaucratic ills—as the antidote to bureaucratic constipation, corruption, and ineptitude.[13] This may be a misconception. Although smaller size and less bureaucratic propensities may give civil societies an edge over the state in many aspects of performance and the delivery of services because they are often closer to the need, they may also be more subject to some of local societies' less desirable influences, such as manipulation or corruption.

Inherent in this Panglossian approach to the efficacy of civil society is the assumption that concepts of power, authority, hierarchy, orthodoxy, and other attributes of administrative control, usually rooted in a cultural context, are different in state and non-state actors within the same society or culture. This assumption is unlikely to be valid. So if power is considered to be finite rather than infinite, and personalized rather than institutionalized; if personal loyalty trumps competence leading to weak institutions; if entourages are required for control and corruption is needed to lubricate these relationships; if leaders speak *ex cathedra* rather than compromise; and if orthodoxy (leading to censorship) seems necessary, the assumption that there will be major differences between civil society organizations and governmental institutions is likely to be erroneous.[14]

In most states, leadership of civil society groups rests on similar traits and concepts of power as groups with state leadership.[15] In multicultural countries, such as Burma/Myanmar, this presents even more formidable problems of analysis. Even if such cultural traits evolve over time, we must be careful about generalizations on the inherent and universal efficacy of civil society as a modernizing force. As Philippe Schmitter has written, "In response to the opportunities (and threats) of democratization, individual associations already existing under the previous autocracy are likely to have to change significantly in their internal structures and operative practices."[16] Concepts of power and authority must undergo modification to reform their operative practices. This is likely to be a lengthy process. As the International Crisis Group report noted: "Since Myanmar has been under military rule for so long, few people today understand the role that civil society is meant to play in a democracy or that a healthy democracy requires broad-mindedness and a dispersion of power. Thus, even organizations outside the regime's direct control tend to replicate the hierarchical organizational structures and lack of tolerance for dissent, which characterize state-controlled organizations."[17]

International-Local Interactions: Who's Space?

Foreign assistance is often driven by the donor's need for the relative ease of bureaucratic management. The relationship among donors and NGO recipients often becomes pivotal. Donors, both governmental and international NGOs, frequently prescribe universalistic goals, patterns of programming, and administrative structures that undercut effective and tailored responses to localized, perhaps unique, conditions and problems. Conceptual convenience for donors—a worldwide development strategy, for example—often becomes translated into standardized bureaucratic responses often detrimental not only to the NGO communities, but also to developmental priorities more broadly defined. The interaction of indigenous non-governmental civil society groups with international NGOs is part of a growing phenomenon that has not escaped the attention of Asian governments, as these relationships have empowered some local groups and caused grave concern to governments that feel their authority and control are diminished. Some, such as Myanmar, believe such activities are sponsored by the "big powers" (e.g., the U.S.) to destabilize the military junta and bring about the previous, often articulated, U.S. goal of "regime change." International environmental and human rights organizations carefully monitor internal Burmese conditions from across the border in Thailand and through extensive networks of informants within the country (Burmese intelligence operatives monitor the reverse). Some of their activities are beamed back into Myanmar though international satellite dishes via BBC, CNN, and other channels, through cell phones, and the Internet, and are beyond the capacity of the state to control completely.

The degree to which indigenous civil society groups are conceptually, administratively, or financially linked to international organizations may have a profound effect on their internal (or external) legitimacy, and these may be in conflict. Thus, an association between local and international environmental NGOs may give an indigenous group some local cachet in addition to programmatic wherewithal, intellectual stimulation, and even international legitimacy, but could occasionally result in anti-foreign and even xenophobic charges against the foreigners. In Myanmar, under the new constitution of 2008, foreign support to individuals or certain groups precludes political registration or running for office. Such people or organizations are deemed the "axe handles" (supporters) of foreign imperialism. Some indigenous NGOs question why international NGOs have to be the intermediary between international bilateral or multilateral donors and local groups, as they often simply siphon off funding.[18]

When international NGOs operate within a society, they rarely can exist independent of local support. Thus, almost inherently, there is a link between the international NGOs and local NGOs, which usually need each other. Few international NGOs can operate in linguistically and culturally diverse societies, so they often partner with or even help create local NGOs, in addition to expanding their local staffs. In a sense, this is both institutional and personal capacity building. Many of the international NGOs have encouraged local personnel to receive advanced training abroad in a variety of fields both for present institutional benefits and for building the future capacity of state and non-state institutions.[19]

Yet, there are dangers in the export of programs from the international NGOs to local ones. A cascade of bureaucratic requirements may skew efficacy as well as local acceptance. International, state-run national or multilateral assistance programs (e.g., USAID, World Bank, etc.) often have imposed their organizational concepts, models, and sometimes fashionably desirable program activities on local governments to make it easier to justify such programs to their internal donor clientele and to monitor compliance. Those aid sponsors have done the same to international NGOs, which have in turn often done the same thing to indigenous NGOs. Thus, the structure and agenda of local groups is often externally shaped, often to the latter's long-term detriment, and sometimes ignoring conformity to indigenous norms, and thus continuity is disrupted, and potentially the lack of positive results occur.[20] As the World Bank noted: "These [operational] requirements have generally meant the creation of special units outside existing government structures solely to implement Bank-funded projects. However, the Bank has found that isolating these projects from local government systems limits institutional strengthening and capacity building and thus the impact of development assistance."[21]

Civil society can exert influence on local affairs, thus filling local needs that the state at some level intentionally ignores or is incapable of providing due to lack of resources, inclination, or both. In effect, the development of civil society groups encourages local, pluralistic centers of programmatic power and autonomy that not only contribute to ameliorating local needs, but also might provide the basis for more representative, perhaps pluralistic, growth. As we have noted, the assumption that this leads to democracy should be tempered by reality checks. Thus, foreign support to civil society organizations as a democratizing tool—in contrast to their role in humanitarian assistance—should be carefully assayed.

One prerequisite for the development of democracy, however defined, is the existence of pluralistic centers of localized power. Although this process of development is likely to be long and arduous in the case of Myanmar, local NGOs serving the needs of local populations can influence the political process over time, and diminish the autocratic nature of the center's unitary power in the geographic or the bureaucratic periphery.

This has not gone unrecognized by donors and recipient states. For example, the United States authorizes funds to be used inside Myanmar and on its periphery for the development of democracy in that authoritarian state (e.g., through the National Endowment for Democracy—NED). This has been a tenet of U.S. foreign policy. Funding usually occurs though international NGOs or the NED to local NGOs to develop pluralistic centers of citizen-oriented activities. This is one of the few ways to begin such a pluralistic process. Several questions present themselves. How may such potential programs be intellectually justified? Are they acts of faith based on the American model? In strong, authoritarian states, are there any other options for foreign programming that might lead to internal political reform or are such alternatives inherently impossible? These are important policy issues.

The dangers of the collusion between international and local NGOs have not gone unnoticed in Myanmar. In January and February of 2006, the state issued a series of regulations severely restricting the activities of international NGOs in registration, ministerial coordination, bank accounts, local hiring, and internal expatriate travel. Such stringent regulations emanated from the top of the power hierarchy. By necessity, they have sometimes been suspended or ignored on the periphery as local officials often know it is more important to get the results (on which their performance is judged) that sometimes only these organizations can provide, than to live up to the letter of imposed, but unrealistic, central regulations. Such regulations may not be rigorously enforced unless political problems develop. This was illustrated in the response to Cyclone Nargis in May 2008, when local military officials ignored regulations and told the NGOs to get on with their relief work.

Civil Society in Non-Democratic Asian Countries

Review of civil society in other authoritarian states in Asia offers insights into the Myanmar situation and potential donor policies. A substantial portion of the burgeoning literature on the roles of civil society in a variety of Asian states has been focused on China, and to a lesser degree, Vietnam.[22]

Various authors have suggested backing away from the Western paradigm of assumptions of civil society in the People's Republic of China (PRC). There, "the elements of civil society are the result as much of accommodations with the state as of resistance to it…. Civil society [in China] might better be thought of, therefore, as a formation that exists by virtue of state-society interaction, not as something between, separate from, or autonomous from either."

The development of civil society in the PRC was severely retarded during the Mao era from 1949 to 1976 because such organizations contradicted the doctrine of the dictatorship of the proletariat.[23] However, over time, with the economic liberalizations enacted by Deng Xiaoping, alternative resources developed outside of state control that allowed the growth of autonomous organizations that did not seem to threaten the state. This also undermined the highly vertical structure of Chinese society under the Chinese Communist Party (CCP), and provided an avenue of horizontal mobility between the countryside and urban areas. By the 13th National Party Congress in October 1987, there was limited acceptance of some policy independence outside of the CCP structure.[24]

Civil society organizations began to expand. Each was required to be registered beginning in October 1987 under Document #43 "Management Regulations on the Registration of Social Organizations."[25] By the end of 1993, 167,506 were registered with provincial and lower-level governmental units, and by October of that year there were 1,460 registered national social organizations and 19,600 branch and local organizations at the county level.[26]

As He Baogang has noted, "The autonomy of Chinese social organizations must be viewed in the context of the special overlapping structure within which state corporatism co-exists with elements of civil society." There are both advantages and problems with this conceptual unity. The state provides considerable financial support to many elements of civil society, which increases the latter's capacity to perform its roles, and at the same time gives these groups greater potential influence and also can assist in checking the CCP's political power. This also results in less than completely autonomous organizations. It is a "mutually penetrative process." Thus, some of these organizations have been called either "semi-civil societies" or "nascent civil societies."[27] During the process of registering civil society organizations, state-sponsored mass organizations became more autonomous to ensure they would not become irrelevant. He Baogang concludes that "civil institution building is well under way at the present in China, though under the vigilant eyes of the CCP and the secret police." Similarly, Bruce J. Dickson observes: "The CCP's implicit strategy is to increase the cost of collective action by arresting political and labor activists and keeping most social organizations dependent on the state for their survival and success. In the process, it aims to prevent the emergence of a "critical realm" of civil society and prevent it from making claims on the state."[28]

Tony Saich, in a cogent analysis of the Chinese situation, expresses concerns that are echoed by many in governmental circles in Myanmar: "It is also clear that no coherent alternative vision has emerged that would fashion either a civil society or a rapid construction of a democratic political order. From the [CCP] party's point of view, what is lurking in the shadows waiting to pounce on any opening that would allow freedom of expression is revivalism, religion, linguistic division, regional, and non-Han ethnic loyalties."[29]

The Chinese experiences do demonstrate a policy dilemma as yet unrecognized in U.S. legislation on Myanmar. The U.S. Congress and administration have prohibited U.S. funding of central or local chapters of either governmental or quasi-governmental NGOs, such as the former USDA (Union Solidarity and Development Associations, now the government's political party) in Myanmar. But the Chinese experience demonstrates that this prohibition may be self-defeating.[30] The efficacy of NGO programming in China is directly linked to their contact with state institutions, but this link is denied in U.S. legislation on Myanmar. Even governmentally linked local institutions or chapters often have better knowledge of local needs than the central government, and thus can be more effective, while also assisting in the growth of the NGOs themselves. Blanket prohibitions against any state sponsored or organized groups in Myanmar should be eschewed and replaced with reviews of individual cases.

The Burma/Myanmar Definition and Realities

Civil Society until 1988

The complex that is contemporary Burma/Myanmar is mirrored in the anomaly of the history of, and contemporary policies toward, its own civil society. Whether civil society existed in pre-colonial Burma will no doubt be a subject of much intellectual debate when Burmese scholars are allowed to freely research their own history, which has been rewritten in part to conform to preconceptions of the historical role of the *tatmadaw* (armed forces). Certainly, civil society existed in the colonial era, although it was carefully circumscribed. Civic organizations flourished, but were limited to those that were apolitical; those potentially political in nature or threatening to colonial rule were proscribed. International NGOs, such as the YMCA and religious-based groups, were active and were mirrored in the rise of Burmese Buddhist organizations that became part of the independence movement. These religious groups were difficult to ban, however, simply because they were ostensibly religious, although their political overtones were ever present.[31]

The civilian period following independence in 1948 until 1962, including 18 months of military rule under the "caretaker" government, saw the proliferation of civil society organizations that were autonomous of the state. Mass political organizations were fostered and run by elements of the Anti-Fascist People's Freedom League (AFPFL), the ruling coalition. These mass organizations (perhaps we should term them "QUANGOs"— quasi-autonomous NGOs) were arms of the AFPFL, or more accurately various factions led by aspiring politicians within the political umbrella grouping that was the AFPFL. The state preempted the rise of civil society organizations that might divert political authority away from the party. Such QUANGOs were used as political springboards for various leaders and factions within the AFPFL. The organizations and institutions for professional, academic, civil, religious, and other populations that were developed during that period functioned as a kind of leavening element, but the political hold of the AFPFL was both ubiquitous and fragmented. Most mass and civil society organizations reflected the personalization of leadership that was endemic in state institutions.

These organizations were essentially destroyed following the coup of 1962 and the introduction of the "Burmese Way to Socialism" under the military auspices of the Burma Socialist Programme Party (BSPP). As this author has written, "Civil society died under the Burma Socialist Programme Party (BSPP); perhaps, more accurately, it was murdered."[32] Local, community-based informal associations did, of course, continue. But if civil society had been defined as advocacy groups that were autonomous of the state, they were in effect terminated both during the period of direct rule by the military from 1962 until 1974, and thereafter under the military-inspired and dominated BSPP—a single-party, mass mobilization system—until its collapse in 1988.

One of the elements of continuity in the volatile political situation has been the army. Its role has been far more important in modern Burma/

Myanmar than it has in most modern Western societies. Another significant motif that continues to reverberate in contemporary Burmese society is a strong nationalist sentiment that affects the way international NGOs and foreign assistance are regarded. The United States Economic Survey to Southeast Asia notes, "Burmese officials and educated leaders are hypersensitive about any imagined infringement of their sovereignty, and extremely suspicious of Western motives of offering them aid."[33] Little has changed in this regard in almost three-quarters of a century.

A strong distrust of any Western ties stemmed in part from a strong legal left-wing force both in and out of the government and the legislature (for example, Burma did not join the Commonwealth on independence, as did India, Pakistan, and Ceylon/Sri Lanka). The extreme nationalism was a product of the colonial experience and the fears of foreign economic and cultural inundation that were likely exacerbated by having been governed as a province of India until 1937. The establishment of an independent state—coinciding with the Cold War and the formation of the People's Republic of China—reinforced fears of being swept up in the turmoil.

Foreign critics who look upon the present junta as being an example of an ultra-nationalistic ruling elite—anomalous in the contemporary world—are missing an important historical link. Today, the military *tatmadaw* stresses national sovereignty and unity as two of its cardinal objectives and ideological pillars, thus illustrating a vision of its premier place in Burmese society that stretches well into the future. The prestige of a strongly nationalist army was always present in independent Burma, as it was evident in the speeches of Chinese leadership and in Thai military thinking. But in the Myanmar case, foreign critics have treated this nationalism—often unfairly—as bureaucratic cant.

Equally important is the personalization of power—an element of Burmese political culture that has made the functioning of organizations autonomous of the state difficult or impossible.[34] Such personalization of power leads to competing entourage groupings that distrust any entities that could undercut the role of the personalized leader. Institutional loyalties are less important than personal ones; a "loyal opposition" is an oxymoron. Both the cult of the leader and the ever-present nationalism make international NGOs subject to careful scrutiny. Although the SLORC/SPDC has tolerated the presence of international NGOs and has even registered a wide variety of indigenous NGOs, organizations that are perceived as providing alternative centers of power to the state or that compete with the state or its institutions are prohibited.

There is no evidence that the Burmese government relented on controlling all elements of its diverse society in the period under scrutiny.

Toleration of the development of local NGOs is probably a result of a variety of factors, including the incompetence of the state to manage a socialist economy. The early reliance on the NGO community after the coup of 1988 may also have been prompted by the financial incapacity of the state to supply goods and services to its diverse populations. With cease-fires in many minority areas, the government effectively promised increased support to those regions, so long denied adequate social services, but inadequate new funding has gone into those areas given their needs. The early fiscal problems of the state have now been replaced with considerable surpluses (some U.S. $5 billion in foreign exchange reserves in 2010) that could have been employed to address these needs, if the state had not chosen other priorities to the detriment of its own population.

After 1962, the military prohibited even the modest self-government of the subordinate political units—the states (minority areas) and the divisions (Burmese areas). Thus, the "Union of Burma" was characterized as pluralistic, although it was in fact unitary. The unitary nature of military control and its failure from 1962 to 1988, both directly under the military-run Revolutionary Council until 1974 and afterwards under the BSPP, likely indirectly prompted the new military government in 1988 to allow the development of local organizations that had the capacity to identify and then ameliorate local problems that the state had ignored or was unable to address. This inadvertent expansion of civil society was perhaps reflected in the proliferation of political parties in preparation for the 1990 elections. Some 243 parties were formed, of which 93 participated in the elections, and their number not only illustrated the political frustration that had been building up since 1962, but also in all likelihood the frustration with the centralized administration that proved to be either unaware of local problems, or inept in dealing with them when they were identified.

Another cause for the expansion of the non-profit sector in minority areas has been the state's lack of interest in local languages and cultures. Although the various constitutions (1947, 1974, 2008) have provisions for the protection of minority languages and cultures, the need for national unity—the foremost objective of the junta—has led to the exclusion of officially authorized minority languages in the school system and a prohibition on publishing in minority languages. In response, many minority groups have established language, literature, and cultural schools and societies to promote what the state has denied. As many in these minority communities attest, these cultural initiatives form the basis of their ethnic identity.

Civil Society Since 1988

Burma/Myanmar studies and relations are highly polarized in the West. In part this stems from the simplified and dualistic dichotomy between the military-dominated state and the opposition, exemplified by Aung San Suu Kyi.[35] To many in the West, she is not only the avatar of democracy, but also the leader of the opposition, and an element of civil society—that is, a critically acclaimed non-state actor. She has, however, never been active in civil society groups but a leader of a political party, which is excluded from the definition of civil society in this chapter. Her party was formally disestablished in early May 2010 when, under her influence, it refused to register to run in the November 2010 elections. In all probability, the party remnants led by Aung San Suu Kyi are likely not to be allowed to register as an NGO, and thus will become an informal, unregistered "social movement" without a recognized organizational structure.

Many expatriate and human rights groups have often viewed both foreign and domestic NGOs operating in the country negatively. The latter, however, have sometimes a reductive understanding of NGOs, perceiving them as tools of the military-dominated state. This is an error that in the past has undercut the reputation of civil society. Yet, a significant increase in the formation of both types of civil society organizations occurred in the late 1980s.[36] Before that time, when civil society was referred to in relation to Burma, it was assumed that it was civil society in exile, often across the border in Thailand.[37] Whether this internal increase was based on the Chinese model (noted above) from 1987 or indigenous factors is unclear. The passage of the Organization of Association Law in Myanmar in 1988 was the legal avenue for those that did register, although anecdotal evidence from a variety of local and foreign NGOs seems to indicate that access, personal avenues, and contacts of support are more important than legal or state institutional requirements. As Taylor has noted:

> The abolition of the one-party political system in 1988 allowed revival of both officially sponsored and privately organized clubs, societies, foundations, and other civic organizations in the town and cities of Myanmar. The promise of development of a thriving civil society held out by the end of the BSPP was not, however, achieved. This promise was encapsulated in the SLORC's sixth legislative act, the Law Relating for Forming Organizations (6/88) enacted ten days after the putsch. It gave such organizations legal form separate from overtly political institutions, thus ensuring that their potential political roles were emasculated at birth. The state thus remained the main organizer of

society through its sponsorship of the largest and most prominent associations. However, small non-governmental organizations (NGOs) established by private individuals and groups to achieve peace, maintain the environment, or assist in economic and social development also flourished. Many had indirect or informal connections with the government, in some cases receiving help and assistance from state personnel, for the provision of reciprocal services. Others sought to remain as independent of the state as possible.[38]

Was the motivation of the state then to preclude political competition, or increase the delivery of services, or both?

Organizations had to be vetted by the Ministry of Home Affairs (which also controls the police), but registration started at the local township level and proceeded up the bureaucracy to the central government. Religious organizations did not have to register (Buddhist sects were already controlled through laws passed in 1980 when monks were first registered), and political parties could not do so.[39] A smaller number of organizations were given the possibility of registering under various other regulations: the Companies Act, Cooperative Law, Partnership Law, and the Code of Civil Procedure (trust funds for charitable purposes). Community-based organizations have not been required to register. Brian Heidel noted that as of 2004, many organizations surveyed had not registered with the government but were operational nonetheless. Heidel estimated that there were some 120 NGOs in Yangon alone, and perhaps 270 in the country. There may have been 214,208 community-based groups, a figure extrapolated from the limited survey that was undertaken. Fifty-two percent of NGOs operated in the religious sector, 30 percent in social welfare, and 26 percent in education (with overlapping).[40] Some 42 percent of local NGOs received funding from International Non-Governmental Organizations (INGOs), and the rural population donated about 2 percent of their income to community-based organizations. About 67 percent of the community based groups did not coordinate with the government at local levels, although the legislation required them to do so.[41]

In 2010, there seems to have been a formal structural process for the registration and operation of NGOs, as outlined above, but one that was often formally ignored. It was in part replaced or supplemented by an effective but highly tenuous set of personal relationships at the ministerial, local, and military levels. Although registration may be required, it is often incomplete, and organizations may operate with or without Memoranda of Understanding for many years, as long as the process is started and verbal approval is forthcoming from some ministerial, local, or military official. Once memoranda of understanding are formalized, then various reports may be required, including those with financial data. These memoranda seem to have no programmatic effect, however, but rather are used to verify adherence to central regulations in case of problems. Observers have pointed out that such memoranda of understanding do not grant privileges.

International NGOs do not seem to have to report on financial affairs, and their funding is mixed, sometimes informal, and often goes through non-governmental channels. Thus, although one must assume that military monitoring of NGOs is maintained in accordance with the long history of suspicion of foreigners (informal checks on bank accounts and other forms of surveillance including tapping of telephones), the system as perceived by the NGOs so affected is personal, informal, and loose—virtually unstructured. Registration of NGOs themselves does not lead to effective programming opportunities, which are at the mercy of local officials and the degree of personal trust that is built up between such officials and the NGO.

Only a small (unknown) percentage of local NGOs are registered. Tom Kramer has written that registration is sometimes a prerequisite for foreign funding, and for opening bank accounts in the name of the organization; these are usually the requirements for foreign donors.[42]

For whatever reasons, the confusion in both the indigenous non-profit field and for foreign NGOs led to the belief that there was a need for some overarching, generalized criteria for administrative aspects (in contrast to programs) of their operations. This was reflected in a suggestion by this writer in the fall of 1994 to the State Law and Order Restoration Council (SLORC)—the ruling military junta—that a conference should be held between the government and the international NGOs to work out procedures for registration, stay permits, duty-free entry of appropriate supplies, and other such administrative desiderata that engaged much of the attention of these groups that should instead have been directed to their individual programs. Although one member of the SLORC believed that this was desirable, the SLORC as a group rejected the suggestion, preferring to deal with each INGO on an individual basis.

The regulations on both local and foreign non-profit organizations were effectively set aside following Cyclone Nargis, when the world, local Burmese, and Burmese expatriates all responded with alacrity to the needs of the affected population. Civil society expanded in quantity and capacity during the crisis.[43] That the cyclone hit on 2–3 May 2008, just before the planned referendum of 10 May on the new constitution, caused a number of problems for the government. They did not want foreigners observing the referendum, and yet there was a worldwide demand to assist the Burmese, which in effect would have made aid workers observers of the voting process, since it is highly unlikely that the government could have changed the date of the referendum, which they

probably picked as an astrologically auspicious day. Cyclone Nargis created a unique Burmese response and foreign interest in the NGO community. Following the cyclone, about 1,000 NGOs were operating in the
affected regions, but now there are only some 20 church-based groups
left and 10 nonreligious NGOs working in those areas.

In view of the Burmese suspicions of the international community and
their "nefarious" designs on Myanmar and the regime, why were these
organizations allowed to function and grow even before the acute emergency of Cyclone Nargis which devastated the Irrawaddy Delta in early
May 2008, killing some 138,000 and leaving 2.5 million homeless? The
reasons are unclear, but some explanation may be sought both in the
nature of the regime and in the responses of the population to state inadequacies in delivering assistance.

Even under the most oppressive Burmese governments that threatened individual rights, Burma was not a "hard" totalitarian state. It lacked
the capacity to control in manners that seem so apparent in North Korea,
for example, or even in China during the Maoist era. One author termed
it an "imperial state" that lacked the "infrastructural power" to penetrate
the society at both the geographic and institutional periphery.[44] It is evident, even if only from anecdotal evidence, that lower-level officials, circumscribed in their abilities to perform adequately because of seemingly
arbitrary or overly-restrictive state regulations, allowed the development
of organizations that would enable them to be seen as successful in the
bureaucracy.[45] Kyaw Yin Hlaing comments:

> While repressing its enemies, the government has also tried to co-opt former
> and potential enemies and to control some societal actors by allowing them
> to undertake social and development activities within a legal space carefully
> monitored by the government or by offering to help with business or other
> problems they might be experiencing.... At about the same time [as minor-
> ity groups formed NGOs], the government allowed international NGOs to
> undertake health and development-related activities in areas of the country.
> Some of these INGOs encouraged local communities and people to form
> NGOs, and even helped them form development organizations. Many of
> these organizations did not get the government's permission to register. The
> government has been aware of the existence of such organizations. Govern-
> ment agents have not disturbed them so long as they confine themselves to
> non-political activities.[46]

Other factors may also play a role. In traditional Theravada Buddhist
societies, where one's well-being and status are believed to be determined in large part by one's own actions in previous incarnations, the
expectations of state support may be minimal.[47] This Buddhist view has
obviously been tempered in contemporary Thailand, where Buddhism

is still pervasive and strong. Increased access to information and modernization have altered and increased rural expectations of state support because of global and internal political influences.[48] Whether, and when, this might happen in Myanmar is unclear.

The inadequacy of state capacities in fields such as education and minority cultures has prompted proliferation of civil society organizations in the beginning of the twenty-first century. Many local parent-teacher associations have been formed to provide additional school and teaching resources that are needed because of the underfunding of education by the state. The role of civil society organizations in minority areas takes on a special saliency. These often involve the preservation of cultural traditions that in some cases are only oral, while in others a unique written tradition continues under duress. Mai Ni Ni Aung makes the case that, "Minorities believe cultural rights are crucial to their survival."[49] Due to historical suspicions between Burmans and minorities, the relationship between the two is tenuous, and the need for interaction between the community based organizations and the authorities is apparent: "What is seen to emerge is a direct correlation between the strength of the community based organization program and the extent of participation by local authorities. The greater the participation of local leadership, the more successful the community based organization activity.... We cannot ignore GONGOs, local authorities, or even seemingly less influential groups such as local fire fighters as is often suggested in the 'with them or with us paradigm.'"[50]

Another opinion is exemplified by the following: "Some local NGOs believe that it is impossible, or less effective, to work without dealing with the government. Some of them deliberately closely coordinate with local authorities to prevent any misunderstanding that would endanger the project, as well as to prevent beneficiaries from getting into trouble."[51] Other observers have noted that if the role of civil society is interpreted as one that is in confrontation with the regime, the organization will be suppressed.

There is considerable local and international NGO activity beyond the myriad community based organizations. One publication lists 82 local NGOs in 2008 and, in addition, four orphanages. In a similar publication for international NGOs, 49 are listed, although there are a number of additional organizations in both categories that either prefer not to be listed or have been overlooked. Although some organizations operate in a variety of fields, and thus listings overlap, some 23 are in the field of health, 14 in environment, nine in microfinance, 11 in agriculture and fisheries, eleven in food security, and four in civil society development. Many of these organizations employ large numbers of local staff: Marie

Stopes employs around 705, CARE 450, Save the Children 279, PACT 233, International Development Enterprises 125, and Population Services International 479. The most notable of the indigenous NGOs are the Metta Foundation and the Shalom Foundation, both of which are registered with the Ministry of Home Affairs.

Internal growth in civil society has been more than matched by the expansion of civil society organizations involving the Burmese abroad. The proliferation of organizations in Thailand for Burmese in refugee camps that house some 150,000 Karen and Mon, and among the two million or so Burmese workers throughout Thailand has been remarkable, and has been spurred by the growth of international NGOs operating humanitarian programs in all of these areas. Some of these Burmese groups, overtly linked to dissident Burmese political movements, have been engaged in cross-border activities inside Myanmar. This is not unknown to the Burmese authorities who seemingly transmit their suspicions about such external efforts to the international and local NGO community within the country.

The GONGO Phenomenon

To meet political, social, or economic needs, states may sometimes establish what have been called GONGOs (governmental owned-or organized-NGOs), or QUANGOs (or quasi- governmental NGOs). These serve a variety of purposes in various places. They mobilize the population locally or nationally for state-sponsored activities ranging from the benign to educational, political, or even violent actions, but they also are often designed to limit the growth of non-state sponsored NGOs by preempting the latter's roles.

In the early 1990s, the government of Myanmar founded the Union Solidarity and Development Association (USDA), in 2010 it transformed into the Union Solidarity and Development Party (USDP), with the intention of furthering military authority. Its patron is the military head of state, and its membership totaled some 24.5 million people, that is to say almost half the population of the country and perhaps two-thirds of the adult population. In essence, it has replaced the Burma Socialist Programme Party as an organizational tool in government hands. Although it carries out educational activities such as computer training and Buddhist classes, it also has a paramilitary function and elements and has sometimes been accused of organizing anti-opposition riots or demonstrations. In the summer of 2010, it became a political party.[52] Observers from international NGOs have occasionally noted that even some local chapters of the national USDA have acted autonomously as they tried to placate the local public by developing appropriate responses to local needs. In Myanmar, some international NGOs have been under pressure to support local USDA activities, but some international donors to those NGOs have balked at that idea. The government has also sponsored and controlled a wide variety of professional or interest groups, ranging from veterans to firefighters to child welfare and women's organizations.

"Thus civil society is created by the state to help it govern, co-opt, and socialize potentially politically active elements in the population." This sentence, describing the situation in China, is equally applicable to Myanmar. In both places, the state recognizes socio-economic changes by both modifying its own policy and keeping political control.[53]

Some of the civil society groups at the local level are able to operate autonomously of the central command as long as their activities in the social arena make the local (military) administration look good. The prohibition against working with GONGOs as a general principle is thus likely to retard the ability of NGOs and INGOs to provide services to some segments of the population. As the report from the Centre for Peace and Conflict Studies states: "The majority of civil society groups we interviewed for this project were balancing working with the Government with their commitment to communities.... An acceptance that organizations can develop a working relationship with Government, and benefit from it, was a key lesson expressed by many of the organizations we interviewed."[54]

All of the above poses a dilemma for any assistance worker. Should a program to improve standards of accounting and probity through a professional organization controlled by the Burmese state be avoided because it indirectly supports the state? This dilemma is not easily resolved.

Transitional Myanmar

With all its tragedies and problems, Myanmar is on the verge of transition. A military-dominated, but civilianized administration has, since elections in 2010, taken over under a new constitution approved, in a manipulated referendum, by 92.4 percent voters. The anticipated internal change, as well as the failure of the Western sanctions to topple the regime, has prompted the reconsideration of Western policies toward Myanmar. What are the prospects for strengthening the monitory role of civil society in post-2010 elections Myanmar?

There would seem to be few in the foreign community who would dispute the need for civil society in Myanmar. Morten B. Pedersen states,

"As much as Burma needs stronger state institutions, it also needs an active civil society that can challenge, support, and complement the state."[55] In theory, the civilianized and largely representative government should be more attuned to the value of civil society in that country. The constitution provides for such organizations and associations:

> 354. Every citizen shall be at liberty in the exercise of the following rights, if not contrary to the laws, enacted for Union security, prevalence of law and order, community peace and tranquility, or public order and morality:
>
> (a) To express and publish freely their convictions and opinions;
>
> (b) To assemble peacefully without arms and holding procession;
>
> (c) To form associations and organizations;
>
> (d) To develop their language, literature, culture they cherish, religion they profess, and customs without prejudice to the relations between one national race and another or among national races and to other faiths.[56]

Yet, there seem to be restrictions on some foreign associations. One "Disqualification for the Pyithu Hluttaw Representatives" in Section 121 (g), applies to a person who "is a member of an organization [and] who obtains and utilizes directly or indirectly the support of money, land, housing, building, vehicle, property, and so forth, from the government or religious organization or other organization of a foreign country." This would seem to preclude members of NGOs that receive foreign assistance from becoming a member of the legislature.

The new constitution's clauses insulate parts of Myanmar society from foreign influence, and INGOs. For example, religious organizations are prohibited from receiving foreign support (as are political parties), and individuals who get such grants cannot run for office. We may well see a growth of local civil society and a diminished role of INGOs.

This chapter has already postulated a number of potential roles for civil society in Burma/Myanmar. They are: to influence political pluralism, economic development and poverty issues, social needs and mobility, as well as cultural continuity and diversity. Taken together, these four fields constitute many of the issues of governance. The effects of civil society efforts in the country should be disaggregated into those of the international NGOs and those indigenous to that state.

The influence of the international NGOs in directly affecting any of these fields is highly limited by the nature of the political system, their access, and the funding available to participate in the activities of the Myanmar society. The INGOs assistance to economic development, praiseworthy as it is, must be considered only marginal in a population of over 50 million. Yet their influence cannot be disregarded. They have funded local NGOs, set models of operations, financed micro-credit groups, helped to train those who will be needed as Myanmar changes—and indicated international good will. As noted earlier, however, the local staffs of international NGOs are not inconsequential in numbers.

The influence of the local NGOs has been more important, as illustrated by the rapid response to Cyclone Nargis and the willingness of the population to unite and help one another in crisis. Some such NGOs have had influence in cultural continuity, especially among minority peoples. Organizations and private schools have been formed to teach indigenous languages precluded from the state-imposed public curriculum. Cultural organizations have been developed to maintain music, dance, and drama traditions. Religious schools and seminaries operate as well.

But the potential of these indigenous civil society organizations is debatable. Their future roles and influence will depend in part on their demonstrated capacities to address critical issues; their ability to influence policy makers (both military and civilian) with regard to the needs of the people; their access to the new legislatures; and whether their actions will be discrete enough to allay suspicions on the part of the military or civilian authorities who replace the current government that they foster separatism by any of the minority groups, or that they are tools of foreigners out to destroy the sovereignty of the state—in other words, the military's stated national fears. This is a delicate balancing act. With a bicameral national legislature, and legislatures at the state and regional levels (i.e., provincial level), as well as six smaller ethnic enclave legislatures (all but one with some opposition voices), legislative authority will likely increase, as will, perhaps, the enhanced monitory roles of local civil society groups. A mutually enhanced status and influence of both types of organizations could be possible.

The NGO community, importantly, can be an avenue of social mobility in a society in which the private sector has not yet fulfilled that role (except perhaps for the Chinese minority), and in which military-dominated avenues predominate. All roads to higher social status (the military itself, higher education, politics, mass organizations, and the *sangha*) are under military domination, and if the military is to assume a less salient role in a future Myanmar, non-military channels need to develop. The NGO community may be such a route.

Civil society can contribute over time to the amelioration of authoritarian government and carries great potential, but this process is long one. As one author wrote, "With Myanmar/Burma's civil society in such an embryonic stage, it would be utopian to consider it a vehicle for early democratization."[57] And as a Chinese task force commented: "Regardless of the structure of any future political set up, the military will be at the center of the country's politics. The politics of Myanmar are the politics of the military elite, and this will remain the case for the foreseeable future."[58]

Policy Implications

The analysis of the political culture and experience in Myanmar indicates that the foreign and Western-based concept of a strict division between the private non-profit sector and other monitory groups—and the state and the state's GONGOs—is likely to be false in parts of Asia, and thus should be carefully examined while considering this division in other non-Western states.

Prohibitions in foreign aid programs, such as those in the U.S., against funding of government or government-sponsored GONGOs, or indeed working with them, are likely to lose sight of the importance of civic organizations at local levels, where local needs and responses to those needs may contribute to the space between the state and local organizations. Rather, such funding should be considered on a case-by-case basis. There have been cases in which the INGOs have found that local GONGOs have done meritorious work for the local population.

It is evident that civil society should not be viewed as the panacea that will resolve the political issues connected with authoritarian regimes. Civic organizations in such regimes are likely to exhibit the characteristics of the political cultures from which they emerge. The concept of civil society as a *deux ex machina* that will introduce democracy into any polity should be regarded with skepticism as an unrealistic leap of intellectual faith. At the same time, political cultures are not bound in concrete; they also evolve, and as they do so civil society in concept and operation also changes. The link between the evolutions of both is unclear, and in some societies either the state, civil society, or intermediary organizations can take a lead.

In spite of the intellectual gap between civil society concepts as they evolved in the West, and concepts of power and hierarchy in Burma/ Myanmar, at this stage little else can be done to foster pluralism than support to civil society in that country; one can only hope to build a *potential* for such pluralism. The role of GONGOs in such an evolution should not be ignored. Prohibitions that are in operation severely limit any process that could enable citizens to have more of a say in how they are governed.

About one percent of Myanmar's total population has emigrated. That group (distinct from some two million laborers in Thailand) tends to be better educated and could have been the backbone of some new administration. This educated elite must be replaced (or voluntarily return) if the state is to function effectively under any new government, and such training opportunities, internal and abroad, can be furthered by civil societies of all stripes. This may be the single most important contribution of INGO and NGO civil societies to the development of Myanmar. Technical training for central or local governments should be considered.

The effects of foreign assistance to expatriate and cross-border groups that have an incipient, and often overt, political agenda, may undercut the very development of effective communications and dialogue between international NGOs inside the country, local NGOs, the state, and the flowering of monitory functions. The role of civil society under authoritarian regimes is delicately nuanced, and hence defying both sweeping condemnations and the enthusiastic support of outside observers.

What is important is that, although the concept of civil society in Burma/Myanmar was never indigenous, except in the field of religious affairs, its presence is now accepted, and its future may well be important for the well-being of the diverse populations of that state, and for effective governance therein. Civil society seems "essential if any negotiated political transition is to be durable," and external support is needed.[59] Civil society may move into more monitory roles, but the process is likely to be slow.

Whatever interactions and openings have existed between the state in its various incarnations and civil society in Burma/Myanmar, their nature has been rather fluctuating. Relations were relatively open in the civilian administration, closed in the socialist period, and ajar under the SLORC/SPDC. As the country enters a new era of military-influenced parliamentary rule, it remains to be seen whether the relationship between civic organizations and the state can involve more generalized political trust and whether civil society in Myanmar can assume a more monitoring role.

Postscript

Since the new administration came to power in the spring of 2011, President Thein Sein has announced a series of well received liberalizing plans. These include changed political party registration laws, allowing the National League for Democracy and Aung San Suu Kyi to run in bi-elections, and a wide variety of edicts and plans for opening up the society, although continuing military autonomy and effective control and power. Most importantly, he stopped construction of a Chinese-engineered major dam on the vital Irrawaddy River, ostensibly because of popular outcries led by indigenous civil society groups, although equally plausible may have been the administration's intent not to appear too close to the increasingly unpopular Chinese economic presence. Civil society, however, may be given more internal space in the new administration.

Notes

The author would like to thank Mr. Daniel Kim, a student at Georgetown's School of Foreign Service for his excellent research assistance in the preparation of this chapter.

1. The name of the state was changed in 1989 by the military from "Burma" to "Myanmar," an old written form. Use of Burma or Myanmar has become a surrogate indicator of political persuasion, with the U.S. siding with the Burmese opposition and using the old name of Burma, while the UN and other nations generally recognize the 1989 change to Myanmar. Here, Burma is used for the period prior to 1989; Myanmar thereafter; Burma/Myanmar to indicate continuity; and Burmese as any citizen (of any ethnic group) of that country, as the national language, and as an adjective. Political connotations are neither intended nor implied.
2. The military would have taken over even if the legislature had not agreed.
3. Jasmin Lorch, "Civil Society under Authoritarian Rule: The Case of Myanmar." *Journal of Current Southeast Asian Studies* vol. 2 (2006): 10, referring to Linz (2000): 70.
4. World Bank, *Civil Society Engagement: Review of Fiscal Years 2002–2004* (Washington D.C., 2005).
5. John Keane, "Chapter 1: Civil Society and Monitory Democracy." (this volume)
6. Johan Saravanamuttu, "Emergent Civil Societies in ASEAN: Antimonies of Discourse and Practices," in *Democracy, Human Rights, & Civil Society in Southeast Asia*, eds. Amitav Archarya, B. Michael Frolic, & Richard Stubbs, eds. (Toronto: Joint Centre for Asia Pacific Studies, 2001): 90.
7. Colin Ball and Barry Knight, "Why We Must Listen to Citizens," in *Civil Society at the Millennium*, CIVICUS (West Hartford, CT.: Kumarian Press, 1999): 19.
8. Alfredo Sfeir-Younis, "The Role of Civil Society in Foreign Policy: A New Conceptual Framework," *Seton Hall Journal of Diplomacy and International Relations* Summer/Fall (2004): 29.
9. Kumi Naidoo and Rajesh Tandon, "The Promise of Civil Society" in *Civil Society at the Millennium*, CIVICUS (West Hartford, CT: Kumarian Press, 1999): 8.
10. Saravanamuttu, "Emergent Civil Societies in ASEAN," 89.
11. Andrew Clayton, ed., *NGOs, Civil Society, and the State: Building Democracy in Transitional Societies* (Oxford: INTRAC Publication, 1996): 126.
12. He Baogang, "The Making of a Nascent Civil Society in China" in *Civil Society in Asia*, eds. D.C. Schak and Wayne Hudson (Aldershot, U.K.: Ashgate, 2003): 129.
13. This was true in the Philippines when Cory Aquino became president. State administration seemed unable to deliver goods and services to local populations, so she said she would turn to civil society with government funding to supply these needs. Immediately, the wives of some governors established local NGOs to administer (and syphon off) governmental largess. Field interviews.

14. See Benedict Anderson, "The Idea of Power in Javanese Culture," in *Culture and Politics in Indonesia* ed. Clare Holt (Ithaca N.Y.: Cornell University Press, 1972). Also David I. Steinberg, *Burma/Myanmar: What Everyone Needs to Know* (Oxford: Oxford University Press, 2010).

15. One might argue that in the United States, for example, the intellectual interlocking leadership of those who easily move between government and the private foundations and universities illustrate this tendency.

16. Philippe C. Schmitter, "On Civil Society and the Consolidation of Democracy: Ten General Propositions and Nine Speculations about Their Relation in Asian Societies." (July 1996. Revised paper).

17. International Crisis Group, "Myanmar: The Role of Civil Society." Brussels: Asia Report No. 27, 6 December 2001.

18. Personal interview, Yangon.

19. See Tom Kramer, "The State of Civil Society in Burma. Development, Limitations, and Opportunities in Myanmar." Transnational Institute, Alternative Regionalisms Project (Amsterdam, February 2009. Draft).

20. Examples abound where donors help create and fund new governmental institutions that attract the talented staff of line ministries, thus decreasing traditional capacities while fostering new programs.

21. World Bank, *Civil Society Engagement: Review of Fiscal Years 2005–2006* (Washington D.C., 2006). The Bank notes that 72 percent of loans for 2006 involved civil society.

22. By 1996, there were said to be no genuine Lao NGOs in that society. Caroline Harper Clayton, "Strengthening Civil Society in Transitional East Asia" in *Civil Society in Asia*, 128.

23. He Baogang, "The Making of Nascent Civil Society in China" in *Civil Society in Asia*, 114.

24. He Baogang, "The Making of Nascent Civil Society in China," 117.

25. The extent to which the Chinese model affected Burmese decisions to regularize NGOs in 1988 is unknown, although such influence has been entirely denied by Burmese authorities.

26. He Baogang, *The Democratic Implications of Civil Society in China* (London: Macmillan, 1997): 162–63. He Baogang notes that in China, one of every 820,000 people have only one national social organization, one of every 60,000 belongs to a provincial social organization, and every 7,500 a local one. In contrast, 7 out of 10 Americans belong to one association, 25 percent to four or more.

27. He Baogang, *The Democratic Implications of Civil Society in China*, 130–133.

28. Bruce J. Dickson, "Dilemmas of Party Adaptation: the CCP's Strategies for Survival" in *State and Society in 21st-Century China: Crisis, Contention and Legitimation*, ed. P. H. Gries and S. Rosen (New York: RoutledgeCurzon, 2004): 153–154.

29. Tony Saich, (2004). *Governance and politics of China*. Palgrave Macmillan.

30. Ezra Mbogori and Hope Chigudu, "Civil Society and Government: A Continuum of Possibilities" in *Civil Society at the Millennium*, 19. A Johns Hopkins study in 1990 found that in eight countries, including Japan, 41 percent of the income to the non-profit sector came from governments.

31. Current civil societies that are today recognized and that were formed in the colonial period include The Myanmar Baptist Churches Union (1860) and the

Myanmar Baptist Convention (1865). Note that these names originally used "Burma" not "Myanmar."

32. David Steinberg, "A Void in Myanmar: Civil Society in Burma" in *Strengthening Civil Society in Burma. Possibilities and Dilemmas for International NGOs*, ed. Burma Center Netherlands (BCN) and Transnational Institute (TNI) (Chiang Mai: Silkworm Press, 1999): 8.

33. "Needs for United States Economic and Technical Aid in Burma." Report No. 3 of the United States Economic Survey to Southeast Asia (Washington D.C.: May 1950. Confidential, declassified 1967).

34. For a discussion of this, see David I. Steinberg, *Burma/Myanmar: What Everyone Needs to Know* (Oxford, Oxford University Press, 2010): Chapter 7.

35. See David I. Steinberg, "Aung San Suu Kyi and the Making of U.S. Policy toward Burma/Myanmar." *Journal of Current Southeast Asian Affairs* vol. 3, no. 10, (September 2010). For a study of the field of Burma/Myanmar, see Andrew Selth, "Modern Burma Studies: A View from the Edge." City University of Hong Kong *Working Paper Series* 96 (November 2007).

36. Brian Heidal, *The Growth of Civil Society in Myanmar* (Bangalore: Books for Exchange, 2006).

37. Mael Ranaud, "Burma's Civil Society between Nargis and the 2010 Elections." Unpublished briefing paper (June 2009).

38. Robert Taylor, *The State in Myanmar* (Honolulu: University of Hawaii Press, 2009): 445.

39. See Heidal, *The Growth of Civil Society in Myanmar*, 17 and Annex B, 77–82. See also Kramer, "The State of Civil Society in Burma," 12.

40. The Asia Foundation, "Constitutional Reform and Democracy in Thailand" (Bangkok 2009): 103. According to them, only 0.2 percent of the urban population and 0.1 percent of the rural population claimed membership in a non-political religious organization. These figures seem suspect given the high religious NGO membership in Burmese circles.

41. The Asia Foundation, "Constitutional Reform and Democracy in Thailand," 103.

42. Kramer, "The State of Civil Society in Burma," 13.

43. Raynaud, "Burma's Civil Society between Nargis and the 2010 Elections."

44. Elliott Prasse-Freeman, "Power, Politics, and Space at the Peripheries for Burma/Myanmar Civil Society." Unpublished manuscript (2009).

45. It is evident that in a number of instances in which this author was involved, lower-level officials complied with the letter of enforced regulations from the central government, but interpreted them in manners that allowed the operation of desirable programs to continue as long as no political backlash was likely. In many cases, as in the aftermath of Nargis, local military simply ignored edicts from Naypyidaw.

46. Kyaw Yin Hlaing, "Understanding Government Repression and Political Change in Myanmar." Paper presented at the City University of Hong Kong-Hiroshima Peace Institute Conference, Hong Kong (December 2009): 5–6, 25–26.

47. See Melford E. Spiro, *Buddhism and Society. A Great Tradition and Its Burmese Vicissitudes* (New York: Harper & Row, 1970).

48. See Steinberg, *Burma/Myanmar: What Everyone Needs to Know*. For the changes in Thai society, William Klausner has commented perceptively on the Northeast,

where traditional views are giving way to more expectations of state support. Personal communication.

49. Mai Ni Ni Aung, "Creating Space in Myanmar/Burma. Preserving the Tradition of Ethnic Minority Groups: A Catalyst for Community Building" in *Active Citizens Under Political Wraps: Experiences from Myanmar/Burma and Vietnam*, ed. Heinrich Boell Foundation (2006): 108.

50. Ni Aung, "Creating Space" in *Active Citizens Under Political Wraps*, 114, 117.

51. Kramer, "The State of Civil Society in Burma," 13.

52. The Burmese seem to have learned from their previous (1962–1988) experience that the sole authorized political party, the Burmese Socialist Programme Party, was an abject failure that led to coup of 1988 that was designed to shore up failing military rule.

53. Archarya, Frolic, and Stubbs, eds. *Democracy, Human Rights, & Civil Society in Southeast Asia*, 228.

54. Centre for Peace and Conflict Studies, "Listening to Voices from Inside: Myanmar Civil Society's Response to Cyclone Nargis." 3 May 2009.

55. Morten B. Pedersen, *Promoting Human Rights in Burma. A Critique of Western Sanctions Policy* (New York: Rowman & Littlefield, 2008), 191.

56. This constitutional reference was kindly made available by Tom Kramer, Transnational Institute.

57. Jasmin Lorch, "Does Civil Society Actors Have Any Room for Manouevre in Burma/Myanmar? Locating Gaps in the Authoritarian System" in *Active Citizens Under Political Wraps*, 134.

58. The Asia Society, "Current Realities and Future Possibilities in Burma/Myanmar: Perspectives from Asia" (New York: The Asia Society 2010).

59. International Crisis Group, "Myanmar: The Role of Civil Society."

Chapter 7

KENYA'S GREEN BELT MOVEMENT
CONTRIBUTIONS, CONFLICT, CONTRADICTIONS, AND COMPLICATIONS IN A PROMINENT ENVIRONMENTAL NON-GOVERNMENTAL ORGANIZATION (ENGO)

Bron Taylor[1]

Introduction

Kenya's Green Belt Movement became internationally famous in 2004 when its founder, Wangari Maathai, was awarded the Nobel Peace Prize.[2] Since 1977, in Kenya and other parts of Africa, the movement has planted millions of trees in an effort to restore ecosystems, promote sustainable livelihoods, empower women, and promote democracy. Increasingly, Maathai has drawn a close connection between all these objectives and the quest for a peaceful society. As a result, Maathai and the movement she inspired are now well known internationally. A more complete picture, however, reveals not only contributions, but also complications and challenges that seriously undermine the movement's objectives. Given the importance of this movement, and because it shares many traits with grassroots environmental and social movements in the developing world, valuable lessons can be gleaned by bringing this important civil society actor into sharper focus.

My hope is that a fresh look at the movement, that is both appreciative and willing to be critical, will give insight into the movement's strengths and weaknesses, thereby positively contributing to the praxis of civil society, which is composed of diverse individuals and groups, outside of governments, who generally promote social justice, environmental health, and democracy. My belief is that by turning to the epistemological and ethical issues that are raised through this case study, we will eventually be able to see more clearly the ways in which environmental knowledge can be integrated within cultures to promote the flourishing of both human beings and the natural communities to which they belong.

In addition to my longstanding interest in the Green Belt Movement and archival research focused on it, my analyses are based on research conducted in Kenya in July 2009. This research included interviews with academic foresters and ecologists, other professors, professional foresters, high officials of Kenya's Environmental Ministry and Forest Service, grassroots activists with the Green Belt Movement, and Maasai villagers near Masi Mara National Park in Southern Kenya. My perspective is informed by decades of close scrutiny of grassroots environmental movements around the world.[3]

The Prize and the Vision

For generations, the Nobel Peace Prize committee and the Norwegian government, which facilitates the process (and in earlier years controlled its selections), has used the prize to not only celebrate visionaries promoting peace, but also empower them and inspire others. Usually, the committee has sought to promote peace between conflicting human groups. On rare occasions, some of the Nobel prizes (not only the Peace Prize but also for literature, for example) have implied that peace depends on healthy natural environments and equitable distribution of natural resources. Still at other times, there have been intimations through these awards that people should pursue peace with other forms of life and with the entire natural world, in other words, that peace is not only about relationships among human beings and their interests.

Early examples of this broader vision of peace include Selma Lagerlöf, the Swedish author who was awarded the Nobel Prize in Literature in 1909, whose writings and acceptance speech expressed her deep love of nature and remarkable intimacy with its creatures.[4] Albert Schweitzer, the famous humanitarian, may have been given the 1952 Nobel Peace Prize in part for his "reverence for life" ethics, which was certainly innovative in its time. By awarding the Peace Prize to Wangari Maathai in 2004, however, the Nobel committee made its most powerful and explicit connection between peace, equity, human rights, and the flourishing of nature. This connection was reinforced just three years later when in 2007, Al Gore (the former Vice President of the United States) and the United Nation's Intergovernmental Panel on Climate Change, shared the Peace Prize in recognition of their efforts to alert the global community to the dangers posed by accelerating global environmental deterioration linked to anthropogenic climate warming.

The case of Maathai and the Green Belt Movement (GBM) she founded is worth special attention. Although some criticized the awarding of the Peace Prize to Maathai, viewing her efforts as tangential to the prize's purpose, through this award the Nobel Committee averred that grassroots organizations like the GBM promote peace, if often indirectly. Viewed holistically, acts of ecological restoration such as planting trees, the defense of ecosystems from destructive forms of logging, and challenges to corrupt governments that do not actively support environmental protection can all contribute to the environmental and social conditions upon which peace depends. Such activities can directly reduce the competition among groups for land, food, and water—competition that has often led to or exacerbated violence among individuals and groups. But is the Green Belt Movement story as unambiguously positive as its activists and admirers have portrayed it? Does it offer comprehensive solutions to the eco-social predicaments widely found in recently independent developing countries? Maathai and the GBM have faced much criticism; does it have merit? Or rather, as movement activists and sympathizers contend, does the criticism actually amount to the mere machinations of politicians—whose power base is often established and maintained by promoting tribal animosities—and greedy profiteers, both of which are indifferent to environmental destruction and the way it harms human communities?

Context & Contributions

Before addressing such questions, the prevalent narrative about Maathai and the GBM should be well in mind. A precocious young woman, born in 1940 and from the Kikuyu ethnic group, Maathai grew up in rural Kenya and easily developed a love of nature. She attended Catholic schools in Kenya, eventually gaining scholarships to study in the United States. By 1966, she had earned a B.A. and M.A. in biology (in Kansas and Pittsburgh, respectively). This sojourn in the United States was during the early and mid 1960s, where she observed the growing environmental movement and experienced the struggle for civil and women's rights. These experiences reinforced and decisively shaped her assertive nature and future focus on gender equity, social justice, and environmental health. As she wrote later:

The United States prepared me to ... critique what was happening at home, including what women were experiencing. My years in the United States overlapped with the beginnings of the women's movement and even though many women were still bound to traditional ideas about themselves at the time, I came to see that as an African woman I was perhaps even more constrained.... It is fair to say that America transformed me: it made me into the person I am today ... The spirit of freedom and possibility that America nurtured in me made me want to foster the same in Kenya, and it was in this spirit that I returned home.[5]

These experiences, combined with Kenyan independence in 1963, made Maathai optimistic about the future when she returned to Kenya. But they also led to challenges for Maathai, as her newfound ideals, including feminism, were considered by many Kenyans as alien to African values and contrary to the best interests of African women.

Upon her return to Kenya, Maathai worked as a research assistant at Nairobi University, before continuing her studies in Germany. By 1971, she had earned a Ph.D. in anatomy, again, at Nairobi University. She continued her work there, while becoming a prominent advocate for women's rights, and in 1977 gained a promotion to Associate Professor.[6] Her feminist work, however, contributed to her marginalization by male colleagues at the university, leading to her departure from academia to found the GBM in 1977. In this risky move, she took up the idea of a tree-planting movement, which had occurred to her the previous year. She built up the movement, drawing prominently from the women's organizations with which she had been engaged, although men were also involved from the outset. By 1986, with the movement well established in Kenya, she began to spread the model to other African countries. Along the way, Maathai married a politician—with whom she had three children—who later abandoned her, claiming she had become uncontrollable and did not act like a proper African woman. The fissure was likely as much because she had become more prominent than he was. Her divorce, given these same gender-related mores, subjected her to the suspicion that she was not a good African woman and that her values were foreign. This was one way her political adversaries denigrated her and the GBM.

Initially, the GBM was not politically controversial; it focused on tree planting on school grounds and private farmlands. But it entered into an adversarial relationship with the state, partly because of the autocratic rule of Daniel Arap Moi, Kenya's President from 1978–2002.[7] As part of his strategy for retaining power, Moi rewarded his cronies with public forestland, precipitating even more rapid deforestation and the intensifying hardships that naturally follow—such as difficulty obtaining water, food, fuel, and forage—which especially impact rural and semi-urban populations. (Estimates of deforestation found in Forestry Ministry publications indicate that about 98 percent of Kenya's original primary forests have been destroyed or converted to agro-ecosystems, human settlements, and commercial zones.) Here the GBM was indeed fulfilling a monitory role—as discussed by John Keane—by exposing the regime's corruption and lack of transparency.

Although Moi authorized multiparty elections in 1991 (a concession to the intense domestic and international pressure that was precipitated by civil society actors), his regime nevertheless often responded brutally to their demands for democracy and environmental conservation. As Maathai and her movement added the protection of public parks and forests to their cause (first related to a large public park in Nairobi in the early 1990s and later in response to Moi's efforts to privatize public forests), Moi's regime began to repress them. Greenbelt activists were among those who suffered violence and incarceration; Maathai herself was jailed several times and badly beaten by police and hospitalized in 1992. This led to the reputation for courage that Maathai and her movement enjoy, both domestically and internationally. The GBM thus played an important role in early efforts to promote uncorrupt, democratic governance in post-colonial Kenya, a struggle that continues to this day.

The GBM thus provides an important example of an environmental organization that deeply connected human rights, democracy, and environmental protection with the quest for a socially just and peaceful society. Combined with the visibility brought at the same time by the struggle for democracy in Kenya and enhanced by the eloquence and courage of its leader, the GBM gained widespread, positive international attention. Long before she was awarded the Nobel Peace Prize in 1991, she received the Goldman Environmental Prize, the Hunger Project's Africa Leadership Prize, and was featured on the cable news network CNN. In 1992, she played a major civil society role at the United Nations sponsored Earth Summit in Rio de Janeiro. She also drew significant financial support from Western environmental foundations and some European nations.[8] But it was the victory in the battle to save Nairobi's Uhuru National Park from development from 1989–1992 that guaranteed Maathai and the GBM's connection to the quest for poverty reduction, democracy, human rights, and the protection of nature.[9]

In 2002, the year Moi left office, Maathai was elected to Parliament and appointed by the new president as an Assistant Minister for Environment and Natural Resources. Many thought, however, she should have been appointed the head of this agency. Nevertheless, in her new role working with civil society allies, she helped shape Kenya's Forest Act of 2005. This was a very progressive policy—compared with other environmental laws around the world—which was designed to promote environmental sustainability, reduce greenhouse gasses, preserve biodiversity, and meet human needs.[10] The strength of this bill, and even its passage, was likely due in part to the enhanced political strength enjoyed by Maathai and her allies after winning the Nobel Peace Prize.

Even given this concrete legislative accomplishment, it may well be that the greatest contribution of Maathai and the GBM has been, and will be, in the area of consciousness-raising. In my extensive experience with the study of deforestation, I have never seen as much concern, recognition of associated problems (declining water resources, biodiversity, and food insecurity, for example), or meaningful action to reverse it, as what I saw in Kenya in 2009. This heightened awareness was nearly omnipresent—in newspapers, television, and radio broadcasts; the agenda of the environmental ministry and Kenyan officials I spoke with; as well as among many other Kenyans that I encountered during my visit.[11] It was also visible in a truly remarkable way in and around Nairobi, Kenya's densely populated urban center, where individual entrepreneurs tended mile after mile of roadside nurseries. This demonstrated the non-subsidized market within that urban center for shrub and tree planting. It is inconceivable that this amount of consciousness and action could have occurred without the work of Maathai and the GBM. This transformation of consciousness, then, has not only made new forest laws possible in Kenya, it has helped to inspire a broad sustainability movement everywhere its accomplishments have become known.

Conflicts

Despite the GBM's accomplishments, the movement has often been criticized, and not only by Moi and his cronies. Some of her constituents, for example, felt let down when she resigned from her position as Assistant Minister for Environment and Natural Resources. They felt this weakened her position as their elected representative and was an insult to President Mwai Kibaki, who had appointed her.[12] This was one reason that, despite her international stature and strong base among social and environmental activists, Maathai lost her seat in parliament by a wide margin in 2007. GBM activists argue the defeat was because she refused to engage in the same corrupt electoral practices as her opponent, such as vote buying in various forms. However, during more detailed questioning, I learned that her opposition also gained traction by claiming that she cared only for the environment and not for human welfare, a common and sometimes effective charge against environmentalists around the world.

During these same elections, the closely-fought battle for the presidency also led to charges of electoral fraud, which precipitated severe post-election violence that took at least 1,300 lives, displaced 600,000 people from their homes, and involved the widespread rape of women, property theft, and the destruction of forests as opportunists took advantage of the lawlessness to cut trees for profit.[13] Despite increasing international pressure, including a demand by the International Criminal Court (empowered to prosecute violations of human rights and war crimes wherever they occur) that Kenya establish a tribunal by October 2009 to investigate and prosecute those responsible for the violence, the Kenyan government had not established a tribunal to prosecute the instigators and perpetrators of the violence, even by spring 2010.[14] It is commonly believed this reluctance has been because high governmental officials and some members of the parliament fomented or were otherwise responsible for the violence. Maathai, by then no longer in the government, while not denying that the court's intervention might be necessary, urged Kenyans to form their own independent commission to prosecute those responsible for the violence. She argued convincingly that Kenya could not develop a democracy in which human rights are respected and violence overcome (let alone restore the environmental systems upon which everyone's well being depends) if it would not end the era of impunity and corruption in which politicians inflame ethnic hatreds as a means to economic and political power.[15] Major newspapers editorialized similarly.

Those who pay attention to Kenyan politics know most if not all of this history. Obviously, this has been a difficult period in which civil society has faced daunting challenges. A closer look reveals additional conflicts. Some officials and business people in the Kenyan Forest Service and the country's forest products industry have criticized Maathai and the GBM for misleading the public and advocating counterproductive forest policies due to the GBM's advocating of a complete logging ban on public lands, urging elimination of exotic tree plantations, and rejecting the use of genetically modified trees. The same critics believe that these practices exacerbate the destruction of the country's remaining indigenous forests by increasing the value and cost of all wood products, along with the incentive to cut down native forests, both legally and illegally. Moreover, they aver that GBM's prescriptions damage the Kenyan economy and put more people in desperate straits, a situation which ironically increases the invasion of forestlands by squatters, who have damaged the country's forest ecosystems. Some social justice advocates—including advocates for certain tribal or other community groups—have articulated similar criticisms of the GBM and other environmental organizations.

Whatever the merits of such charges and the strength of the rejoinders from the GBM architects and activists, it is clear they are all increasingly voicing alarm based on an intensifying eco-social calamity unfolding throughout the country. Indeed, Kenya is growing to be an exemplar of the Club of Rome's thesis in Limits to Growth, which in 1972 predicted widespread eco-social collapse would occur around the world during the twenty-first century, "if present trends continue."[16] Although sometimes criticized as unduly apocalyptic, recent empirical evaluation of the benchmarks modeled in the report indicate that it was remarkably prescient.[17] Meanwhile, a growing body of analysis, spearheaded by Thomas Homer-Dixon, has been illuminating the role of environmental scarcity in precipitating and exacerbating social conflict, violence, and even genocide.[18] Much of this analysis is based on case studies where, unlike in Kenya, there is no obvious evidence that climate change has been an exacerbating factor. In Kenya, however, there is evidence that intensifying environmental stresses, including those brought on or worsened by climate changes, is causing social instability and violence.

There is little doubt, for example, that struggles to gain or retain land played a role in the post-election violence in 2007, which was related to both Kenya's complicated colonial history and long-standing tribal conflicts among Kenya's forty-two ethnic groups. By the time I visited Kenya in July 2009, and afterward as I continued to follow developments there closely, the major news stories were of the ongoing desiccation of rivers and dams; the consequent decline of hydropower as a resource; the beginning of electricity rationing; and the ways in which the drought was directly causing the death of many domestic animals by reducing both water and food supplies, as well as indirectly starving wild predators such as lions and baboons that then preyed upon domesticated animals. This predation, in turn, led to a violent reaction by people who depend directly on domestic animals for their own livelihoods and survival. Indeed, some of these people starved to death as a result of the potent mix of shrinking per-capita land availability (due to rapid population growth), and long-term environmental degradation exacerbated by drought, which reduces the caloric productivity of the land. This drought, in a vicious feedback loop, is almost certainly related to global warming which climate models indicate will hit many areas of Africa, including Kenya, particularly hard.[19]

Critique and Culture

Given Kenya's critical situation, it is important to get accurate diagnoses of the roots of these problems and create effective solutions to—or at least ways of mitigating—the environmental and climate crisis. Far less well known than the main outline of the story of Maathai and the GBM is their assessment of the roots of the problem and what, apart from promoting women's rights, democracy, and environmental restoration, might address them. The deeper diagnosis and prescription Maathai and the movement offer is significantly more radical than most people know.

The GBM's basic historical and analytical chronology runs as follows: Colonial powers dominated African countries militarily and used what they considered to be their superior religion to denigrate and suppress African respect for indigenous cultural and religious traditions. Inexorable changes in land distribution and use accompanied this martial and cultural attack and together led to devastating environmental and social decline. Reversing these trends requires a revival of respect for and practice of native traditions, including African traditional religions, which more than the colonial religions and traditions, according to GBM, tend to promote environmentally sustainable behavior. Over the years, Maathai has escalated her criticism of colonial Western religions and epistemologies, which, in her view, lead to a commodification and desacralization of life, and ultimately, to people treating nature only as means to their own material ends. In contrast to her view of the colonial influences, Maathai's teaching and writing have promoted an organicist and holistic worldview—in which all of nature is understood as interrelated and sacred—as well as a sense of belonging, a connection to nature, and an animistic and biocentric kinship ethics.

This kind of spirituality I have labeled dark green religion, which involves pantheistic or quasi-pantheistic worldviews that embrace scientific understandings of ecological interdependence, as well as animist perceptions in which communication and even communion with non-human organisms is possible.[20] Such spirituality may—but need not—involve beliefs in non-material divine spirits or beings. But it always includes the belief that all life has value, apart from its usefulness to human beings, and the concomitant belief that all life is interrelated, which is in turn usually grounded in an understanding that all life shares a common ancestor and came to be the way it is through the evolutionary process. This evolutionary understanding is the basis for kinship ethics; the belief that humans have moral duties to their diverse earthly relatives. These beliefs often evoke feelings of belonging to the earth's living systems and even to the entire universe. Such spirituality is increasingly common among diverse environment-focused civil society actors around the world (as well as among some politicians and business leaders) and it is evident in Maathai's lifework, including in her Nobel Prize acceptance speech:

> Today we are faced with a challenge that calls for a shift in our thinking, so that humanity stops threatening its life-support system. We are called to assist the Earth to heal her wounds and in the process heal our own—indeed, to embrace the whole creation in all its diversity, beauty, and wonder. This will happen if we see the need to revive our sense of belonging to a larger family of life, with which we have shared our evolutionary process. In the course of history, there comes a time when humanity is called to shift to a new level of consciousness, to reach a higher moral ground.... That time is now.[21]

Maathai wrote a more detailed exposition of her views about culture and religion shortly before this speech, after she was elected to Parliament in 2002. It shows that for her, the necessary transformation to a new level of moral consciousness requires the revitalization of traditional cultures and a rejection of many Western beliefs and values:[22]

> As I tried to encourage women and the African people in general to understand the need to conserve the environment, I discovered how crucial it is to return constantly to our cultural heritage. Mount Kenya used to be a holy mountain for my people, the Kikuyus. They believed that their God dwelled on the mountain and that everything good—the rains, clean drinking water—flowed from it.... Then the missionaries came [who] ... said, "God does not dwell on Mount Kenya. God dwells in heaven." [But] Heaven is not above us: it is right here, right now. So the Kikuyu people were not wrong when they said that God dwelled on the mountain.... If people still believed this, they would not have allowed illegal logging or clear-cutting of the forests.
>
> After working with different Kenyan communities for more than two decades, the [GBM] ... also concluded that culture should be incorporated into any development paradigm.... Cultural revival might be the only thing that stands between the conservation or destruction of the environment, the only way to perpetuate the knowledge and wisdom inherited from the past. Until the arrival of the Europeans, communities had looked to nature for inspiration, food, beauty, and spirituality. They pursued a lifestyle that was sustainable and that gave them a good quality of life.... Communities that have not yet undergone industrialization have a close connection with the physical environment, which they often treat with reverence.... Their habitats are rich with local biological diversity, both plant and animal. However, these are the very habitats that are most at threat from globalization, commercialization, privatization, and the piracy of biological materials found in them. This global threat is causing communities to lose their rights to the resources they have preserved throughout the ages as part of their cultural heritage. These communities are persuaded to consider their relationship with nature primitive,

worthless, and an obstacle to development and progress in an age of advanced technology and information flow.

During the long, dark decades of imperialism and colonialism [European] governments told African societies that they were backward. They told us that our religious systems were sinful; our agricultural practices inefficient; our tribal systems of governing irrelevant; and our cultural norms barbaric, irreligious, and savage. ... Of course, some of what happened, and continues to happen, in Africa was bad and remains so. Africans were involved in the slave trade; women are still genitally mutilated; Africans are still killing Africans because they belong to different religions or ethnic groups. Nonetheless, I for one am not content to thank God for the arrival of "civilization" from Europe because I know from what my grandparents told me that much of what went on in Africa before colonialism was good.

There was some degree of accountability to people from their leaders. People were able to feed themselves. They carried their history, their cultural practices, their stories, and their sense of the world around them in their oral traditions, and that tradition was rich and meaningful. Above all, they lived with other creatures and the natural environment in harmony, and they protected that world.

Maathai thus contended that to overcome the pernicious impact of European cultures and colonial violence, Africans must revitalize their own cultures, including the use of indigenous pastoral and agricultural practices (by using native plants, for example, rather than the supposedly superior non-native species introduced by Europeans, let alone genetically modified organisms). They must also recognize that their colonizers, by viewing African traditional agricultural practices and food production processes as primitive, actually "contributed to food insecurity at the household level and diminishment of local biological diversity."

Here, Maathai was reflecting an increasingly influential school of thought among ecological anthropologists and ethno-biologists who have found that "traditional ecological knowledge"—namely, knowledge embedded in the cultural and religious mores of many indigenous and traditional peoples—generally promotes environmentally beneficent behavior.[23] Their perspective has become common within the global environmental milieu including grassroots organizations, international development experts, and social and natural scientists, some of which are affiliated with the United Nations Environmental Programme (UNEP).[24]

I know from interviews with GBM movement activists in 2002 and 2009 that many of them share Maathai's ideas. During the 2002 United Nations Summit on Sustainable Development (in Johannesburg, South Africa), for example, I interviewed two leaders of the GBM. One of them, Gathuru Mburu, like Maathai, emphasized the need to develop an environmental strategy that respects and draws on African culture and indigenous knowledge. In 2009, when I met him again in Kenya, he had established his own organization, the Institute for Culture and Ecology, to focus especially on this part of the environmental cause, while also coordinating the African Biodiversity Network.[25]

At the 2002 United Nations Summit on Sustainable Development in Johannesburg, South Africa, I met with Nanga Tiango, who was an attorney for the GBM at that time. Tiango expounded on the philosophy animating the GBM and much of grassroots African environmentalism, articulating a strong biocentric kinship ethics. Tiango stressed that we must "reconnect" to nature and recognize that: "we are all part of the universe, that man is not superior to the other animals.... We are all part of the earth and we should preserve it, both for use by other species, and for future generations."[26] Then he explained how he and other Africans were blending traditional African religion, Christianity, and environmentalism. "Christians are for the protection of the Universe.... Christians want to be linked with the ancestors [and to] preserve nature for future generations."

Especially noteworthy in this conversation was Tiango's musing about how colonizers once suppressed African traditional religions but now champion their value. Like Maathai, Tiango stressed that Africa's native religions contained positive environmental values and ecological knowledge about how to protect the environment. He even said that these traditional religions teach "how to communicate with the mountains," while also expressing surprise that some Europeans had come to respect traditional African beliefs and practices. Tiango was delighted that it was becoming acceptable to fuse beliefs traditional in African culture with his ecological concern as well as with Christianity.

Complications

Tiango, like Maathai, was in sync with the trend toward looking to traditional knowledge systems for insight into ways to think about and relate to nature. But their examples raise a critical question: On what basis does one arbitrate between incompatible aspects of the world's diverse cultures? This is a difficult conundrum for Maathai and others who feel torn between their respect for traditional cultures and Western cultural streams that have promoted democracy and universal human rights, including gender equality.[27] She tends to emphasize the positive in world cultures: "Humanity needs to find beauty in its diversity of cultures and accept that there will be many languages, religions, attires, dances, songs, symbols, festivals, and traditions. This diversity should be seen as a universal heritage of humankind."[28] So, despite her harsh critique of European civilization and its destructive role in Africa, and given her long, positive relationships with many Western organizations, governments, and individuals, it is clear that she believes that all societies have positive dimensions. But what does she think about the negative aspects of certain human cultures?

After repeating in her Nobel Prize speech the idea that "culture may be the missing link in the development of Africa," she added that over time, it is self-corrective. "Culture is dynamic and evolves over time, consciously discarding retrogressive traditions, like female genital mutilation (FGM), and embracing aspects that are good and useful." Then, she added: "Africans, especially, should rediscover positive aspects of their culture. In accepting them, they would give themselves a sense of belonging, identity, and self-confidence."

This begs two sorts of questions; the first one empirical: When, to what extent, and why is culture self-corrective? The second one is both epistemological and ethical: How do we identify the positive and negative streams? To my knowledge, Maathai has not addressed the first and seems to assume that the good and bad dimensions of a culture should be obvious. The case of female genital mutilation suggests these assumptions may not have merit. Although most Westerners and many Africans today condemn the practice—the Kenyan government outlawed it, but only for minors, in 2001 and the African Union's 2005 Maputo Protocol required member states to ban the practice—it is still commonplace.[29] Indeed, in Kenya and other African countries, it is defended on cultural, religious, and moral grounds, especially in culturally traditional (usually more rural) places. It remains a common cultural and religious practice in part because it is considered important for community cohesion and well-being. It is, moreover, "widely believed to increase a girl's chances of marriage, prevent promiscuity, and promote easy childbirth," and the endurance of the practice is in part because of the belief that "women who do not circumcise their daughters run the risk of being seen as irresponsible, immoral imitators of Western culture."[30]

Maathai's clear condemnation of this cultural practice, which is most prevalent in West and East Africa, complicates her belief that to promote the well-being of people and nature, Africans must revitalize their traditions. The complication may be due, in part, to the understandable desire to not only achieve political independence, but also to shed a colonial mindset that devalues Africa and Africans. Maathai states: "Cultural liberation will only come when the minds of the people are set free and they can protect themselves from colonialism of the mind. Only that type of freedom will allow them to reclaim their identity, self-respect, and destiny. Only when communities recapture the positive aspects of their culture will people relearn how to love themselves and what is theirs. Only then will they really appreciate their country and the need to protect its natural beauty and wealth. And only then will they have an understanding of the future and of generations to come.[31]

Ironically, some defenders of genital cutting blame imperialists, colonialist Christians, for denigrating and seeking to abolish what they consider an authentic and positive African tradition.[32] Maathai has been unpersuaded by this anti-colonial critique, but in another important and in some ways analogous case, she may have been persuaded by such critique. In 2004, as she was about to receive the Nobel Prize, a controversy erupted over comments attributed to her about HIV/AIDS in a Kenyan newspaper.

> News media in Africa—including the [East Africa] *Standard* ... reported that Maathai has claimed Western scientists, to decimate the African population, deliberately created HIV/AIDS. Maathai denied making such allegations. In a statement issued by the Nobel Committee, she stated that she does not believe the virus was developed by white people to destroy Africans. Such views, she wrote, "are wicked and destructive." She also expressed hope that scientists will find conclusive evidence about the source of AIDS in order to dispel the belief that the disease was the result of a laboratory accident.[33]

In the same year, however, Maathai responded to questions in an interview published in *Time* magazine in a way that cast doubt about the strong scientific evidence present at the time, which became even stronger in the subsequent five years, that HIV/AIDS originated in simian populations and crossed over into human populations, probably in the early twentieth century.[34]

> Time: You've said AIDS is a biological weapon manufactured by the developing world to wipe out the black race. Do you still believe that?
>
> Maathai: I have no idea who created AIDS and whether it is a biological agent or not. But I do know things like that don't come from the moon. I have always thought that it is important to tell people the truth, but I guess there is some truth that must not be too exposed.
>
> Time: What are you referring to?
>
> Maathai: I'm referring to AIDS. I am sure people know where it came from. And I'm quite sure it did not come from the monkeys. Why can't we be encouraged to ask ourselves these questions?[35]

By doubting the disease came from another species, and attributing it to an as yet unknown human creator, Maathai leant credence to the idea that Western scientists may have been responsible for the pandemic.[36]

The fundamental question posed by these two cases—of genital mutilation and the origin of AIDS—is what to do about Western values and science when there are many cogent critiques of the ways in which both have harmed African people and the environment. The result has been that both Western values and science have been brought under suspicion. Although suspicion is common among grassroots civil society actors and some scholars, it risks the construction and reification of a new kind of dualism, this time between the values (and ways of knowing) characterized as Western and non-Western, with the latter considered superior to the former. This dynamic can hinder the appropriation of Western knowledge, such as from the environmental sciences, which are important to current efforts to manage social and environmental systems. In seeking to revitalize the environmental knowledge in non-Western contexts—knowledge that has been accumulated through careful human observation and experimentation often over long time periods and integrated into everyday cultural practices—it is possible to denigrate the value of knowledge gained by people in Western contexts.[37] While techniques may differ, what can be generalized as Western and non-Western ecological knowledge both depends on the human capacity to observe and theorize the world, and subsequently, to test whether the impressions gained are replicable.

Other issues with which the GBM has been involved amplify this concern. Maathai has contended that Europeans should not denigrate traditional pastoralism and the ways many people in Africa equate wealth with cattle possession. Indeed, the Maasai, the best known and most culturally intact of these pastoral groups, had co-evolved with wildlife in a way that had, more so than many other groups around the world, promoted biological diversity and provided for their needs. Yet both in the past and present there have been dimensions of these lifeways that have been unsustainable, including overgrazing, a reality worsened in recent years by drought and the shrinking pastoral land base, which is due to increasing human numbers throughout East Africa, including the Maasai population.[38] So, while there is much to admire in Maasai culture, given the rapidly changing environmental and social conditions in the habitats they depend upon, it is clear that the Maasai need to understand that the drier climate and declining soil moisture and productivity is likely to endure and intensify, as predicted by the IPCC's climate scientists.[39] It would exacerbate an already tragic situation if suspicion of Western science and scientists hindered such a realization.

The declining productivity of East Africa's grassland is far from the only threat to Maasai well-being, which some longstanding cultural practices now worsen. Their rites of manhood, for example, involve a collective lion hunt by male adolescents. The one responsible for the kill gains great respect from the community, and welcome attention from young women. Although this does not lead to the death of many lions, it does contribute to the rapid decline in lion populations. The participation of Maasai pastoralists in the poisoning of lions and other predators that kill their cattle is a far bigger threat.[40] Yet the Maasai also rely on income from the tourists who come to see the animals and visit their villages to learn about Maasai culture, often purchasing Maasai arts and crafts during the visit. Ironically, their contributory role to wildlife depreciation, while protecting cattle, likely harms the long-term viability of their society's economic base.

The best outcome for the Maasai—and the non-human organisms who share their landscapes—would happen if all stakeholders, the Maasai themselves and regionally or nationally based land managers and politicians, were fully informed about the challenges they face. This means the Maasai should both preserve the most useful aspects of their unique cultural knowledge of how to survive in their eco-region and merge their own understandings with relevant knowledge from outsiders, including scientists, development experts, or governmental officials. If suspicion prevents a full vetting of facts and ideas about what might be done in these regions, however, many opportunities to ameliorate the calamity will be lost. This calls for an approach capable of reducing historical suspicions of one another, which are difficult to forget or forgive. Here, democratic political processes, across diverse regional and cultural divides, are both a worthy goal and useful tool for moving toward what some call integrative adaptive management.[41]

The same types of issues that are found on Kenya's grasslands exist in the tensions between GBM activists and professional foresters and resource managers. The limited perspectives and narrow knowledge of the professional experts were roundly and properly criticized by the GBM activists I spoke with during my visit in 2009. These activists faulted foresters and agency personnel for not taking a holistic, ecosystem centered approach when assessing forest health and devising forest-related policies. Instead, in the view of these activists, the misguided priority has been to increase the "sustained yield" of forest products. Some of these foresters, in turn, harshly criticize GBM activists for advocating logging bans and other measures that, they believe, fail to recognize that plantation forestry takes pressure off the native forests, thereby helping native forests to flourish (or recover) and thus provide the ecosystem services that the activists contend plantation forests destroy. I believe that both the activists and the agency professionals have important points to consider. The present danger, however, is insularity between two factions—activists and their allies (including some scientists), on the one side, and professional foresters and agency officials (and the scientists and disciplines they typically draw upon), on another. These groups do not seriously consider and incorporate the knowledge of their adversaries as they develop their understandings of how best to proceed. The result of the mutual suspicion and antagonism—often rooted in valid criticisms from both sides—leads to epistemological myopia and unnecessary social tension. Africans schooled in Western approaches to forest management are often criticized for selling out to former colonial masters, while grassroots activists are considered naïve, anti-scientific, anti-development, and even misanthropic.

Perhaps the most alarming example of the danger of not integrating all relevant data sets into a holistic view of humans in nature, a dynamic to which grassroots civil society groups sometimes contribute, is the failure to integrate an understanding of carrying capacity and population dynamics into a comprehensive analysis. This pattern can be seen nearly everywhere government officials and civil society actors intersect to address environmental and social problems. The conflict is due to the combination of very strong taboos against such integration in both highly developed and less developed countries.[42]

Specifically, these taboos are rooted in two problems. The first is a failure to understand human beings as part of nature, whose existence and survival is the result of the same evolutionary processes as other organisms, and thus subject to nature's laws. These under-appreciated laws include the idea of carrying capacity and population dynamics: when populations grow and consume the available calories or produce too much waste, their populations will decline (through a decreasing birth rate, increasing death rate, or both).[43] On the contrary, many believe there are few if any limits to the growth of human numbers, and that if the people get their practices right, populations can increase without an eventual reduction. Often reinforcing the first problem is a second problem, the belief that the roots of social and environmental problems are inequities between affluent and non-affluent individuals and cultures; this is often linked to the belief that affluence is the result of exploitation by the affluent of the poor (through colonialism, capitalism, or some other reviled system). Whether this exploitation is believed to have resulted from the activities of currently affluent individuals does not matter so much as the prescription: that affluent groups and individuals should provide assistance to those who are not. Since, from this perspective, the root of environmental degradation and poverty is overconsumption by the affluent, it is considered wrongheaded if not pernicious to assert that population growth increases environmental and social suffering. Those who do pose the population issue are often accused of being Malthusians or social Darwinists. This strategy has been effective in reducing attention to the role of increasing human numbers, who increasingly consume natural resources and precipitate a concomitant decline in the resources that the world's ecosystems provide to all forms of life.[44]

I saw this longstanding failure to understand the importance of carrying capacity and population growth, and a corresponding belief that the solution to environmental and social ills is a redistribution of resources, in Kenya first hand when interviewing top officials in Kenyan environmental ministries and in ENGOs there, including prominent individuals currently and formerly in the GBM. On the one hand, the Environmental Ministers and other governmental officials I spoke with were promoting an ambitious reforestation campaign, and they were deeply involved in and committed to significant and important reforms within the Kenyan Forest Service under the 2005 Forest Act, including measures to reduce corruption and deforestation. On the other hand, they spoke of Africa as a resource rich continent and did not believe that population growth was a problem or that carrying capacity was a barrier to it. I (gently) expressed incredulity at this to one high Kenyan government official, mentioning this was difficult to believe when, for example, it is so difficult to get anywhere in Nairobi due to the terrible traffic. In response I was told that if the government gets the environmental practices right, there could be a repopulation of the rural areas, and traffic in urban centers would abate. This was similar to what I heard from some (but not all) GBM activists.

Having had the opportunity to visit their projects and read about the ways in which tree planting can halt deforestation and enable repopulation of devastated land, it was easy to see that the human carrying capacity of the land can be increased in some areas due to the reformed practices. This is one of the wonderful things about the model the GBM has promoted—they are demonstrating how rich life can be when tree planting is integrated in an intelligent way with native food crops. They have shown that even watercourses can return when watersheds are restored. This demonstrates that it is possible to develop sustainable practices that are informed by traditional agronomy and pastoral knowledge in a way that is judiciously supplemented by more recently acquired knowledge. It also illustrates that cultural transformation, including respect for traditional lifeways and cultures, can be critical to the success of such sustainable models. It is, nevertheless, telling and tragic that important members of Kenya's intelligentsia minimize the contributing role that increasing human numbers play in creating and worsening their eco-social predicaments. Consequently, they are doing little to prioritize population stabilization at levels consistent with environmental sustainability. It is, moreover, discouraging that those most focused on addressing Kenya's environmental predicaments base their prescriptions on the idea that best environmental practices can be comprehensively and perfectly implemented.[45] This is a hope that finds no exemplars, anywhere.

It is beyond the scope of this analysis to provide detailed evidence for the contributing role of increasing numbers in the increasingly desperate situation of people and other living things in Kenya and beyond. Here I will simply note several pertinent facts: It is true that by some measures Africa and Kenya are both resource rich. The amount of photosynthetic productivity of the continent its people use, for example, is low compared to Asia, Europe, and America.[46] Yet Kenya has one of the highest human fertility rates in the world and its people are experiencing increasing food and water shortages and consequent social unrest.[47] Although land redistribution could reduce the numbers who are landless or land poor, this is unlikely to occur. Seldom have social movements secured significant land reform and even if it were to occur this would only temporarily mitigate the problem. Moreover, the common prescription from environmentalists, that everyone should live simply, is widely ignored despite a growing awareness that the human consumption of nature is eroding the planet's life support systems.

With the population issue, as with so many others, the needed holism is rarely incorporated comprehensively into eco-social diagnoses and prescriptions. While the contributions of ENGOs, including the GBM, are many, they are not enough. By not prioritizing a broader educational and cultural agenda, they ignore a number of critically important variables.

Conclusions

The preceding analysis of the difficulties and complications faced by the GBM suggests that the movement might be able to be even more effective if it were able to overturn some of the patterns and myths that lead to inadequate diagnoses and prescriptions in response to the unfolding, global environmental crisis, which is also deeply related to the world's intensifying economic and social strains. While I have merely introduced some critical perspectives on the GBM and kindred movements, my hope is that such analysis can be helpful to those involved in these struggles. My critical comments are not intended to distract from appreciation for the intellectual and practical accomplishments of Maathai and her compatriots, and no one should overlook their resolute courage when facing repression and violence. Few individuals or movements have done as much to demonstrate to the world the close connections between a healthy environment and the hope for a socially just world where conflicts are ameliorated nonviolently.

More specifically, the most important of GBM's contentions have been vindicated. It is now widely understood in Kenya that healthy forests are exceptionally important for the well being of people and the wider community of life. This is a growing realization around the world, also recognized by the very professions, like forestry, which have often contributed powerfully to deforestation. This realization was nearly inevitable, and would be well underway even in the absence of groups like the GBM. Yet it is inconceivable that without Maathai and the GBM, this shift in thinking would have occurred as rapidly as it has. The same could be said of the role of forest activists in many regions of the world.[48] Moreover, where such groups have struggled to protect and restore forests, generally speaking, forest health is much better than it would have been the case in their absence. If the government had been persuaded a generation ago, there would now be more forest, food, and water available today, and significantly less suffering by humans and other sentient creatures.

Wangari Maathai and the GBM have been adept at changing their strategies from education to ecological restoration and from cooperation with governmental sectors—when such opportunities arise—to uncompromising resistance. The international stature that came with the Nobel Prize increased the power of the GBM, and the movement became all the more effective, by both maintaining pressure for reform and supporting the implementation of official policies they considered salutary. They could have never achieved their objectives without winning over many in the government and thus securing greater resources than they could get from outside donors or income generating activities. One of their major accomplishments is that, despite the obstacles posed by the country's trenchant corruption, they have still significantly influenced forest policy.

The tragic reality is, however, that these positive contributions appear small in scale and importance compared to the overwhelming destructive inertia of an increasingly globalized market society with its ever-growing number of producers and consumers. Little time remains to make the comprehensive changes that are needed. What then is the most critical role for civil society ENGOs such as the GBM? Very possibly, it is the role of visionary. Perhaps the most important contribution of Maathai and the GBM, and their allies in the global environmentalist view, will be the work of cultural transformation. Maybe a change is needed in the way people think and feel about their place on earth; about what living well means, about what a rich life involves. The increasingly obvious crisis might help precipitate the needed change—in consciousness, policies, and behaviors—that many in the environmentalist milieu have been

promoting: spiritualities and ethics that value all life and recognize ecological interdependence. If the transition from crisis to sustainability is to
occur in the most humane possible way, it may be that the civil society
ENGOs will lead the way by modeling this transformation in consciousness and practices.

The quest for sustainability in a world characterized by multiple crises, most of which are exacerbated if not precipitated by environmental
decline, has the greatest chance when people remain open to rethinking
everything. To do this, strides must be made to include all points of view,
and then to integrate and hybridize them in the most intelligent fashion
possible. The genetic fallacy must be avoided: the value of an idea is
independent of the place it first took root, whether it is understood as
Western or otherwise.

It is difficult to reconsider long cherished assumptions and beliefs.
But this does not mean we must be cast adrift on seas of uncertainty. Although epistemological and ethical guideposts may be difficult to obtain,
given the diversity of perspectives around the world, we can find them.
There is, for example, a gold standard when it comes to sustainability
that can provide epistemological and ethical principles—and it comes
from nature herself. All organisms must properly seek to adapt to their
habitats if they are to flourish and survive. The ideas and practices that
should be retained are those that promote the resilience and fecundity
of ecosystems, and thus respect the evolutionary process and the life
prospects of all species. Other beliefs and practices should be jettisoned
through an ongoing pragmatic process of careful observation and the
testing of the resulting hypotheses.

In my view, this is a type of natural law—focused on natural processes
rather than immutable, static facts—that is compelling and defensible.[49]
This is a process to which civil society actors have made significant positive contributions. They will do so all the more effectively as they become
more reflexive about the process and the epistemological principles that
are best for arbitrating between competing perceptions, diagnoses, values,
and prescriptions. They will do so all the more easily when they recognize that the task now is to hybridize the best of human experience,
knowledge, and practice, without regard to where it first emerged.

Notes

1. I am grateful for Daniel Keeter (in Florida) and Leah Junge (in Kenya) for diverse
forms of research and logistical assistance during this research, and for financial
support from the Centre for Environment and Development at the University

of Oslo, the University of Florida's College of Liberal Arts and Sciences, and the Center for African Studies at the University of Florida. Events in Kenya are unfolding rapidly. I am also grateful to Junge as well as Drs. Celia Nyamweru and Koi Muchira-Tirima, for their insightful and helpful critiques. I am sure there are points where I have not been able to respond adequately to their suggestions, some due to space constraints, and others due to my limited expertise with regard to Kenya's complicated history. I nevertheless hope that my observations and reflections, which are informed by long observation of grassroots eco-social movements globally, will be of some value in thinking about the Kenyan context and the challenges facing people and other living things there.

2. Maathai died on 25 September 2011, well after this article was written in August and September of 2009 and was finalized after copy editing. The movement she founded was originally known as the "Kenya Green Belt Movement," but it expanded to support similar efforts in many African countries and so the name was shortened.

3. See, for example, Bron Taylor, *Ecological Resistance Movements: The Global Emergence of Radical and Popular Environmentalism* (Albany, N.Y.: State University of New York Press, 1995). Among the Greenbelt activists I spoke with were David Mutinda, Julius Githaiga, and Lydia Gathii. I also drew on conversations with many other people I met and talked with during the month-long visit. For two reasons I have elected not to quote individuals: (1) there is insufficient space for my contribution to this volume to quote from these interviews in a more ethnographic genre and (2) the political situation is fragile enough that, until I gain approval to quote specific passages from them, I will not do so, so as to not precipitate reprisals for their speaking freely with me. Even while revising this article in the spring of 2010, the Kenyan government had not moved to prosecute the offenders.

4. Of the books that led to the award perhaps the best exemplar is Selma Lagerlöf, *The Wonderful Adventures of Nils*, trans. Velma Swanston Howard (New York: Doubleday, Page & Company, 1907). For its influence on a contemporary photographer and naturalist, see Frans Lanting, *Eye to Eye: Intimate Encounters with the Animal World* (Köln, Germany: Taschen, 1997): 14–15; and further analysis in Bron Taylor, *Dark Green Religion: Nature Spirituality and the Planetary Future* (Berkeley, C.A.: University of California Press, 2010): 169. (See also the revealing praise in the award speech by Claes Annerstedt, *http://nobelprize.org/nobel_prizes/literature/laureates/1909/index.html.*)

5. Wangari Maathai, *Unbowed: A Memoir* (New York: Knopf, 2006): 96, 97.

6. See the United Nations Convention to Combat Desertification for a short biography, at *http://www.unccd.int/IYDD/documents/iydd_docs/WANGARIMAATHA ICV.pdf.*

7. Moi followed Jomo Kenyatta, who led the nation from independence.

8. Major funders have included the Rockefeller Brothers Foundation, the Gaia Foundation, many European government agencies, and other major funders. By 2004, the organization's budget exceeded two million U.S. dollars per year.

9. Although, as one Kenya specialist who read a draft of this article pointed out, Kenyan schools have taught about environmental degradation and conservation for many decades, this has not prevented the steady erosion of forest cover in Kenya since independence, and other forms of severe environmental degradation.

10. See *http://www.kenyaforestservice.org/*, for the text of the act, located at the Kenya Forest Service website.
11. Most of those I spoke with were urban, relatively well educated, and not a part of the perpetual, unemployed, underclass.
12. This perception was based on conversations Celia Nyamweru had with constituents in Maathai's district, which she related to me when reviewing a draft of this paper.
13. These figures are the ones typically reported in Kenyan news sources in 2009, as for example, in an article describing President Obama's pressure on Kenyan officials (and the Kenyan President's negative reaction to it) to move forward with anti-corruption efforts and prosecution of those responsible for political violence; see Anthony Kariuki, "Kibaki Protests Obama letters," (Kenya) *Nation*, 26 September 2009, online at *http://www.nation.co.ke/News/-/1056/663684/-/item/0/-/ochtdlz/-/index.html*
14. The court was created by a 1998 United Nations Treaty, which went into force in 2002 and is located at The Hague in the Netherlands; see *http://untreaty.un.org/cod/icc/index.html*.
15. Wangari Maathai, "Ending Impunity: Why I Support Special Tribunal," *Daily Nation* (Kenya), 6 September 2009, at *http://www.nation.co.ke/oped/Opinion/-/440808/653760/-/4nr3ae/-/index.html/*. The conclusion to this opinion well summarizes her argument and underscores how difficult it is to overturn decades of intertribal violence and build national unity: "The only effective deterrent is to call those who have committed the crimes to account. The rule of law must be restored. The special tribunal will help us get justice. It will encourage us to have confidence in our judicial system, believe in our country again, and develop the courage to deal with our own demons."
16. Donella Meadows, Jørgen Randers, and Dennis L. Meadows, *Limits to Growth: a Report for the Club of Rome's Project on the Predicament of Mankind* (New York: Universe, 1972).
17. Graham M. Turner, "A Comparison of the Limits to Growth with Thirty Years of Reality," in *Global Environmental Change*, vol. 18 (2008): 397–411. See also Donella Meadows, Jørgen Randers, and Dennis L. Meadows, *The Limits to Growth: The Thirty Year Update* (White River Junction, V.T.: Chelsea Green, 2004).
18. Thomas Homer-Dixon, "Across the Threshold: Empirical Evidence on Environmental Scarcities as Causes of Violent Conflict," *International Security* vol. 19, no. 1 (1994): 5–40; Thomas Homer-Dixon, "On the Threshold: Environmental Changes as Causes of Acute Conflict." *International Security* vol.16, no. 2 (1991): 76–116; Thomas Homer-Dixon and J. H. Boutwell, et al., "Environmental Change and Violent Conflict," *Scientific American* vol. 268, no. 2 (1993): 38–45; Thomas Homer-Dixon and J. Blitt, eds., *Ecoviolence: Links among Environment, Population, and Security*, (Lanham, M.D.: Roman & Littlefield, 1998). See also Robert D. Kaplan, *The Coming Anarchy: Shattering the Dreams of the Post–Cold War* (New York: Random House, 2000).
19. See the 2008 special technical report by the IPCC, "Climate Change and Water," *http://www.ipcc.ch/*, especially chapter two and its chart on p. 27, which focuses on precipitation, soil moisture, and runoff. This research indicates that East Africa is one of many places only now beginning a long period of protracted warming and drought.

20. For more on such religion and an argument that it is growing rapidly, increasingly influential, and may decisively and positively shape the future of religion and nature on earth, see Taylor, *Dark Green Religion.*

21. For the entire speech see: *http://nobelprize.org/nobel_prizes/peace/laureates/2004/maathai-lecture-text.html*

22. The extended quotes beginning here are among the most revealing of Maathai's views of the cultural dimensions of her work and how she positions it against the West. I first found this article, entitled "Nature, Nurture, and Culture," at AlterNet's environmental news website, *http://www.alternet.org/story/20492*, with the subtitle, "A Nobel Peace Laureate Says Cultural Revival May be the Only Thing that Stands between the Conservation or Destruction of the Environment" (which I put in italics for emphasis). The GBM posted the article on its own website with a different title, "The Cracked Mirror" on 11 November 2004; see *http://www.greenbeltmovement.org/a.php?id=28*. Both places attribute the article to the spiritual-environmentalist magazine *Resurgence, http://www.resurgence.org/*, although in 2009 I could not locate the article on its website.

23. Traditional peoples, in this way of thinking, are those on the periphery of the global market system or who, at least, have not been entirely overwhelmed by it and subsumed into it. Key sources include Fikret Berkes, *Sacred Ecology: Traditional Ecological Knowledge and Resource Management* (New York, Routledge, (2008 [1999]). Gerrardo Reichel-Dolmatoff, "Cosmology as Ecological Analysis: A View from the Rainforest," *Man* vol. 2, no. 3, (1976): 307–18. Roy Ellen, Peter Parkes, and Alan Bicker, eds., *Indigenous Environmental Knowledge and its Transformations* (Amsterdam: Harwood Academic Publishers, 2000). Stephen S. Lansing, *Priests and Programmers: Technologies of Power in the Engineered Landscape of Bali* (Princeton, N.J.: Princeton University Press (1991); Gerrardo Reichel-Dolmatoff, *Amazonian Cosmos* (Chicago, I.L.: University of Chicago Press, 1971); R. E. Schultes, "Reasons for Ethnobotanical Conservation," in *Traditional Ecological Knowledge: A Collection of Essays*, ed. R.E. Johannes, (Geneva: International Union for the Conservation of Nature, 1989).

24. For example, UNESCO, *Man belongs to the Earth: International Cooperation in Environmental Research* (Paris: UNESCO-MAB 1988); Darrell A. Posey, *Cultural and Spiritual Values of Biodiversity* (Nairobi, Kenya: United Nations Environmental Programme, 1999).

25. Also in our conversation was Gathuru Mburu, who later wrote in a similar way, see Gathuru Mburu, "Kenya Greenbelt Movement," in *Encyclopedia of Religion and Nature*, ed. Bron Taylor (London and New York: Continuum International, 2005). See also the interview, "Agriculture-Africa: Bring Back a Culture of Sharing; Terna Gyuse Interviews Gathuru Mburu, Coordinator of the African Biodiversity Network," *Interpress News Service*, 3 March 2009, *http://ipsnews.net/africa/nota.asp?idnews=46015*

26. Also worth noting, Tiango spoke in a way similar to that of other activists at a "Decade of Commitment" session held earlier at People's Earth Summit, a conclave of grassroots environmental, anti-poverty, human rights, and anti-globalization campaigners, who had gathered near the UN Summit in order to put pressure on those politicians to respond aggressively to the environmental crisis and all the ways in which it contributes to human misery and social injustices. Excerpts from this interview are now available at *www.brontaylor.com*, and under the supple-

mentary materials for Chapter 8, in Taylor, *Dark Green Religion*. For more about the People's Earth Summit, see pp. 182–88.

27. In the final paragraphs of her reflection, Maathi focused on the positive, "Of course, no one culture is applicable to all human beings who wish to retain their self-respect and dignity; none can satisfy all communities."

28. Maathai, "Nature, Nurture, and Culture."

29. Background and quotes in this paragraph about female genital mutilation are from Ochieng' Ogodo, "FGM in Kenya: Outlawed, Not Eradicated," *WeNews* (Women's ENews), 2 August 2005, *http://www.womensenews.org/article.cfm/dyn/aid/2177*.

30. When commenting on the practice when reading the manuscript, Dr. Koi Muchira-Tirima argued that the persistence of the practice is in part because most policies banning the practice "did not provide room for the social/cultural training" that takes place during the process surrounding the rite. The lack of an alternative rite of passage, she seemed to be suggesting, accounts for some of the resistance to change. Interestingly, some young Maasai I spoke with in July 2009 at a village near Masi Mara National Park, well understood this. Although their culture had long practiced the genital cutting that Maathai condemned, some of those (with external education and encounters), are now are seeking to convince their elders to eliminate the practice and to develop alternative rites of passage to adulthood. This approach could apply to other environmental practices that today need to be left behind, such as lion killing as a rite of passage to manhood, which is soon discussed in text.

31. Maathai, "Nature, Nurture, and Culture." In this, Maathai was likely influenced by Thiongo Ngugi Wa, *Decolonising the Mind* (London: Heinemann, 1986).

32. Theodore Natsoulas, "The Politicization of the Ban of Female Circumcision and the Rise of the Independent School Movement in Kenya. The KCA, the Missions, and Government, 1929–1932," *Journal of African Studies* vol. 33, no. 2 (1998): 137–158.

33. See Daisy Sindelar, "World: Africa's First Female Nobel Peace Laureate Accepts Award amid Controversy Over AIDS Remarks," Radio Free Europe/Liberty (online, 10 December 2004), *http://www.rferl.org/articleprintview/1056339.html*.

34. See, for example, Michael Worobey, et al., "Direct Evidence of Extensive Diversity of HIV-1 in Kinshasa by 1960," *Nature* vol. 455, 2 October 2008: 661–664, DOI:10.1038/nature07390; Brandon F. Keele, et al., "Chimpanzee Reservoirs of Pandemic and Nonpandemic HIV-1," *Science* vol. 313, 28 July 2006: 523–526, DOI: 10.1126/science.1126531; and the earlier studies Tuofu. Zhu, et al., "An African HIV-1 Sequence from 1959 and Implications for the Origin of the Epidemic," *Nature* vol. 391, 5 February 1998: 594–597, DOI:10.1038/nature35400; Bette Korber, et al., "Timing the Ancestor of the HIV-1 Pandemic Strains," *Science* vol. 288, 9 June 2000: 1789–1796, DOI:10.1126/science.288.5472.1789.

35. See "10 Questions: Wangari Maathai," Sunday, 10 October 2004, *Time Magazine*, at *http://www.time.com/time/magazine/article/0,9171,901041018-713166,00.html*. AIDS-related conspiracy theories are alive and well on the Internet; for a journalistic overview and example, see "AIDS Conspiracy" at *SourceWatch*, *http://www.sourcewatch.org/index.php?title=AIDS_conspiracy*.

36. Many conspiracy theorists specifically blame pentagon biowarfare specialists for the disease, a view that may have been propagated by Soviet propagandists, but

for which no credible evidence has emerged. An Internet search reveals a wide variety of speculation about devilish Western plots leading to HIV/AIDS.

37. This is highly ironic since, as Dr. Koi Muchira-Tirima noted in her comments to this manuscript, as the world shrinks through globalization processes, "the distinction between western and non-western is becoming blurred and harder to identify."

38. That the Maasai lost land to the Kikuyu on independence I learned from Celia Nyamweru.

39. See the 2008 special technical report by the IPCC, "Climate Change and Water," *http://www.ipcc.ch/*.

40. CBS *60 minutes*, "Poison Takes Toll on Africa's Lions."

41. Such approaches can be found where indigenous peoples are involved in co-management of ecosystems with scientists and government land managers. The possibilities are exemplified by the notion of integrative adaptive management, wherein western scientists work hand in hand with local people to fuse knowledges in the quest for sustainable livelihoods. See, for example, Lance Gunderson, and C. S. Holling, *Panarchy: Understanding Transformations in Systems of Humans and Nature* (Covelo, C.A.: Island Press, 2002). Also in this vein is Berkes, *Sacred Ecology.*

42. Without an evolutionary/ecological worldview it is much easier to maintain the fiction that *Homo sapiens* are not subject to nature's laws and thus, that there are no carrying capacity limits to the their numbers. Peter M. Vitousek, Jane L. Mooney, and Jerry M. Melillo, "Human Domination of Ecosystems," *Science* vol. 277 no. 5325, (1997): 494–499; Peter M. Vitousek, Paul R. Ehrlich, Anne H. Ehrlich, and Pamela A. Matson, "Human Appropriation of the Products of Photosynthesis," *Bioscience* vol. 36, (1986): 368–73.

43. Critically important texts include: William Catton, *Overshoot: The Ecological Basis of Revolutionary Change* (Urbana and Chicago I.L.: University of Illinois Press, 1980); Garrett Hardin, *Living within Limits* (New York: Oxford University Press, 1993); Jared Diamond, *Collapse: How Societies Choose to Fail or Succeed* (New York: Viking, 2005). See also Mathais Wackernagel, et al., "Tracking the Ecological Overshoot of the Human Economy," *Proc Natl Acad Sci* vol. 99, no. 14, (2002): 9266–9271. Wakernagel is a leading scholar promoting what is known as ecological footprint analysis, which has an accessible website, *http://www.foot printnetwork.org/en/index.php/GFN/page/world_footprint/*. As put simply there:
    "Today humanity uses the equivalent of 1.3 planets to provide the resources we use and absorb our waste. This means it now takes the Earth one year and four months to regenerate what we use in a year. Moderate UN scenarios suggest that if current population and consumption trends continue, by the mid 2030s we will need the equivalent of two Earths to support us. And of course, we only have one. Turning resources into waste faster than waste can be turned back into resources puts us in global ecological overshoot, depleting the very resources on which human life and biodiversity depend."
    It may be true that population growth need not lead to deforestation, as argued by Paul E. Waggoner and Jesse H. Ausubel, in "How Much Will Feeding More and Wealthier People Encroach on Forests?" *Population and Development Review* vol. 27, no. 2, (2001): 239–257. They accurately note that forests have expanded in many countries simultaneously with population increases, in part because of im-

proved crop yields. They conclude that with best practices up to a third of today's cropland could revert to forest. Although true, as is so often the case with technological improvements, this would at most only halt or delay deforestation, while the human population grows, fueled by the calories from the touted innovation.

44. Garrett Hardin, *Stalking the Wild Taboo,* third ed. (Petoskey, M.I.: Social Contract Press 1996); David Nicholson-Lord, "The Silence of the Greens: Why Do Environmentalists Choose to Ignore the Undeniable Connections between the Food Crisis and Over-population of the Human Species?" *Resurgence* (2008) *http://www.resurgence.org/magazine/article2651-The-Silence-of-the-Greens.html.*

45. Another comment from Dr. Koi Muchira-Tirima helps to make my case: "I don't understand what this idea is as you have described it, or why you are so surprised by this belief. It seems to me like best practices are always being developed and implemented in all fields. What is so utopian about finding a good way of doing something and implementing it?" It is, of course, good to spread and keep refining "best practices" in all fields. But my point was that to *expect* widespread success of the kind of social engineering that the Kenyan officials were assuming was possible is not a rational expectation, given the weight of evidence. At best, even when some people have a good idea of what best practices are, these are rarely perfectly implemented. I think the reviewer's comment was grounded in an imprudent and unfounded optimism about human beings accurately accessing and ameliorating environment-related risks.

46. Vitousek, Mooney, and Melillo, "Human Domination of Ecosystems," 494–499; Vitousek, Ehrlich, Ehrlich, and Matson, "Human Appropriation of the Products of Photosynthesis," 368–73.

47. In 2009, UNICEF estimated Kenya's population at 37.538 million, see *http://data.un.org/Data.aspx?q=kenya+population&d=SOWC&f=inID percent3a105 per cent3bcrID percent3a75,* while the U.S.'s Central Intelligence Agency estimated 39,002,772. The CIA also estimated annual population growth rate at 2.8 percent (24th highest in the world), and the fertility rate at 4.56 children born per woman (38th highest) of 224 countries analyzed; *see https://www.cia.gov/library/publications/the-world-factbook/rankorder/2054rank.html?countryName=Kenya& countryCode=ke&regionCode=af&rank=31#ke.* Kenya is surrounded by countries with some of the highest rates of birth and population growth in the world, which provides its populations, and that of the nearby countries, no place to go as ecosystems become more stressed. Meanwhile, United Nations data estimated that in 2004, 30 percent of the Kenyan population was undernourished, a figure that was no doubt higher by 2009; see *http://data.un.org/Data.aspx?q =kenya+population&d=MDG&f=seriesRowID percent3a566 percent3bcountryID percent3a404.* The UN's latest, posted growth rate for Kenya, 3.9 percent, is also from 2004, see *http://data.un.org/Data.aspx?q=kenya+population&d=SOW C&f=inID percent3a78 percent3bcrID percent3a75.* Another daunting projection is that Kenya's population will rise to 51,261,167 by 2025 and 65,175,864 by 2050. Even potentially worse if one compares the high versus the low variants in the United Nations table provided at: *http://data.un.org/Data.aspx?q=kenya+po pulation&d=PopDiv&f=variableID percent3a12 percent3bcrID percent3a404.* With ecosystems already strained, these projections appear cataclysmic in a country already characterized by high unemployment and over 30 percent of the population undernourished.

48. For examples see Taylor, *Ecological Resistance Movements*.
49. Most helpful in this respect is H.L.A. Hart, *The Concept of Law* (Oxford: Claren-
    don, 1961). I began developing my thoughts on natural law in Bron Taylor, "On
    Sacred or Secular Ground? Callicott and Environmental Ethics," *Worldviews* vol.
    1, no. 2, (1997): 99–112.

Chapter 8

A NEW DIRECTION IN TRANSNATIONAL CIVIL SOCIETY
THE POLITICS OF MUSLIM NGO COALITIONS

Zeynep Atalay

Introduction

In recent decades, civil society has been one of the most debated concepts within and across various academic disciplines. Its capacity and political functions, as well as its normative values, have stimulated much research and debate in both academic and political fields. John Keane's article on emerging "monitory democracy"—the centerpiece of this volume—considers civil society to play a significant role in the post–Westphalian era of global politics. Keane argues that civil society, today, has become a power-scrutinizing mechanism, "by putting politicians, parties, and elected governments permanently on their toes, complicating their lives, questioning their authority, and forcing them to change their agendas."[1] As an institution of monitory democracy, civil society enforces public standards and ethical rules for preventing corruption, and strengthens the diversity and influence of citizens' voices and choices in decisions that affect their lives. Located outside the domain of the state and the market, Keane's civil society restrains state power by keeping its operations in check. It safeguards individual freedom and constitutes a counterforce against the state, which holds, "a potential for domination, intervention, regulation, collectivism, and positive law imposed arbitrarily from above."[2]

Civil society has become a blanket term for an array of organizations and networks including economic, informational, professional, developmental, issue-oriented, and civil associations. The vast diversity within civil society is customarily grouped under two categories: service- and advocacy-oriented civil society. The former is associated with humanitarian, social aid, charity, and philanthropic organizations and networks that provide education, housing, health services, and material goods to populations in need. The latter refers to professional think tank type groups dedicated to causes such as human rights, minority issues, women's issues, environmental protection, and civic education. This classification considers the "service" strand neutral and impartial, and therefore non-political, while the "advocacy" strand is granted the political potency to develop and consolidate democracy. It is the political advocacy and contestation function of the latter that pushes civil society to the forefront of Keane's thinking about monitory democracy.

This chapter argues that the dynamics between the "service" and "advocacy" functions of civil society are far more complex than much of the civil society literature readily suggests, and calls for a more contextualized approach to the understanding of the political role of diverse groups within civil society. It should be noted that there are overlaps between the service and advocacy organizations even in contexts where civil society has carved out autonomous spaces for themselves. In order to better understand the dynamic between civil society and democracy, researchers should carefully examine the ways in which humanitarian and service organizations function as political agents.

The current formation of civil society networks and alliances in the self-labeled Muslim World is a noteworthy example. The state surveillance and legal restrictions in the majority of Islamic states, especially the Gulf region, define the limits of civic engagement. Although some researchers call attention to the political transition that some Arab countries have been undergoing, paths to free debate and dissent remain blocked in others. In most Muslim countries, non-governmental organizations are constrained by law, political authorities control the media, and human rights violations continue. The constricted space for civil engagement in these countries obliges organizations to claim political neutrality. Most organizations claim to operate in "harmless" areas of social aid and humanitarianism such as human relief, health care, and religious education.

For theorists of the NGO field, such humanitarian organizations constitute the first generation in the evolution of NGOs from "service" to "advocacy."[3] According to David Korten's typology, NGOs start out as welfare organizations that provide immediate relief to humanitarian emergencies and do not overtly engage in political advocacy work.[4] The first generation of NGOs continue on the path towards the second generation small-scale, self-reliant, local development projects, followed by the third generation strategies of creating policies or institutional settings that facilitate sustainable development. Only in the fourth stage do NGOs shift their efforts from specific policies and institutional sub-systems to mobilizing collective action towards social and political change.

This chapter takes the Union of the NGOs of the Islamic World (UNIW) as its case and analyzes how its 185 member NGOs sidestep the linear evolution from charities to political agents described in this typology and devise an alternative route for political action. Rather than positioning themselves as political agents vis-à-vis the state, these organizations limit their local work to service provision. Yet, they form coalitions and perform political advocacy on a global level as a collective monitory agent. In other words, as individual local NGOs, they bypass national politics and act on global politics as a Muslim NGO coalition. They transform local faith-based activism into global monitory agency.

In order to trace service oriented organizations' trajectory towards global monitory agency, I will first introduce the UNIW and sketch out the perspectives and issues of its member NGOs in major activity areas. In this introductory section, I focus on how these organizations employ religion as a source of motivation and a vehicle of engagement by integrating religious norms with the discourse of civil society. In the remainder of the chapter, I discuss the ways in which these organizations join forces to consolidate the Muslim civil society sphere as a global coalition, raise political awareness, and promote advocacy on issues such as Islamophobia, discrimination against Muslim minorities, and the Palestinian problem.

Data and Methods

The data for the study comes from the analysis of documents published by UNIW and its member organizations; 52 semi-structured, in-depth interviews in Turkey, Germany, and the U.S.; and participant observation of internal meetings of UNIW in Malaysia, and of its field operations in Cambodia.

Published material—including periodicals; press releases; bulletins; brochures; mission statements; and reports that address the activities, projects, and opinions of UNIW and its members—has been an essential part of the research since the circulation of most written material is limited to the members of the NGOs. Such material reveals insider information that might otherwise be brushed aside or remain undisclosed in interviews with an outsider researcher. At the same time, face-to-face interviews and participant observation presented the most critical data for this research. My lack of personal connections with any religious network and my affiliation with an American university initially raised questions and concerns among interview subjects. Furthermore, being a female researcher occasionally brought about discomfort in all-male conservative settings. Nevertheless, my preliminary interviews with UNIW executives between 2007 and 2008 allowed me to establish a relation of trust over the years and facilitated my contact and communication with representatives of member NGOs.

Between June 2008 and May 2010, I conducted a total of 52 interviews with people including UNIW's secretary general, executive council members, and representatives of member NGOs from 28 different countries. The majority of the interviewees had university degrees and came from middle to upper-middle class backgrounds in their countries. The age of the interviewees ranged from 19 to 62, with a median of 42. The younger interviewees were in the lower positions in the organizational hierarchy. Tenure of interviewees in their organizations ranged from one to 18 years. Of the 52 interviewees, only 18 were women who were the representatives of either women's organizations or the women's branches of larger organizations.

In May 2010, I was invited to attend and observe UNIW's 9th Council Meeting in Malaysia and its subsequent field work in Cambodia. UNIW's council meetings are periodical summits intended for member NGOs to convene, review projects and activities of the previous year, and discuss new business. Many of the UNIW's members participated in the meeting, which involved presentations by spokespeople, open discussions about issues and projects, and decision-making sessions for further action. Throughout these meetings, I had the opportunity to observe the ideological and operational heterogeneity across the member base of the UNIW.

UNIW's council meetings are held in a different country each time and a select delegation from the meeting travels to a neighboring country to visit other members and provide support. In the days following the council meeting in Malaysia, the UNIW delegation traveled to Cambodia. During their stay, the delegation visited the Cambodian Muslim Intellectual Alliance in Phnom Penh, had a meeting with the Cambodian Secretary of State, and visited a Muslim village 50 km out of Phnom Penh to observe the living conditions of Muslim communities in Cambodia. I had the rare opportunity to shadow the UNIW delegation for the duration of their stay in Malaysia and Cambodia, and to observe the decision-making, agenda setting, strategy building, and networking processes of the organization in action.

Background

The Civil Society and Islam debate

The concept of civil society is associated with Enlightenment ideals, individualism, and the existence of autonomous institutions. It is conceptualized as a formation whose prerequisites are derived from Western political and historical conditions. The essential prerequisites of civil society are widely believed to include neoliberal economic programs, independent and self-autonomous individuals and political groups, vertical organization between state and society, a legal bureaucratic system that acknowledges public debate and association, and participatory democracy of Western political traditions. In other words, in prevailing scholarly literature, civil society is associated with "what the West has." The logical conclusion of this assumption is that the existence of civil society and its institutional arrangements in non-Western, specifically Islamic, contexts are problematic, if not impossible.

In fact, an array of Orientalist scholars has vigorously argued that the very existence of civil societies in Muslim contexts is an oxymoron. For William Watt, the totalistic characteristic of Islam requires a totalitarian state that is hostile to the emergence of a functioning civil society.[5] According to John Hall, Islam as a religion is essentially "monotheism with a tribal face" that blocks the development of a true civil society and democracy.[6] Patricia Crone argues that Islamic civilization refuses to legitimize political authority.[7] Islam, according to this perspective, discourages the formation of groups that might resist despotism since "Islamic law knows no corporate legal persons; Islamic history shows no councils or communes, no synods or parliaments, nor any other kind of elective or representative assembly."[8] As a consequence, Robert Springborg argues, social associations in Muslim societies are "informal, personalistic, and relatively inefficient as a means of winning support and extracting resources from the populace."[9] The most influential scholar of this perspective, Ernest Gellner, argues that civil society cannot arise in Muslim societies because Islam is unique among the major world civilizations and religions in terms of its immunity to secularization.[10] Islam "exemplifies a social order which seems to lack much capacity to provide political countervailing institutions or associations, which is atomized without much individualism, and which operates effectively without intellectual pluralism."[11]

In response to the literature's stance on the incompatibility of Islam and civil society, alternative voices have started to raise their criticisms.[12] One strand of the alternative scholarship points to the civil nature of institutions such as guilds, bazaars, associations, trusts, and foundations in Islamic history and argues that these are the possible equivalents of civil society in pre-modern Arab and Middle Eastern cities.[13] The proponents of this argument state that despite the absence of bureaucratic organizational models and individual autonomy, these institutions provided a counterbalance to the power of the state and enjoyed a significant degree of autonomy from the state, thus fulfilling civil society's raison d'être.[14]

Another strand of literature that studies contemporary civil action in Muslim societies suggests that informal networks serve as functional civil societies in these contexts. These analyses apply social movements theory to Islamist movements[15] and argue that in the repressive political climates of most Muslim states, informal sectors of social networks and personal ties serve as viable civil societies.[16] Civic activism, according to this perspective, should not only be sought in the formal political structures of political parties, legal institutions, and bureaucratic NGOs, but also, and primarily, in the politics of daily life.[17] In this framework, spheres that are typically left out of civil society discussions—such as familial ties and networks,[18] daily struggles of squatters, the unemployed, and street-vendors[19]—are all located within the boundaries of politics.

Proliferation of NGOs in the Muslim World

The longstanding debate on the compatibility of Islam and civil society notwithstanding, associational life has a long history in Muslim societies. Trusts and foundations funded by philanthropic endowments have served as humanitarian organizations for centuries. Social networks of religious communities and personal ties have functioned as vivid, informal civil societies within communities.

In the 1980s and 1990s, however, during the Russian invasion of Afghanistan and the War in Bosnia, civic action in the Muslim World underwent a major transformation. The previously informal religious communities started mobilizing within the framework of formal non-governmental organizations. During this period, the number of humanitarian Muslim NGOs increased rapidly as Muslim countries and communities around the world came together to provide humanitarian relief to Afghans under invasion. Yet, the major turning point for Muslim NGOs was the War in Bosnia. In 1992–1993, NGOs from all over the Muslim world mushroomed in an effort to provide aid and raise awareness about the Bosnian situation. Today, most Muslim humanitarian NGOs trace their origins to mostly amateur field work in Bosnia in the early 1990s. The Bosnian case came to be the training ground for organizations to acquire the skills and proficiency that were extended to other areas in the years to come.

Political and economic dynamics also have a direct influence on the increasing number of NGOs in Muslim countries, specifically in the Middle East. The implementations of structural adjustment policies and neoliberal economic programs have resulted in massive migration to urban centers that were not equipped to serve the unprecedented needs of such populations. Local and national governments' inability to provide services such as housing, healthcare, and food subsidies has led NGOs to fill the vacuum.[20] Islamic medical clinics in Egypt are one of the most successful examples of Islamic grassroots social-welfare activities. Located in or beside mosques throughout the city of Cairo, these clinics provide millions of people with "an intermediate form of healthcare between the expensive private hospitals and the government's often inadequate services." [21] In countries such as Iraq, Lebanon, Palestine, and Sudan, where states are absent or in crisis, NGOs provide almost all social services. In Palestine, for instance, NGOs provide up to 60 percent of primary health care services; nearly 50 percent of hospital care; 100 percent of disability care; 100 percent of all agricultural extension, training and research; and 30 percent of educational services.[22]

Until recently, however, the majority of Muslim NGOs worked in isolation, relying on their own funding, skills, information networks, and human capacity. The dispersed nature of civil society in the larger Muslim world has been especially challenging for the small organizations that work on a local scale and suffer from lack of credibility and legitimacy with their national governments. However, since the mid-2000s, the face of civil society in the Muslim world has taken a striking turn. Not only are extant civil initiatives transforming into formal NGOs at an unprecedented rate, but they are also joining forces and forming coalitions to speak with one voice and devise common plans of action and agendas.

The Union of the NGOs of the Islamic World, established in 2005, is the first and largest NGO coalition to bring together a large number of Muslim NGOs around issues that concern specifically Muslim communities around the world. As of September 2010, UNIW's membership has reached 185 NGOs from 43 countries in the world. Even though UNIW's mission statement, which aspires to achieve "sustainable progress; an environment of justice, peace, and stability; fundamental rights and freedoms; and a strong civil society through collaborative economic and social activities" is similar to that of many civil society initiatives, its members distinguish themselves by orienting their projects towards the Islamic world. As a coalition of Muslim faith-based NGOs, UNIW aims to consolidate unity across Muslim populations around the world and to establish a common, cohesive voice in global civil society.

Faith-based Humanitarianism and Social Aid

Today, UNIW demonstrates significant diversity in geographical distribution, areas of work, membership size, funding sources, and political influence. There are international relief organizations, local organizations, and youth and alumni associations within its composition.[23] What brings such a wide array of organizations together is their self-definition as faith-based organizations and their shared concerns over the Muslim world. Faith-based or religious NGOs are formal organizations whose identity and mission are self-consciously derived from the teachings of one or more religious or spiritual traditions.[24] Although religious NGOs carry out projects in diverse activity areas, they share defining characteristics such as being affiliated with religious bodies, having mission statements with explicit references to theology, acquiring financial support from religious sources, or basing decision making processes on religious values.[25]

All members of the UNIW have: (1) mission statements that explicitly identify Islamic doctrine or tradition as the ideological framework, (2) agendas that focus on the mobilization of Muslim populations, (3) activities that aim to disseminate theological information and (4) activities that are exclusively aimed at Muslim persons or groups.[26]

Although the extent to which religious faith is reflected in the activities and projects of Muslim organizations varies, the focus remains almost exclusively on implementing projects in and providing services to areas with a strong Islamic presence. The humanitarian NGOs of the coalition are concerned about poverty and its effects: hunger, malnutrition, lack of access to safe potable water, illiteracy, lack of access to health service, social isolation, and exploitation. Those who work with families and children call attention to threats to traditional family structure and the increase in drug abuse in Muslim societies. Human rights NGOs emphasize the discrimination against Muslim minorities in Southeast and Central Asia as well as Europe and North America.

Humanitarian and Social Aid

In the international humanitarian aid system, faith-based organizations are increasingly recognized and have become significant actors in the Muslim world. Although faith-based and secular humanitarian NGOs reveal many similarities in terms of the projects and conditions they deal with, faith-based NGOs distinguish themselves through their discourse. Whereas secular NGOs employ a rights-based language in their actions, faith-based NGOs routinely invoke a language of religious duty and obligation when explaining individual civic action. For the members of Islamic NGOs, civil society is not a liberal category framed by a language of rights, but refers to a morally loaded category framed by the duty-oriented language of religion.[27] The notion of *hizmet* (service to God and humanity) pertains to religious duty in assistance to fellow Muslims in particular and to humanity in general. To perform such a duty in the form of humanitarian action "is a way of receiving help from heaven, of erasing sins, and of meriting paradise."[28] One informant states: "In Islam there is a strong tradition of foundations. For centuries people established foundations, small or large, to provide help in all kinds of issues. The culture of Islam encourages that. People know that if they do a good deed in this world, they will be rewarded in the afterworld. This is what nourishes civil society today. It is not a hobby for us. It is about being human, being a Muslim, being concerned about the afterlife."[29]

Some of the projects adopted across the board are urgent food aid programs, orphan care programs, shelter and clothing programs, vocational training programs, and assistance in drilling wells and canals in areas with water shortage. Each of these projects has their roots in Islamic theology, as they are explicitly encouraged in the Qur'an and *hadiths*.[30]

Food aid programs are omnipresent in the world of Muslim NGOs, especially during the Muslim holidays of Ramadan and Eid-ul-Alha. Local and international organizations establish mobile and temporary soup kitchens, food deliveries to the crisis regions, fast-breaking dinner organizations during Ramadan, and arrangements for animal sacrifices and meat deliveries for Muslim families around the world during the Feast of Sacrifice. Meat deliveries and animal sacrifices are powerful projects for Muslim NGOs as they are a religious obligation in Islam. Muslim NGOs emphasize the significance of this practice in their calls for donors by arguing that it is imperative for any Muslim to share his or her fortune with the poor by donating money for animal sacrifices around the world. One NGO arranges animal sacrifices in over a hundred countries within the four days of Eid-ul-Alha. Another one does so in forty-five countries during the same days. These countries include almost all Muslim countries in addition to Muslim communities in Europe, North America, Latin America, East Asia, and even Oceania.

Similarly, projects that provide safe and clean water have a particular resonance among Muslims. Most humanitarian organizations run projects to provide clean water and sanitation to water shortage areas in Africa and Southeast Asia. Water and sanitation services are typical projects for both faith-based and non-faith based organizations. The common objectives of these projects are to limit hygiene related deaths and preventable diseases, to decrease the daily burden of carrying water, and consequently, to improve girls' chances of getting an education or women's prospects of keeping jobs. Another objective is to decrease the cost of obtaining an unpredictable supply of water.

For Muslim religious organizations, having or providing access to water is a religious duty mandated by the teachings. Water is a necessary element of Muslim purification rituals, most commonly those performed before prayer.

Additionally, according to the Muslim beliefs and practices, "one who founds a public fountain on Earth for the poor or passers-by is promised relief in the afterworld."[31] WEFA (Weltweiter Einsatz für Arme), a humanitarian organization based in Cologne, Germany, collects donations to drill wells in areas with water shortages such as Bangladesh, Burkina Faso, Nigeria, Sierra Leone, and Chad. The project advertises that "for 110 Euros a donor can sponsor a surface, hand operated well in his/her name or the name of a deceased family member in Bangladesh."[32]

Most Muslim humanitarian NGOs under UNIW employ the long-term development-oriented jargon emblematic of development NGOs in the West. The International Islamic Charitable Organization of Kuwait, for instance, has the mission of "providing global and humanitarian aid, aiming and assisting the poor communities and helping them develop their resources in the most efficient ways so that they become self-sufficient [*sic*]."[33] However, the focus of most Muslim humanitarian organizations outside the UNIW remains short-term and charity-oriented. Easily implemented charity-oriented projects which provide services in the form of material or financial aid and health services are favored over the longer-term projects oriented towards the achievement of social and economic rights, self-sustainability, and the elimination of the root causes of poverty. The majority of longer-term projects are in the healthcare field. In collaboration with state agencies and transnational humanitarian networks, NGOs build health facilities, set up mobile clinics, medical buses, permanent hospitals, and temporary tent hospitals; deliver medication and medical equipment aid; and provide health services such as health screenings, voluntary health personnel, and cataract surgeries.

Family, Women, and Children

As the foundation of the Islamic sociocultural structure and the fundamental social unit, the family institution is central to Islamic social order. It reproduces and disseminates codes of social morality, transmits Islamic values through generations, prevents illicit sexual activity, secures a peaceful emotional and psychological atmosphere for men and women, tightens the bond between generations, and ensures the expansion of the *Umma*, or the global Muslim community.

Marriage is not only encouraged in the Qur'an, but also considered a duty for a man who has the means to pay the dowry and to support a wife and children.[34] The Qur'an explains in detail the structure and function of the family, principles of choosing a spouse, conditions of marriage and financial maintenance of the household, conditions of divorce or dissolution of marriage, rules of child support and custody, and rules for remarriage. In the same vein, any obstacle, such as exorbitant dowries or economic injustice, should be combated in defense of family and marriage institutions.[35]

Member NGOs of the UNIW are mainly concerned about the delayed marriage age, reduction in birth rate, rising divorce rate, dissolution of ties across generations, and increasing isolation of the nuclear family in metropolitan areas due to the pressures of liberal capitalist globalization and "westoxification." For concerned NGO leaders, such trends lead younger generations to be fascinated by prevailing attitudes of consumerism, remaining ungrounded in their own traditions, and unaware of the possibility of a culturally rich Islamic life.

In order to keep young generations closely connected to the community, UNIW's members provide extra venues of socialization and moral education for children and teenagers. Several member NGOs that focus on women, family, and children offer day care facilities for younger children, as well as organizing picnics, art and culture trips, movie hours, book clubs, tea times, and sports events for teenagers. The main objective of these activities is to help generate a peer group for children and young adults within the community, and "to encourage them to socialize with kids from the neighborhood rather than random ones they meet at Internet cafes or arcades."[36]

UNIW's members uniformly value the survival of the family institution in Muslim societies and agree on women's vital role in keeping marriages and families intact. Some NGOs organize projects to educate marriage-age and newly-married women about the role and responsibilities of spouses, as well as the keys to managing a successful marriage. Erdem-Der, a member NGO based in Istanbul, Turkey, has held a nine-week long seminar series every year for single young women titled "Is Your Dowry Ready?" In the program director's words: "We use dowry as a pun to get attention. We teach young women skills and information that will be useful their entire married life. We know of so many couples that stay engaged for years and divorce in the first six months of the marriage. We have to do our part to stop marriages from dissolving at this rate."[37] The seminar topics include home economics, interior decoration, skin care, makeup, and wardrobe as well as religious education, conditions of an Islamic marriage, and constructive communication methods between spouses.

NGOs that work on women and family uphold the mothers' role as the essential building block of the Islamic family structure and the guardian of its moral order.[38] The woman's position as mother is highly praised, since raising virtuous and morally grounded children for the future of the individual family, the community, and the *Umma* is considered the most rewarding task. Therefore, motherhood transcends the private sphere of the family and enters the civil sphere of Muslim society, reinforced with the legitimacy of social responsibility. One NGO member expressed her concerns about the devalued role of motherhood in modern society: "Motherhood is more important than being a high-level executive; you are raising a person. But it is not valued as much anymore and that is very dangerous. After all, the hand that rocks the cradle runs the world."[39] Regardless of their particular areas of activity, most Muslim NGOs share concerns and develop projects for the well-being of the family structure in their societies. Since the survival of the family and its moral values is one of the key priorities of Muslim organizations, most members of the UNIW offer assistance to families in crisis. Marriage counseling, reproductive health assistance, financial support, and vocational training are some of the wide-ranging programs offered by the organizations to local communities.

Religious Education

Muslim NGOs that work in the field of education are responding to UNIW's concerns about the dissolution of Islamic values and the dispersion of the *Umma*. In countries where the state does not provide religious or Islamic education, NGOs take it upon themselves to offer Qur'anic and moral education courses to local communities. Most of these courses are designed for children of primary school age. The common curriculum in these courses emphasizes Islamic studies and a greater understanding of Islamic principles governing the day-to-day lives of Muslims. The Qur'an, Islamic law (*fiqh*), the Prophet's sayings (*hadith*) and traditions (*sunna*), and interpretation of the Qur'an (*tafseer*) constitute the majority of curricula.

Educational projects devised for students of high-school and college age are mostly limited to providing financial assistance in the form of scholarships. NGOs that fund students from modest backgrounds are not limited to the organizations that work in the educational field. Various NGOs act as bridges between private donors and students in need. Although some NGOs do not seek to establish personal relationships with the students, most organizations involve students in their events in order to create a community. They frequently pay home visits to students; hold community events such as picnics, dinners, and seminars; and establish connections with similar organizations. In that sense, educational scholarships serve as a means to form strong links with the students and the local communities.

Promoting the Umma ideal

For the founders of UNIW and its member NGOs, the religious duty of serving humanity surpasses the national boundaries of states and requires them to serve the Islamic world in general. This term is not a geographical definition. The "Islamic world" is defined in relation to *Umma*, which is no longer restricted to national borders because of the migratory flows of Muslims all around the globe. Therefore, the founders maintain that they are concerned about the troubles of each Muslim wherever in the world he or she may be.

The rhetoric of *Umma* in Islamic movements is not a recent one. Having its roots in the Qur'an, the term has been used in modern Islamic discourse, from the nineteenth century pan-Islamist movement of Jamal al Din al-Afghani throughout many twentieth century movements, including the Muslim Brotherhood and the Iranian Revolution.[40] As a blanket term that covers all countries, regions, and societies in which Muslims live as a majority, the idea of *Umma* assumes a unifying cultural bond among the global community of Muslims and it has maintained its appeal as a discursive ideal. Although the strong nationalisms of the twentieth century have complicated the coexistence of "local" and "global," the flexibility and expediency of the concept still provide a vision of shared identity and tradition beyond the immediate experiences of Muslim communities. In the words of Abdullahi An-Na'im, the imagination and shared identity of *Umma* is "sufficiently present in the consciousness of present generations of Muslims to be mobilized in support of overlapping national and global citizenship."[41]

In view of that, the state of the *Umma* today is the leading concern for the founders of the UNIW and each member NGO; "it is dispersed, disintegrated, and poverty stricken."[42] A growing awareness of the weakness, poverty, and backwardness of the Islamic world as compared to the advancing West is the key mobilizing factor for the Muslim NGOs. For the leaders of the UNIW and its member organizations, vitalizing and uniting civil societies in Muslim geographies is the key to solving *Umma*'s pressing problems. UNIW leaders assert that civil society is the "rising value of the century and it is only civil society that can fight against the injustices the Muslim world faces."[43] NGO leaders argue that civil society is in the unique position, in the contemporary world, of being one of the most active, dynamic, and flexible elements of societies and of being the major force of mobilization. They argue that NGOs possess a great deal of political power in today's world, and therefore, they must reorganize and renew themselves, and must realize that their power has immense influence on the global scale. They state the need to make use of their resources; support their own civil initiatives; and take the lead to overcome the social, economic, and political infirmities that make Islamic countries vulnerable to foreign interventions. In that way, UNIW and its members assert that they are obliged to join forces with each other.

Exchange programs for college-age Muslim students are held in high regard by UNIW. For member NGOs, hosting college level students from the Middle East, Africa, the Balkans, or Central Asia through exchange programs materializes UNIW's foremost goal of uniting the *Umma* by bringing together the future leaders of the Islamic world. The declaration issued by the 150 participants from 25 countries at UNIW's 4th Youth Gathering articulated the mission to achieve unity, solidarity, and mutual understanding among Muslim youth as follows: "We strongly emphasize the development of the youth, with respect to their vocation to materialize their Islamic visions. We will have to start encouraging Muslim talents to be part of a cross border organization that would gather competent people and help them serve the Islamic World, wherever and whenever required."[44] For the organizations that work with youth run transnational exchange programs, promoting the unified *Umma* ideal is an essential goal. In fact, "we are one nation" is uttered frequently during meetings and events that bring together young people from different parts of the Muslim world.[45] Transcending the racial, language, and national barriers facing the future of the *Umma*, students are encouraged to imagine themselves as a unified community and as the future leaders of a strong Muslim world.

Political Advocacy through Coalition

As a global Muslim NGO coalition, UNIW's mission is to unify Muslim populations around the world and to establish a single voice in global civil society. While most of UNIW's faith-based members work to provide services such as orphan care, religious education, health, and youth within their respective countries, their global coalition provide a platform for political advocacy.

In what follows, I discuss the fluid dynamics between humanitarian action and political agency. The argument here is that humanitarian action opens fertile areas for political action precisely because it is considered non-political. In the remainder of this section, I illustrate the ways in which the global alliance of humanitarian and social aid organizations function as a global political platform to act on issues such as the Palestinian problem, Islamophobia, and discrimination against Muslim minorities.

Direct Political Action in Humanitarian Form

Humanitarian action and service provision are by and large dismissed as non-advocacy work for civil society groups. However, all humanitarian work has political grounds and consequences, thus, it is inherently political. Among social aid organizations, the very decisions about which population to help, and with what kind of projects and sponsors, all involve ideological reasoning and political strategy, be it faith-based or non-faith-based. Humanitarian action has always had a political element, although its pretense of being impartial and neutral—and therefore seemingly non-political—has been essential.[46] Indeed, the "harmless façade" of humanitarian action allows organizations to maneuver within a wider range of politics. The best example of how humanitarian pretense lends itself to effective political action is the Freedom Flotilla operation, which was intended to draw attention to the Israeli blockade of Gaza, and broke it to the detriment of the Turkish-Israeli relations.

In May 2010, the Humanitarian Relief Fund (IHH), which is one of the largest members of the UNIW, organized a six-ship flotilla in collaboration with the Free Gaza Movement to "make a deliberately attention-grabbing effort" to deliver 10,000 tons of humanitarian aid to 1.5 million Palestinians in Gaza and to break Israel's blockade of the territory.[47] IHH is a faith-based humanitarian relief organization based in Turkey. Their social humanitarian projects include donating mosques and religiously oriented schools in Africa and animals for Muslim religious sacrifices to Muslim minorities all over the world, as well as aid and food for the poor during Ramadan.

In recent years, humanitarian aid groups have sent supply ships and activists to Gaza. The Free Gaza Movement itself has organized no less than five voyages since 2007. The flotillas carry aid and activists from a wide range of countries. While the earlier ones were allowed to reach Gaza, others were directed and landed at the port of Ashdod by Israel before delivery to Gaza. The very purpose of the Freedom Flotilla operation was to land at the port of Gaza to serve as a precedent. On 22 May 2010, a six-ship flotilla including the *Mavi Marmara*, owned by the IHH, set sail toward Gaza. Seven hundred activists from 38 countries participated in the mission.

On 31 May, 130 kilometers from the Israeli coast in international waters, the Israeli navy demanded the convoy to reroute to Ashdod. When the convoy refused to reroute, Israeli commandos raided it. The confrontation resulted in eight Turks and one Turkish-American being killed, in addition to more than 20 passengers and ten commandos who were injured. The incident sparked an unprecedented crisis in Turkish-Israeli relations. Turkey recalled its ambassador to Israel, cancelled joint military exercises with Israel, scaled back previously extensive intelligence cooperation, and banned Israeli military flights over its airspace. Turkey demanded an Israeli apology, compensation for the victims, return of the ships, and an international investigation. Israel blamed the incident on IHH in public, but put responsibility on the Turkish government in private.[48]

Although the political aftershocks are still being felt in the international relations arena, IHH and UNIW consider the operation a victory. The net result of the political scandal and human casualties was heightened attention focused on the humanitarian crisis in Gaza. It should be noted that the primary reason why this operation could be made in the first place is that it was organized by a humanitarian organization delivering humanitarian aid. Yet, it was political action in purpose and effect, albeit a covert one, given the political circumstances. Israel's strict state surveillance on the activities of NGOs that operate in Gaza and its scrutiny on Gaza's corridors of contact with the outside world provoked shifts in the boundaries of civil society's composition.

Global Political Advocacy through Coalition

UNIW's member NGOs direct the political power that is forged through the alliance towards global political advocacy. The most prominent of UNIW's pursuits in the sphere of political advocacy is increasing awareness about the rise of Islamophobia around the world after 9/11. Following the events of 11 September 2001, Muslim groups consistently reported increased hostility and discrimination, especially in North America and most EU countries. Stereotypical and sensationalist depictions of Muslims in mass media, negative images of Muslims promoted by the news sources and political leaders, religiously motivated abuse experienced by Muslim groups, and exclusory political practices are addressed by UNIW's member NGOs in assembly meetings and internal summits.

As a Muslim faith-based NGO coalition, the UNIW lists "fighting Islamophobia around the world" as its leading mission. It works to organize and mobilize public opinion to raise awareness in the international community of the dangers of Islamophobia, and calls to develop mechanisms against defamation of religions and discrimination against Muslims. With the use of its supposed mandate as the "voice of Muslim civil society," UNIW officially responds to activities that insult, discriminate, or violate the human rights of Muslims because of their faith.

In order to expose Islamophobia in the international community and media, UNIW holds international conferences with the participation of political leaders, academics, media personalities, international organizations, and representatives of its member NGOs. In December 2007, UNIW organized a high profile international conference on Islamophobia in Istanbul, Turkey. Turkish Prime Minister Recep Tayyip Erdogan opened the conference and the Organization of Islamic Cooperation (OIC) Secretary General, Ekmeleddin Ihsanoglu, gave the keynote speech. The Final Communiqué announced the launch of a Monitoring Center Committee to inform international decision-making mechanisms, press organs, and the international community with periodical reports. Since the establishment of the committee, the UNIW General Secretariat has issued statements; met the political leadership of numerous countries, international organizations, and think-tanks; addressed letters to the United Nations and the European Union; organized workshops and symposiums; and made demarches to the Danish embassy following the caricature controversy and to the Dutch embassy regarding the release of the film *Fitna* by a Dutch parliamentarian.

In addition to increasing awareness of Islamophobia on a global level, UNIW works to publicize the humanitarian condition of Muslim populations in the world. UNIW's Secretary General, Necmi Sadikoglu, describes the coalition's purpose with regards to alleviating the conditions of Muslim minorities facing discrimination as, "gathering Muslim communities who became alienated and even hostile to each other in some places around our common principles within the frame of our religion and civilization, and to establish and reveal a will that uses the potentials of the Islamic World for the prosperity and welfare of Islamic World."[49] In that framework, UNIW considers "the chaos in Iraq; the denial of rights in Palestine and Kashmir; the state of lawlessness in Somalia; the security situation in Afghanistan; and the situation of Muslim minorities in the Philippines, southern Thailand, Myanmar, and Eastern Turkistan" of primary importance. In order to guide international public opinion regarding such crisis regions, UNIW organizes international symposiums, conferences and workshops, publishes reports, and holds press conferences.

One example of a high profile political awareness event on Muslim minority issues is the East Turkistan Symposium. In March 2010, UNIW co-organized the East Turkistan Symposium in Istanbul to put the spotlight on the Uighur population in China. Bringing together the international chapters of the East Turkistan Solidarity Associations, researchers, academics, representatives of asylum seekers in Turkey, and political figures, the symposium drew attention to the humanitarian crises and human rights violations in the region. The participants highlighted restrictions on religion, prayer, and Uighur language; restrictions on freedom of expression, information, and communication; violations against women; forced labor; and migration. The final declaration made statements about the lack of attention from the international community to the situation in East Turkistan and made suggestions for action. In the intergovernmental sphere, the UNIW delegation and the NGO leaders accused the UN Security Council of hesitating to display the required sensitivity over the issue due to the veto power of China and invited the General Assembly of the UN to take a position in favor of the people of East Turkistan. On a country level, some of the suggestions for Islamic countries included reconsidering economic and political relations with China in favor of East Turkistan, as well as opening consulates, offices of humanitarian organizations, and faculties of Islamic universities in East Turkistan. The delegates agreed to run effective lobbying activities through communication devices and propaganda channels to disseminate information, to publish and translate books in East Turkistan, and to prepare exhibitions and short movies to depict the humanitarian situation in the region in order to influence popular opinion.

The UNIW body works most efficiently on raising awareness about the conditions of Muslim populations around the world, on monitoring crisis regions in the Islamic world, and motivating its members to contribute to the solutions. The UNIW considers symposiums and conferences as illustrated above to be a key strategy to determine a common attitude towards pertinent issues. After all, the "dispersed state of the *Umma*"[50] that UNIW leaders frequently mention is most apparent in the lack of intercommunication and awareness of information among its constituents. As the president of the Algerian delegation declared in the aforementioned East Turkistan Symposium: "Believe me. We are not really aware of what is happening in East Turkistan and to our Muslim brothers there. It is so, because we do not have sufficient and reliable information about the situation in this occupied Muslim territory. With such symposiums, the awareness level increases among the people who have capability to change this unacceptable brutal situation. I will take this as my topic in Friday lecture at the mosque Insha'Allah [God willing]."[51]

While most of UNIW's member NGOs find that they have to limit their work to humanitarian aid and service provision in their home countries, they find UNIW a productive platform for performing political advocacy. Muslim NGOs of more than 40 countries mobilize and take active part under the same roof because they share common values, goals, and concerns regarding the state of the Muslim world. UNIW is more than a mere network of NGOs that are loosely connected on a symbolic level. UNIW is effectively an NGO coalition as it has a broader strategic aim rather than focusing on a single issue. It promotes stronger and longer lasting links among members, allows for meaningful collaborations rather than sporadic exchange, and takes an overarching political stance. The member NGOs benefit from and meet their individual needs by participating in a large scale alliance that shares resources, information, and expertise, while reducing costs as a result of group specialization. That way, the overarching faith-based ideology of the coalition serves a purpose that is larger than the camaraderie of an average NGO network by mobilizing organizations of all sizes towards political goals on a global scale.

Conclusions

As Keane observes in this volume, democratic governance involves more than the territorial state, parties, or legislatures. An array of "non-party, extra-parliamentary, and often unelected bodies operate within and underneath and beyond the boundaries of territorial states"[52] and scrutinize all fields of social and political life. Therefore, the transparency, representativeness, accountability, and legitimacy of power blocs are kept in check by a multiplicity of national and transnational mechanisms.

Civil society is one of the key actors in this political configuration. While the politics of civil society were conceived as limited to national or regional scales until the end of the Cold War, the interconnected nature of the globalization process has extended its domain. As the boundaries and interdependencies of politics transcend local and national territories toward regional and global spheres, actors multiply and transform as well. The transnational inter-reliance of civil society organizations and political movements forms sites of socio-political power and legitimacy, presenting an alternative to power structures of the nation-state.

This transformation opens new venues for diverse civil society groups to act as political agents. The work of the UNIW analyzed in this chapter demonstrates that such venues provide opportunities to the smaller-scale, faith-based humanitarian and social aid organizations to extend their networks to a global scale. More importantly, these venues allow seemingly non-political organizations to exert political agency and operate as global monitory actors on issues that concern Muslim populations around the world. In other words, the lines between the service and advocacy work of civil society blur to the extent that humanitarian work and political action overlap.

In view of the complex nature of civil society as a political sphere, further work is required to understand the intersections of humanitarian work and political activism. Following Keane's perspective on the role of civil society as a political agent, we need to delve deeper into how humanitarian organizations serve as monitory organs. The conditions that enable and force NGOs to claim harmless humanitarianism and yet to engage in political action need further analysis. Also, the ways in which humanitarian NGOs directly contribute to monitory democracy should be exposed in contexts other than the Muslim world. Considering ways in which "service" and "voice" groups diverge and converge points to innovative research venues in studies of democracy and civil society. Such venues contribute to the understanding of civil society as a complex platform, rather than as one whose internal categories and boundaries are mistakenly considered cut and dry.

Notes

1. John Keane, Chapter 1 (in this volume).
2. Lars Tragardh, "Rethinking the Nordic Welfare State through A Neo-Hegelian Theory of State and Civil Society," *Journal of Political Ideologies* vol. 15, no. 3 (2010): 231.
3. See David C. Korten, *Getting to the 21ˢᵗ Century: Voluntary Action and the Global Agenda* (West Hartford, C.T.: Kumarian, 1990) and Charles Elliot, "Some Aspects of Relations between the North and South in the NGO Sector," *World Development*, vol. 15 (Supp. 1987): 57–68.
4. Korten, *Getting to the 21ˢᵗ Century*: 113–132.
5. William M. Watt, *Islamic Political Thought* (Edinburgh: Edinburgh University Press, 1968): 120–123.
6. John Hall, *Powers and Liberties: The Causes and Consequences of the Rise of the West* (Harmondsworth, U.K.: Penguin, 1985): 89.

7. See Patricia Crone, *Slaves on Horses: The Evolution of the Islamic Polity* (Cambridge: Cambridge University Press, 1986).

8. Bernard Lewis, *The Shaping of the Modern Middle East* (New York: Oxford University Press, 1994): 45–46.

9. Robert Springborg, "Patterns of Association in the Egyptian Political Elite," in *Political Elites in the Middle East*, ed. G. Lenczowski. (Washington D.C.: American Enterprise Institute Press, 1975): 87.

10. Ernest Gellner, *Conditions of Liberty: Civil Society and Its Rivals* (New York: The Penguin Press, 1994): 15.

11. Gellner, *Conditions of Liberty:* 29.

12. See Augustus R. Norton, eds., *Civil Society in the Middle East* (Leiden, The Netherlands: Brill, 1996) and Chris Hann and Elizabeth Dunn, *Civil Society: Challenging Western Models* (London: Routledge, 1996).

13. See John L. Esposito and Francois Burgat, eds., *Modernizing Islam: Religion in the Public Sphere in the Middle East and Europe* (London and New Bunswick: Hurst Publications and Rutgers University Press, 2003).

14. For the former, see Saad E. Ibrahim, "Egypt's Islamic Activism in the 1980s," *Third World Quarterly* vol. 10 (1988) and Sami Zubaida, "Islam, the State and Democracy," *Middle East Report* vol. 179 (1992). For the latter, see Masoud Kamali, "Civil Society and Islam: A Sociological Perspective," *Archives Europeennes De Sociologie* vol. 42, no. 3 (2003).

15. See Asef Bayat, "Activism and Social Development in the Middle East," *International Journal of Middle East Studies* vol. 34, no. 1 (2002); Shaul Mishal and Avraham Sela, *The Palestinian Hamas: Vision, Violence, and Coexistence* (New York: Columbia University Press, 2006); and Judith Palmer Harik, *Hezbollah: The Changing Face of Terrorism* (London: I.B. Tauris, 2004).

16. See Quintan Wiktorowicz, *The Management of Islamic Activism: Salafis, the Muslim Brotherhood, and State Power in Jordan* (Albany, N.Y.: State University of New York Press, 2001).

17. See Bayat, "Activism and Social Development in the Middle East."

18. Diane Singerman, *Avenues of Participation: Family, Networks, and Politics in Urban Quarters of Cairo* (Princeton, N.J.: Princeton University Press, 1995).

19. Asef Bayat, "Un-Civil Society: The Politics of the "Informal People,'" *Third World Quarterly* vol. 18, no. 1 (1997).

20. Ghada H. Talhami, "Whither the Social Network of Islam?" *Muslim World* vol. 91, nos. 3/4 (2001).

21. Janine A. Clark, "Islamic Social Welfare Organizations in Cairo: Islamization from Below?" *Arab Studies Quarterly* vol. 17, no. 4 (1995): 11.

22. See Bayat, "Activism and Social Development in the Middle East": 16.

23. UNIW's members include international relief organizations, such as Islamic and Muslim Relief based in the U.K., European Muslim Union based in Germany, the International Islamic Relief Organization based in Saudi Arabia, the IHH Humanitarian Relief Foundation based in Turkey, and the Eurasian International Development Association based in Azerbaijan There are local organizations such as the Zam Zam Foundation in Somalia, the Cambodian Muslim Intellectual Alliance, and Al-Awn Development and Relief Association of Ethiopia. There are also youth and alumni associations such as Assembly of Muslim Youth in Saudi Arabia, the Muslim Youth Movement of Malaysia, the National Union of Kuwait Stu-

dents, and the All Ceylon Young Men's Muslim Association in Sri Lanka. Finally, there are human rights and peace organizations such as the National Organization for Defending Rights and Freedoms based in Yemen, the Global Peace Mission in Malaysia, and the Awareness and Consolidation Association in Lebanon.

24. Peter Berger, "Religion and Global Civil Society," in *Religion in Global Civil Society*, ed. M. Juergensmeyer (Oxford: Oxford University Press, 2005): 16.

25. Elizabeth Ferris, "Faith-based and Secular Humanitarian Organizations," *International Review of the Red Cross* vol. 87 (2005): 312–313.

26. While there is not a single generally-accepted definition, faith-based organizations are characterized by their core philosophy, programmatic approach, funding source, and membership. For the purposes of this chapter, I propose a four point criteria based on the organizations' mission statement, mobilization agenda, theological objectives, and the target population. The first three of these points are loosely based on Evelyn Bush's [Evelyn Bush, "Measuring religion in global civil society," *Social Forces* 85(4): 1645–1665 (2007)] criteria to measure religious mobilization in global civil society. The fourth point is based on a self-identified characteristic that each 185 member of UNIW shares.

27. See Richard Falk, *On Global Governance: Toward a New Global Politics* (University Park, P.A.: Pennsylvania University Press, 1995).

28. Jamal Krafess, "The Influence of Muslim Religion in Humanitarian Aid," *International Review of the Red Cross* vol. 85 (2005): 327.

29. Interviewee 7 (UNIW executive committee member), personal interview by author, 4 September 2009.

30. Hadith is the collection of traditions attributed to the Prophet Muhammad that include his sayings and acts. Jamal Krafess (2005), the Director General of Islamic Relief, provides a detailed treatment of the Quranic texts and hadith pertaining to humanitarian aid. Qur'an (Surah 13:29) encourages charitable acts in verses such as "For those who believe and do charitable works is every blessedness and a beautiful place of final return." Similarly, Surah 2:83 states "[and be good] to the orphans and the very poor, speak kindly to men, make prayer, and give in charity." Charitable giving is not only ordered to the members of the Islamic faith, but also suggested as a way to erase sins and obtaining God's satisfaction: "Alms extinguish sins exactly as water extinguishes fire" (Al Bukhari, *Sahih Al Jami'e*, Hadith No. 2951, in Krafess 2005: 329). Food aid is encouraged in hadith as "the best of alms is to feed the hungry" (Al Baihaki, *Chouab Al Iman*, Hadith No. 3367, in Krafess 2005: 332). Similarly, sharing one's food is commended in hadith as "He who sleeps with a full stomach knowing his neighbor is hungry is not a believer" (Al Baihaki *Chouab Al Iman*, Hadith No. 3389, in Krafess 2005: 333). The Prophet encourages believers to look after orphans: "God's favorite residence is that in which an orphan is well-treated" (Al Bukhari, *Alfath*, Hadith No. 5304, in Krafess 2005: 333). NGOs which run water provision programs frequently refer to the Prophet's hadith on the issue: "Whoever digs a well will be rewarded until the Day of Judgment every time a human, a genie, or an animal drinks from that well" (Al Bukhari, *Sahih Al Jami'e*, Hadith No. 5757, in Krafess 2005: 334).

31. Interviewee 15 (WEFA spokesperson), personal interview by author, 4 January 2009. The interviewee is paraphrasing the hadith on water use: "He who sinks a well in Rawma will go to Paradise" (Al Hafid, *Al Fith*, vol. 5, p. 510, in Krafess 2005: 335)

32. Weltweiter Einsatz für Arme. *http://www.wefa.org/de/projekte/wasserbrunnen .html.* (Accessed 3 June 2011).
33. International Islamic Charitable Organization of Kuwait. http://www.iico.org/ home-page-eng/index-eng.htm. (Accessed 1 June 2011)
34. Quintan Wiktorowicz and Suha T. Farouki, "Islamic NGOs and Muslim Politics: A Case from Jordan," *Third World Quarterly* vol. 21, no. 4 (2000): 689–91.
35. Wiktorowicz and Farouki, "Islamic NGOs and Muslim Politics."
36. Interviewee 36, (Gul-Der spokesperson), personal interview by author, 12 December 2009.
37. Interviewee 39, (Erdem-Der spokesperson), personal interview by author, 7 December 2009.
38. Ayse Kadioglu, "Women's Subordination in Turkey: Is Islam Really the Villain?" *Middle East Journal* vol. 48, no.4 (1994).
39. Interviewee 36, (Gul-Der spokesperson), personal interview by author, 12 December 2009.
40. Fred Halliday, "The Politics of the *Umma*: States and Community in Islamic Movements," *Mediterranean Politics* vol. 7, no. 3 (2002): 21.
41. Abdullahi An-Na'im, "Global Citizenship and Human Rights: From Muslim in Europe to European Muslims," in *Religious Pluralism and Human Rights in Europe: Where to Draw the Line?*, eds. M.L.P. Loenen and J.E. Glodschmidt (Antwerp-Oxford: Intersentia, 2007): 25.
42. Interviewee 7 (UNIW executive committee member), personal interview by author, 4 September 2009.
43. Interviewee 4, (UNIW Secretary General), personal interview by author, 12 June 2008.
44. Fourth Youth Gathering, 2010, UNIW, Bursa Declaration. (Accessed 3 June 2011) *http://idsb.org/en/index.php?option=com_content&view=article&id=436: bursa-declaration&catid=1:haberler&Itemid=2*
45. "We are one nation" *The Pen Magazine.* Interviews from 3rd Youth Gathering, 2009. (Accessed 9 June 2011) *http://www.thepenmagazine.net/we-are-one-nation/*
46. Nicholas Leader, *The Politics of Principle: The Principles of Humanitarian Action in Practice* (London: Overseas Development Institute, 2000): 3.
47. Crisis Report, *Turkey's Crises over Israel and Iran* (Europe Report: International Crisis Group, 2010): 4.
48. Crisis Report, *Turkey's Crises over Israel and Iran:* 8.
49. Necmi Sadikoglu, Pakistan Consultation Meeting, Istanbul. 9 October 2010.
50. Interviewee 41 (UNIW executive committee member), personal interview by author, 16 May 2010.
51. Presentation by President of the Algerian delegation, East Turkistan Symposium, Istanbul. 20-21 March, 2010.
52. John Keane, Chapter 1 (in this volume).

Chapter 9

ANTI-TOTALITARIAN FEMINISM?
CIVIC RESISTANCE IN IRAN

Haideh Daradeh and Nina Witoszek

Introduction

In the mass protest demonstrations that broke out in Iran in the wake of the contested presidential elections in June 2009, the conspicuous presence, and role, of women more than fulfilled the expectations of those who were aware of the long and gradual build-up to this eruption. Official reports and amateur citizen journalist films captured the level-headed courage of the women who confronted the Revolutionary Guards and militiamen, and stood between them and the demonstrators they were about to beat up and take away. The women acted as buffers to the spread of violence by standing between the angry crowd and the odd militiaman who had been separated from his unit and fallen into people's hands. More importantly, they challenged gender apartheid by participating in the demonstrations alongside the men and by defying the regulations of compulsory veils, which the Islamic Republic imposed over the course of its thirty years of existence.

The present chapter aims to provide insights into the ongoing feminist revolt in Iran as an instance of civil society action in a totalitarian state.[1] In doing so, we shall draw on Hannah Arendt's analysis of totalitarianism, specifically in relation to Nazi Germany. The Islamic Republic's humiliation and suppression of women in Iran is clearly a political ploy to control the society as a whole. In some sense, it is analogous to the Nazi's treatment of the Jews in Nazi Germany. It may be tempting to compare the role of the veil for women in Iran to that of the yellow Star of David on Jewish clothes during the Third Reich. The objection here may be that the predicament of Iranian women cannot be compared to the fate of Jews, Romas, and other human objects of Nazi contempt that were ultimately exterminated. By contrast, Iranian women are kept alive—as a species of eternal *Untermensch*. This being granted, the legal basis of ethnic discrimination in the Third Reich—the 1934 Nuremberg laws which robbed Jews of all citizen's rights—bears structural similarities to the redefinition of women's social standing in the Islamic Republic. In both cases, social groups that once enjoyed equal citizen's rights were reduced to thralls and became objects of abuse. In the Iranian case, their subservience was justified, not by pseudo-scientific racial theories of Nazi ideologues, but by reference to verses from the Koran, the *Hadith* (stories attributed to the behavior of the Prophet), the Sharia law, and 1,400 years of clerical interpretation of these texts and related narratives. Their ongoing revolt has been a challenge with which the Islamic Republic has had to grapple during the entire course of its existence. If Iran under the Islamic Republic can be defined as a totalitarian state, then the Iranian women's movement should be viewed as a form of civil resistance with implications far beyond the national boundaries of the country.

In the following argument, we wish to offer two contentions. The first one, founded on an analysis of the historical roots of Iranian feminism, is the often occluded—or even ignored—presence and intellectual influence of Iranian female dissidents at the early stages of modern history. The second contention is more theoretical and conceptual. Although modern Iranian feminism borrows concepts and tropes from Western feminist theory, its nature today clashes with the reality of mainstream Western feminism. As we shall argue, there are various reasons for this "mismatch." The Iranian political opposition with women in leading positions is *an anti-totalitarian movement*. This is a fact that Western observers hardly register and that Iranian women dissidents themselves sometimes hardly realize. In fact, the very label of the "feminist struggle" may today be used or understood to the Iranian activists' disadvantage. To the extent that the Iranian women's movement seeks radical political change, its goals and conditions differ from Western feminism. Similar to "socialism"—a concept that denoted noble causes, and is now an antiquated phrase in social democracies—so "feminism" has acquired new connotations in the West. In the second decade of the twenty-first century, Swedish or Dutch "feminists" ask for more kindergartens for children or more leadership positions for women. By contrast, feminists in Iran struggle for acceptance as humans with dignity and rights. For this demand they are thrown into prison, tortured, or stoned—no Western "feminist theory," however accurate, has so far captured their predicament. In short, a temporal asymmetry exists between the radical days of Western feminism and the current human rights movement in Iran. This may have led to a misunderstanding of—if not sheer disregard for—the first anti-totalitarian revolution with a female face. It is enough to read Negin Nabavi's *Intellectuals and the State in Iran* (2003) to see the gender-blindness (or complicity with official sponsors) of contemporary research on civil society in Iran.[2] Perhaps we need a set of new concepts to describe the Iranian dissent?

We shall return to this point later in the chapter. Hannah Arendt believed that "no matter how abstract our theories may sound or how consistent our theories may appear, there are incidents and stories behind them which, at least for ourselves, contain as in a nutshell the full meaning of whatever we have to say."[3] The question is: what is the story behind the official story?

Iranian Feminism: Founders and Mentors

The anti-totalitarian opposition in Iran has been highly complex and includes male leaders like Mir Moussavi and Mehdi Karroubi. Their political as well as ideological connection with the establishment, however, makes them, at best, problematic figures. Unlike other civic upheavals in human history, in twenty-first century Iran, it is the women protagonists who have become the international forefront of dissent and defense of human rights: Parvin Ardalan, Shadi Sadr, Shirin Ebadi, Mansoureh Shaojai, Nasrin Sotoodeh, and Shiva Nazar Ahari to mention but a few. These women seem to have replaced the old male Eastern European dissidents—the Havels, the Michniks, and the Sakharovs—and they add a novel dimension to the nature of modern civic movement, both in Iran and in the world. To understand the legacy that has empowered the female opposition, it makes sense to delve into the nineteenth century history, narrated at the time mostly by non-Islamic or non-Iranian historians.[4] In these works we find the powerful image of one woman, Fatemeh Baraghani. Since she played a formative role in a suppressed religious movement, most of her writings have been lost or destroyed, and efforts have been made to erase her from history. Her wider recognition is, for the most part, the result of research within the secular feminist movement of the last thirty years in Iran.

A literary historian of our time described Fatemeh Baraghani as having "a constitution made up of revolt."[5] This sums up the short life of one of the most extraordinary women in modern history. Fatemeh Baraghani— nicknamed as Ghorratulein (The light of the eye) and Tahereh (The pure)—was the first woman in the Islamic world who, more than a hundred and sixty years ago, took the veil off her head in public. She believed that all wealth was theft, wrote poetry and scholarly treatises, and while still under thirty, taught religious scholars from behind a curtain in the holy city of Karbala.

Ghorratulein was born in 1814 in the city of Ghazvin in central Iran, to a well known and well-to-do religious family. Her passion for learning gave her father the incentive to appoint tutors to teach her the basics of the knowledge of the time. Thus, by her early teens she had a grasp of Arabic and Persian poetry, rhetoric, theology, Islamic jurisprudence, and the interpretation of the Koran. Her father bemoaned the fact of her being a girl: "Alas! Were you born a son the praise of the world would have been showered on me."[6] At the age of fourteen, she was married off to her cousin, who belonged to the fundamentalist side of the family, and in the course of her married life bore him two sons and one daughter. Ghorratulein was attracted to the reformist ideas of the Sheikhi school (centered in Karbala, in present day Iraq). She divorced her fundamentalist husband unilaterally as a matter of principle, and after a period in Karbala, where she had the chance to teach Shiite scholars, joined the Baabi reformist religious movement that had developed out of Sheikhism.

Baab, the founder of the new faith, was the advocate of an indigenous brand of socialism. He believed that: "The world belongs to God. All property belongs to Him, while a small group of people have expropriated what should be divided between you equally. We believe that ownership is the biggest social evil." The Baabis held that peasants should not pay taxes on land to the land owners. Baab advocated the expansion of public means of communication, such as post and telegram; a single currency; and the founding of printing presses, hitherto a novelty in the country. He was in favor of compulsory education and against capital punishment, as well as the beating of small children. He also amplified the importance of women, as suggested by the Sheikhi scholars. He banned polygamy, stood for the consent of both parties in marriage, endorsed social contact between men and women, and, in the words of a historian of the Baabi movement, "he set women free from the bondage of the veil." The popularity of his ideas among progressive religious intellectuals, as well as the poorer sectors of society, alarmed the court and the clerical establishment. He was arrested and remained in jail until his execution at the age of thirty. At a Baabi general assembly in 1850, Ghorratulein tried to persuade leading Baabi figures to break with Islamic traditions. Since she wore no veil at the meeting, she pulled down the curtain from behind which women were allowed to address a male audience, to illustrate her points. This was a striking symbolic gesture hinting at the necessity to both uncover the truth and to tear down the main accessory of women's subjugation.[7]

The Baabis were defeated, and their leaders put to death in brutal ways that defy description. Ghorratulein, falsely accused of killing her fundamentalist father-in-law, was arrested and thrown into jail. Here she received visitors, some of them women who had turned to Baabism through her teaching. One of her visitors was an emissary from the court who offered her life if she denied her faith in the presence of a number of handpicked Mullahs. By rejecting the offer, Ghorratulein did not only sign her own death warrant; she defied the Shiite provision of *taghia* that permits a Muslim to deny his faith if his life is in danger. Her executioners came in the middle of the night and moved her to the Ilkhani garden in Tehran. Since there is no consensus in Islam about shedding a woman's blood, they pushed a scarf down her throat, threw her into a well while still alive, and filled the well with stones. She was thirty-six at the time of her death in 1850.

Ghorratulein's emancipatory legacy has marked every aspect of the women's liberation movement in Iran: from being non-persons and hence easily susceptible to brutality and violence, to being marked by the veil and denied access to education and participation in politics. It would not be far-fetched to claim that the present secular feminist movement traces its genealogy back to her. Her example made it possible for others, such as Tajossaltaneh (the crown of the royalty) born in 1881, the daughter of Naseroddinshah, the third king of the Ghajar dynasty, to express their condemnation of the condition of women. Tajossaltaneh left behind a book of memoirs that she wrote at the age of forty-three, making it easy to follow the development of most of her life and thought. She rejected the traditional education for girls, and through the teaching she received from an enlightened tutor, she learned about modern science and rebelled against the way religion explains the world. Brought up in the king's harem by black nannies that she obviously loved, she grew up with an intense sense of indignation toward discriminating people on the basis of what she called "the color of the cover." She spoke some French and harbored socialist ideas. But the most moving parts of her memoir are her revolt against the position of women and her description of the veil as a shroud, reflecting the death-in-life condition of women's lives. Toward the end of the memoirs, she describes a period in her life when she turned to religion as her biggest folly, "I turned to faith, that is, I turned stupid."[8]

There are more women like Ghorratulein and Tajossaltaneh, whose existence has barely been noticed by Iranian historians, influenced as they are by orthodox religion, canon, or, occasionally, state support. Nonetheless, we cannot speak of a women's *movement* prior to the beginning of the Constitutional Revolution (1906), when modernity officially entered Iranian politics in an atmosphere ripe for social and political change. Women, including those in the Shah's harem, showed astonishing political awareness and involvement. They engaged in the boycott of tobacco against the monopoly sold by the Ghajar king to a British company. They spread vital information and participated in demonstrations. Mirza Malkolm Khan, one of the major intellectual driving forces of the movement, paid tribute to them in 1905 in his newspaper *Qanun* (published abroad) for their courage and better grasp of the humanitarian ideal of the constitution than men. Morgan Shuster, the American who had been invited to Iran to organize the finances of the constitutional government in 1911, praised them in his book, *The Strangling of Persia*, as the most progressive women in the world.[9] When the Russians delivered an ultimatum to the Iranian parliament that they would occupy the country if Shuster was not expelled, the women went to meet the head of the parliament alone, with weapons under their veils, making it clear that they were prepared to shoot the deputies if they gave in to the threat. Meanwhile, around the turn of the century, there was hardly a constitutionalist newspaper, poet, or writer who did not deplore the subjugation of women and condemn the veil as its symbol and the shame of Iranian society. One of the many famous cartoons in the satirical magazine *Mulla Nasruddin*—published in Baku for twenty-one years and smuggled into Iran—portrays a poor woman in a black veil, bent under the weight of a huge bundle containing her numerous children as well as her husband, who sits comfortably and drinks tea out of a samovar. On the side is a corpulent mullah, who, with an outstretched arm, sanctions this family idyll. The paper considered the harrowing situation of women as the main obstacle to modernity, and as early as 1906, when the election for the first Iranian parliament was under way, it demanded that women get the right to vote.

After the defeat of the constitutional government (largely through the intrigues of Tsarist Russia and Britain), the constitutional assembly denied Iranian women the right to vote, alongside minors, criminals, and the insane. Nonetheless, despite staunch opposition by the clergy, formal education of women started when, in 1906, the American missionary school in Uroomieh accepted girl students from Muslim families for the first time. Other girls' schools were founded after a conference in Tehran which took up the question of women's education. The first magazine featuring a woman editor, called *Danesh* (knowledge), came out in 1910, and was followed by a large number of similar journals. From the beginning of the constitutional period, women had organized themselves in what was called "women's associations."[10]

Another female dissident from that time who had a tremendous influence on the Iranian opposition was Sedigheh Dolatabadi, born in 1882. She was involved in all areas of the struggle of women by starting a school for girls, a publication dedicated to the cause of women, and a women's civic organization. Dolatabadi attended all the important women's conferences of the time. Upon her return to Iran from Paris and the International Women's Conference in 1926, she took off the veil. She and two others represented Iranian women in the first conference of Muslim women in Damascus in 1930, and again at the Congress of Oriental women in Tehran in 1932 with Tajossaltaneh, who was still alive at the time. She was accused of being a Baabi and stones were cast at her house because of the publication of a magazine called *Zabaan-e Zanaan* (The language of women). She died in 1961, having mentioned in her will that it would be against her wishes for any woman with a veil to visit her grave. Many years later, during the most recent wave of the Iranian women's movement under the Islamic Republic in the early 2010s, The Women's Cultural Center, founded by two young Iranian feminists, remembered Dolatabadi by choosing her out of the many activists as the patron of the Center's library and giving her bust to the author of the best feminist work of the year.

When Reza Khan, an officer in the Iranian army, seized power through a military coup in 1923, he used the model of Kemal Ataturk's modernization reforms in Turkey. Many of his reforms were related to women, the most important among them being the prohibition of hijab in 7 January 1936 and the establishment of his own official Women's Day. But modernity's assault on cultural symbolism was bound to provoke a mixed reaction. While the opposition to the veil from women activists and grassroots organizations was one thing, pulling the veil off women's heads by armed police and giving them a free hand to insult and humiliate veiled women was another. There were older women, embittered and alarmed by the new "head regime," who chose to remain indoors for the rest of their lives.

The clergy and a considerable part of the religious establishment were opposed to every aspect of the Shah's reforms. Having lost the bulk of their traditional areas of influence, they made Reza Shah a symbol of modernity's evils. It is important to note that Ayatollah Khomeini used these reactions and the ensuing bitterness to build up support for himself as a liberator. He also used the Shah's gender reforms to justify his vendetta against Reza Shah's son and successor, Mohammad Reza Pahlavi. In 1963, Khomeini equated women's emancipation with prostitution and issued an edict inciting his supporters to revolt against the Shah's "White Revolution." The latter gave women the right to vote and reformed the feudal ownership of land. The revolt was quelled and Khomeini was exiled to Iraq.

Under Reza's iron rule, the judiciary was secularized in 1931, but the area of family life was left to the jurisdiction of the clergy and the dictates of Sharia law. This led to a curious "gender schizophrenia" in Iran's modernity. On the one hand, mandatory organizations of women absorbed a large number of the major figures of the existing women's movement. On the other, women were allowed into higher education, and in 1935, into the University of Tehran. On the grassroots level, some women went back to wearing the veil, but to younger women who were brought up without the veil, the head scarf was generally considered either as unfashionable, or as the outfit for the poor, or as a sign of devout religiosity that they distanced themselves from.

Both Reza Shah's and Mohammad Reza Shah's reforms—carried out from above—served as a double-edged sword from the point of view of women's rights. They facilitated the entrance of women into the job market but—intolerant of any form of democratic activity and freedom of expression—they stifled spontaneous grassroots organizations of any sort. This situation intensified under Mohammad Reza Shah after the 1953 CIA coup that toppled the democratically elected government of Prime Minister Mosaddegh. The return of the Shah was accompanied by creating the Shah's notorious secret police (SAVAK), trained by the CIA and Israel, and turning Iran into the most docile ally of the U.S. in the region.[11]

Mohammad Reza Shah's reforms in relation to women went beyond those of his father; the new law allowed women to enter the hitherto entirely male-dominated field of law. In 1976, five women, including Shirin Ebadi (years later the winner of the Nobel Peace Prize) were appointed judges. The so-called "Family Protection Law" was introduced in 1967. It challenged the existing jurisdiction in matters such as divorce and the custody of children which was taken out of the hands of the clergy. The Sharia law was replaced by civil courts; abortion was tolerated; birth control pills could be sold over the counter. Iran boasted one female ambassador, one female interior minister, and two women senators.

These reforms were important in the sense that they made a differ-ence in the living conditions of middle class women,[12] but they were as mandatory as they were inconsistent. For instance, women still had to have written permission from their husbands to travel abroad. In a coun-try where parliamentary elections were a sheer formality, and where the candidates were preapproved by the Shah, giving voting rights to women was something of a farce. In a famous interview with Oriana Falacci, the Shah emphasized the inferiority of women to men by declaring that, compared to the achievements of men, women had failed throughout his-tory to produce even a single first class cook—cooking, apparently, being their main area of activity.[13] The Shah continued the tradition of auto-cratic modernization. Not only was the mass media entirely censored and controlled, but many books—including Khomeini's treatise on Islamic rule (*Velaayat-e Faghih* [The Guardianship of the Jurisprudent] along with the rest of his writing such as *Tahrir-ul Vasileh*), rife with edicts re-lated to family life and the rules for marriage and sex with child girls and infants—were banned and known only within narrow clerical circles.[14] Lack of access to Khomeini's true beliefs was one of the reasons for the general public support for his opposition to the Shah's 1963 reforms. To the general public, Khomeini's reactionary ideology and antagonism toward modernity were eclipsed by his compelling anti-imperial, anti-Western stance and seemingly egalitarian stance. He would say, "God Himself is a Worker," and many people wanted to believe that he was expressing his support for working class aspirations in his own way.

Reactionary Radicalism da Capo

After the successful 1979 revolution, Khomeini assumed the status of the great leader and embarked on the project of reversing the Shah's modernization of Iran.[15] The anti-imperialist politics facilitated his res-toration of what he considered the Prophet Mohammad's rule of eq-uity in Mecca 1,400 years previously, in the name of social, political, and economic justice.[16] Admittedly, under pressure from the democratic demands of the 1979 revolution, the first draft of the constitution was secular. But, before being put to the vote several months later, the second document was procured, and it was this text that prevailed. As a con-sequence, the Islamic Constitution is ridden with tension between two antithetical entities. Modern democratic institutions—such as elected parliament and elected presidency—are recognized but subjected to the supervision of several clerical bodies above them, all appointed by the Supreme Leader. Women's rights seemingly exist, but hinge on the verse in the Koran—explicitly placing men above women—from which all Islamic laws related to women emanate.

It did not take long for millions of people to discover that they brought down one dictatorship only to replace it with what, from the vantage point of the present, was a totalitarian system. Khomeini's state was very much in line with the structure described by Hannah Arendt in *The Origins of Totalitarianism*—it involved a total theocratic control of all aspects of individual existence. It was a "sandstorm on a desert" that covered and stifled all life.[17] Paradoxically, the process of destruction of human dignity was justified by invoking history and tradition. Totalitarian states, as Arendt maintains, can succeed more easily if they base their propaganda on existing elements within the history and culture. Thus Hitler and his ideologues drew upon the existing anti-Semitic tendencies in Europe—and on the return to the greatness of "pure *Germania*"—in forming the Nazi ideology. Khomeini, in turn, relied on fourteen centuries of Islamic history and tradition for the success of his idea of the new/old Islamic regime, even though to some Shiite scholars this was an unacceptable precedence.

Arendt's description of the distinction between a dictatorship and a totalitarian state captures the difference between the totalitarian Islamic Republic and the autocratic rule of the Shah: Mohammad Reza Shah curbed all political freedoms without trespassing into the private sphere of life. By contrast, the Islamic Republic left no area of political, public, or private life to the discretion of the citizens. Khomeini invoked the idea of the *Umma*, a nation of believers, irrespective of geographical borders. In the name of implementing the Sharia law, ordinary habits of everyday life had to be transformed and *Umma* members, irrespective of whether they were believers or not, had to adjust to what he considered the Islamic way of life. Music was banned and dancing was considered immoral; playing cards, chess boards, and backgammon boxes were confiscated. Manufacturing dolls was considered decadent, and Khomeini advised that little boys should play war games, rather than silly games with balls. Drinking alcohol was punishable by flogging and the production of pork sausages was stopped. Women, their appearance, social standing, and behavior, became the primary objects of control in the new political order.

Khomeini's rule reignited the issue of the veil. The "re-veiling" of women, faced with extensive opposition that forced a setback on it at the start, was not only a part of Khomeini's revenge for Reza Shah's compulsory un-veiling of women in 1936, but also a reflection of the self-image of the Islamic state. To a large number of secular people—or those on the left who had harbored illusions about the nature of the Islamic state and the democratic intentions of Khomeini—his decree about the veil, announced twenty-four days after his coming to power, on the evening nine o'clock news on 7 March 1979, came as a rude awakening. In *Going to Iran* (1982), Kate Millett, the American writer and feminist who was invited to Tehran by a Trotskyist group to hold a lecture on 8 March, provides a vivid picture of the turmoil all over the Tehran University compound and heated discussions among the leftist activists about the wisdom of opposing the "anti-imperialist" Khomeini over such a "trivial matter" as the veil.[18]

The importance of the "trivial matter" of the veil in the history of the Iranian feminist movement cannot be exaggerated. One should bear in mind that, as distinct from most of the Arab world, Iran was never directly colonized and the veil has never assumed the status of an anti-colonial symbol. There is hardly any advocate of modernity in Iran, particularly after the Constitutional Revolution, which, while opposed to any form of foreign intervention in the affairs of the country, would not connect the concept of modernity to the liberation of women. Not surprisingly, there have been frequent references to "the shackle of the veil." Many prominent Iranian feminists such as Shahin Nawai and Shahla Shafigh have written self-critical essays for not having taken a strong enough stand against the veil at the start of the 1979 revolution. Among the younger generation, Shadi Sadr, who gave a lecture on the subject in Hanover in 2009, posed the question why, despite a radical resistance to the veil, the Iranian opposition had failed to make it the major issue around which women would rally and organize. Her only speculation was the high level of risks involved and their prohibitive effect, in view of the centrality of the veil for the prestige of the Islamic Republic. The secular opposition to the regime, in an overall reappraisal of the enlightenment values, has put the question of women's rights on their agenda and declared the compulsory veil as a violation of the basic human rights of half of the population. Both the veil and diverse methods of dealing with it are a constant theme of feminist debates, publications, and websites.

The 1979 protest demonstrations to which Millett refers started on 8 March and went on for six days, ending with a gathering outside the building of Tehran television. The latter refused to report on the event and claimed that the women on the streets were no more than a bunch of mink-wearing call girls. A team of French feminist journalists recorded the fifth day of the demonstration in a film that, together with Kate Millett's book which came out three years later, documents how women were the first social group to sense the totalitarian threat.[19] In the film interview with two veiled demonstrators, one woman complains that she has worked hard all her life so that her daughters could be educated and not to have to wear the veil. The other insists that, having participated in the revolution, it was time for women to fight for "our own rights." Should the authorities try to force the veil on women, she would be prepared to give up her faith. The mood of the demonstration was reflected in slogans and messages on hand-made placards: "We did not make a revolution to go backward," "At the dawn of freedom women's rights are missing," "The freedom of women is the measure for freedom in society," and, "Freedom is neither Eastern or Western, it is universal."

As distinct from the situation that had given Hitler infinite authority over human lives, Khomeini had come to power on the shoulder of a revolution with deeply rooted democratic demands, stretching back to the Constitutional Revolution. While the revolutionary social environment—from the women's movement through the new, freedom-hungry media, to the autonomous councils in factories and schools—was ripe for change, it was not the kind of change Khomeini and his civil and clerical entourage had in mind. The expressions of grassroots democracy were quelled by force. Offices of independent newspapers were attacked;[20] yellow working class councils (Islamic factory and work place councils) were set up to neutralize the independent ones; universities were closed to be Islamicized by the so called "Cultural Crusade"; and leftist students and lecturers were purged and arrested. The full military invasion of Kurdistan, which started in August of 1979, was resumed in April 1980 in the wake of indiscriminate executions by the Sharia judge Khalkhali, who was directly appointed to the job by Khomeini.

Women, whom Khomeini had presumably considered the easiest target for control, proved to be a hard opponent. Khomeini never referred to his initial failure to impose the veil, or commented on the six day demonstrations. Rumor spread that the "Imam" had been misinformed. More moderate clergy, such as Mahmoud Taleghani, jumped forward to say that in Islam there was no compulsion to wear a hijab. Instead, the Islamic state should concentrate on encouraging and convincing women to put it on. However, when the majority of the relatively small number of women who worked in the army refused to go to work veiled, they were immediately sacked. The Khomeini regime employed the same tactic in government departments and offices, and gradually in sectors with a large number of women employees, such as healthcare, education, and shops. Women were controlled at the entrance of work places and checked if they were properly veiled, used makeup, or carried perfume in their hand bags. Special morality police squads patrolled the streets for "badly veiled" women and, at times, used pins to press the veil on the forehead of women who had not covered all their hair. Powdered glass was rubbed into the lips of women suspected of wearing lipstick. Women who were arrested were fined and often subjected to intimidation, such as being shown the dangling corpse of a hanged man. The measures of what came to be called gender apartheid included segregating men and women at the work place, in public transportation, cinemas, food lines, and, for a short period, even on the pavement. School books were rewritten and illustrations redrawn to reflect the different tasks and positions of men and women in society. Walls around girls' schools open compounds were raised to prevent male neighbors from seeing the children. Films were allowed to be shown on television and cinemas only if they had no female protagonists, or if unveiled actresses were first blacked out from the scenes. The film director, Mohsen Makhmalbaf, published a pamphlet which trained camera men on how to marginalize even fully veiled women in the shots they took. Mobs were mobilized and armed, and charged with finding offenders. Morality police could barge into private parties in people's homes to check the relationship of male and female guests.

Meanwhile, in the shadow of the Iran-Iraq War that broke out in 1981, all secular legal provisions securing women's rights were abolished as judiciary power became the domain of Sharia law and the clergy. Legislation passed by the Islamic parliament reduced the marriageable (and punishable) age of girls to nine and of boys to fifteen. Women lost the right to divorce, and the custody of their children was given to the man, or, in the absence of the father, to his male relatives. Daughters' share of inheritance was reduced to half that of their brothers'. Male polygamy was allowed and the Shiite tradition of *sigheh* (ceased marriage)—a form of legal prostitution that allows men to "marry" a woman for a short or long period of time against payment—was encouraged by Islamic leaders, particularly after the Iran-Iraq War that left scores of widowed women behind. Medieval laws, such as stoning for adultery, were introduced for the first time in modern Iranian history, and the penal law of retribution (eye for eye) ruled that since a woman's blood was worth half that of a man, a man who killed a woman could not be punished unless the family of the dead woman first paid him half of a full person's blood money.[21] This policy, in practice, sanctioned the killing of poor women with impunity. To crown it all, 12 June, allegedly the birthday of the Prophet's daughter Fatima, was declared the Islamic Women's Day.

As Hannah Arendt has argued, totalitarian regimes constantly require enemies to define their own existence. For Khomeini, the supreme enemy was, predictably, the U.S., or the "Big Satan." Another easy target of hate was—and continues to be—Israel. The Iran-Iraq War, that Khomeini called "a blessing for us," and lasted for eight years and killed one million Iranians and Iraqis, started with Saddam Hussein's air attack, and provided Khomeini with an enemy on the actual battlefield. The war allowed the Islamic Republic to build up its propaganda machine to perfection. School boys were encouraged to enroll in the ranks of the Holy Defense and sent to the war front after scant training. With plastic keys to paradise hanging on their necks, they left for the battlefront with promises that they would qualify for the lofty status of a martyrs when they were killed in the mine fields. Women were given a new role as mothers who should bring up their sons for martyrdom. In a multicolored poster called *Isaar* (self-sacrifice), using the idea of a pieta, the centerpiece is a pale, expressionless woman in two layers of veil holding the corpse of her son on her outstretched arms. On the left hand side are fetuses which had passed through the red area in the middle of the picture, presumably the woman's womb, and transfigured into the martyrs of Islam on the right side of the picture. In the foreground there is her prayer mat and behind her are the white, headless bodies of the martyrs in paradise. The edges of the poster are inscribed with verses from the Koran about the benefits of killing and getting killed for a Godly cause.[22]

Like in the case of Hitler, the paramount concern of Khomeini was the survival of the *nezam* (the system) to which all cost in human life and suffering was irrelevant. When, as he said, he drank "the cup of poison"—i.e. accepted the UN resolution for the end to hostilities with Iraq in 1988—the Islamic Republic, having squandered so many lives to a war it had lost, was weakened and discredited. Thousands of members of the opposition who had not been executed or forced into exile were serving prison terms in various parts of the country. On Khomeini's direct order, those who refused to repent were put to death and buried in mass graves whose locations remain unknown to this day. [23]

During these years—and up to the present day—one of the most fascinating developments in the history of civic mobilization in Iran has been the consistent reactivation of the 8th of March Day, usually accompanied by demonstrations. This Western emblem of women's struggle for emancipation became a focal point of Iranian women's demands in 1979 and the early 2000s. In 2005, after the election of Ahmadinejad, there was a massive 8th of March gathering held in Daneshjoo Park. The new government responded with brutal violence directed at women. To quote one incident: Simin Behbahani, an eighty-two-year-old poet and women's rights activist, was among those who were beaten severely. She commented on the event by saying that Iran was the kind of country in which the International Women's Day had become the day for woman beating. Parvin Ardalan, the feminist journalist, one of the founders of Women's Cultural Centre, and the winner of the 2006 Olof Palme prize, has recorded the sequence of events leading to that day in her "Women's Movement in the Streets," "We realized we had become a big enough force for them to have to attack us the way they did."[24]

The 2000s have signaled a new phase of activism for the women's movement. The "Campaign for One Million Signatures for the Repeal of Discriminatory Laws against Women" started in the fall of 2006. Its organizational method was networking, both as an experiment in decentralized organization and as a safety measure. The campaigners printed a pamphlet that mentioned discriminatory laws and explained the reasons why it was imperative to change them. Using the experience of Morocco, the activists worked mostly with a face to face contact, taking the pamphlet to the streets and parks, from door to door, and from workplace to workplace, entering into a discussion with the women or men that they met. They published the minutes of their discussions on the Internet to find out how people thought and to learn from each other. At its height, the Campaign was active in twenty different cities. The year 2006 also witnessed the founding of the campaign against stoning of women, "End Stoning Forever." Its *spiritus movens*, the Iranian journalist and lawyer Shadi Sadr, has been part of the women's website group, *Women's Field*, whose objective has been to change the Islamic Penal Code of Iran so that stoning will neither be issued as a sentence nor be practiced as a punishment ever again.

Dissidents' International

It is impossible to review the history of the women's opposition to Iranian totalitarianism without mentioning a vast network of Iranian feminists abroad, growing rapidly among the four to six million Iranian political exiles and their families. At the UN women's conference in Nairobi in 1985, when the Islamic government still had some remnants of international prestige as the representative of an "anti-imperialist" revolution, a small group of Iranian women from Sweden, Britain, and the U.S. exposed the treatment of women in Iran in the non-governmental sessions of the conference. When the fully veiled governmental representatives tried to quiet one of these exiled speakers by chanting "war, war, till victory," they were thrown out of the room. In response, the Iranian government worked hard to organize some thirty-five non-governmental groups of its own, in coordination with a number of women from Islamic organizations elsewhere in the world. At the 1995 UN women's conference in China, the women representing these "official" non-governmental organizations had to face the eloquent Iranian exile feminists who contradicted their platitudes with facts about the condition of women in Iran. Over the last twenty years, national and international conferences of Iranian women abroad have invited and promoted activists from Iran, serving as a link between the home-based and exile parts the women's movement. Internet magazines as well as individual and collective blogs and mailing lists have been established to disseminate information and create a forum for recognizing the "power of the powerless."

The "One Million Signature Campaign for the Repeal of Discriminatory Laws against Women" was the most publicized initiative in the period of 2006–2010. Occasionally, it led to clashes between inside and outside activists. Many of the home campaign activists were well aware that the signatures had little chance to change the laws, but they regarded their work as a form of public education in feminism. However, since a political system such as the Islamic Republic provides no scope for reform or compromise, those on the outside found it easy to accuse the activists of creating an illusion that there could be a systemic change. Worse still, the merciless suppression of the demonstrations after the 2009 elections, and the long prison terms meted out to women activists and to their lawyers, was meant to demonstrate that the idea of a women-led civil society was a chimera, at least in the Islamic Republic.[25] While the Campaign and its advocates received world-wide recognition and were awarded prestigious prizes by human rights and pro-democracy organizations, for reasons we shall mention below, the importance and consequences of the Campaign have never made front page headlines in Western European media.

An unprecedented development in the history of world feminism has been the collaboration of many young men within the ranks of the Iranian women's movement. As the Iranian exile feminist Nahid Husseini pointed out in her lecture at the 21st Iranian Women's Studies Foundation Conference 2010 in Paris, the Islamic Republic, and most other political Islamic groups, musters the support of the male population for their policies by giving the men sway over women.[26] There are, however, men who refuse to play the part of the oppressor and reap the benefits. Yet another speaker at the conference, Ali Abdi (a young man surprisingly knowledgeable in feminist theory and history) put it this way: "I entered the women's movement as a human rights activist. But now I am fighting for my own rights. I refuse to be the creature they are making me into." After the arrest of a male student dissident who had spoken at a rally in the fall of 2009, Iranian television showed him in women's clothes and a veil, claiming that was the way he had wanted to sneak out. This claim was, from the perspective of the authorities, the ultimate humiliation for a man. The move backfired on the regime, however, when hundreds of Iranian men, some with thick moustaches, put on veils and posted their images on the Internet, with captions that read: "I also am a woman!"

To summarize, the Iranian case shows a new face of modern dissent. There is no doubt that the heroism and rectitude of women's opposition in Iran transcends anything that had been endured by Eastern European dissidents. In a speech delivered in the Swedish parliament in November 2009, entitled "Women and the Women's Movement after the Post-election Popular Revolt," Shadi Sadr quoted the case of Elham, a woman who was arrested in the demonstrations and was Sahdi's former cellmate. Elham's father was a retired army officer whose pension did not cover the cost of his big family. At fifteen, Elham was taken out of school and married off to a man who subjected her to various forms of abuse. She managed to divorce him fifteen years later, with numerous scars over her body and a number of broken teeth. She was left with a small sum of money as an alimony and lost the custody of her two daughters, aged ten and fourteen, by the ruling of the Sharia judge. In spite of these challenges, she managed to finish her basic school education to give herself the chance of getting a job. When the demonstrations broke out, she and her sister joined the protestors out of curiosity. Soon they turned into the leaders of street defense. They tied their head scarves in such a way that only their eyes could be seen, and so that security guards could not identify them. Elham was arrested as she was encouraging several young men to neutralize a group of security forces by leading them to a side street around the Revolution Square. Sadr tried to find out why Elham, a woman who made no claims to being a political activist and who had no access to a computer, had used the only luxury in her life, her mobile telephone, to film several of the marches and become so deeply involved in the popular movement. Recounting their interaction, Sadr stated: "Elham said that she had long ago found out that in our society a woman was not considered a full human being, that she had no rights whatsoever. She piled up resentment against the system that had for years treated her unfairly, but to the same extent she had developed a will to resist injustice. 'I can take beatings,' she said. 'This is nothing compared to what I got from my husband and my brothers. Human life is not worth much, I've found out.'"[27]

This, if nothing else, evokes Hannah Arendt's statement that, "Only those who can endure the passion of living under desert conditions can be trusted to summon up in themselves the courage that lies at the root of action, of becoming an active being."[28]

Feminism in a Totalitarian State

As we have argued, although Iranian feminism has its own founding mothers and its unique genealogy, there is no doubt that its main inspiration has been Western European rites and scribes—from the International 8th of March Day, to Simone de Beauvoir and Kate Millet's writings. Springing from these diverse origins, there are two difficulties that lie at the basis of feminism in Iran. The first one is conceptual and internal, and the second is related to the current state of Western feminism. Starting from Iran: the "Iranian Women's Movement" aspires to be internationalist and secular. However, a considerable number of women with religious background have defined themselves as feminists. They range from the conservative Azam Taleghani, daughter of the late Ayatollah Taleghani, to Shirin Ebadi, the Nobel Peace laureate who depicts herself as a believing Muslim as well as an advocate of a secular state. Further, efforts have been made to include in "Islamic feminism" women groups that, even though close to the Islamic power elite, consider excesses in relation to women as the wrong interpretations of Islam. Thus, by general consent among Iranian secular feminists, "Islamic feminism" is often regarded as a contradiction in terms,[29] even though the use of the concept itself can point to a growing ideological and religious diversity of dissent in Islamic countries. However, lurking in the background is the unresolved question of the potential for reform of the Iranian Islamic Republic into a state including women as full-fledged political citizens. Would not such a reformed, women-friendly state then need to omit the word "Islamic" in its self-definition? Having founded its ideology, structure of power, and the bulk of its propaganda on the inferior position of women, what other claims to authenticity or religiosity is left for the Islamic state? These questions are pertinent, considering that both the gender apartheid and the ongoing debasement of women have rested on religious justification.

The second difficulty in trying to identify the true nature of the Iranian feminist opposition stems from Western misperceptions. For all its conceptual refinement and theoretical sophistication, the dominant tendencies within current Western feminism lack both the insight and the sensitivity to accommodate present day feminism in non-Western countries. Though it has supported the conventional wisdom that regards the oppression of women as universal, it tends to "culturalize" feminism in non-Western countries. It may well be that the radical, postmodern respect for cultural difference has somehow overshadowed the plight of the female underdog in the Islamic Republic. Or that sisterhood is global, but the globe ends up having a parochial shape. Whatever the reason for the current myopia or indifference, feminism in Western countries has been largely oblivious to the political, anti-totalitarian dimension of women's movement in Iran. While the tribute to individual Iranian feminists has been paid in the form of prestigious prizes, no pressure from the women's movement in the West has been put on governments and political parties to recognize the Iranian women's movement as a serious political force. As it is, curbing Islamism, rather than supporting grassroots movements—the strongest among them the Iranian women's movement—tends to predominate in the political propaganda in the West. Like the Western Left—largely oblivious to totalitarian threats—dominant Western feminism itself seems to have lost a sense of what an anti-totalitarian struggle is about. Absorbed in "academism" and diverted for the last three decades into state feminism, it seems to be unperturbed by what Arendt called the "conditions of the desert." It has largely ceased to be the grassroots civil movement it once was, and has become local and provincial, losing most of its earlier muscle.[30] This is a far cry from the political position of the Iranian women's movement that, at the beginning of the twenty-first century, cannot, even if it wanted, be co-opted into a political system that owes its identity to the suppression of women. With all its disparities, the civic opposition to Iranian totalitarianism has developed what Arendt, referring to the American Revolution, described as a "grammar of action" and "syntax of power." By the first she meant "that action is the only human faculty that demands a plurality of men." By a "syntax of power" she referred to the power "that is the only human attribute which applies solely to the worldly in-between-space by which men are mutually related, combine in the act of foundation by virtue of the making and keeping of promises, which, in the realm of politics, may well be the highest human faculty."[31]

Like previous totalitarian regimes, the Iranian authorities have done their best to disregard or trivialize the women's agenda. When in 2009 President-elect Ahmadinejad conceded the strength of the women's movement and tried to emulate Western state feminism by posing with his fully covered, indistinguishable wife and including women in the list of ministers for his cabinet, he responded to the criticism of the conservative clergy by saying that the presence of a woman would prevent the male cabinet members from using obscene language at meetings on the governmental level. Moreover, the few token female representatives in the Islamic Parliament (The Women's Parliamentary Faction), have systematically condoned the anti-women legislation passed over the last thirty-two years.

To conclude, at the first decade of the twenty-first century, the very concepts of Iranian "feminism" and "Iranian opposition" require some revaluation. The current revolution in Iran is, like any anti-totalitarian revolution, less about gender and more about totalitarianism's denial of basic human dignity, both to men and women. True, it is women who are the new "proletariat" in the Iranian case; they have nothing to lose but their chains. They are also the avant-garde of the civic opposition to totalitarian rulers and face the challenge of safeguarding their rights after the regime's collapse. Hence, they are potentially the embodiment of political revolution where, in Arendt's terms, "the act of foundation is identical with the framing of a constitution."[32] Perhaps it is not gender, but *dignitas* that should be the key to the Iranian civic movement? To invoke Arendt again, the right to membership in a political community should rest on the notion of human dignity which transcends cultural specificity. Further, Arendt has argued that human dignity needs a guarantee that can be provided only by a new law on earth whose validity must comprehend the whole of humanity.[33] Following Arendt, although the opposition in Iran defines itself as "feminist," we in the West should understand it as a driver of an anti-totalitarian revolution which is about reclaiming human dignity. Such a revolution transcends cultural and gender boundaries. It should not be relativized because of its gender bias or so-called "Western inspiration." The stakes behind it are so high that the very concept of "feminism" may be misleading, if not downright embarrassing.

The new, unique revolution in Iran has a woman's face—but it is, in essence, the Arendtian revolution which has as its objective to restore human dignity to the whole population, men, women, homosexuals, and children. If even partly successful, it can transform the politics of the entire region. Such a transformation is as much an exciting as a challenging project. On the one hand, the 2011 political upheavals in North Africa—sometimes compared to the 1979 and 2009 uprisings in Iran—reflect the fragility of oppressive regimes in the face of a determined and politically mature population. But, as the African Awakening, or the Arab Spring have shown, the specter of a possible fundamentalist take-over after the manner of the Iranian revolution, haunts the fledgling democracies. The women-led "monitory democracy" in Iran may provide an inspiration for other oppressed communities in the Middle East, but it still faces the challenge of creating a compelling vision which will gain popular support at home and abroad. This project will be well nigh impossible, if citizens and media in affluent democracies do not stand up to the test of solidarity and the necessity of speaking truth to power.

Notes

1. Many of the events related to the post-revolutionary period referred to here are based on Haideh Daradeh's first-hand, personal observations, documented and corroborated by other activists. We also quote articles, addresses, blogs, and interviews which are available only in Persian. Full accounts of this period, including scholarly analysis and interviews—edited by Nasser Mohajer and Mahnaz Matin—are forthcoming in two volumes in Persian.
2. Nabavi mentions only one woman intellectual: Simin Daneshvar. See Negin Nabavi, *Intellectuals and the State in Iran: Politics, Discourse, and the Dilemma of Authenticity* (Gainesville, F.L.: Florida University Press, 2003).
3. Hannah Arendt, "'Action' and 'The Pursuit of Happiness,'" in *Politische Ordnung und menschliche Existenz. Festgabe für Eric Vögelin zum 60. Geburtstag,* ed. A. Dempf (München: Beck, 1962): 2.
4. See the orientalist Edward Brown's 4 volumes of *The Literary History of Persia,* and *Selections from the Writings of E.G.Brown on the Baabi and Bahai Religions,* ed. M. Momen (Oxford: Oxford University Press, 1987). See also Conte de Gobineau, *Les Religions et Philosophies dans L'Asie Central,* vol. 2. (Paris, 1865).
5. Ali Akbar Moshir Salimi, *Zanan-e Sokhanvar* (Tehran: Elmi Publishers 1946).
6. Mo'inuddin Mehrabi, *Ghorratulein Sha'ere-ye Azadibakhsh va Melli-ye Iran* (Köln: Royesh Publishers, 1949).
7. Abbas Amanat, *Resurrection and Renewal: The Baabi Movement in Iran 1844–1850* (Ithaca, N.Y.: Cornell University Press, 1989): 295.
8. Mansoureh Ettehadieh and Cyrus Sadounian, eds., *The Memoirs of Taj os Saltaneh* (published in Persian), (Waldorf, M.D.: Iranbooks, Inc., 1991).
9. The English translation of the full Persian title is: *The Strangling of Persia: Story of the European Diplomacy and Oriental Intrigue that Resulted in the Denationalization of Twelve Million Mohammedans* (1812; rpt. Waldorf, M.D.: Mage Publishers, 2006).
10. About women's associations at this time see Janet Afari, *The Iranian Constitutional Revolution: Grass Roots Democracy, Social Democracy, and Origins of Feminism* (New York: Columbia University Press, 2005).
11. For the analysis of the nature of the Shah's dictatorship see Homa Katouzian, "The Iranian Revolution at 30: The Dialectic of State and Society," *Critique* vol. 19, no. 1, (2000): 35–53. See also Abbas Milani, *The Shah* (New York: Palgrave, Macmillan, 2011).
12. See Eliz Sanasarian, *Women's Rights Movement in Iran: Mutiny, Appeasement, and Repression from 1900 to Khomeini* (New York: Praeger Press, 1982).
13. "Oriana Falacci's Interview with Mohammad Reza Shah on Religion," available at: *http://www.iranian.com/main/blog/masoud-kazemzadeh/oriana-fallaci-inter view-mohammad-reza-shah-religion*
14. For translations of Khomeini's ideas see *Imam Khomeini, Islam and Revolution,* ed. Hamid Algar (New York: Mizan Press, 1981): 27–166.
15. In this he benefitted largely from the work of a number of earlier intellectuals who made no distinction between modernity and colonial or imperialist political, economic, and cultural exploitation. The writer Jalal Al-Ahmad (1923–69) in his famous essay "Westoxication," (1962) taking his cue from Franz Fanon, at-

tacked Western dominance and advocated return to Eastern values and domestic industries such as carpet weaving. The factual mistakes and misrepresentations of his essay were challenged immediately after its publication, but this did not prevent Khomeini from using some of Al-Ahmad's arguments in his speeches many years later. Ali Shariati (1933–77) in his less sophisticated and more emotionally charged writing promoted Shiism. The Iranian journalist and political activist Khosrow Golsorkhi (1944–74)—sometimes compared to Che Guevara—in his televised trial prior to his execution, referred to Imam Hussein, the Shiite martyr of the early years of Islamic history, as his spiritual mentor.

16. For a selection of Khomeini's writing in French see Ruhollah Khomeini, *Principes Politiques, Philosophique, Sociaux et Religieux* (Paris: Editions Libres-Halliier, 1979).

17. Hannah Arendt, *The Origins of Totalitarianism* (New York: Harcourt Brace, 1979).

18. Kate Milllet, *Going to Iran* (New York: Coward, McCann, & Geoghegan, 1982).

19. The film, *Tehran Anne´ Zero* (1979), was made by four French women—Michele Mouler, Sylviana Boiasuna, Claudine Mular, and Sylven Rey—from the group Psychanalyse et Politique, a division of Moouvement de Liberation des femmes.

20. The daily *Ayandegan* and the weekly *Peygham-e Emrooz* never came out again. The extremely popular satirical weekly *Ahangar* managed to continue for two more months by being printed inside a moving container before it was stopped.

21. Some of these measures have changed, for better or for worse, over the years. A moratorium on stoning was announced following the pressure by the European Union but it did not last. The demand for the sum of blood money becoming equal for men and women is one of the demands of the One Million Signature Campaign. Some of the clerical members of the Islamic parliament have been pushing for male polygamy which has been conditional—and dependent on the consent of the first wife—to become unconditional.

22. The poster is the work of Kazem Chelipa and published by the Masjed-e Jame-e Abbasi and the Ministry of Guidance.

23. When Ayatollah Montazeri, Khomeini's heir-apparent, argued with him that his execution order undermined the authority of Islamic judiciary and the Sharia judges who had passed the initial prison sentences, Khomeini, in an unpublished film that now exists on YouTube, rejected all appeals for clemency by referring to Imam Ali, the fourth caliph (and according to Shiites the first legitimate heir to Mohammed). Ali, Khomeini argued, had personally put 700 men to the sword in a single day. The outcome of Montazeri's appeal was that he was deprived of his position as Khomeini's successor, and the position went to the less qualified Khamenei, the present Supreme Leader, after Khomeini's death in 1989.

24. Parvin Ardalan, *Name-ye Zanan*, Newsletter of the Women's Cultural Centre, no. 5&6, March 2006: 85–96.

25. It is just as well to recall that when the anti-government demonstrations were shaking the foundations of the system, the Iranian Islamic Parliament was pushing to abolish a clause in the polygamy law that makes taking of a second wife dependent on the approval of the first one.

26. Nahid Husseini, *Impact of Culture on Iranian Female Education* (London: Satrap Publishing, 2010).

27. The present quote comes from Shadi Sadr's blog *Meydan-e Zanan*, transl. Haidah Daradeh.

28. Hannah Arendt, "Epilogue" in *The Promise of Politics* (New York: Schocken, 2005): 202.

29. The main criticism leveled against the Campaign by secular feminists was that it had sought the approval of the more liberal high ranking clergy and thus limited its space for maneuver.

30. In a widely debated book, *The Death of Feminism* (2006), Philis Chesler announced that the mainstream feminism, dominant in Western academia and in the media, is morally bankrupt because it does little or nothing to oppose or criticize communities and regimes which reduce women to cattle, practice gender apartheid, or condone genital mutilation. According to Chesler, the original courage and creativity of feminism has today been replaced by cowardice: fear of being branded as racist, imperialist, or arrogant. She mourns the "Stalinization and Palestinianization of the feminist postcolonial and postmodern academy." See Philis Chesler, *The Death of Feminism* (New York: Palgrave, Macmillan, 2006).

31. Hannah Arendt, *On Revolution* (London: Penguin Books [1963], 1990): 175

32. Arendt, *On Revolution:* 125.

33. For an insightful discussion of this question see Jeffrey C. Isaac, "A New Guarantee of Earth: Hannah Arendt on Human Dignity and the Politics of Human Rights," *American Political Science Review,* vol. 90, no. 1, (1996): 61–73.

Chapter 10

ASSOCIATIVE DEMOCRACY IN THE SWEDISH WELFARE STATE

Lars Trägårdh

Introduction

From a Nordic perspective, John Keane's notion of "monitory democracy" seems more quaintly familiar than radically novel. With an ancient and constitutionally enshrined protection of freedom of speech, a well-established right to association, and the world's oldest freedom of information legislation—Sweden's Freedom of the Press Act of 1766, granting public access to government documents—one might even claim that Nordic democratic governance fundamentally rests on the pillars of what Julian Assange and Wikileaks now call "information activism." Indeed, lacking a tradition of constitutionally embedded separation of powers, or a bill of rights protecting individuals and minorities from majoritarian "dictatorship," Sweden and the other Nordic countries depend on the free press and a critical civil society to challenge and balance state power highly centralized in parliament and government.

   In this chapter I will, using Sweden as my primary case, attempt to lay bare the fundamental logic of the Nordic social contract with respect to the interplay between state and civil society in a broader comparative and theoretical context.[1] The underlying question, directly relevant to the broader concerns of this book, is whether the Nordic historical experience can be of help in analyzing current developments in countries where the emergence of a strong civil society is more recent.

The Nordic countries also pose a particular challenge to theorists of civil society since they can be understood simultaneously as founded on large and vital civil societies; as characterized by unusually extensive public sectors (and by an unusually positive view of the state); and as quintessential, vibrant, market societies with open and export-driven economy. Indeed, as I write these words in the spring of 2011, the Nordic countries are undergoing an interesting image transformation: traditionally famous for their cradle-to-grave welfare states, they have recently been labeled as the "Nordic tiger economies," and the mystery of high-octane Nordic capitalism was one key theme at the 2011 World Economic Forum in Davos, Switzerland.[2] But equally true, in the wake of global comparative surveys on social trust and the size and character of civil society, theorists of social capital and civil society have come to herald the Nordic countries, along with the Netherlands, as shining examples of social orders founded on the firm pillars of societal self-organization.[3]

In focus will be a number of themes and issues central to this book: an attempt at unpacking the concept of civil society at the empirical level, in particular its political "voice" versus its aid and charity "service" dimensions; an analysis of the political position of civil society in relation to the state, especially contrasting narratives of "autonomy" and "opposition" with those of "representation" and "co-governance"; and finally a discussion of how these tensions can be theorized by pitting a neo-Hegelian conception of civil society against the currently dominant neoliberal account.

The Paradox of Swedish Political Culture: State and Civil Society in Sweden

The Swedish political tradition is marked by a seemingly mysterious paradox. On the one hand, many historians have emphasized the early emergence of a modern, centralized state since the sixteenth century. Indeed, Sweden is at times viewed as one of the first and most fully realized examples of an absolutist state, one that served as a model for the Prussian and Russian state builders in the centuries that followed. On the other hand, Sweden is also often celebrated as an open democratic society in which citizens enjoy easy access to political leaders and the political process. In particular, the historical role of the oppositional Swedish civil society, the so-called popular movements of the nineteenth century (*folkrörelserna*), has been stressed as crucial to the formation of a modern democratic political order. In this reading, the hallmark of Swedish political culture is a productive tension between a state representing the universal or national interest and a plethora of civil society organizations that speak for and protect the interest of particular groups and classes in society.

The notion that Swedish political culture is particularly statist has shown itself to be an enduring one, not least among critics of Sweden. In his controversial book *The New Totalitarians*, Roland Huntford developed this thesis to its extreme conclusion.[4] Viewing Sweden as the incarnation of Aldous Huxley's *Brave New World*, Huntford castigated the Swedes, who he deemed to be "not quite of the West," for their "worship of the State." According to Huntford, they possessed the trappings of constitutional democracy, "but they do not have democracy in their hearts." Rather, he went on, "they have a preference for government by bureaucrats rather than by politicians," and like true denizens of a Brave New World, they do not even suffer under the rule by central administration, instead, "they love their servitude."[5] Most serious academics would not go as far as Huntford. Nevertheless, ever since the 1950s, even leading Swedish political scientists, from Gunnar Heckscher in the 1950s to Bo Rothstein in the 1990s, have described Sweden as a "corporatist" state, even though they would carefully distinguish Swedish "democratic" corporatism, however statist, from its fascist cousins.[6]

In marked contrast to this conception of a state dominated society stands another equally potent and deep-rooted conception, that of Sweden as a quintessential popular democracy. At times, this essentialist narrative about Swedish national identity has rivaled even English and American "exceptionalism," the self-celebratory tales of being the "chosen land" of democracy and freedom. The unique status of the Swedish peasantry—which never suffered under feudalism—would be emphasized, along with long-standing traditions of rule of law, local self-government, social trust, and personal freedom. Building on a tradition going back to the father of modern Swedish history, Erik Gustaf Geijer, it was in the 1930s and 40s common to depict an unbroken tradition that linked legendary peasant leaders from the distant past to popular movements of the nineteenth century and the breakthrough of modern democracy in the twentieth.

From this perspective, what scholars like Heckscher and Rothstein describe as corporatism is instead conceived as a particularly vibrant form of participatory, deliberative, or, to invoke Keane, "monitory" democracy, in which the free associations, not least the unions, the cooperative movement, and the employers organizations, critically watch and effectively co-govern Swedish society in close but free cooperation with the representatives of the state. Indeed, the liberty of Swedes was the result of centuries of struggles by "the little people" (*småfolket*)—peasants and workers—to keep at bay the threats from above, from the aristocracy of the past to the capitalist upper class of modern times. Another Swedish political scientist, Hilding Johansson, who was a contemporary of Heckscher, calls this "a democracy of popular movements, or associative democracy." Rejecting the label "corporatism," Johansson emphasized that, "in Sweden the organizations are free and self-governing." They primarily "pursue their own purposes and seek to safeguard the interests of their members. The cooperation with the state is voluntary."[7]

Whether one wants to conceive of modern Sweden and the other Nordic countries as closed, state dominated societies or as associative democracies in which the state is but a set of open institutions, where free associations negotiate with each other under the helpful and neutral guidance of state representatives, is to a great extent a matter of political taste and interpretation. Asle Toye's chapter in this book is one example of the more critical view in the case of Norway. But beyond political rhetoric, the two perspectives are not incompatible. Empirically speaking, both Heckser and Johansson appear to be right. Sweden and the other Nordic countries score comparatively very high when it comes to measures of trust, social capital, and membership in voluntary associations. At the same time, there is no doubt that the state plays a major role in the affairs of the Nordic countries, or that taxes and public sector spending is very high.

Swedish Political Culture and the Role of the State

What is clear is that the case of Sweden appears to undermine the idea that the struggle between state and society is a zero sum game—that a strong state will typically undermine popular self-organization and democratic governance, and that a large public sector stands in opposition to a vibrant civil society. Symptomatically, until very recent times, coinciding with the introduction of the civil society concept, the words for "state" and "society" were often, if not usually, used as synonyms. The simultaneous presence of an exceptionally large public sector and an unusually vital civil society in Sweden thus poses an interesting and important conceptual and theoretical challenge with serious political and policy implications.

The way in which many Swedes have come to understand the proper relationship between "state" and "society" is in fact central to what we may call "the Swedish social contract." That is, Swedish national identity has come to be tightly linked to a positive view of the role the state, understood not simply as a set of institutions but as the realization of the vision of *Folkhemmet*, the "people's home," the central organizing slogan of the Social Democrats that dominated Swedish politics from 1933 until 2006. The "Swedish Model" as it came to be known, has been characterized by a particular form of statism built on a vision of an alliance between a strong and good state, on the one hand, and emancipated and autonomous individuals, on the other.

The historical roots of the Swedish iteration of the ethos of modern democracy can be traced to the legacy of the strong position of the peasantry. Since the Swedish peasantry largely escaped feudalism and even retained its rights to be represented as a separate estate in the *Riksdag*, it could play a decisive role in the political affairs of the country. In particular, the peasant estate formed an enduring alliance with the quasi-absolute monarchy against the common enemy, the nobility. As a consequence, the Swedish gentlemanly class never came to play the same leading role that it did in Western Europe, and Swedish political culture came to be cast in a mold very different from that of other Western democracies. Far from generalizing noble or bourgeois privilege, the organizing principle was that of leveling, of eliminating rather than extending privileges and special rights. Ultimately it was a process of universalizing the egalitarianism of the peasant community, of reducing noble and bourgeois "rights" until there were but "peasants"—"the people"—left. If in the West the ideal type was the honorable gentleman, in Sweden it was the modest but proud peasant.[8]

It was the luck (or, some would claim, the political genius) of the Swedish and other Nordic Social Democrats to be able to tap into this potent tradition, half-myth, half institutional reality, during the high age of statist nationalism after the World War I. Thus, during the famous "deals" between the peasants' and workers' parties during the early 1930s, the Social Democrats managed to shoulder the mantles of both monarchical statism and peasant populism by becoming, on the one hand, the party of the state and, on the other, the voice of the people's movements. The time-honored tradition of seeing the king/state as an ally against the upper classes mutated and deepened with the democratization of the political system and the rise to power of the workers' and peasants' parties. Instead of seeing "civil society" as the crucial, even sole repository of freedom and protection against the power of the state, the state was seen as having a legitimate and decisive role to play in eradicating the inequalities and remaining privileges of the upper classes that were deeply embedded in many, if not most, of the institutions of civil society.

The Character and Composition of Swedish Civil Society

In sharp contrast to Continental Europe, the social contract on which the welfare state was built is therefore one between the individual and the state at the expense of the family and the intermediary institutions of civil society, such as the churches, and private and voluntary charity organizations. Many of the latter are associated not first and foremost with pluralism and freedom, but with demeaning private charity, unequal patriarchal relations, and informal abuses or uses of power. In Sweden, the state is conceived as the liberator of the individual from such ties of dependency, an order of things I have termed "statist individualism."[9] While a rhetoric concerning social equality and individual autonomy is also present in British liberalism or, for that matter, in French Republican thought, the radical emphasis on individual autonomy and equality that is embodied in the institutions of the Swedish welfare state, especially in the realm of social and family policy but also in taxation policies, is not remotely equaled outside the Nordic countries.

In this schema, the position of civil society was ambiguous. Through the institutions of the modern welfare state, the individual was liberated from one set of civil society institutions—such as the traditional family, the churches, and the charity organizations—that were associated with inequalities and relations of personal dependency. The ideals of social equality, national solidarity, and individual autonomy were thus associated with the beneficial power of the state. This is a social contract that profoundly differs from those of most other Western countries outside of Scandinavia.

This suspicion of the liberal, anti-statist notion of civil society does not, however, mean that organizations and associations are and were not important in Scandinavia. Indeed, as noted earlier, the role of the popular or social movements, as well as of the interest organizations, have long been viewed as central to the democratic system. However, two broad points, relevant not just to Sweden but to a general understanding of what civil society is, must be made here about both the character of civil society associations and their relationship to the state.

The first point concerns the type of associations and organizations that have been most common in different countries. Comparative data show that while Swedes and other Nordics are very active as association members, they tend to flock to associations of a different type than is the case in other countries, such as the United States. Unions, clubs that cater to sports and leisure, as well as associations that focus on adult education and culture tend to attract the largest number of members, whereas religious institutions, charities, and non-profit social welfare organizations do not figure as prominently.[10] One way in which one can illuminate this difference is to distinguish between associations whose primary function is political, to express voice, and to promote and protect the interest of a particular constituency; those that provide services to its own members or to particular groups; and those whose focus lie on modes of economic production and consumption that involves non-profit and cooperative forms of organization.

In the first group one can find political parties, social movements, interest organizations, unions, etc.; in the second, charities, aid organizations, faith-based organizations, etc.; and in the third, non-profit organizations, cooperatives, and other types of "social economy" endeavors. A related defining characteristic is the way in which associations are organized. In the Nordic countries, the ideal-typical association has been membership based, democratically organized, and largely run on a volunteer basis. This is in contrast to the currently dominant U.S.-style non-profit corporation/NGO model, which lacks democratic infrastructure and tends to have a much larger proportion of paid employees. To some extent, this second dimension coincides with the first, meaning that democratic and membership organizations often either express political interest, or focus on sports and culture, whereas the service-producing non-profit corporations and NGOs more often have a hierarchical, corporate structure.

The second point concerns the relationship between civil society organization and the state. In the globally dominant (neo)-liberal conception and practice, the emphasis is on a normative ideal in which civil society is autonomous from and in opposition to the state. In the Nordic political culture, civil society organizations are, however, not seen to simply occupy an adversarial position in relation to the state, however crucial of a dimension this is. Rather, they have been viewed as an intrinsic part of a broader democratic structure, exhibiting democratic practices internally and linking up to the national democratic structure externally. In practice this principle has been institutionalized through the longstanding practice of inviting and involving organizations in the long process of turning a proposal into a law or policy through the ubiquitous use governmental commissions.[11]

Governance and Government Commissions in Sweden

As the Swedish political scientist Rune Premfors has observed, "virtually every important piece of legislation is prepared through the work of specially appointed government commissions."[12] The commissions also enjoy considerable autonomy, once constituted. As Premfors notes, since both interest organizations and opposition parties are routinely represented and able to affect the outcome, "the Swedish commissions make up an important arena for political negotiation."[13]

The commissions are also very common. Exact numbers have fluctuated greatly over the past two hundred years, increasing dramatically since the beginning of the twentieth century; in recent decades between two hundred and three hundred commissions have been at work at any given moment. As these numbers suggest, we are not talking about commissions set up just to handle extraordinary and pressing matters, such as is usually the case with Royal Commissions in the U.K. or similar commissions and hearings in the U.S. Rather, the range of topics is very broad, ranging from the most narrowly technical matters to the most basic constitutional issues.

Another hallmark of the commissions is that they engage in both politicking and fact-finding. This once led the American political scientist Thomas Anton to describe Swedish political culture as particularly deliberative, rationalistic, and consensual.[14] The Swedish word for commission, *utredning*, itself suggest not political debate or compromise, but rather rational (*saklig*) investigation of a particular problem or question through the medium of scientific knowledge accumulation and analysis in order to arrive at factual truth and rational solution. And indeed, many commissions do in fact engage natural and social scientists, as well as other experts, to assist in the work of the commission.[15] At the same time, however, the commissions are profoundly political, and while facts unearthed by social scientists are not exactly ignored, they do not trump politically motivated compromises.

A particularly celebrated, yet strangely understudied, aspect of the commissions is the so-called *remiss* system, often described as both the most uniquely Swedish and the most democratic aspect of the commission process.[16] This is the procedure whereby the reports produced by the commission are sent out to a large number of affected government agencies and interest organizations. The *remiss* system is not formally inscribed in law, but it is a long-established praxis. Anyone, even an individual citizen, is free to send a written comment, which then will be included in the final report that becomes part of the record, the basis on which the government will write a bill for the parliament to consider. This process, with its open feedback cycle, not only serves to alert the commissions to ideas, information, and political opinions they might otherwise have missed or neglected, but also legitimizes the final policy or law by giving a hearing to a maximum number of views.

The Commissions: Cooptation by the State
or Democratic Governance

In her book on state-civil society relations in Sweden, the political scientist Michele Micheletti concludes that: "The system of commissions is an important pillar of Swedish political culture, corporatism, and strong society. It symbolizes the Swedish model."[17] By invoking both the notions of "corporatism" and "strong society," Micheletti captures a crucial ambivalence or tension that, as we noted earlier, runs through much of the academic debate as it has unfolded during the past eighty years or so about the character of the Swedish political culture. Her own work is suffused by this ambivalence: one moment she worries about the state dominating civil society ("corporatism"); next she emphasizes the open political opportunity structures that allow for a "strong society" to share and balance power with the state.

In this she is not alone. If we go back to two influential books on the Swedish political system cited earlier, by Gunnar Heckscher (1946) and Hilding Johansson (1952), we see this tension reflected in both their key concepts and their analyses. Thus Heckscher, in writing about civil society organizations, uses the neutral word "organizations," whereas in describing the political system as a whole he chooses the rather more controversial term "corporatism," although he crucially adds the qualifier "free" to set this Swedish variant of corporatism apart from what he calls "the corporative experiments of the dictatorships" (writing in 1946). Johansson, on the other hand, prefers the positively charged term *folkrörelserna*, meaning "popular or people's movements," to designate civil society organizations. Turning to the Swedish social and political order, he argues that the position of the popular movements constitutes "the very peculiarity of the present Swedish social order," which he goes on to describe as "a democracy of popular movements, or *associative* democracy" (his emphasis in the English summary of the book; in Swedish he uses the term *folkrörelsebaserad demokrati* or *folkrörelsesamhälle*[18]).

Johansson rejects Heckscher's use of the term "free corporatism," a concept that other, later scholars have alternately used or rejected but nearly always taken as a point of departure. Nils Elvander, for example, in his influential book *Intresseorganisationerna i dagens Sverige* from 1969, finds the expression inadvisable even as he also avoids the quasi-romantic term *folkrörelse* and instead describes the civil society organizations as "interest organizations."[19] Victor Pestoff, on the other hand, relates to Heckscher's terminology via Schmitter's distinction between state corporatism and societal corporatism.[20] Bo Rothstein, finally, largely echoes Heckscher by using the term corporatism in his book *Den Korporativa staten,* where, just like Heckscher, he carefully draws a line separating the democratic Swedish variant from the odious, fascist one.[21]

While the difference in conceptual usage and analytical emphasis between Heckscher and Johansson, and those who follow in their respective tracks, is a real one, it should also be noted that the gulf that separates them is not particularly wide. They share, one might say, the same enthusiasm and the same worries; on the one hand, that a too close relationship may become corrupting, and on the other, that a collaborative, if also competitive, relationship can be highly productive for society at large.

Heckscher is careful to extol the role played by the organizations in safeguarding the Swedish democratic form of government. His notion of a "free" corporatism is, he writes, meant to suggest a fundamental equality between state and society: "In a democratic society one might say that the state, the organizations, and the individuals are all equal rather than there existing an unambiguous relation of subordination with the state on top."[22] He even appears to foreshadow Robert Putnam in emphasizing that if they are to sustain their position, the organizations must protect and develop the "trust capital" they hold.[23]

Johansson, on the other hand, while predominantly confident in celebrating the virtues of Swedish "associative democracy," also warns that once the organizations themselves cease to be internally democratic, then great dangers lie ahead: "Should the members no longer have real influence on their organizations, then not only would the organizations lose their democratic character, but there is also the risk that the national democracy too would become in fact a dictatorship ruled by the bosses who run the parties and organizations."[24]

Conclusions

We are now in a position to draw conclusions with regards to Swedish political culture and what I elsewhere have called a neo-Hegelian conception of state-civil society relations. By Hegelian I refer to a theory of state-civil society relations that differ profoundly from the dominant Anglo-American account. In the latter, civil society is associated with civic and communitarian virtues such as altruism, charity, volunteering, philanthropy, religion, non-profit organizations, and a host of activities deemed to serve the common good and providing public benefits, such as education, healthcare, and social welfare. The state tends, by contrast, to be viewed with suspicion as a threat to the autonomy of civil society and the freedoms and liberties of the citizens. In a logic that follows from this binary and oppositional conception, it is also argued that a large public sector will "crowd-out" civil society based initiatives and that such a "colonization" by the state constitutes a threat to the vitality and survival of civil society.

By contrast, in the Hegelian scheme, civil society is conceived of as the sphere in which private interests, needs, and desires play out. Inspired by his reading of Adam Smith, Hegel embraced the market as a legitimate, necessary, and ultimately positive force for enabling the private pursuit of gain, pleasure, and self-expression in addition to its laudatory aggregate effect on societal wealth creation.[25] Instead of ascribing to civil society social virtues such as voluntarism, altruism, communitarian impulses, non-profit economic imperatives, freedom and liberty, etc., Hegel had a far more cold-eyed view of civil society. By retaining the market squarely within civil society, Hegel made clear that political parties, unions, voluntary associations, and even what is today called non-profits, ultimately were vehicles for asserting a particular interest, not the common good. They were not there simply for altruistic reasons, to "do good," and they did not embody some kind of different moral logic or rationality that set them apart from for-profit businesses.

This analysis led Hegel to conclude that the internal contradictions of civil society, including poverty, atomistic individualism, and social disorder, could never be resolved by civil society itself. Only the state could promote and safeguard a greater purpose of rationality, by which Hegel meant the "unity and interpenetration of universality and individuality."[26] Thus, for Hegel, the state was not a threat to individual freedom, quite the contrary, it was only through membership in the state and through the superior rationality of the state that the highest form of individual freedom was made possible. In concrete daily life, this merging of individual freedom and the state's universalist rationality was mediated and realized in what Hegel called the "corporations." These were the various associations that individuals, otherwise isolated as atoms in the market system, joined to pursue common interest. In the very act of joining, the individual began the journey to transcend self-interest, forge a social identity, and begin to contribute to the welfare of society as a whole.

By neo-Hegelian, I refer to the strengthening of the democratic element over the more expert dominated and directed statism that often is ascribed to Hegel's original vision by many writers.[27] For Hegel, the state was clearly the top dog, forever trying to corral the mischievous sheep—black and white—romping about in civil society. In the neo-Hegelian conception, on the other hand, state and civil society are more equal partners even as they play different roles, one promoting special private and political interests, the other safeguarding the general interest.

We may also note a few other important principles that seem central to the particular Swedish inflection of this neo-Hegelian social contract. These include: (1) the importance of key values and practices that focus on individual autonomy and social equality; (2) how these have been secured through an alliance between state and individual; (3) that this moral and political logic focused on notions of autonomy and equality also characterize Swedish civil society organizations; and (4) that civil society and the state are linked in a network of ongoing governance structures—the system of commissions—that allow state and civil society to co-govern in a comparatively cooperative manner that is consistent with the neo-Hegelian theory of state and civil society. The key, in terms of democratic governance, then becomes not the extent of strict separation of civil society *from* the state, as in the Anglo-American account, but rather the character of relations *between* civil society and the state.

Finally, let me add a few caveats. First, with respect to Sweden, the discussion of civil society has emphasized the predominance of membership-based, democratic associations whose primary function has been to voice interests and to act as political agents. This is an ideal typical description that tends to underplay the extent to which in Sweden there always also existed charities, churches, and foundations whose primary purpose has been to provide social and welfare services. Indeed, even those associations which primarily performed a voice-function often also provided services to its members.

A second point concerns the actual consequences of a close and collaborative relationship between the state and the associations of civil society, in particular the system of governmental commissions that I have already alluded to above (and written more extensively about elsewhere).[28] The commissions exemplify "governance" as opposed to "government," with representatives of the state—elected officials as well as civil servants—governing in cooperation with a range of civil society actors. As I noted at the outset of this chapter and as also argued by Toje in this book, the move towards close relations between civil society actors and government agents is not unproblematic: will it in fact open up the political system to more actors from civil society, or will it rather entail cooptation and insidious abuse of government power? Ultimately this question must be answered on the basis of empirical evidence. This also applies for the Swedish governmental commissions, which have in fact, been seen both as the epitome of deliberative democracy and, more cynically, as a quasi-corrupt and secretive system whereby a cabal of insiders representing privileged organizations have been able to strike favorable deals with agents of the state.

A final and related point concerns current trends that, according to some observers, suggest a shift from (political) voice to (social) service among Swedish and other Nordic civil society organizations.[29] This is a development that has been noted for some time and that may be accelerating today. One indication of this is the increased usage of the American concepts of "nonprofit" and "charity" in the Swedish language, not least when it comes to discussions about how to reform and restructure the provision of welfare. A debate that in turn is inspired by the British experiment with the Compact, the purpose of which is to set new rules for the cooperation and division of labor between the public sector and civil society by defining their respective rights and responsibilities.[30] Again, it is ultimately an empirical question whether closer collaboration between state and civil society deepens or cheapens democracy.

However, I would like to end by emphasizing the importance of how an ideologically loaded concept like "civil society" structures the debate. As a key concept, civil society is both enabling and limiting, depending on how it is defined and understood. It has a generative power that sets the terms of the discussion. For this reason it is crucial to be clear on how it is ideologically embedded. The recent move to export the "non-profit sector" idea to the Nordic countries is thus in no way innocent but represents a major shift in how civil society is understood, what its relation to the state and politics should look like, and how it is defined in relation to the market.

Notes

1. Here I draw on previous work; see Lars Trägårdh, ed., *State and Civil Society in Northern Europe: The Swedish Model Reconsidered* (New York and Oxford: Berghahn Books, 2007); Lars Trägårdh, "Rethinking the Nordic Welfare State through a neo-Hegelian Theory of State and Civil Society" *Journal of Political Ideologies* vol. 15, no. 3, (2010): 227–239; and Henrik Berggren and Lars Trägårdh, "Pippi Longstocking: The Autonomous Child and the Moral Logic of the Swedish Welfare State" in *Swedish Modernism: Architecture, Consumption, and the Welfare State*, eds. Helena Matsson and Sven-Olov Wallenstein (London: Black Dog Publishing, 2010).
2. See, for example, the pamphlet *The Nordic Way* (*http://www.globalutmaning.se/wp-content/uploads/2011/01/Davos-The-nordic-way-final.pdf*) presented at the World Economic Forum at Davos 2011 and its reception (Bagehot 2010) in *The Economist* (*http://www.economist.com/blogs/bagehot/2011/01/britain_and_nordic_world_0*).
3. Douglas Baer, "Voluntary Association and New Social Movement Association Involvement in Comparative Perspective," in Trägårdh, *State and Civil Society in Northern Europe:* 67–125.
4. Roland Huntford, *The New Totalitarians* (New York: Stein and Day, 1971).

5. Huntford, *New Totalitarians:* 347–348.
6. Gunnar Heckscher, *Staten och organisationerna* (Stockholm: KFs Bokförlag, 1946) and Bo Rothstein, *Den korporativa staten* (Stockholm: Nordstedts, 1992).
7. Hilding Johansson, *Folkrörelserna och det demokratiska statskicket i Sverige* (Karlstad: Gleerups, 1952): 244.
8. Maciej Zaremba, "Byalagets diskreta charm eller folkhemmets demokratiuppfattning" in *Du sköna gamla värld*, ed. Sekretariatet för Framtidsstudier (Stockholm: Liber Förlag, 1987).
9. Lars Trägårdh, "Statist Individualism: On the Culturality of the Nordic Welfare State" in *The Cultural Construction of Norden*, eds. Øystein Sørensen and Bo Stråth (Oslo: Scandinavian University Press, 1997); Henrik Berggren and Lars Trägårdh, *Är svensken människa? Gemenskap och oberoende i det moderna Sverige* (Stockholm: Norstedts, 2006) Berggren and Trägårdh, "Pippi Longstocking."
10. Erik Amnå, "Associational Life, Youth, and Political Culture Formation in Sweden: Historical Legacies and Contemporary Trends" in Trägårdh, *State and Civil Society in Northern Europe;* Baer, "Voluntary Association Involvement"; Eva Jeppsson Grassman and Lars Svedberg, "Civic Participation in a Scandinavian Welfare State: Patterns in Contemporary Sweden" in Trägårdh, *The State and Civil Society in Northern Europe.*
11. Lars Trägårdh, "Democratic Governance and the Creation of Social Capital in Sweden: The Discreet Charm of Governmental Commissions," in Trägårdh, *The State and Civil Society in Northern Europe.*
12. Rune Premfors, "Governmental Commissions in Sweden," *American Behavioral Scientist* vol. 26, no. 5, (1983): 623–642.
13. Premfors, "Governmental Commissions": 628.
14. Thomas Anton, "Policy-Making and Political Culture in Sweden." *Scandinavian Political Studies* vol. 4 (1969): 88–102; Thomas Anton, *Administered Politics: Elite Political Culture in Sweden* (Boston: Martinus Nijhoff, 1980).
15. Lars Foyer, "The Social Sciences in Royal Commission Studies in Sweden." *Scandinavian Political Studies* vol. 4 (1969): 183–204; Premfors, "Governmental Commissions"; Olof Ruin, "Att komma överens och tänka efter före. Politisk stil och 1970-talets svenska samhällsutveckling," in Research Report No. 1 (University of Stockholm, Department of Political Science, 1981).
16. Lars-Erik Erickson, Marja Lemne, and Inger Pålsson. *Demokrati på remiss.* (Stockholm: SOU, 1999): 144; Nils Nilsson-Stjernquist, "Organisationerna och det statliga remissväsendet," *Förvaltningsrättslig Tidskrift* (1947); Victor Pestoff with U. Swahn, "The Swedish Organizational Community and Its Participation in Public Policy-making: An Introductory Overview." in Research Report No. 6 (University of Stockholm, Department of Political Science, 1984).
17. Michele Michelletti, *Det civila samhället och staten* (Stockholm: Fritzes, 1984): 76.
18. Johansson *Folkrörelserna*, 296.
19. Nils Elvander, *Intresseorganisationerna i dagens Sverige* (Lund: Gleerup, 1969).
20. Pestoff, "The Swedish Organizational Community."
21. Rothstein, *Den korporativa staten.*
22. Heckscher, *Staten och organisationerna:* 227.
23. Heckscher, *Staten och organisationerna:* 258.
24. Johansson, *Folkrörelserna:* 258.

25. Norbert Waszek, *The Scottish Enlightenment and Hegel's Account of "Civil Society"* (Dordrecht, Netherlands: Kluwer Academic Publishing, 1988).

26. G.W.F. Hegel, "Elements of the Philosophy of Right," in *Elements of the Philosophy of Right,* ed. Allen Wood (Cambridge: Cambridge University Press, 1991).

27. Hegel's political philosophy was long condemned by liberals and leftists for its alleged worship of the authoritarian, and more specifically, Prussian state. A more nuanced view, which recognizes Hegel's concern to preserve civil society and the domain of individual self-determination, emerged in the 1970s and 1980s with works like Shlomo Avineri's *Hegel's Theory of the Modern State* (Cambridge: Cambridge University Press, 1972), Charles Taylor's *Hegel and Modern Society* (Cambridge: Cambridge University Press, 1979), Z.A. Pelczynski, ed. *The State and Civil Society: Studies in Hegel's Political Philosophy* (Cambridge: Cambridge University Press, 1984), and Manfred Riedel, *Between Tradition and Revolution: The Hegelian Transformation of Political Philosophy* (Cambridge: Cambridge University Press, 1984). For the controversy about the meaning of Hegel's political philosophy among both left and right-wing German thinkers in his own period, see Warren Breckman, *Marx, the Young Hegelians, and the Origins of Radical Social Theory: Dethroning the Self* (Cambridge: Cambridge University Press, 1999).

28. Trägårdh, "Discreet Charm."

29. Tommy Lundström and Filip Wijkström, "Från röst till service? Den svenska ideella sektorn i förändring," *Sköndalsinstitutets Skriftserie* vol. 4 (1995).

30. The "compact" was introduced in 1998 by the Labour government under Tony Blair, as part of his attempt at creating a "third way" between traditional statist labour policies and the neoliberal policies of Thatcherite conservatives.

Chapter 11

STATE CAPTURE OF CIVIL SOCIETY
EFFECTS OF PATRONAGE
IN THE NORWEGIAN AID INDUSTRY

Asle Toje

Introduction

Civil society is the totality of civic and social organizations and institutions that form part of the basis of a functioning democratic society, distinct from the commercial institutions of the market and legally enforced structures of the state. Civil society organizations, including research institutions, are considered in most democracies to be independent of the government. They belong neither to the public sector nor to the private sector, but are rather something in between. Yet in a little over two decades, the Norwegian government has come to be the indispensable financier of Norwegian non-governmental organizations.

In return for state funding, civil society organizations are expected to work towards politically defined policy objectives. The government relies on private organizations to realize the many goals of the public sector. This is the case in a variety of policy areas from foreign aid to healthcare; for example, the Norwegian Red Cross receives government funding to run nursing homes or to achieve Norwegian foreign policy objectives in Haiti. Sociologist Håkon Lorentzen has mapped this dependency on government money. A 2010 survey showed that fourteen different ministries have eighty-one grants available, which amounted to 4.7 billion NOK ($800 million) in the 2009 budget.[1] These grants have quadrupled over the last 25 years, and the culture and sports sectors have been primary beneficiaries. Had the study included the aid sector, the figure would have been doubled to 10 billion NOK ($1.7 billion).

A civil society bankrolled by the government invites a number of important questions with regard to financial dependence and political independence. If civil society's cordial relations with the government are a result of economic dependence, and if civil society has the role of being an extended arm of the central government, this raises the question as to whether this compromises the independence of civil society or the national interest that is the mainstay of the state. It also raises the question as to the extent to which close ties with the government translate into partisanship in civil society. These questions are all the more pressing because of allegations of public practice for private gain. In sum, has political control of the funding of aid NGOs prevented them from playing their corrective role—that is, their speak-truth-to-power function?

In Norway, such questions are rarely asked.[2] One example can stand in the place of many. Atle Sommerfeldt, the head of Norwegian Church Aid the, in 2011, largest recipient of government largesse, responded to questions regarding the effects of dependence, "It has not succeeded, for scientists to point out specifically how the state has affected Norwegian aid organizations working in a way that undermines their independence and critical role for government policy in the field." He went on to claim, "Government money will ensure that operations are increasingly professionally managed and not dependent on commercial collection strategies and the whims of wealthy patrons."[3] The validity of this claim is dubious. Several seminal studies have demonstrated that high levels of government funding can significantly restrict independence of action and independence of spirit.[4]

There is, in other words, a clear case for inquest. Using clienteles as the point of entry into five interconnected challenges—(i) institutional capture, (ii) agenda chasing, (iii) partisan politics, (iv) moral hazard, and (v) crowding out—this chapter will seek to flesh out the main challenges that arise when civil society is primarily funded by the government. Examples will be provided from the Norwegian aid industry. This segment is singled out because it is the civil society sector that receives the largest amounts of state funding relatively and in absolute terms. The ties to the government are tight and the dependence is concrete. The study is all the more relevant because the Norwegian shift towards fully state-funded NGOs can be seen to have originated in the aid industry.

This is not an attempt to provide a comprehensive account of government-civil society relations; rather it intends to shine a light on a particular problem—the adverse effect of government financed NGOs. The examples provided illustrate the relevance of these challenges for the

Norwegian case. The ambition is, in other words, limited—to persuade the reader that challenges associated with clientelism are also relevant in the specific case of government funded aid NGOs. In order to assess the scope or depth of these challenges, a more comprehensive study will be required. The scope of analysis could have been broadened to include the media and state-financed research institutes—but the focus here will be narrowly on the state-NGO nexus. The main argument of this chapter is that potential problems stemming from a state-funded civil society are greater—both for the government and for non-governmental organizations—than are generally acknowledged.

The Norwegian model

Since not all readers are familiar with the dominant role of the state in Norwegian society, a few words on the so-called Norwegian foreign policy model may be helpful. The Norwegian model refers to the idea that government, civil society organizations, and research institutions are mobilized for concerted foreign policy engagement, in particular in such a way that the shared effort remains directed by the state. Political scientist Iver B. Neumann explores several reasons for this. He argues that Norwegian diplomacy changed after the end of the Cold War and that the involvement of civil society actors is an integral element of this change. The state took on new responsibilities, more than the state bureaucracy could reasonably be expected to handle. The additional manpower was found in civil society. This has led to what he calls "dual-track diplomacy," where one track concerns traditional governmental actors and the other the NGO sector.[5]

One reason for the increase in using NGOs was that the state, by fostering civil society, dramatically increased its own administrative resources, allowing for a more ambitious foreign policy than one might otherwise expect from a state with less than five million inhabitants. A second reason was the belief that NGOs are able to efficiently and cost-effectively implement projects in a sustainable manner, particularly those close to the grassroots. The historian Terje Tvedt has pointed out that both substantial government funding for the NGOs and an extensive interpenetration of elites distinguishes the Norwegian model, including exchange of personnel.[6] He is supported in this assessment by Neumann, who concludes that we "might just as well, even preferably, treat such organizations as part of the state formation," when most of their budgets are received from the same government to which they are accountable.[7]

What distinguishes the Norwegian model from similar aid-oriented systems in other countries is, according to Tvedt, that the system is disproportionally larger in Norway in the sense that the number of organizations involved is larger.[8] The aid segment is also relatively larger in the civil society sector and the government gives more, relatively, through the civil society than is the case in other states. In addition, the political consensus between the government and the civil society actors is greater in Norway than in other countries. The circulation among elites within the Norwegian model is more pervasive and the leaders in the civil society organizations have an unusual degree of flexibility when it comes to administering the funds that they are given from the government. One reason for this is that the Norwegian model enjoys relatively stronger popular support than is the case in other comparable countries.[9]

In 2010, the Norwegian aid segment comprised of more than 200 organizations with over 3 billion NOK ($500 million) in annual government support. These organizations encompass more than traditional relief and missionary work.[10] Norwegian Church Aid, the Red Cross, Norwegian People's Aid, and Save the Children are the largest recipients. Individually, over the period from 1990 to 2010, these four organizations received between four and five billion kroner from the state budget, or almost 20 billion NOK ($3.3 billion) in total.[11] Norwegian Church Aid alone received NOK 452 million ($75 million) in 2009. The actual amounts received may be greater still, however, due to discrepancies in self-reported figures and government figures. For instance, the annual government budget operates with a higher figure, of NOK 489 million ($82 million) in 2009 given by the government to the Norwegian Church Aid.[12] Other organizations, such as Norway's sports federations, have also received several hundred million NOK in state aid to conduct projects in accordance with political development goals.

Clientelism

Much, perhaps even most, of the debate about the relationship between civil society and the state is concerned with the old Bolshevik question: *Kto kovo*—who [dominates] whom? Economic dependence carries with it an inherent potential for clientelism. Clientelism refers to a form of social organization characterized by patronage. In such places, relatively powerful and rich "patrons" provide relatively weaker "clients" with jobs, protection, infrastructure, and other benefits in exchange for vocal support and other forms of loyalty, including labor.[13] While this definition suggests a kind of "socioeconomic mutualism," these relationships are fundamentally asymmetric, often resulting in indebted clients.[14] Clientelistic relationships are often seen as providing perverse incentives and are therefore at odds with institutional or individual independence.

According to political scientist Simona Piattoni, clientelism is found "in a variety of political systems characterized by allegedly different [political] cultures and social systems in connection to the transformation of the set of incentives that make them viable and acceptable."[15] She carried out a seminal study on the incentives that make political clientelism and patronage into viable and acceptable strategies. This is a question of particular salience for the Norwegian model: why would civil society actors part with their main distinguishing feature and prized asset—their nongovernmental nature? Part of the answer to this may be found in political scientist Robert Putnam's study of Italian regional institutions. He asserts that the polities can be neatly divided into two broad categories: those with particular interests that are promoted at the expense of the general interest, and those in which particular interests manage to be expressed as cases of broader general interest.[16] The Norwegian model is very much based on an assumption that, in the words of one Ministry of Foreign Affairs (MFA) official, "we are all in the same boat," and that "insofar we are driven by shared idealism, ordinary rules of independence have not been seen to apply."[17] Former Prime Minister Einar Gerhardsen perhaps best summarizes this notion when, in the parliamentary debate that took place when Norway first became an aid donor, stated that Norwegians have "from their whole culture and history represented freedom and democracy, everyone knows that we cannot be suspected of having any interest in exploiting anyone."[18]

Terje Tvedt calls this consensus 'the regime of moral excellence' where the moral justification of the endeavor crowds out critical perspectives on misused funds, low goal attainment, and bad governance.[19] As the government money has surged into development NGOs, other sources of funding have dwindled. In practice, all the large aid organizations are today completely reliant on government funding. While countries such as Britain attempt to keep the ratio of government support for development activities below 50 percent, no such rules exist in Norway. This is worth noting because there has been no lack of guidelines as to the balance between public and private money in the organizations so as to ensure institutional independence. Since 1962, the percentage of private money fell from 50 percent in 1962, to 20 percent in 1972, to 10 percent in 2001. Today organizations are often not asked to provide any funds of their own. According to aid consultant Ian Smillie, the average Norwegian NGO has "a very high level of financial dependency on government."[20]

For the organizations, the dwindling part of private funding has not lead to a scaling down of activities, on the contrary there have been frequent and vocal demands that the government should compensate for the limited fund raising—out of concern for the world's poor.[21] The government money has allowed the organizations to significantly enlarge the number of staff and their wages. For example, Norwegian Church Aid has gone from being mainly a volunteer organization financed by church collections with 8 employees in 1977 to become one of the "Big Four" aid organizations with 150 paid employees in Norway and 33 abroad.[22]

In an economic sense, there clearly exists a patronage relationship between the government and civil society organizations in the aid sector. The nature of this relationship is that the government provide funds and the organizations carry out government objectives. This is significant since it goes to the heart of whom the organizations are actually representing. As economic independence has dwindled, leading aid organizations have been at pains to profess their independence prominently in printed and online material. A former state secretary drew a mischievous parallel: "No country that has the word 'democratic' in its official title has ever been a democracy."[23] Let us then ask the question, as Sommerfelt did—so what? If the NGOs are funded by the state, are they not united in an altruistic endeavor? The following section will look at five challenges of clientelism that have affected the Norwegian aid industry since adopting of the Norwegian model.

Institutional capture

In his doctoral dissertation, "Clientelism," political scientist Samuel Huntington described how federal agencies, exemplified by the Interstate Commerce Commission, get taken over by the very industries that they are supposed to regulate.[24] Institutional capture is defined as the ability of powerful actors to create broad laws and institutions that protect their advantages in the future and allow for their continued power and enrichment. It refers to the de facto take-over of entire state institutions by an elite cartel, which will often manifest itself in these actors' ability to block laws or reforms that would level the playing field. The term was coined by researchers at the World Bank Institute, who noted that institutional capture involved "so-called oligarchs manipulating policy formation and even shaping the emerging rules of the game to their own, very substantial advantage."[25]

Looking back over the last two decades, it is striking how much the Soviet collapse opened a space for Norwegian foreign policy. The result was the so-called engagement policy.[26] A key to understanding the logic of the engagement policy is Jan Egeland's *Impotent Superpower: Potent Small State from 1985*.[27] In this book, Egeland argues that Norway should spend its foreign policy resources on humanitarian endeavors. The claim is that the goodwill generated from state idealism would further national interest objectives. This engagement policy meant that Norway directed its foreign policy resources to help it to play the role of a "humanitarian great power."[28] This was made possible by directing disproportionate foreign policy resources to idealistic endeavors. One figure that illustrates the gravity of this shift is that in 2008, Norway used a historically low proportion of GDP for defense spending (1.3 percent), yet a historically much higher proportion of GDP (an estimated 1.2 percent) on engagement policy, of which civil society has been the primary beneficiary.

The state took up the means, ends, and, importantly, the vocabulary of civil society and elevated them to the heart of foreign policy.[29] Any explanations about how this came about are bound to have a great number of variables. On a practical level, one factor—elite circulation—stands out. At the center of the aid system, and in the border zones of both state and industry, are a surprisingly large number of prominent figures who circulate within the aid industry. A single career typically spans jobs in the government, the research institutions, and in the aid NGOs. This not only applies to the top tier, but also the administrative level. In the aid sector, the three spheres (i.e., state apparatus, research institutions, and the NGOs) form a coherent career progression in which a given person will sit first on one side of the table, and then on the other.

The authors of the three-volume Norwegian foreign aid history underline close links between state aid bureaucracy, aid organizations, and research institutions.[30] Political scientist Øyvind Østerud has pointed out that within this group there is a tendency to consistently overestimate the positive aspects of aid and peace building, while underestimating the negative. He believes that "practitioners from government, NGOs, and research will be a pressure group that blocks objections."[31] The three sides of the triangle have found a common cause in demands for more money to be directed to the aid industry. Resulting growth has been spectacular. Helge Pharo argues that the level of activity exceeds the administrative resources and that this is the single biggest quandary in Norwegian aid policies.[32] This also means that limited MFA personnel resources are spent on donor activities. One diplomat interviewed lamented: "In Oslo we are spending very little time on national interests—extracurricular activity (*valgfag*) has become the core.... The logic and language of Norwegian foreign service has become that of the NGO."[33]

The logic is that the development lobby has succeeded in convincingly arguing that the good of humankind is synonymous with the aid industry's self-interest, and that this in turn is synonymous with Norway's national interests, what might be labeled the "NGO-ification" of Norwegian foreign affairs. The other side of the coin is a "governmentification" of the NGOs. The state-NGO consensus from the 1990s was increasingly seen by many NGOs as a logical extension of their project activities. The idea is that their efforts may have an important community impact in poor countries, but which alone have little general impact unless carried out in a concerted manner. Over past decade, NGOs have dealt with the policy challenge in an ambivalent manner. The growing ambivalence has much to do with the operations in Afghanistan and the notion of "integrated missions" where the NGOs have been expected to formally or informally (the case of Norway) provide support for the military mission. Some have simply denied that there is any potential conflict of interests. Others, concerned about cost and possible government and donor reaction, have somewhat unrealistically argued that coordinating bodies such as The Norwegian Development Network (*Bistandstorget*), the Norwegian Missionary Council (the *Atlas Alliance*), or Forum for Women and Development (*Fokus*) can reasonably be expected to accept the risks associated with voicing concerns. It is a pertinent question whether the near-absence of a debate regarding Norway's disproportionally large military contribution in Afghanistan would have come under greater debate had not the NGOs been so intimately linked with the Norwegian government.

Institutional capture is often assumed, rather than studied; the out of sight nature of the processes involved makes this a difficult issue to pursue. One reason for this is that the group tends to develop a shared set of norms and values. Sociologist Dorothy E. Smith points out that "[i]nstitutional capture can occur when both [involved parties] are familiar with institutional discourse, know how to speak it, and can hence easily lose touch with experiential knowledge."[34] This is no doubt bolstered by the privileges involved in the granting of well-paid jobs. A critical mindset can lead to expulsion, not from one, but from three different work arenas, though this is not to suggest a conspiracy. As political scientist Russell Hardin points out, no intent is necessary for institutional capture—it can result from the structure, or the formal rules, or from the unintended consequences of standard practices within the agency.[35]

Agenda chasing

Agenda chasing, sometimes referred to as "rent seeking" or "ambulance chasing," refers in the simplest terms as directing efforts to the goal of achieving visibility or securing funding.[36] The aid industry has on occasions been accused of focusing on the crisis that represents the best fundraising opportunities, and of responding in a manner that gives the highest public profile to the home country. The International Crisis Group roundly criticized aid organizations for clustering in the countries and regions where there are many television cameras, while harder-hit regions, such as Banda Aceh, received less attention. Industry insiders readily admit to participating in ambulance chasing because of the financial rewards. As a Christian NGO leader once put it, "When a major disaster occurs that captures media attention, our donors respond with incredible generosity."[37] Journalist Linda Polmann has called this phenomenon a "crisis caravan" that "moves on whenever and wherever it sees fit, scattering aid like confetti."[38] As Jan Egeland, in his capacity at the time as UN under-secretary said: "aid is a lottery ... you have twenty-five equally desperate communities taking part in this lottery for attention every week. Twenty-four lose and one wins."[39]

Jan Egeland was himself caught up in a case study conducted by Professor Terje Tvedt. The former was accused of, while serving as the head of the Norwegian Red Cross, securing 100 million NOK in funding from the State Department to send 367 derelict military trucks to Africa. The salient point was that the trucks were sent to alleviate a "humanitarian disaster" that most reports agree had been grossly exaggerated in the Norwegian media with representatives from the government and the NGO community lending authority to the claims.[40] To what extent the Norwegian aid industry is more or less culpable in agenda chasing in comparison to their international counterparts is unclear. What is certain is that leading NGOs are remarkably attuned to changing government priorities, claiming expert competence in areas that, until a change in government priorities, had previously gone unmentioned. Another revealing example is that of former Minister for Development, Erik Solheim. After receiving a second government portfolio as Environment Minister in 2008, he announced that he would treat climate change and development as interlinked questions. In a remarkably short time, all of the "Big Four" government-funded aid organizations developed an environmental focus, accepting and evangelizing Solheim's hypothesis that saving the environment and encouraging development are two sides of the same question.

The most obvious challenge is that this arrangement has weakened the NGOs functions as evaluators of government priorities. Furthermore, both because priorities change at a rapid pace in accordance with the Norwegian political debate (as opposed to in accordance with the priorities of the recipient countries), and because the ambitions are often unrealistic, the situation is all the more worrying. In 2004, the Norwegian Parliament adopted a "Comprehensive Development Policy" explicitly based on the notion that everyone around the world can agree on development goals and how they are to be achieved. The message was centered on good intentions and a directory of unrealistic goals. One goal stated an aim to ensure third world gender equality in primary education, "preferably by 2005."[41] Norwegian aid organizations rarely question the wisdom of the political priorities that come attached to the money they covet. Money has not flown to the organizations with the largest membership or public support. On the contrary, the organizations that have grown the fastest are those that have most whole-heartedly supported political priorities. One example is Norwegian People's Aid, which, by specializing in clearing mines, bolstered its budget by some NOK 255 million in the period 1991–1996, after the Red Cross had turned the government's invitation to meet government objectives in this area down.

It is not possible to draw conclusions about how exactly the NGOs are influenced by this growing proximity to the state: there is simply a gap in the research. Political scientist Janne Haaland Matlary observes that any suggestion that the close ties between leaders of the civil society organizations and the political elites that influence funding decisions might impair the former's impartiality is generally dismissed as impertinent innuendo. She notes: "NGOs are logically based on the thesis of opposition, as a critical corrective to government and politics, in short, on independence. But Norwegian NGOs aspire to the state's money, the major [aid organizations] have intimate relationships with the ministries, especially the Ministry of Foreign Affairs. The principle and fundamental problem is that [he who pays the piper calls the tune]: If you have 90 percent of your income from the government, it is easier to swallow the criticism rather than bite the hand that feeds you."[42]

Partisan politics

With civilians functioning as both "militarized" actors and strategic targets in modern-day conflicts, the relief activities of humanitarian organizations in war-torn regions have become increasingly politicized. Factions targeting civilians view any kind of aid to these civilian "opponents" as supporting the enemy. As an aid donor, Norway has a long list of cases where Norwegian aid money has been used for political gain, and Norwegian NGOs have even taken part in the war effort in some areas—as was the case with Norwegian People's Aid in southern Sudan.[43] This challenge also presents itself in the donor country where civil society actors can take on the role of "political Sherpas," providing political support, or as partisans, needling the opposition. The politicization of civil society occurs when government, business, or advocacy groups use legal or economic pressure to influence the findings or the way information is disseminated, reported, or interpreted. The politicization of civil society may also negatively affect personal and institutional freedom of opinion.[44]

In politics, a partisan is a committed supporter of a political party.[45] Majority governments elected through representative democracy, whether they consist of one party or a coalition of parties, are in this sense inevitably partisan. There is in a democracy, a constant tension between partisan politics and the need for a universalistic government—political responsiveness has to be tempered with a degree of neutrality.[46] Much of the research into the effects of partisanship has been carried out on British "quasi-autonomous non-governmental organizations"—QUANGOS.[47] Sommerfeldt's previously mentioned assertion that QUANGOs provide a "democratic gain" has been challenged on a number fronts: with regard to the undemocratic selection of leaders of QUANGOs; the lack of effective structures for scrutinizing QUANGOs' focus and performance; and the secrecy surrounding them, which tends to restrict access to information on the work of QUANGOs.[48]

The state funding of the aid establishment has coincided with a seeming rise in the employment of politicians in the industry. This parachuting of ex-politicians into leadership positions of NGOs is, I hasten to add, not a new phenomenon. Many of the aid organizations have historical ties to political parties, notably, the Socialist Left Party, the Christian People's Party, and the Labor Party. What is new is that as party funding has dried up and government funding has taken its place, the politicization of the aid industry has continued tacitly. There are a great many examples of former politicians being recruited to the leadership of civil society organizations: the head of the Red Cross, Børge Brende, is a former conservative politician; Helen Bjørnøy, General Secretary of Plan Norway, is a former socialist (SV) minister. It should be noted that these posts come with (in a Norwegian context) high wages.[49] A senior MFA official observed: "Several political parties have in fact used the dependence on subsidies as a lever to place partisans in key positions. The positions are used as privileges, as rewards to loyalists. Let us have no illusions about this. This is problematic. Not least because it is consequently the main opposition party that suffers partisan ambushes masking as civil society critique, while Labor usually get off scot-free."[50]

This new form of politicization of humanitarian aid is seen to challenge these principles, by "subordinating humanitarian objectives to political and strategic ones."[51] This has taken the form of members of the aid industry using their role as independent civil society actors in the political discourse to condemn or support political parties. On general election day in 2009, the leader of Norwegian People's Aid, Petter Eide, claimed that statements made by the Progress Party (*Fremskrittspartiet*, also known as *Frp*) "about asylum seekers [are] at odds with the Penal Code." The implication was that the Progress Party was a criminal party.

Eide did not mention that he is a former SV politician. When the government later adopted the *Frp* policy, Eide did not repeat his accusation. Another example from the 2009 election was the Peace Council's "peace policy audit" of parties, where the governing coalition came out most favorably. Naturally, the Peace Council was aware that intentions expressed in the party program are not the same as actual policies, but they still drew far-reaching conclusions, claiming that a win for the opposition would make for less peace in the world. They failed to mention that the previous government cut funding to the organization, while the incumbent government had brought them back to life.

No survey has been carried out in relation to partisanship in the aid sector. Aid organizations have accepted that Minister Solheim's claim that, "apolitical aid is nonsense," not only holds true in the recipient country, but also in Norwegian domestic politics. [52] The head of the Norwegian Agency for Development Cooperation (Norad), Poul Engberg-Pedersen, concurred: "We should embrace being politicized." [53] In May 2009, the author of this chapter was present at a meeting to discuss aid evaluation where representatives from the aid organizations made up the audience. Erik Solheim gave a speech and ended his address by stating that it was the obligation of the aid industry to work for a continued left-wing government "because if we do not win, you will lose!" The clear implication was that a right-wing government might be less generous with government funding. Rather than protesting the suggestion that the organizations were the clients of a political system, the minister was roundly applauded. One interviewee at Norad argued that the main element of partisan politics in the aid segment is not the attacks on the opposition, but the failure to criticize the government, "when the NGOs accepted that the government placed the costs of running asylum camps in Norway on the aid budget, the lack of independence lead them to keep quiet, when they should have spoken out." [54]

Moral hazard

Moral hazard occurs when a party insulated from risk behaves differently than it would behave if it were fully exposed to the risk. [55] Moral hazard arises because an individual or institution does not take the full consequences and responsibilities of its actions, and therefore has a tendency to act less carefully than it otherwise would, leaving another party to hold some responsibility for the consequences of those actions. For example, a person with insurance against burglary may be less cautious about locking their house, because the negative consequences of theft are the responsibility of the insurance company. Economists explain moral hazard as a special case of information asymmetry—a situation in which one party in a transaction has more information than another. In particular, moral hazard may occur if a party that is insulated from risk has more information about its actions and intentions than the party paying for the negative consequences of the risk.[56] Moral hazard can occur when upper management is shielded from the consequences of poor decision-making.[57]

The economist Bertin Martens explains: "Like every contract, aid contracts are necessarily incomplete and some of the activities and results will be costly to verify. As a result, moral hazard and adverse selection are inherent in aid delivery."[58] He continues with the argument that due to the "broken feedback loop" in foreign aid, inserting an explicit evaluation function in foreign aid programs is necessary to overcome the moral hazard of the aid service suppliers. He warns against those who see this as a panacea for performance problems, noting that evaluation is itself subject to moral hazard, induced by the same institutional and political incentives that affect aid performance.[59] This points toward one of the great, unresolved questions of foreign aid: How can so many positive evaluations lead to so little development? For example, overall development assistance to Africa is estimated at $350 billion a year. Yet the real income per capita in Africa today remains lower than it was in 1970.[60] The number of poor has doubled since 1990. "The development that disappeared" is one of the great mysteries in aid research. Norad's "great effort" to combat corruption uncovered NOK 12 million in the wrong hands, that is, 0.0004 percent of the budget was largely directed towards the world's most corrupt states. According to economist William Easterly, moral hazard creates incentives for donor country NGOs and the recipient countries to keep the lid on bad news.[61]

Author and former aid worker, Tone Ellefsrud provides a recent testimony of moral hazard in the novel *Monsoon* (*Regntid*). This story, which takes place in Tanzania and Sri Lanka, describes how the aid agencies fail to take responsibility for the direct negative consequences of their actions. She describes the fueling of corruption and aid giving in ways that short circuit market mechanisms and democratic accountability.[62] Part of the challenge is that what was once a job for shoestring idealists has, over time, come to resemble the lifestyle of diplomats. Shielded from the population they are intended to help, the aid workers in Ellefsrud's book pass time in an almost neo-colonial fashion. The opinions placed in the mouths of the civil society experts are dishearteningly cynical. Rector of Buskerud Community College, Morten Eriksen, made a similar observation about the lack of "idealists" in the Norwegian aid industry. He laments a lack of will to cut back on the lavish lifestyles of NGO personnel in developing countries.[63]

In an in-depth interview, a former director of Norad explained that the problem is that the volume of money is greater than the administrative resources; this creates perverse incentives. The result is a culture of accepting misallocation, misspending, and outright theft.[64] The moral hazard inherent in the Norwegian model is that bad practice goes unpunished. A cursory survey of the aid industry by the newspaper *Bistandsaktuelt* for 2006–2010 shows that although in the reported cases of bad practice two-thirds relate to the "Big Four," the inflow of government aid to the same organizations has continued to grow year-on-year. Organizations caught up in bad practice, such as the misappropriation of funds, are not given smaller budgets the following year. Philip Gourevitch notes that—while some flinch at the tone of the debate, and others still insist that they don't need to be told—NGOs "are all too aware of the moral risks of their work and are their own fiercest critics."[65] This last argument is arguably part of the problem: a public institution that is self-policing is effectively un-policed, and deflecting the critique by claiming the critique is not viable is not a serious form of reckoning.

Crowding out

In economics, crowding out is any reduction in private consumption or investment that occurs because of an increase in government spending. While there are many reasons for giving foreign assistance, a major argument for such aid is that this assistance will increase the rate of economic growth in the recipient countries. The growth predictions of aid proponents, however, have often been disappointing. While much of this disappointment may be due to initial expectations that were unrealistically high, numerous reasons have been given as to why traditional aid might be largely ineffective in generating growth. The oldest explanation is that aid largely goes to consumption, crowding out domestic savings and investment.[66]

In development studies, "crowding out" refers to the market dominance of the big aid organizations that corner so much of the available finance that they prevent alternatives from emerging. For this reason they are sometimes referred to as "ferns"—a plant that kills off the green shoots under its dense foliage. A key finding in Håkon Lorentzen's survey is that the big national umbrella organizations that have been created, in part, to facilitate the allocation of funds from the public to smaller organizations, have an intermediate position that is potentially problematic. Umbrella organizations protect members' interests. In this context, Lorentzen suggests, it might be tempting to limit the number of new recipients in order to secure funds for themselves.[67] It is a distinguishing trait that the organizations that make up the backbone of a sector that is worth some $5.8 billion (NOK 35 billion) annually depends only to a limited degree on funding from private individuals, corporations, funds, foundations, and other parts of civil society. Few attempts have been made to foster such a culture. Norway lacks, for example, a system of tax deductions for gifts similar to that in the U.K. or in the United States.

One example of crowding out is found in the case of the new segment of "philanthrocapitalists" in Norway. The term philanthrocapitalism was first introduced by the New York bureau chief of *The Economist*, Matthew Bishop, as a prescription to solve the world's problems in areas where governments, NGOs, and the business sector have failed: "[it is] a new way of doing philanthropy, which mirrors the way that business is done in the for-profit capitalist world."[68] Examples of Norwegian organizations falling into this category are *Stiftelsen et rikere liv* (Literally; *Foundation a richer life*), *Kolibri Kapital*, and *Voxtra*. In interviews, respondents note that especially civil society actors frequently view Norwegian hybrid organizations with skepticism. A recurring view was that the new sector was seen as unwelcome competition, and efforts were made to prevent the philanthrocapitalist from gaining access to the state apparatus and laboring in a system where many have come to see development to be a government issue.[69]

Tvedt notes that although the large aid organizations are part of the same neo-corporate structure, they do not coordinate their relations with the government. Instead, they compete with each other and with smaller organizations. The main competitive advantage of the "Big Four" is the sheer size of their administrative resources, which means they can handle larger volumes of money—an important factor in a sector so well-funded that "getting rid" of the money is a primary challenge for government bureaucrats. From this perspective, it is advantageous to transfer larger sums to organizations with personal experience of the routines and habits of Norad. As one member of a small human rights organization put it—it is so much easier to apply for 2 million NOK than for 200,000. The handlers make no secret of the fact that the two represent the same amount of work—and that they would rather do it once than repeat it twenty times.[70]

Conclusions

The Norwegian aid-sector's culture of economic dependence predisposes it to accept government primacy in the organizations area of expertise.

The political setting with little accountability and government guarantees, and the various negative aspects of clientelism, be they in the shape
of institutional capture, agenda chasing, partisanship, moral hazard, or
crowding out are all present in the Norwegian case. To use Huntington's
reasoning, clientelism is a rudimentary response to decision-making in-
sufficiencies, the consequent social and political instability caused by
an imbalance between the advances in political participation and rising
standards of democratic governance, and the slowness of political institutionalization and administrative modernization to respond to those
changes.[71]

Dependence leads easily to servility, for real criticism requires freedom
from addiction. It weakens an entire sector when it is funded so heavily by the state, because "who pays the piper calls the tune." Questions
need to be asked whether Norwegian civil society has slipped too far
into public policy. This is a problem if the sector is to be corrective and
not a tool of public administration. A case can be made for strengthening
other power centers in society, away from politicians and key government offices. It is not necessarily easy to achieve this in a country where
government is often confused with society, and where private generosity
sometimes falls short of societal ambitions.

But this does not explain why the aid NGOs have given themselves
so freely and so completely to the government. One possible explanation
can be found in Columbia professor Jack Snyder's study on domestic
politics and international ambition.[72] Snyder explains why some states
throw themselves into breakneck expansionist policies. He finds the answer lies with the interest groups in public, private, and academic sectors, which reap the benefits of escalation. These factions bind together
in coalitions that grow so strong that they can put pressure on those in
power. Through horse-trading, political support is exchanged for promises on foreign policy activism. He finds that the sum totals of the many
discrete ambitions are often greater than any single actor had wished. No
one planned to deprive Norway of a civil society in a traditional sense; it
happened as a sum total of a great many expediencies.

A question that springs from this analysis is: Where is what political
scientist Morton Grodzins called "the tipping point" located?[73] In sociology, the tipping point is when a once rare phenomenon becomes quickly
and dramatically more common. In our context, the tipping point could
be the percentage of funding where the NGO cannot be seen to be independent, but the issue is perhaps not so much whether the dependency
ratio is 10, 50, or 60 percent, it is the ability to remain one's own master
while remaining responsive to a multitude of needs and pressures. Some
NGOs, such as *Bellona* (international ENGO based in Norway) and Am-

nesty International have clearly achieved this, while others—notably the "Big Four" Norwegian aid organizations—cannot claim a similar reputation for independence. Their freedom to function implies that NGOs can do what governments ought not, or will not do: for example, for exposing aid corruption, addressing the abuse of power among cooperation partners, or asking questions about the impact of development projects on the local economy. There is good reason for asking whether many Norwegian NGOs are in fact guilty on this count. When reliance on government support reaches 80 or 90 percent, any perceived independence can no longer be taken for granted.

Notes

1. Håkon Lorentzen, *Statlige tilskudd til frivillige organisasjoner—en empirisk kartlegging*, Senter for forskning på sivilsamfunn og frivillig sektor, Rapport 2010: 4.
2. K. O. Åmås, "Er frivilligheten fri?" *Aftenposten* vol. 05, no. 10, (2010): 2.
3. "Staten må være en engasjert aktør," *Aftenposten* Morgen vol. 07, no. 10, (2010): 4.
4. Steven Smith and Michael Lipsky, *Nonprofits for Hire: The Welfare State in the Age of Contracting* (Cambridge, Massachusetts: Harvard University Press, 1993).
5. Iver B. Neumann, "Norsk sørpolitikk: den disaggregerte stats diplomati," *Internasjonal politikk* vol. 57, no. 2 (1999): 185.
6. Terje Tvedt, *Utviklingshjelp, utenrikspolitikk og makt: den norske modellen* (Oslo: Gyldendal Akademisk, 2009).
7. Tvedt, *Utviklingshjelp, utenrikspolitikk og makt:* 190.
8. Tvedt, *Utviklingshjelp, utenrikspolitikk og makt:* 80–81.
9. Tvedt, *Utviklingshjelp, utenrikspolitikk og makt:* 80–81.
10. Dutch scholar Sara Kinsbergen categorized the different types of non-governmental organizations operating in the developing world into QUANGOs (quasi-autonomous NGOs); BONGOs (business NGOs); ENGOs (environmental NGOs); INGOs (institutional NGOs); GONGOs (government NGOs); and of course the ubiquitous MONGO (my own NGO)—one-off charities set up by individuals. Sara Kinsbergen, Lau Schulpen, and Anneke Smeets, *De Anatomie van het PI: Resultaten van vijf Jaar Onderzoek naar Particuliere Initiatieven op het Terrein van Ontwikkelingssamenwerking.* (Amsterdam: [etc: Nationale Commissie voor Internationale Samenwerking en Duurzame Ontwikkeling] [NCDO], 2010) etc.
11. In the 2011 aid budget, 1.2 billion NOK ($0.2 billion) is earmarked for the NGOs. The same organizations also gain additional funds for emergency relief and humanitarian aid to the tune of 2.6 billion NOK ($0.4 billion). Peace and reconciliation get 1.2 billion NOK ($0.2 billion), environment and sustainable development get 2.5 billion NOK ($0.4 billon), and 6.8 billion NOK ($1.1 billion) is earmarked for "other" aid objectives.
12. *Prop. 1 S (2009–2010)* Statsbudsjettet, Appendix 4: 343. In this (the Norwegian government's budget) support for 2009 is estimated at NOK 453 million.

13. James A. Robinson, Thierry Verdier, and Centre for Economic Policy Research (Great Britain), *The Political Economy of Clientelism* (London: Centre for Economic Policy Research, 2002).
14. Georges Casamatta and Charles Vellutini, "Clientelism and Aid," *Journal of Development Economics"* vol. 87 (2008).
15. Simona Piattoni, *Clientism, Interests, and Democratic Representation: The European Experience in Historical and Comparative Perspective* (Cambridge: Cambridge University Press 2001): 2.
16. Robert D. Putnam, Robert Leonardi, and Raffaella Y. Nanetti, *Making Democracy Work: Civic Traditions in Modern Italy* (Princeton: Princeton University Press, 1993).
17. Interview, senior MFA official, The Norwegian Ministry of Foreign Affairs, Oslo, 23 November 2010.
18. Quoted in Knut Gunner Nustad, *Gavens makt: norsk utviklingshjelp som formynderskap* (Oslo: Pax Forlag, 2003): 4.
19. Tvedt, *Utviklingshjelp, utenrikspolitikk og makt:* 26
20. Ian Smillie, "Changing Partners: Northern NGOs, Northern Governments," *Voluntas* vol. 5, no. 2 (1993): 155–192; 174.
21. One high profile case was when the government banned slot machines and the NGOs that operated them demanded to be compensated in full on an annual basis.
22. Aud V. Tønnessen, *Kirkens nødhjelp: bistand, tro og politikk* (Oslo: Gyldendal Norsk Forlag, 2007): 213.
23. The practice of boosting the aid budget by adding asylum costs began in 2005 and is widely seen in the NGO community as reprehensible, but few chose to criticise the government. Interview, Norad—Norwegian Agency for Development Cooperation, Oslo, 23 June 2010.
24. Samuel P. Huntington, *Clientelism: A Study in Administrative Politics*, Thesis (Harvard University, 1950).
25. Sanjay Pradhan and The World Bank, *Anticorruption in Transition: A Contribution to the Policy Debate* (Washington D.C.: World Bank, 2000): 45.
26. The term was coined in Rolf Tamnes, *Oljealder. Norsk utenrikspolitikks historie*, Bind 6 (Oslo: Universitetsforlaget, 1997): 69.
27. Jan O. Egeland, *Impotent Superpower—Potent Small State*, (Oslo: International Peace Research Institute, 1985).
28. For more on this see Asle Toje, "Norsk utenrikspolitikk: en kritikk," *Nytt Norsk Tidsskrift* vol. 1, no. 2, (2010): 206–217.
29. The 2004 government white paper on development illustrates this point. Utenriksdepartementet, *Felles kamp mot fattigdom: en helhetlig utviklingspolitikk* (Oslo: Det Kongelige Utenriksdepartement, 2004).
30. Jarle Simensen, Arild Engelsen Ruud, Frode Liland, and Kirsten A. Kjerland, *Norsk utviklingshjelps historie* (Bergen: Fagbokforlaget, 2003).
31. Øyvind Østerud, "Lite land som humanitær stormakt," *Nytt Norsk Tidsskrift* vol. 23, no. 4 (2006): 303–316.
32. Helge Ø. Pharo and Monika P. Fraser, *The Aid Rush. Vol. 1, Aid Regimes in Northern Europe during the Cold War* (Oslo: Unipub 2008).
33. Interview, senior MFA official, The Norwegian Ministry of Foreign affairs, Oslo, 23 November 2010.

34. Dorothy E. Smith, *Institutional Ethnography: A Sociology for People*, The Gender Lens Series (Walnut Creek, C.A.: AltaMira Press, 2005): 225.
35. Russel Hardin, *Distrust*, Russell Sage Foundation series on trust, vol. 8, (New York: Russell Sage Foundation 2004): 109.
36. Gordon Tullock, *Public Goods, Redistribution, and Rent Seeking* (Cheltenham, U.K.: Edward Elgar, 2005).
37. Paul W. Brand and Philip Yancey, *In His Image* (Grand Rapids, M.I.: Zondervan Publishing House, 1984): 302.
38. Linda Polman, *The Crisis Caravan: What's Wrong with Humanitarian Aid?* (New York: Metropolitan Books, 2010): 157–158.
39. Jan Egeland quoted in *Africa Renewal*, United Nations Department of Public Information 2006, vol. 19, no. 4: 7.
40. Terje Tvedt, "De Hvite Hjelperne i de Hvite Bilene," *Aftenposten* 5 March 2007.
41. *Felles kamp mot fattigdom. En helhetlig utviklingspolitikk.* St.meld. nr. 35 (2003–2004), Innst. S. nr. 93 (2004–2005).
42. Janne Haaland-Matlary, "Avhengighet leder lett til servilitet," *Aftenposten*, 10 October 2009.
43. Bengt Nilsson, *Sveriges afrikanska krig* (Stockholm: Timbro, 2008): 46–49.
44. Geoffrey Garrett, *Partisan Politics in the Global Economy* (Cambridge: Cambridge University Press, 1998).
45. Edward B. Portis, Adolf G. Gundersen, and Ruth L. Shively, *Political Theory and Partisan Politics*, SUNY series in political theory (Albany: State University of New York Press, 2000).
46. James Allan and Lyle Scruggs, "Political Partisanship and Welfare State Reform in Advanced Industrial Societies," *American Journal of Political Science* vol. 48, no. 3 (2004): 496–512.
47. Liz Sperling, "Public Services, QUANGOs, and Women: A Concern for Local Government," *Public Administration* vol. 76, no. 3 (1998): 471.
48. Stuart Weir, "QUANGOs: Questions of Democratic Accountability," *Parliamentary Affairs* vol. 48, no. 2 (1995): 306–22; David Wilson, "QUANGOs in the Skeletal State," *Parliamentary Affairs* vol. 48, no. 2 (1995): 181–92; Wendy Hall and Stuart Weir, *The Untouchables: Power and Accountability in the QUANGO State* (London: The Scarman Trust, 1996); Leo Pliatzky, "QUANGOs and Agencies," *Public Administration* vol. 70, no. 4 (1992): 555–63.
49. "God Lønn for Fred og Bistand" online news NRK (the Norwegian Braodcasting Company): "Flere Tidligere Samfunnstopper Jobber Med Freds- Eller Hjelpe- og Bistandsspørsmål." *http://www.nrk.no/nyheter/okonomi/skattelister/1.7343945.*
50. The Norwegian Ministry of Foreign affairs, Oslo, 3 November 2010.
51. Devon Curtis, *Politics and Humanitarian Aid: Debates, Dilemmas, and Dissension*, HPG Report 10 (Humanitarian Policy Group, Overseas Development Institute, London 2001): 13.
52. *Bistandsaktuelt* 8 (2010): 9 and 11.
53. *Bistandsaktuelt* 8 (2010): 9 and 11.
54. Interview, Norwegian Ministry of Foreign Affairs official, Brussels, 19 November 2010.
55. Arantxa Jarque, *Repeated Moral Hazard with Effort Persistence* (Richmond, V.A.: Federal Reserve Bank of Richmond, 2008).

56. Bengt Holmstrom, "Moral Hazard and Observability," *Bell Journal of Economics* (1979): 74–91.
57. Allard E. Dembe and Leslie I. Boden, "Moral Hazard: A Question of Morality?" *New Solutions 2000* vol. 10, no. 3, (2000): 257–279.
58. Bertin Martens, "Why Do Aid Agencies Exist?" *Development Policy Review* vol. 23, no. 6, (2005): 644.
59. Bertin Martens, *The Institutional Economics of Foreign Aid* (New York: Cambridge University Press, 2002): 27–28.
60. Dambisa Moyo, *Dead Aid: Why Aid Is Not Working and How There Is A Better Way for Africa* (New York: Farrar, Straus, and Giroux, 2009): 37.
61. William Easterly, *The White Man's Burden: Why the West's Efforts To Aid the Rest Have Done So Much Ill and So Little Good* (New York: Penguin Press, 2006), 204–205 and 117–119.
62. Anders Nordstoga, "Norsk Hjelpearbeider i Tanzania:—Norge Bør Stoppe All U-hjelp," *Aftenposten*, 25 July 2009.
63. *Bistandsaktuelt* 8 (2010), 2 "letters."
64. Interview, Former Norad official, Oslo, 28 November 2010.
65. *Philip Gourevitch*, "The Moral Hazards of Humanitarian Aid: What Is to Be Done?" *The New Yorker*, 4 November 2010. *http://www.newyorker.com/online/blogs/news desk/2010/11/the-moral-hazards-of-humanitarian-aid-what-is-to-be-done.html*
66. Michael P. Shields and Monash University, *Foreign Aid and Domestic Savings: The Crowding Out Effect* (Clayton, Victoria, Australia: Monash University, Department of Economics, 2007).
67. Lorentzen, *Statlige tilskudd til frivillige organisasjoner.*
68. Matthew Bishop, "The Birth of Philanthrocapitalism," *The Economist*, 23 February 2006.
69. Quotes from data collected for the commissioned report "Private Actors in the Norwegian Aid Landscape" (Anne Welle-Strand, Pernille Dehli, Erik Kimmestad, and Christen Torp 2009) that was carried out in 2008/2009 by researchers at the BI as a part of the multilateral World Bank Study "Private Actors in the Aid landscape."
70. Interview, Deputy leader of Norwegian Human Rights organization, Brussels, 19 May 19th 2010.
71. Samuel P. Huntington, *Political Order in Changing Societies* (New Haven, C.T.: Yale University Press, 1968).
72. J. L. Snyder, *Myths of Empire: Domestic Politics and International Ambition.* Cornell studies in security affairs (Ithaca, N.Y.: Cornell University Press, 1991).
73. Morton Grodzins, *The Metropolitan Area As A Racial Problem* (Pittsburgh: University of Pittsburgh Press, 1958).

Chapter 12

CIVIL SOCIETY AS A DRIVER
OF GOVERNANCE INNOVATION
A MONTESQUIEU PERSPECTIVE

Atle Midttun

Introduction

Following the neoliberal turn in the 1980s, the world has witnessed a fundamental change in business orientation in the late 1990s and early 2000s. Leading global companies and business organizations have engaged with a social and environmental agenda on an unprecedented scale. Distancing itself from the doctrine of profit maximization constrained only by public regulation, there has been a trend of businesses adopting the doctrine of corporate social and environmental responsibility (CSR). Firms have been establishing CSR divisions and are developing CSR visions and ethical guidelines. They have started reporting on social and environmental performance like never before, and have flocked to join prestigious clubs of the do-gooders like the World Business Council for Sustainable Development or the United Nations' Global Compact. This has not been achieved without battles, however. As I shall argue, the core drivers of this development have been civil society and civil society organizations (CSOs), which have worked to expose business malpractice in the media and mobilize action against social and environmental abuses.

Using this evolution of business as a point of reference, I propose that we have to fundamentally rethink economic governance and the way we conceive of business in society under the classical doctrine of *regulatory governance*, where social and ecological responsibility lies with

public policy regulation of purely profit-seeking firms. The argument I
will present is that we need to adopt a much wider concept of "*multi-
polar governance*" where civic engagement, facilitated by open media
communication, is included alongside government and business. There is,
in other words, a need to reframe economic governance as an act of balancing the power of the state, business, and civil society along the lines of
Montequieu's eighteenth century argument for balancing the three state
powers: the legislative, the executive, and the judiciary. In Montesquieu's
own words:[1]

> In every government there are three sorts of power; the legislative; the execu-
> tive, in respect to things dependent on the law of nations; and the executive,
> in regard to things that depend on the civil law.
>
> ...
>
> When the legislative and executive powers are united in the same person, or
> in the same body of magistrates, there can be no liberty; because apprehen-
> sions may anse (be considered), lest the same monarch or senate should enact
> tyrannical laws, to execute them in a tyrannical manner.
>
> Again, there is no liberty, if the power of judging be not separated from the
> legislative and executive powers. Were it joined with the legislative, the life
> and liberty of the subject would be exposed to arbitrary control, for the judge
> would then be the legislator. Were it joined to the executive power, the judge
> might behave with all the violence of an oppressor.
>
> There would be an end of every thing were the same man, or the same body,
> whether of the nobles or of the people to exercise those three powers that of
> enacting laws, that of executing the public resolutions, and that of judging the
> crimes or differences of individuals.

I suggest a Montesquieu "version 2.1"—a paraphrase of his original theory—to suit the twenty-first century, where his insights in state theory are
transferred to a broader theory of societal governance that encompasses
the state, markets, and civil society in rivaled interplay. The approach to
civil society as a significant force alongside the classical polity and the
liberalist economy rests on Charles Taylor's understanding of society
as a rich web of traditions and institutions with deep historical roots[2].
These traditions go back to medieval notions of an independent religious
sphere, subjective rights inscribed in feudal relations of authority, and
later to the natural rights doctrine launched in the seventeenth and eighteenth centuries. This means that civil society today is not just a dynamic
player in the global and local politics, but, unlike the market, it is imbued
with values, habits, and memories which are to be reckoned with. It is
not the objective of this chapter to explore the full implications of the

cultural dimension of the civic realm. Rather, it is to focus on a dynamic interplay between the civic and political domains, which has not been considered under regulatory governance. The intrusion of the civic into the political and economic sphere also introduces additional potential checks on global multinationals that escape government regulation.

There is a clear parallel between my concept of multi-polar governance and John Keane's concept of monitory democracy. They both feed on the new possibilities for civic engagement in the modern communication and information society. While Keane's analysis focuses on monitory democracy and its effects on our political system, I shall focus on its impact on economic governance.[3]

CSR and the Logic of Civic Engagement with Business and Markets

Civic engagement and the contours of a new multi-polar governance structure have emerged from a series of business malpractices. Business scandals—such as Nestlé's aggressive powder milk campaign in developing countries; Nike's child labor scandals in the 1990s and early 2000s[4]; and Enron's financial reporting fraud in the U.S., among many others—triggered civic action that pushed multinational companies to demonstrate a renewed commitment to corporate social responsibility on an unprecedented scale. In all these cases, industrial practices violated widely held norms, first in the North/West, but also increasingly in the South. Parliamentary democracy initially failed to deal with the problem, both because of a lack of global outreach and because of priorities given to other political party-constituting agendas. As a result, CSOs engaged, voiced claims, and staged action against industry. As the media picked up and broadcast these claims, civil society subsequently maintained a continued level of monitoring and pressure until they were gradually incorporated into industrial and public agendas.

The logic of multi-polar governance can be observed in three central initiatives: the Extractive Industries' Transparency Initiative, the Forest Stewardship Initiative, and the Ethical Trading Initiative, all of which have codified central parts of new governance practice. In the case of petroleum and extractive industries, CSO-driven initiatives were launched to counteract business practices that distorted the economy and propped up corrupt and autocratic governments that exploited their control over revenues. Transparency International and Global Witness initially pioneered the Extractive Industries' Transparency Initiative, EITI. Its report, *A Crude Awakening,* released by Global Witness in 1999, formulated central premises for actions that followed. It presented a critical examination of corruption, placing blame on both the Angolan government and the international petroleum industry. As the main generators of revenue to the government of Angola, it argued, the international oil industry and financial world needed to acknowledge their complicity, change their business practices, and create new standards of transparency. The report was followed up by Publish What You Pay (PWYP), a campaign organization that mobilized stronger civic power through a broad CSO coalition. Pressured by NGO initiatives and extensive media debate, the PWYP initiative provoked industry engagement by British Petroleum (BP). However, after an almost immediate attack from Sonangol, the Angolan national petroleum company, BP recognized the commercial implications of unilateral disclosure and backed down. The CSO campaign then targeted the U.K. government, which was compelled to engage because of public pressure, but also to support British firms. Following the early U.K. government buy-in, Western governments gradually decided to support the campaign. Later, considerable buy-in also followed from oil-rich development states.[5]

The EITI case illustrates how CSOs have deployed democratic norms in autocratic states: they did it by targeting Western firms as leverage. The firm then became a tool for engaging Western home country public opinion and governments to take action, and this in turn spilled over to broader international initiatives. In this case, it led to the establishment of a new multi-polar governance regime anchored in traditional regulation.

In the case of the forestry, paper, and pulp industry, CSOs mobilized public opinion against existing forestry practice and launched a new forest stewardship program. The program described the industry as one of the main forces behind the reduction of forests, as well as the loss of biological diversity, and a threat to the global environment. The CSOs also mobilized public opinion, so that printers and publishing houses were pressured to take ecological action against their supply chains and force these to adopt ecological stewardship principles. A coalition of NGOs focusing on environmental issues waged criticism at financial institutions through a report entitled "Broken Promises," which provided evidence that the World Bank Group contributes to the damage of the world's forests.[6]

The CSO initiatives were crystallized in the establishment of the Forest Stewardship Council (FSC), which codified its demands for responsible forestry in a set of principles and criteria for forest management.[7] The scheme met with critical opposition from leading forest industry groups, often in alliance with host/home governments. Nevertheless, the FSC challenge sparked industrial initiatives to develop forest stewardship standards. In North America, the American Forest & Paper Association (AF&PA) adopted the Sustainable Forest Initiative (SFI) program.[8] Similarly, in Scandinavia a government-partnered industrial standard for the Norwegian forest industry was developed under the heading "Living Forest" Initiative.[9] The European Programme for the Endorsement of Forest Certification schemes (PEFC) was established in 1999 as an umbrella organization for certification.[10]

The Forest Stewardship Council case illustrates how CSO engagement to build up new multi-polar governance triggered traditional regulatory initiatives from industry and their home governments. This has fostered a regulatory competition, where the FSC pushes the regulatory avant-garde, while government and industry standards are improving mainstream practice.

A third focus of multi-polar engagement has been on increasing industrial responsibility for labor conditions in their supply chains. This push comes out of the expansion of global markets and accompanying access to cheap labor in Asiatic countries, which has boosted Northwestern industrial outsourcing to an unprecedented scale. The monitoring pressure focused particularly on Western brand retailers and design firms in the garment and food industry. Perhaps the most well-known CSO initiative to target poor supply chain conditions is Nike, where, following active NGO campaigning and strong civic engagement, the company admitted to having serious workplace problems at sub-supplier factories in Indonesia, China, Thailand, and Vietnam, including sexual harassment, mandatory 72 hour working weeks, and sub-standard working conditions that affected more than 300,000 people.[11] The banana and fruit company Chiquita was also heavily criticized for poor working conditions and submitted to similar scrutiny.[12]

Civic exposure of bad work conditions in Western multinationals' supply chains eventually led to the formation of the Ethical Trading Initiative (ETI), a collaboration between CSOs, trade unions, and industry to further the cause of responsible work conditions. The apparent success of the ETI lies in its combination of civic pressure on Western brands and their leverage in supply industry across world markets. The combination of reputation and brand building makes firms vulnerable to civic pressure and gives global industrial systems incentives to deliver. Through the larger retailer's direct multinational managerial systems and contractual relations, they have essential infrastructure in place to deliver credible results beyond the reach of territorially bound national legislatures.

To sum up my argument so far, multi-polar governance involves several conditions, which include:

a. *A socially shared normative basis.* The claims against industrial practice and the voicing of social and environmental concerns must
resonate with public sentiment and appeal to widely held norms.
Civic engagement in what John Keane calls the monitory democratic mode, a post-parliamentary democratic phenomenon, here
paradoxically touches base with pre-democratic political theory.
Already in the eighteenth century, Rousseau advanced the idea of a
"social contract" between the sovereign and his people that obliged
him to respect widely held social norms, irrespective of formal
codification.[13] Rousseau claimed that a breach of such norms gave
people the right to rebel and overthrow the ruler. Civic engagement
against immoral, but formally legal, business behavior thus rests on
classic political theory, penetrating the commercial markets in the
EITI, FSC, and ETI cases. Under social contract thinking, advanced
segments of industry have in fact come to recognize that, in addition to their duties under written law, they must respect basic social
norms and values. Reform-oriented business groups such as the
World Business Council for Sustainable Development (WBCSD)
have in fact explicitly picked up the social contract idea.

b. *An open communicative basis.* The contestation of formal rights and
established institutional practice rests on access to communication
channels, both for information and mobilization as indicated in all
three cases. The evolution of a media-society and its capacity to
mass-market also facilitates mass communication of business malpractice. Furthermore, the new media have lowered the threshold
and opened global information systems to less endowed civic activists—although large disparities still remain.

c. *The CSO's acquisition of moral legitimacy and bargaining rights* in
their respective fields. As custodians of moral concerns, CSOs need
to acquire symbolic moral bargaining rights against industry on the
public's behalf in order for multi-polar governance to work. The
moral legitimacy bestowed on CSOs to bargain on the public's
behalf, often through media "canonization" (support), has a parallel in Ronald Coase's libertarian theory of governance without a
state. Coase argued that social and environmental spillovers from
economic activity could be internalized through bilateral negotiation between the firm and its stakeholders, if appropriate property
rights are allotted to representatives of all resources involved.[14]
Once such property rights were established, this model would effectively individualize social and environmental responsibility to
be settled through negotiations or court litigation. I argue that the
moral bargaining rights bestowed on CSOs through media and

public debate allow them to stand up for their causes in much the same way as Coase assumed for property rights.[15]

d. *Civic capability for strategic action.* The emergence of strong CSOs with strategic action capability, many with a global outreach, is vital for successful civic influence. Having become strategic catalysts of public sentiment in the media, CSOs need to skillfully exercise their Coasian "bargaining rights," building on their comparative advantage. CSOs are, for instance, often capable of acting more flexibly across national jurisdictions than current national jurisprudence. The threat of brand damage through CSO-mobilized media exposure of global worst practices within advanced home markets with high social and environmental standards is something corporations with global supply chains clearly wish to avoid. Global Witness and Publish What You Pay, the Forest Stewardship Council, and CSOs participating in the Ethical Trading Initiative all strategically used media exposure of global value chains to gain bargaining leverage on industry and governments.

The transposition of Montesquieu's concept of rivalry between state powers on to a broader societal arena, where civil society is included alongside politics and markets, provides an added governance potential and additional potential checks and balances, not the least on global multinationals that escape government regulation. In addition, the inclusion of a civic dimension introduces a richer, cultural, historical dimension to governance than the traditional state-market centered regulatory model. Although facilitated by the discourse and visual impact of modern media, civil society engagement draws on a rich web of traditions and institutions with deep historical roots and brings them to play a role in multi-polar regulation.

Civic Engagement and Governance Innovation

Civic engagement has a particularly important role to play in governance innovation. Just as the entrepreneur is a critical factor in bringing about new technological and economic breakthroughs, civil society is essential in fostering new governance. In a dynamic perspective, and in parallel with new product ideas, new governance initiatives emerge in early experimental forms. If successful, they spread and become institutionalized and mainstreamed into formal governance arrangements, just like products are diffused, scaled up, and gradually consolidated into mass production for mainstream markets.

The flexible creative and experimental character of civic initiatives makes them particularly apt to pioneer governance innovation. For later stages of scaling-up and formalized implementation, I suggest formal institutionalization in public administrative and business routines may be required to consolidate governance. This line of reasoning draws on widely recognized insights from the innovation literature, that the organizational challenges vary dramatically from early product conceptualization, via early product deployment in rapid growth firms, to mass production of mature products. By analogy, I argue there is a need for similar shifts in the organization of governance. There we also encounter innovation moving from early exploration to standardization, growth, and mature institutionalization. A flexible civic engagement meets an important need for creative governance response to an increasingly dynamic modern world.

I have chosen to illustrate the role of civil society in dynamic governance innovation through a deeper examination of the EITI over time. This case illustrates the forms of civic engagement through several phases in the innovation process, where actors and arenas shift as the process proceeds from early civic initiatives to a later stage commercial and political engagement. The first phase, set in motion by civil initiatives, illustrates their critical role in early conceptualization and initial experimentation of new governance initiatives. The second phase, representing growth and early institutionalization, involves civil society "chasing" industry and maneuvering to trigger early business and political engagement. The third phase entails political institutionalization of the governance initiatives in mature advanced economies. This precipitates the fourth phase of broader international institutionalization of commercial engagement.

The EITI study is based on a series of interviews with representatives of the EITI secretariat, as well as civil society representatives and former employees in British Petroleum and the British Department for International Development (DFID), who were involved in critical phases of the Initiative's development.[16] The interviews were supplemented with written sources.[17]

Phase I: Conceptualization and Initial Experimentation

The early conceptualization of the EITI initiative was launched through the report *A Crude Awakening*, released by Global Witness in 1999. It presented a critical examination of corruption placing blame on both the Angolan government and the petroleum industry. The report emphatically blamed the oil industry. As the main generators of revenue to the government of Angola, it argued, the international oil industry and financial world needed to acknowledge their complicity, change their business practices, and create new standards of transparency.

Global Witness then proceeded to mobilize stronger civic power through Publish What You Pay (PWYP), a campaign organization founded in June 2002 along with the Catholic Agency For Overseas Development (CAFOD), Open Society Institute, Oxfam GB, Save the Children U.K., and Transparency International U.K. The founding coalition of NGOs was soon joined by others, such as Catholic Relief Services, Human Rights Watch, Partnership Africa Canada, Pax Christi Netherlands, and Secours Catholique/CARITAS France, along with an increasing number of groups from developing countries. In the wake of *A Crude Awakening*, PWYP was contacted by civil society and community groups from countries that faced the same challenges described in the Angolan report. As a result, PWYP assumed a co-coordinator role to facilitate its work. This further contributed to the global spread of the movement for transparent accounting.

The early phase of the Global Witness initiative illustrates the creative flexibility of multi-polar governance innovation. It has sought to overcome blatant regulatory failures in both host and home countries with regard to money flows from the multinational oil industry. This has been done by using novel combinations of actors, arenas, and media attention. The initial focus on the resource curse of oil rich countries and coupling it with a new governance initiative has proved highly effective in attracting media attention. It has also succeeded in linking the campaign to Western policy concerns regarding good governance, corporate accountability, and poverty reduction. In this way it gained basic acceptance from Western political elites, although these ideals were not always adhered to in their political and commercial practice. By their initiatives, the entrepreneurial CSOs outlined a governance approach with a promising potential to overcome major regulatory hurdles. Last but not least, their interventions have empowered the civic initiators. As they were projected in the media as custodians of widely held norms and values, they became bearers of unique moral rights and gave voice to the public concern with unacceptable industrial practice.

Phase II: Growth and Early Institutionalization

In the second phase, CSOs brought the governance challenge more directly onto business and policy agendas. The report and active NGO campaigning mounted pressure on the oil industry—in the U.K. in particular—to act on principles to which they were committed. The media drew more attention to both corruption and NGO initiatives, which compelled politicians to put their ideals into practice. As momentum increased inside Western oil companies, NGOs also lobbied for revenue transparency, in both their home countries and oil-rich countries. They saw the Western companies as more likely to engage in dialogue with NGOs than, for example, state-owned companies from developing countries, which may be less compelled to maintain the "social license to operate" as seen by NGOs or community groups.

Human Rights Watch (HRW) added another dimension to the already complex case of transparency in countries suffering from the resource curse: the link to human rights. This put additional pressure on Western firms operating in oil rich countries in the developing world. A report published by Stratfor Global Intelligencefocused on human-rights issues facing oil, gas, and mining companies.[18] The report addressed government security forces and security arrangements around their operations, as well as companies' impact on the economy and environment of communities.

Pressured by NGO initiatives and extensive media debate, the PWYP initiative provoked industry engagement and BP—with strong influence from public opinion, as well as U.S. regulatory pressure—prepared to disclose its payment to the Angolan government. But, as already mentioned, following the strong attack from the Angolan national petroleum company, with a threat to withdraw BPs Angolan license, BP backed down.[19]

The growth and early institutionalization phase illustrates the importance of persistent learning and adaptation in scaling up and consolidating the civic component of multi-polar governance. Having successfully scaled up pressure on industry to make the first move, the PWYP initiative faced reversal after the Angolan government's reaction and BP's retreat. The NGOs then realized that they could not force Western-based multinationals to abandon their contracts. Nevertheless, the flexible organization of the civic initiative allowed it to rapidly change strategic focus and redirect its efforts towards public policy.

Phase III: Mainstreaming and Political Institutionalization

Having successfully launched the PWYP initiative in public media, but failing to push industry into unilateral action, the next move of civil society was to launch the initiative into public policy, thereby attempting to mainstream the new governance initiative through political institutionalization.

In parallel with their engagement with industry, Global Witness and later the PWYP campaign mobilized pressure on policy-makers. This campaign was met with considerable support in the U.K. DFID. At the time, reports from several U.K. embassies in oil rich developing countries also expressed concern about the transparency and corruption associated with the oil industry and potentially also affecting British firms. Following BP's problematic experience with unilateral company initiatives and the expectations for strong British multi-stakeholder initiatives at the Johannesburg Summit in 2002, the British government decided to launch the Extractive Industries' Transparency Initiative. The British Prime Minister stated in Johannesburg that he wanted to initiate a dialogue about the issue of revenue transparency that would bring together not only oil, gas, and mining companies, but also NGOs, the "Publish What You Pay" campaign, and relevant host and home country governments.

The successful engagement of British policy makers in promoting transparency in extractive industries was also due to a network of individuals who played specific roles in the formation of EITI and the buy-in from companies and governments. Global Witness and the PWYP campaign found support from DFID, which had a number of engaged individuals who believed in the cause and who were sympathetic towards the NGOs. This included the head of the Business Alliances Team in DFID, Ben Mellor, and its Secretaries of State, Hillary Benn and Clair Short. The U.K. Africa Minister, Peter Hein, also made use of his strong ties to the region and his particular interest in Angola. Prime Minister Tony Blair himself was highly influenced by George Soros, the founder of the Open Society Institute and supporter of both Global Witness and PWYP. The Nigerian President, Obasanjo, worked closely with Shell because of his position at the Transparency International advisory board and the Ford foundation. Nigeria also hired a former World Bank employee as finance minister to help fight corruption. This network of people and politicians was committed to the initiative's values and did not want to see EITI fail once it was established.

It was, however, hard to reach a broader consensus among Western countries. According to Global Witness activists, the U.S. and France had been pulling in different directions over EITI. The U.S. stance was that this was an issue for government-to-government dialogue, not their companies. An even stronger factor for the U.S. government at that time was access to resources, particularly in countries outside OPEC. The French stance, on the other hand, was that corruption in another country only concerned companies and had nothing to do with the French government. The French government, however, soon turned around on the EITI and was willing to move forward.[20]

The mainstreaming and political institutionalization phase illustrates the difficult tradeoffs that have to be made when civic governance initiatives seek to engage traditional governance arenas. The advantage of partnering with national government and international institutions is clearly the increased outreach and stable implementation that it entails. The cost is the compromise that has to be made to achieve this. The EITI emerged from the political process with quite a few of the PWYP campaign's goals, but stopped short of the stronger policy measures that PWYP campaigned for. While EITI took a voluntary approach, the NGO initiative had focused on mandatory regulation. They had hoped to make mandatory transparency rules a precondition for listing on the stock exchange. They also wanted rules and accounting standards to be imposed on extractive industries in their home countries. Lastly, they demanded similar criteria to be used for the World Bank, the IMF, and anyone else who lends money, such as the export credit agencies who fund infrastructure developments. In spite of the soft voluntary approach taken by governments and international institutions, the PWYP coalition nevertheless continued to support and monitor the EITI process as a collaborating body.

Phase IV: Further Diffusion and International Institutionalization

After the U.K. initiative, EITI has received extensive international support. The World Bank pioneered pressure for structuring revenue transparency in several high-profile extractive industries projects in the first years of the twenty-first century, including its official endorsement of the EITI on 9 December 2003. A number of Western governments—including Australia, Belgium, Canada, France, Germany, Italy, the Netherlands, Norway, Spain, Sweden, the U.K., and the U.S.—support the EITI. The EITI has also been endorsed by the United Nations (UN), the European Union (EU), and the Organization for Economic Co-operation and Development (OECD). One may therefore conclude that the EITI has enjoyed remarkable success in creating an institutional framework for revenue transparency among Western nations. In 2007, the International EITI Secretariat opened in Oslo, under the leadership of former Swedish diplomat Jonas Moberg, again indicating an internationalization of the initiative within the West.

On 30 March 2004, the EU parliament became the first parliamentary institution to pass legislation dealing with the issue of revenue transparency in mainstream financial services legislation. An amendment to the "Transparency Obligations Directive" reads, "EU states should promote public disclosure of payments to governments by extractive companies listed on European stock exchanges."[21] In March 2004, the "Publish What

You Pay Act" was launched in the U.S. House of Representatives, with the goal of using stock market disclosure rules to mandate the disclosure of payments to foreign national governments by American extractive companies.[22]

The EITI has also managed to mobilize considerable financial support. The Multi-Donor Trust Fund (MDTF) for the EITI was established in August 2004 through an agreement between DFID and the World Bank. In 2005, the governments of Germany, the Netherlands, and Norway joined. France joined in 2006 and Australia, Belgium, Canada, and Spain followed in 2007. The U.S. government and the European Commission joined in 2008, and Finland and Switzerland in 2009. The fund is also supported by oil, gas, and mining companies; institutional investors; and to a lesser extent foundations and NGOs. A Memorandum of Understanding (MoU) was signed between the MDTF and the EITI International Secretariat in early 2008. The EITI has also managed to attract a number of resource-rich Southern countries, particularly in Africa, in addition to the support of the African Union (AU). It has to be noted, however, that few countries have taken the step from candidacy to full compliance, which would require extensive scrutiny and verification by designated auditors.[23]

The diffusion and international institutionalization of civic initiatives fully illustrate hurdles of international diplomacy in further mainstreaming civic governance initiatives. In this turmoil, the civic entrepreneurs face the difficult tradeoff between preserving their vision and ideas and the benefits of international regulatory implementation. This tradeoff becomes more difficult as the initiative spreads to new states and institutions with local agendas that modify the original vision.

Let me sum up the successes and limitations of civil society as the agent of political innovation: On the positive side, innovation in the era of multi-polar governance may be effectively triggered by civic initiatives directed at industrial malpractice. They avoid taking the cumbersome route of political voice through established party-channels, followed by legislative processing in parliament, to only thereafter trickle down into regulatory practice. They bypass this route through disclosing industrial malpractice and political neglect directly to the public and they are generally accompanied by a focused demand for immediate action. When successful, civic initiatives may jumpstart governance innovation, set agendas, and force businesses and established political institutions to react. In other words, they replicate the logic of technological and commercial entrepreneurship, where radically new ideas often come from critical outsiders who succeed because they meet important needs and capture the interest of consumers, not to mention their uses of their freedom to act. The ability to project the initiative into the established political and business arenas and to diffuse it widely, especially in the Western world, has been remarkable. Industry and governments had to accept extraordinary institutionalization of supervisory functions on top of traditional decision-making and include civic engagement to promote new transparency ideals.

On the negative side, the institutional success came with a policy cost: Civil society organizations found themselves having to compromise on mandatory legislation in order to participate in supervisory functions on the national EITI boards. Neither industry nor home governments were willing to unilaterally implement transparency through hard law. Furthermore, the institutionalization of EITI in global governance has also had its limitations. As noted by the EITI Secretariat itself, few major emerging economies have shown interest in EITI so far.[24] South Africa did attend the 2005 London Conference as observers, but no progress has been achieved in subsequent dialogue. Russia also attended the 2005 London Conference as an observer—their companies are signatories to the Kazakhstan and Azerbaijan memorandum of understanding—but there has been no unequivocal support for EITI from either the Russian government or companies. Petrobras has up until 2009 been a member of the EITI International Board, but there was no Brazilian representation at the 2005 London Conference. Neither India nor China sent representatives to the Conference, although the EITI has worked hard on networking and lobbying embassies, foreign ministers, country representatives, and Western oil company headquarters.

In multi-polar governance, civil society is not supposed to carry the whole burden of achieving success. Its identity is based on an adversarial role vis-à-vis the political and commercial establishment and pushes them towards embracing good causes and taking regulatory measures to meet social and environmental challenges. As innovative governance initiatives are picked up by industry and by established institutions, they become responsible for successful implementation.

Montesquieu for the Twenty-First Century

I have argued that in multi-polar economic governance, civic engagement is not a substitute for traditional political regulation of business, but a challenging supplement and an innovation driver. As mentioned in the beginning of this chapter, Montesquieu's doctrine of balance of state powers provides a relevant conceptual framework for understanding multi-polar governance when the doctrine is transferred from the state to the societal level. At this level, the question is that of balancing politics, markets, and civil society and not the powers of the state.

Montesquieu's doctrine has its roots in seventeenth and eighteenth century political philosophy, especially in John Locke's *Second Treatise of Civil Government*. Locke noted the temptations of corruption: "And because it may be too great [a] temptation to human frailty, apt to grasp at power, for the same persons who have the power of making laws to have also in their hands the power to execute them, whereby they may exempt themselves from obedience to the laws they make. And suit the laws, both in its making and execution to their own private advantage…"[25] Inspired by Locke's views, Baron de Montesquieu articulated the foundations of the separation doctrine after visiting England between 1729 and 1731.[26] In *The Spirit of the Laws*,[27] Montesquieu argued that English liberty was preserved by its institutional arrangements. He saw the separation of powers not only between the three main branches of English government, but also within them, such as the decision-sharing power of judges with juries, or the separation of the monarch and parliament within the legislative process.

The doctrine of societal balance of powers implied in multi-polar governance entails a rivalry between politics, markets, and civil society. Montesquieu argued for the three branches of the state; pluralism of societal powers may entail a constructive competition that keeps all powers alert and creative. For example, the civic challenge to the forest industry provoked a new industrial practice and improved regulation. Strategic alliances between CSOs and the printing industry that included ecological constraints led to inclusion of ecological standards in their supply contracts. This proved a powerful tool in reforming the forestry and paper industry and later trickled down into government regulation.

Multi-polar rivalry has created new roles for each of the three players. The role of the state has changed, as new multi-polar practices are inserted on top of traditional legal procedure. The EITI case illustrates how civic participation and third party auditing was introduced alongside traditional contracting and public accounting: British Petroleum, abiding by Angolan law, was chosen by Global Watch as a target. Principles of state sovereignty in petroleum regulation came under fire and the company found its legal Angolan contracts portrayed as illegitimate in the public eye. As a result of successful civic pressure, both BP's home state (Britain), followed by other European countries, as well as a number of resource-rich developing countries, were forced to expand their regulatory repertoire with measures that included more transparency as well as broader stakeholder participation. The petroleum companies were also pushed to comply. Democratic guarantees are no longer just provided by the political mandating of administrative procedures, but by open and transparent engagement by stakeholders in regulatory practice.

Business has also had to change its role in a confrontation with multi-polar realities and has to legitimize commercial practice in a broad public debate. This comes on top of its traditional obligation to play according to formal legal rules. Some businesses see extended multi-polar governance as an opportunity for differentiation, where higher social and environmental standards become part of a quality production and branding strategy with products aimed at the high end of the market. Other businesses, particularly those that compete on cost in lower quality segments, see this as a threat and attempt to minimize compliance if the pressure on them is not sufficiently strong. In the cases previously discussed concerning forestry and petroleum industries, both strategies were observed. A few early movers took on the FSC standards, while mainstream U.S. and European industry was far more reluctant and developed less demanding standards. In the petroleum industry, European companies moved fairly early into compliance with the EITI payment disclosure policy. U.S. companies, however, maintained a traditional position that obliged them only to follow formal host-country rules for a long time.

For civil society, multi-polar economic governance implies a strong and targeted activist role. As CSOs rely on indirect bargaining power derived from their standing in the public debate, they must engage with clear and critical voices and stir up public debate. The need to derive moral bargaining rights, through media visibility, remains a critical factor for civic action. As already noted, informal organization and flexibility allows civil society to take the entrepreneurial role. Its independence from established politics and vested market interests often makes it well suited to take a critical role and spearhead change. The civic initiation of EITI with the *A Crude Awakening* report and the "Publish What You Pay" campaign, the mobilization around new ecological principles for forest management and establishment of the Forest Stewardship Council, and the civic engagement for labor rights in supply chains leading to the formation of EITI all triggered extensive change processes and governance reform.

Multi-polar governance is strongly driven by the new media, and would in fact be unthinkable without the "digital revolution." The ability to blend traditional media such as film, images, music, spoken and written word with the interactive power of computer and communications technology creates a powerful tool for popular participation in governance, with easy access any time, anywhere.[28] The new media have therefore, in many ways "democratized" the creation, publishing, distribution, and consumption of communication. They have also facilitated civic governance in public life. They have lowered the information gathering costs (Internet search) as well as the communication costs, and thereby facilitated introduction of alternative perspectives and agendas. Specialized forums, such as Norwatch, Human Rights Watch, etc., publish critical overviews that provide information for civic campaigns and regulatory intervention.

The new media have also drastically reduced the mobilization and organization costs and thereby enabled strategic implementation of the civic challenge. In all three cases—the FSC, the EITI/PWYP, and the ETI—virtual civic communities were established across geographical boundaries and helped mobilize pressure on the official regulatory forums. Orchestrated by strategically focused CSOs, new media have also been used to facilitate and activate "old" mass media in broader mobilization of public opinion to bring pressure on established governance elites. The establishment of the ETI was inspired by a series of newspaper articles and TV programs that exposed shocking work conditions in the supply chain of Western multinationals, particularly in the garment and food industries. The PWYP campaign and FSC engagement also made extensive use of traditional mass media to engage the general public opinion in building up pressure on industry and regulatory authorities.

In any democratic country, with brand-sensitive industry and public opinion, bad press is a serious challenge to the established regulatory practice. The combination of information and mobilization efficiency of the new media orchestrated by clever CSOs and the potential public exposure through mass media represents valuable leverage towards the wider opening of the regulation process to new stakeholders and a move towards multi-polar governance.

Conclusions

Given its flexibility and swift reaction, civic media-facilitated engagement allows a quicker response to new regulatory challenges than the traditional legalistic approach. The combination of civic engagement and media pressure may in some cases suffice to change industrial behavior irrespective of formal regulation. When CSOs acquire sufficient moral bargaining rights through media "canonization/blessing" they may short-circuit legal procedure and challenge industry sufficiently to directly change practice. In other cases, they can trigger rapid and unconventional political action taken to the same effect. Admittedly, regulation will eventually need to be formally institutionalized to become a stable practice.

The capacity to transcend national boundaries is also one of the advantages of multi-polar regulation. The traditional regulatory model, with its parliamentary-democratic component is not easily replicated at a transnational level. Civic initiatives typically cut across territorial boundaries and, therefore, frequently spearhead international regulation. By targeting the social and ecological upgrading of supply chains of global industry, NGOs have been important precursors to later international regulation. Similarly, civic protest against embezzlement and corruption has challenged later engagement by international institutions. Civic initiatives have subsequently partnered with friendly states and international institutions in governance initiatives that increase their global outreach.

A central contribution of multi-polar governance is that it brings important new checks and balances into the governance approach. The core argument of this chapter has been that there is a parallel between the eighteenth century concept of division of powers and the need to engage and balance the powers of the state, industry/markets, and civil society in governance today. In both cases, complementary and somewhat adversarial power bases can be used to increase transparency while minimizing monopoly and the rule of dogma. The substitution of the triadic, multi-polar governance for the dyadic, regulatory governance marks a need for connecting to a broader understanding of society, where the rich web of civic traditions and capacities are included.

In other words, the "Holy Trinity" of state, business, and civil society in multi-polar governance has the potential to civilize the global market economy through extended outreach while also keeping checks and balances against one another. Given their diverse capacities, the three powers, if mobilized properly, may have a larger governance range in the global economy than traditional state governance could achieve. Civil society transcends national boundaries; nation states have powerful institutions and implementation capability; business has resources and strategic skills. However, following Montesquieu, we need the three powers to keep each other in check; states that are too strong may lead to monopolistic economic development with efficiency problems and dynamic incapability, as well as public disengagement and pontification of political elites. Overly strong markets may generate uncontrolled profit seeking, destabilization, and under-regulation by the state, as well as disengaged and overruled civil society. Overly strong civil societies may become the basis of populism and disrespect for the rule of law, and may even cerate inefficiencies in populist-governed markets or, in a worst-case scenario, deteriorate to mob-rule. Finally, multi-polar governance has inserted swift moving civic entrepreneurship into the much slower legalistic expert-driven governance. This allows faster response to modern technological and social realities in today's globalized world.

The challenge of regulation in a world with complex, inter-regional links and levels in both economic and political domains necessitates a broader engagement of the rich web of civic relations. The theory of multi-polar governance inspired by Montesquieu codifies the relationship between three societal realms, and thereby enriches the perspectives on modern governance and its regulatory tools.

Notes

1. Baron de Montesquieu, *The Spirit of the Laws*, vol. 1, trans. Thomas Nugent (London: J. Nourse, 1777): 221–237, passim.
2. Charles Taylor, *Philosophical Arguments* (Cambridge: Harvard University Press, 1995).
3. Although John Keane discusses general democracy and I explore industrial regulation, we share common focus on civic engagement and new extra-parliamentary monitoring, largely facilitated by new media. However, we differ in our interpretation of the relative weight of the new and old governance forms. Keane's notion of "monitory democracy" argues for a new post-parliamentary form of democracy, where old parliamentary institutions are transcended but linger on as a ceremonial tradition, more or less like constitutional monarchy. The concept of "multi-polar governance" which I propose, points to civic governance as a third pole in addition to industry and government. Drawing on Montesquieu, I argue for a balance of the three components.
4. Steve Boggan, "Nike Admits to Mistakes over Child Labor," *The Independent* (World edition), 20 October 2001. *http://www.independent.co.uk/news/world/americas/nike-admits-to-mistakes-over-child-labour-631975.html*
5. Based on EITI *Report of the International Advisory Group* (2006): *http://eiti.org/files/document/eiti_iag_report_english.pdf* (accessed 1 September 2009); Global Witness, *A Crude Awakening* (1999): *www.globalwitness.org/media_library_detail.php/93/en/a_crude_awakening* (accessed June 2009); Publish What You Pay (2009): *www.publishwhatyoupay.org/en/resources/energy-security-through-transparency-act-2009* (accessed September 2009).
6. Jon Buckrell, *Broken Promises: How World Bank Group Policies and Practice Fail to Protect Forests and Forest Peoples' Rights.'* (Washington D.C.: The Rainforest Foundation, 14 April 2005). Available through the web-sites of the Forest Peoples Programme and the World Rainforest Movement: *<http://www.wrm.org.uy/actors/WB/brokenpromises.pdf>*
7. *Forest Stewardship Council (FSC)* (2010): *www.fsc.org/en*
8. *Sustainable Forest Initiative*: *http://www.sfiprogram.org/*
9. *Levende skog (Living forest)*: *http://www.levendeskog.no/*
10. The European Programme for the Endorsement of Forest Certification schemes (PEFC): *http://www.pefc.org/*
11. Based on Nike's "CSR report" (2004): www.nike.com/nikebiz/gc/r/fy04/docs/FY04_Nike_CSR_report_full.pdf
12. Based on Chiquita, "Corporate Responsibility Report" (2005*): www.chiquita.com*

13. James Rosenau, *Along the Domestic-Foreign Frontier* (Cambridge: Cambridge University Press, 1997).

14. Ronald H. Coase, "The Problem of Social Cost," *Journal of Law and Economics* vol. 3 (1960): 15–25.

15. Furthermore, the establishment and execution of moral bargaining rights are probably less susceptible to transaction costs than individual property rights applied to social and environmental externalities.

16. Interviews with: Jonas Moberg (Head of EITI Secretariat), 12 June 2009; Sefton Darby (Formerly with DFID and World Bank), 30 September 2009; Graham Baxter (Former VP Corporate Responsibility, BP), 14 October 2009; Alan Dethridge (Former VP External Affairs, exploration and production, Shell), 19 October 2009; Mona Thowsen (PWYP Norway), 22 September 2009.

17. EITI, Report of the International Advisory Group: *http://eiti.org/files/document/ (2006) eiti_iag_report_english.pdf* (accessed 1 September 2009). "A Crude Awakening" in *Global Witness*: *www.globalwitness.org/media_library_detail. php/93/en/ a_crude_awakening* (accessed 16 June 2009); Interview with Joe Schumacher in *Global Witness*: *www.monitor.upeace.org/archive.cfm?id_paper* ¼ 58 (accessed 28 July 2003); Publish What You Pay, "Publish What You Pay": *www.publishwhaty oupay.org/en/resources/energy-security-through-transparency-act-2009* (accessed September 2009).

18. Stratfor Global Intelligence, "Human Rights: A New Lever for Angolan Oil Transparency?": *www.stratfor.com/memberships/84157/human_rights_new_lever_ angolan_oil_transparency* (accessed 15 September 2009).

19. Terry Macalister, "'Ethical' BP linked to Angola Claims" *The Guardian*, 27 February 2002: *http://www.guardian.co.uk/business/2002/feb/27/oilandpetrol.bp* (accessed February 2011).

20. Interview with Joe Schumacher, Global Witness, available at: *www.monitor .upeace.org/archive.cfm?id_paper* ¼ 58 (accessed 28 July 2003).

21. Extractive Industries' Transparency Initiative (EITI) (2006): *www.eitransparency .org/section/abouteiti/keydocuments*

22. This bill was never passed, but there have been several attempts later at launching similar Acts, the most recent being "The Energy Security through Transparency Act" of 2009. If passed, the bill would require energy and mining companies to reveal how much they pay to foreign countries and the U.S. government for oil, gas, and other minerals (Publish What You Pay, 2009), Publish What You Pay: *www.publishwhatyoupay.org/en/resources/energy-security-through-transparency-act-2009* (accessed September 2009).

23. Dilan Ölcer, "Extracting the Maximum from EITI", Working Paper no. 276 (Paris: OECD Development Centre); Stefan Bauchowitz, "Measuring EITI's Success," available at: *www.voxeu.org/index.php?q* ¼ *node/3088* (accessed September 2009).

24. EITI: *http://eiti.org/files/document/eiti_iag_report_english.pdf* (accessed September 2010).

25. John Locke, *The Legislative, Executive, and Federative Power of the Commonwealth; Second Treatise of Government*, chapter XII (1690; New Jersey: Barnes and Noble Books, 2004): 86.

26. Graham Spindler, "Separation of Powers: Doctrine and Practice," originally appeared in *Legal Date* (March 2000): *www.parliament.nsw.gov.au/prod/parlment/*

publications.nsf/0/E88B2C638DC23E51CA256EDE00795896 (accessed 10 October 2009).

27. Charles L. Montesquieu, "The Spirit of the Laws" (1748) in *Cambridge Texts in the History of Political Thought*, eds. A.M. Cohler, B.C. Miller, and H.S. Stone (Cambridge: Cambridge University Press, 1989).

28. WAPMEDIA—Wiki New Media *http://wapedia.mobi/en/New_media* (accessed March 2011).

AFTERWORD

PREFATORY REMARKS

Nina Witoszek and Lars Trägårdh

If John Keane, whose essay opens and ignites the debate in this volume—
were looking for a living incarnation of a "global civil society," Bill McKibben's environmental movement, 350.org, would be the ideal example. So
far nobody has explored in detail McKibben's innovative breakthrough
in creating an international, "post-carbon community" concerned with
climate shift, though his is probably the most successful—and the most
global—of all grassroots movements ever. Hence, we decided to treat his
essay as a practitioner's conclusion to our volume—a sort of test case for
the prospects of monitory democracy.

Inspired by world climatologist James Hansen's alarming ideas about
the rising levels of CO_2, McKibben has embarked on a mission which
has as its ultimate goal the possibility for humanity "to preserve a planet
similar to that on which civilization developed and to which life on Earth
is adapted." Though a charismatic leader and inspired speaker, McKibben
has an unsullied communitarian soul. His ego is buried in the global "we";
the ancient notion of a particular *Volk* has lost its ultimate power. His environmental sermons display a demanding, breathlessness cosmopolitanism of a digital visionary for whom cultures and continents are not about
difference, but about a common aspiration. Here is a sample:

> We need to rouse the world to a new sense of urgency and of possibility. Our
> plan—again, with your help—is to take the number 350 and beat it into every
> head and heart on planet Earth, to tattoo it into every brain. If our fellow earth-

lings know nothing else about climate change, they need to know that 350 lies in the direction of safety. We are busy trying to find artists, musicians, activists, preachers, athletes, and, well, normal people in all corners of the globe who will figure out how to make 350 the most well-known number on the planet. ... I was in Honolulu yesterday, where activists are figuring out how to put red tarps on the roofs of 350 homes in a single neighborhood that could have solar PV panels if only the utility would get out of the way. In Maui today, people promised to assemble 350 surfers off the beach for a photo. At an evangelical conference last week, pastors were talking about ringing their bells 350 times. We've heard from Mongolian cartoonists, Chinese universities, Canadians. *Canadians!* ... We think that if we can take that meme—350—and spread it everywhere, it will almost subconsciously set the bar for these negotiations much higher than it currently stands. We think it will nudge them sharply to the left, in the direction that physics and chemistry would indicate. We think 350 is the most important number in the world."[1]

The comments which we include point to the crucial dilemmas of the impact of civil society on government and industry. On the one hand, 350.org demonstrates that, thanks to the new media, global civic mobilization for an urgent cause is possible. It also proves that civil society capital is not entirely uprooting, flattening, homogenizing, or deterritorializing—as it is sometimes presented by radical critics. However, in the essay below, McKibben strikes a note of caution, "It's possible that the fight over global warming represents the ultimate test for emerging ideas about monitory, post-electoral democracy—and if so, it's not entirely clear that those ideas will be vindicated." According to him, monitory democracy may be able to raise questions, but not perhaps to answer them when confronted with the powerful, fossil-based industry on the planet.

Perhaps this is too pessimistic? As Atle Middtun has argued in this volume, civil society's ultimate goal is not to provide concrete deliverables, but to start an often long process of social and environmental innovation. In his "relay" theory, Midttun has further argued that civil society is the first, innovative runner in a multi-stage race, whose final destiny today is the green transition generated by the industry and institutionalized by governments.[2] At the same time, however, McKibben gestures towards a more entrenched dilemma which haunts new attractive options of global citizenship and cosmopolitanism which his environmental gospel requires. Is it so that even that which relates to humanity's future fate has little meaning—and perhaps reduced impact—without attending to deep structures of belonging which are at their most effective at the micro-level of particular cultures? If that is the case, then the catchword of making the earth our home is perhaps overambitious.

An Ounce of Action is Worth a Ton of Theory

Bill McKibben

The rise of the Internet has transformed many parts of human life in the last decade. I will argue here that it offers new opportunities for political organizing, but only if our sense of how movements work undergoes a serious shift. In particular, I will describe the ways new technologies allow for the easy and powerful agglomeration of local actions into global movements, using our work at the 350.org global warming campaign as a prime example. Then I will also describe the particular challenges—so far unmet—of trying to take that mobilization and use it to dramatically shift political outcomes on a scale commensurate with the particular problem we face right now: the fast-moving and devastating upheaval of the earth's climate system.

Let's think first of how movements have been conceived, especially in an American context, in the latter half of the twentieth century. Their key moments have usually been great centralized events: the March on Washington of the Civil Rights Movement, with Martin Luther King Jr.'s famous oratory; the giant nuclear freeze demonstration in New York's Central Park; and so on. This kind of concentration was necessary primarily to generate media attention: only by gathering a massive show of force in one place could you persuade television and elite print journalists to treat the event as a major story, a possible game-changing moment. The same kind of events happened regularly in many of the world's capital cities in the last few decades of the century—in fact, the last great moment for this strategy may have come in 2000 with the World Trade Organization gathering in Seattle, when a huge number of demonstrators surprised the world community with their vociferous opposition to new international trade legislation.

This strategy, however, produced far more fizzles than spectacular successes, for a variety of reasons:

    i. After a few repetitions, it became more difficult to sustain media interest. If gatherings were not larger than in the past, or if they didn't offer some other point of novelty, the coverage for them declined—even gatherings of 100,000 on the mall in Washington often failed to win coverage in even the *Washington Post*. Such gatherings began to suffer from sameness.

ii. It was difficult for a message of any subtlety to get through. Lacking an orator of the distinction of Dr. King, the only idea that would penetrate was blunt, for example: We are against the War in Iraq.

iii. Politicians, a key audience for such gatherings, tended to discount their meaning. In the United States, for instance, legislators from the rest of the country tended to think that very few participants in such gatherings were from their states or districts, and that they were dominated by liberal elites from the northeastern U.S. (In smaller and more homogeneous countries, this was likely less of a drawback).

iv. Small fringe groups were often able to dominate what news coverage there was of such gatherings. In the 2010 protests that accompanied the G-20 meetings in Toronto, Canada, for instance, a small group of anarchists smashed shop windows and overturned and burned a police car. Those images played endlessly on local and global TV coverage, and obscured the critique of the meetings that organizers hoped to offer.

v. Almost by definition, such gatherings were hard to internationalize, since travel restrictions and costs meant most participants would be local. There were occasional attempts to mount mass demonstrations simultaneously in many locales, the most successful being a day of protests prior to the U.S. invasion of Iraq in 2002, but most of these were confined to European and developed world locations.

With the spread of the Internet, new modes of activist organization began to emerge. The simplest made straightforward use of the new technology to send electronic petitions or encourage email letters to politicians—the cleverest use of such means was made by Moveon.org in the United States and its imitators in other countries such as the Australian Getup.org, and internationally by Avaaz.org. In addition, blogs and community political sites, led in the U.S. by examples like Dailykos.org, emerged to monitor and influence political campaigns and activist organizing—clearly the Barack Obama presidential campaign in 2008 drew on such models both to raise money and to organize volunteer efforts, with enormous success.

However, the structure of the Internet also allowed the conception of other activist forms. Those of us trying to deal with global warming face several interesting challenges that required creative thinking:

i. The problem is unavoidably global. Effective action can only be achieved with international agreement on a strategy, but that international agreement is predicated on consensus in various national capitals. Thus, the target for activism is somewhat unclear at any given moment.

ii. Many of the most obvious early victims of climate change are located in small and powerless nations that normally would have little way of reaching international media.

iii. The traditional approach of big national demonstrations, at least in a large nation like the United States, carries an additional burden in this case: it runs counter to the conservation message inherent in such a gathering to encourage people to travel long distances to attend.

350.org was formed in an effort to take advantage of these openings and constraints. We took our name from a paper published in January of 2008 by the planet's foremost climatologist, James Hansen, and his NASA-led team. Their paper, "Target Atmospheric CO_2: Where Should Humanity Aim?" was the first study to put a firm number on the planet's peril. They concluded that, "If humanity wishes to preserve a planet similar to that on which civilization developed and to which life on Earth is adapted, paleoclimate evidence and ongoing climate change suggest that CO_2 will need to be reduced from its current 385 ppm to at most 350 ppm." This, obviously, is strong language for scientists—it demonstrates that there is already too much carbon in the atmosphere, that global warming is not a future problem, and that we must in fact put the system in reverse quite quickly to have any hope of avoiding disastrous outcomes.[3]

Choosing a scientific data point as the banner around which to rally a movement is a novel idea, and presents certain difficulties compared with organizing around a slogan or demand. But 350 held certain advantages. One, it defined for policy makers and for our constituent audience the magnitude of necessary change: we didn't need "action on climate change," we needed *this much* action. Two, it allowed us to imagine a global strategy for organizing, since Arabic numerals, unlike slogans, cross language boundaries easily. 350 is as meaningful in Beijing, Boston, Barcelona, and Bergen. And so we made it the basis for our organizing efforts.

Our effort to conceive of new tactics was necessary, in part to deal with the fact that we had very few resources when we began our campaign in the winter of 2008, and in large measure because funders had difficulty imagining a global scale campaign. Also, organizing a single giant gathering was beyond our logistical ability—we began with myself and seven twenty-four-year-old recent college graduates, each of whom was assigned a continent to organize. It was not a beginning guaranteed to produce success, but we did have one advantage: experience in using the Internet in political change, gained the year before when we had organized a large domestic campaign (Step It Up) in the United States that had coordinated 1,400 rallies across all 50 states. That proved to be a useful dry run for our 350.org efforts because we had a good sense of how to make use of social media (which—Twitter, for instance—continued to emerge as our campaign unfolded) for something beyond electronic petitions and emails to leaders. We believed that it might be possible to coordinate widespread days of global action with dispersed events taking place across the earth, linked together by the web.

We set the date for the first such event in October of 2009, picking a weekend about six weeks in advance of the pivotal Copenhagen climate summit. Eighteen months of organizing led up to that event. Much of it was traditional—though we used the Internet to communicate with far-flung supporters, and to spread materials and updates—we also relied heavily on face to face interaction, in particular training camps for young leaders that we organized in central Asia, the Caribbean, Africa, and elsewhere. However, we decided at the outset for a radically decentralized day of action on 24 October—instead of trying to coordinate a few mass gatherings, we decided instead to aim for a widespread geographic diversity, with small, medium-sized, and large gatherings in as many places as possible.

In the event, we were successful in our efforts to catalyze this dispersed day of action. On 24 October, there were 5,200 events in 181 countries, which CNN called "the most widespread day of political action in the planet's history," and *Foreign Policy* magazine described as "the largest coordinated global rally of any kind." The demonstrations took place in a wide variety of settings. For instance, the president of the Maldive Islands, Mohammed Nasheed, organized an underwater cabinet meeting set against the dying coral reefs of his island nation; in Los Angeles, throngs of people formed human tidelines along beaches to show where the water would rise in a globally warmed world; along the Dead Sea, Israeli activists formed a giant 3 on their beach, Palestinians a 5 on theirs, and Jordanians a 0 on theirs.

The pictures of these activities were crucial to our plan. Our theory was that if people quickly uploaded the images to our website, we could in essence show that we'd just held a global rally far larger than could be accommodated on any of the planet's plazas, squares, and malls.

The rallies had several interesting outcomes. They demonstrated the enormous diversity of the environmental movement, which in the past had often been typified as western, white, and affluent. Instead, most of the participants were poor, black, brown, Asian, and/or young, because of course that is what most of the world looks like. In addition, there was enormous religious diversity, with high profile participation by leaders and adherents of all the world's faiths. Many of the 25,000 images uploaded to our Flickr account (and easily seen at 350.org/photos) looked unlikely to Western eyes: large demonstrations, for instance, composed entirely of women covered in burqas or chadors, or rallies in the remotest parts of, say, the Masai homelands of Africa.

The rallies were not captured by disruptive fringe groups because the scattered nature of the protests meant that extremist acts were diluted in their effect. Only one arrest was reported, oddly enough in Massachusetts in the United States. Due to the localized nature of the events, people's creativity was brought to the fore, with an almost endless selection of different ways of communicating the day's message about the need to return the planet's atmosphere to 350 parts per million carbon dioxide. In coastal cities, people erected sandbags against rising waters; in glacial uplands, they built ice sculptures that melted in the sun; in the desert, they made giant numbers out of solar panels; and so on.

As a media strategy, the plan worked well. We were the top story on Google News for more than 24 hours, meaning that there were more stories about our events than anything else happening on the planet. That success was due in no small part to the fact that reporters for local media were covering the individual events, and as their stories aggregated, major global media decided that they were witnessing a major world story.

Not trivially, we managed to pull off an event of that scale on a very limited budget, mostly thanks to the fact that the main web-based tools were free. The total cost was around a million dollars (U.S.), which given the size of and attention paid to the day's events was a small cost indeed.

The day's events gave us strong momentum approaching the Copenhagen conference, and we managed to convince 117 nations to sign on to a 350 target at that gathering. However, they were the wrong 117 nations, mostly weak and vulnerable, not rich and addicted. So we continue to press forward with this model of a globalized but dispersed campaign. The effort continues to expand; in the fall of 2010, for instance, we coordinated a Global Work Party, where people were asked to do more than demonstrate. They needed to also do something constructive in the climate fight, be it erect solar panels on a community center, dig a community garden, or lay out a new bike path. Despite the extra effort involved, this day of action was even more widespread than the first, with more than 7,400 work parties in 188 countries—virtually the entire planet. In 2011, we continued with some of the same tactics; that year the global mobilization focused on bicycles, one of the few tools shared by rich and poor.

However, we continue these efforts chastened in certain ways. It's possible that the fight over global warming represents the ultimate test for emerging ideas about monitory, post-electoral democracy—and if so, it's not entirely clear that those ideas will be vindicated. The issue, essentially, is that global warming is an unavoidable problem, one that can't be ducked. That's because of its overwhelming nature—left unabated, the steady increase in temperature guarantees to overwhelm every other effort to improve our lives. That is, you can build a remarkable local food system with highly democratic participation at every step, one attentive to the needs of the poor and of producers, but if it doesn't rain once in forty days, or rains every day for that stretch, then you won't be growing anything. And both scenarios, as the brutal summer of 2010 illustrated in places like Russia and Pakistan, become ever more likely as the temperature increases.

And here's the rub: it seems unlikely that you can solve global warming without invoking the power of governments, indeed of many many governments. The essential cause of climate change is that the business model of the fossil fuel industry has traditionally allowed it to vent the waste from its product directly into the atmosphere—the atmosphere has served as a free open sewer, an arrangement that has helped make the industry the most profitable the world has ever seen. A small fraction of those profits usually suffices to produce favorable political outcomes. For instance, Exxon Mobil made $40 billion in profit in 2009, and the industry as a whole had to spend about $500 million in lobbying fees to defeat mild climate legislation in the U.S. Congress, a defeat that also made international progress all but impossible.

This essentially nineteenth century industry must be defeated for climate legislation powerful enough to make a difference to be enacted—in essence, that legislation would charge the fossil fuel companies for the right to use that sewer, reducing their profitability, and inducing a rapid switch to other technologies. The extra-legislative efforts to put pressure on these industries are difficult, given the ubiquity of fossil fuels in our lives: it would be hard to know how or what to boycott. Conceivably, people could build lives and communities that use much less fossil fuel—the Transition Town initiatives are an excellent example—but the chances of it adding up to appreciable changes in the atmosphere's carbon concentration in the time allowed by physics and chemistry seems remote. (And that is not their main intention, though they have been excellent allies—they are preparing for a world that runs out of oil and whose thermostat has become unpredictable).

In short, we are left using a series of extra-legislative and post-electoral tactics to try and accomplish extremely twentieth century ends: a legislative solution. And a particularly difficult one, in that most of the major countries in the world must both agree internally on plans, and then reach some kind of enforceable joint agreement. It is perhaps not surprising that Copenhagen was a less than total success, and that subsequent talks at Cancun in December 2010 were judged a victory simply because they kept the process on track.

And so we carry on, probing for weaknesses in that seemingly impenetrable exterior, looking for new alliances, and new tactics. Later in the fall, we planned a massive global-scale art show, visible from outer space, in an effort to remind people just how interconnected the planet was. And we began laying more serious plans for mass civil disobedience in the year ahead.

We're drawing inspiration from a wide variety of contemporary thinkers. Naomi Klein's ongoing account of a worldwide movement has instructed our thinking, and we are heartened by Paul Hawken's informed insistence in *Blessed Unrest* that, "if you meet the people in this unnamed movement and aren't optimistic, you haven't got a heart." Probably more than any other such effort, we have met those people. And yet we remain unclear about how to translate the power of the movement we're building into legislative victories against powerful foes. We're building a movement without a sharp sense of how to put it into action—waiting, perhaps, for openings provided by the natural world or unforeseen political opportunities, but cognizant that we can't wait too long or else this particular game is lost.

It's possible that in the end, the power of this movement can only play out fully, at least in countries like the U.S., in conventional electoral politics. For that to happen, however, we will have to raise the salience of the issue high enough to overcome the inherent advantages of money in that arena. To that end, we are increasingly focused on the role of the United States, and on the role of political money within the U.S. The fight for climate legislation has been held back by the financial power of the fossil fuel industry, but that financial power is beginning to come under examination. In California, in the fall of 2010, we collaborated with many groups in the fight against the repeal of the state's landmark global warming law. The repeal effort was led by two Texas oil companies, and their participation became the most controversial part of the referendum fight. It was anger at their intrusion into political decision-making that helped turn the tide. We are trying to figure out how to nationalize such anger; in 2011, for instance, we' planned a campaign against the intrusive lobbying of the national Chamber of Commerce, which has been a convenient front for a few large oil and coal companies.

What this would suggest is that monitory democracy is a strong enough force to raise questions, but not perhaps to answer them when the concentration of wealth and power on the other side is so large and so ubiquitous (granted, a situation that pertains perhaps uniquely to the fossil fuel industry, the most powerful enterprise on the planet). Making the transition from bearing witness to producing measurable change is our next challenge, as yet unfulfilled.

In summary, I think we've demonstrated that there are interesting new possibilities for political organizing offered by emerging technologies, in particular the ability to aggregate local events around a common theme that presents the chance to unite voices around the planet. Whether or not this form of activism—or indeed any form of activism—will prove strong enough to play a major role in reshaping climate policy remains to be seen.

Notes

1. Available at: *http://www.utne.com/Politics/Utne-Reader-Visionaries-Bill-McKibben-350-Org.aspx#ixzz1QbWZnSCB*
2. Atle Midttun and Anne L.Koefoed, "The Effectiveness and Negotiability of Environmental Regulation," *International Journal of Regulation and Governance* (2001). See also Atle Midttun, "The Greening of European Electricity Industry:A Battle of Modernities, *Energy Policy,* special issue on "Frontiers of Sustainability," 48 (2012): 22–35.
3. A variety of other papers in subsequent years have concluded that the 350 number is approximately correct. See for instance: "Statement on the Science and Management of Coral Reef Ecosystems in a Changing Climate," version released by the technical workshop of leading world marine and climate change scientists, hosted by ZSL, IPSO, and the Royal Society, July 2009.

CONTRIBUTORS

Zeynep Atalay is an assistant professor of sociology at St. Mary's College of California and a visiting scholar at the Abbasi Program in Islamic Studies at Stanford University. She received her PhD in Sociology at the University of Maryland in 2012. The title of her PhD dissertation is Global Islam in the Age of Civil Society: Transnational NGO Networks, Religion, Power. She received her bachelor's and master's degrees from Bogazici University in Istanbul, Turkey in 2002 and 2004. Recent work includes the forthcoming "Civil Society as Soft Power: Islamic NGOs and Turkish Foreign Policy" in Turkey between Nationalism and Globalization by Riva Kastoryano (2012), Readings in Globalization: Key Concepts and Major Debates, edited with Professor George Ritzer (2010), as well as the book chapter "Global Majority–Minority Relations: Race,Gender and Ethnicity in the Global Age" in Globalization: Textbook by George Ritzer (2009). Her areas of research interest are in the fields of political sociology, sociology of religion, globalization, and culture. She has published on globalization, civil society, and Muslim NGO networks and her current research focuses on the global networks of faith-based Muslim civil society organizations.

Cathy Baldwin is a post-doctoral associate in anthropology at the University of Oxford, from where she holds a doctorate in social and cultural anthropology. Her thesis explored the role of information from the U.K. and international media and life experiences in shaping perceptions of identity, ethnicity, community and place among Indian Sikh, English, and Polish adults in an English town. Cathy also works as a Social Impact Consultant for the corporate environmental sector. She is a member of the Academic Assessment Committee for EDU, an intergovernmental organization (IGO) validating education in territories lacking in educational infrastructure worldwide. She was previously a factual and documentaries reporter for the BBC's World Service radio, Radio 4 and 3. She reported for and presented over thirty reports and full-length programs throughout Europe. Cathy studied for her master's degrees at the Universities of Oxford, Sussex and Iceland, lecturing at the latter, and holds a bachelor in music and media from Sussex. She has worked in media relations for NGOs Christian Aid, Article 19, and the British Refugee Council; and been a project director in Belarus for the British Council. Her interests are social and environmental sustainability, ethnic relations, international cultural diplomacy, and the intersection of research and practice.

John Clark is an independent consultant and principal at The Policy Practice. He specializes in the roles of civil society in development and participatory governance. Prior to 2009, he was at the World Bank (as head of its civil society program and then lead social scientist for East Asia) and in Oxfam GB (leading its campaigns and policy functions). He has advised Kofi Annan on UN-civil society relations; served on Tony Blair's Africa Task Force; and written five books on civil society and other topics, including *Worlds Apart: Civil Society and the Battle for Ethical Globalization* (2003) and *Democratizing Development* (1991). From 2000 to 2003, he was visiting fellow at the Centre for Civil Society at the London School of Economics (LSE). Recent academic publications include the book chapter "The World Bank and Civil Society: An Evolving Experience" in *Civil Society and Global Finance*, ed. J. Scholte and A. Schnabel (2002); the book chapter "NGOs and the State" in *The Companion to Development Studies*, ed. V. Desai and R. Potter (2002); and "The State, Popular Participation and the Voluntary Sector" in *NGOs, States, and Donors: Too Close for Comfort?* ed. D. Hulme and M. Edwards (1997).

Paddy Coulter is a specialist in media and sustainable development working as communications director for the Oxford Poverty & Human Development Initiative (OPHI), a research centre within the University of Oxford's Department of International Development. He is also a partner in the Oxford Global Media consultancy. He was formerly director of studies at the Reuters Institute for the Study of Journalism at Oxford, responsible for the international journalism program. He is a fellow of Green Templeton College, University of Oxford as well as a visiting fellow of Bournemouth Media School, Britain's largest media training school at the University of Bournemouth.

Previously, Paddy was director of the independent television production company, the International Broadcasting Trust (IBT), between 1990 and 2001 (and its deputy director 1987 to 1990), where he produced over a hundred television program for leading broadcasters on global environment and development issues. Paddy has a strong interest in media and civil society. He has had a lengthy involvement with UNICEF and

Oxfam (including as Head of Oxfam Communications) and is currently a member of the Board of Directors for UNICEF U.K. Enterprises. He is a founder trustee of the Media Trust and is also a trustee of the African social justice network, Fahamu, publisher of *Pambazuka News.*

Haideh Daragahi was a professor of English literature at Teheran University when Khomeini took power. She has lived in Sweden since 1984 as a scholar and women's activist. Haideh Daragahi was born in 1949 in Tehran, Iran. She studied English literature in Britain and received her doctorate in English literature from the University of East Anglia in 1978. She was offered a professorship at Tehran University upon her return to Iran the same year. This was the year of the revolution that overthrew the government of the Shah and brought the Islamists to power. As a result of her activities as a feminist and left activists, Haideh, together with a large number of lecturers with similar activities, was purged from her university job, and, shortly afterwards, had to leave the country and come to Sweden as a political refugee.

With a few exceptions—such as her piece on Satanic Verses: "Reclaiming Satanic Verses as Literature"—most of Haideh's writing, social, and political work have been centered around the question of women. Her latest article, "Three Pictures: An Analysis," that deals with the role of women in the protest demonstrations after the Iranian presidential elections in June 2009, was published in Swedish, Norwegian, English, German, and Tamil.

John Keane was born in southern Australia and educated at the Universities of Adelaide, Toronto, and Cambridge. John is professor of politics at the University of Sydney and at the Wissenschaftszentrum Berlin (WZB). In 1989, he founded the Centre for the Study of Democracy (CSD) in London. Among his many books are *The Media and Democracy* (1991), which has been translated into more than twenty-five languages; *Democracy and Civil Society* (1988; 1998); *Reflections on Violence* (1996); *Civil Society: Old Images, New Visions* (1998); the prize-winning biography *Tom Paine: A Political Life* (1995); and a study of power in twentieth century Europe, *Václav Havel: A Political Tragedy in Six Acts* (1999). Among his most recent works are *Global Civil Society?* (2003); *Violence and Democracy* (2004); *The Life and Death of Democracy* (2009); and (with Wolfgang Merkel and others) *The Future of Representative Democracy* (2010).

In recent years, he has held the Karl Deutsch Professorship in Berlin, co-directed a large-scale European Commission-funded project on the future of civil society and citizenship, and served as a Fellow of the London-based think tank the Institute for Public Policy Research (IPPR). He recently held a Major Research Fellowship awarded by the Leverhulme Trust and is a fellow of the Fudan Institute for Advanced Study in Social Sciences in Shanghai. More information can be found at *http://www .johnkeane.net/pictures/pictures.htm*

Bill McKibben is the Schumann Distinguished Scholar in Environmental Studies at Middlebury College in Middlebury, Vermont. The founder of the global climate campaign 350.org, he is the author of a dozen books about the environment, including *The End of Nature* (1989), widely regarded as the first book for a general audience about global warming. In 2007, Bill published *Deep Economy: the Wealth of Communities and the Durable Future*. It addresses what the author sees as shortcomings of the growth economy and envisions a transition to more local-scale enterprise. In 2010, the Boston Globe called him "probably the nation's leading environmentalist" and *Time* magazine described him as "the world's best green journalist."

Atle Midttun is professor at the Norwegian School of Management, Institute of Innovation and Economic Organization; Director of the Center for Corporate Responsibility; and Co-Director of the Center for Energy and Environment. Before joining the Norwegian School of Management, he worked at the Group for Resource Studies under the National Research Council at the Institute for Social Studies, Oslo and the Institute of Sociology, University of Oslo. He was a visiting professor at the Université Paris Sud, the University of Michigan, and a visiting scholar at the University of California, Berkeley, and the Max Planck Institute for Social Research.

His research contributions and teaching are within regulation and governance, corporate social responsibility, innovation, strategy, and economic organization. Much of his empirical work has focused on energy and the environmental issues. Recent publications include *Reshaping of European Electricity and Gas Industry: Regulation, Markets, and Business Strategies,* (ed. with Dominique Finon) (2004), *Approaches to and Dilemmas of Economic Regulation* (ed with Eirik Svindland) (2001).

James Miller is associate professor of Chinese Studies in the School of Religion at Queen's University, Canada. He is a specialist in Daoism (aka Taoism), China's indigenous religion, and has published four books and numerous articles and essays related to Chinese religions, nature, and ecology. His current research focuses on the intersection of religion, nature, and modernization in the People's Republic of China.

David I. Steinberg is the distinguished professor of Asian studies, School of Foreign Service, Georgetown University, and was previously director of that program (1997–2007). He was a representative of The Asia Foundation in Korea, Hong Kong, Burma, and Washington, as well as president of the Mansfield Center for Pacific Affairs. Earlier, as a member of the Senior Foreign Service, Agency for International Development [USAID], Department of State, he was director for technical assistance for Asia and the Middle East, and director for Philippines, Thailand, and Burma Affairs. Professor Steinberg is the author of thirteen books and monographs including one translation, and over one hundred articles/chapters. Among these books are: *Burma/Myanmar: What Everyone Needs to Know* (2010); *Turmoil in Burma: Contested Legitimacies in Myanmar* (2006); *Stone Mirror: Reflections on Contemporary Korea* (2002); *Burma: The State of Myanmar* (2001); and *The Republic of Korea. Economic Transformation and Social Change* (1989). David I. Steinberg was educated at Dartmouth College; Lingnan University [Canton, China]; Harvard University, where he studied Chinese; and the School of Oriental and African Studies, University of London, where he studied Burmese and Southeast Asia.

Kathryn Stoner-Weiss is senior fellow at Foreign Service Institute, deputy director at the Center on Democracy, Development, and the Rule of Law, and (as of 1 September 2010) faculty director of the Ford Dorsey Program in International Policy Studies at Stanford University. Prior to coming to Stanford in 2004, she was on the faculty at Princeton University for nine years, jointly appointed to the Department of Politics and the Woodrow Wilson School for International and Public Affairs. At Princeton, she received the Ralph O. Glendinning Preceptorship, awarded to outstanding junior faculty. She also served as visiting associate professor of Political Science at Columbia University and assistant professor of Political Science at McGill University. She has held fellowships at Harvard University as well as the Woodrow Wilson Center in Washington, D.C. In addition to many articles and book chapters on contemporary Russia, she is the author of two single-authored books: *Resisting the State: Reform and Retrenchment in Post-Soviet Russia* (2006), and *Local Heroes: The Political Economy of Russian Regional Governance* (1997). She is also coeditor (along with Michael McFaul) of *After the Collapse of Communism: Comparative Lessons of Transitions* (2004). She received bachelor's and master's degrees in political science from the University of Toronto, and a PhD in Government from Harvard University.

Bron Taylor is president of the International Society for the Study of Religion, Nature, and Culture and editor of the Journal for the Study

of Religion, Nature, and Culture. He has written widely about environmental ethics and grassroots movements, with special attention to their
religious, moral, and political dimensions. His works include *Dark Green
Religion: Nature Spirituality and the Planetary Future* (2009); the *Encyclopedia of Religion and Nature* (2005); and *Ecological Resistance Movements* (1995). Bron was appointed as the Samuel S. Hill Ethics Professor
at the University of Florida in 2002, where he teaches in its graduate program focusing on religion and nature. He is also the host of http://www
.religionandnature.com, which is a gateway to his initiatives, research, and
teaching.

Asle Toje is acting research director at the Norwegian Nobel Institute
(Oslo) where he works on the intersection between security and de-
velopment studies. Since graduating in 2007 from Pembroke College,
Cambridge, he has published extensively on different aspects of Euro-
pean security and development policy. Among his most recent works
are *America, the EU, and Strategic Culture: Renegotiating the Transatlantic
Bargain* (2008) and *The European Union as a Small Power: After the Post-
Cold War* (2010).

Lars Trägårdh is professor of history and civil society studies at Ersta
Sköndal University College in Stockholm, Sweden. He received his PhD
in history from University of California, Berkeley in 1993 and worked
for ten years as assistant professor in history at Barnard College at Columbia University, New York. He co-directs a major research project on
social trust at Ersta Sköndal University College in Stockholm and has
also served as a coordinator for an EU funded program on social capital
and social policy at the London School of Economics. In 2011, he was
appointed to the Commission on the Future of Sweden, led by the prime
minister of Sweden, Fredrik Reinfeldt. Publications include *State and
Civil Society in Northern Europe: The Swedish Model Reconsidered* (2007);
*After National Democracy: Rights, Law, and Power in America and the New
Europe* (2004); and *Culture and Crisis: the Case of Germany and Sweden*
(with Nina Witoszek, 2002).

Nina Witoszek is research professor and research director at the Center
for Development and the Environment at the University of Oslo. Before
joining Oslo University, she worked at the Universities of Oxford, the
National University of Ireland in Galway, and the European University
in Florence. She also held visiting professorships at the University of
Cambridge (1995) and the University of Stanford (2010). Her research
interests include comparative history of cultures, Scandinavian studies,

and cultural innovation for a sustainable future. Her studies include *Culture and Crisis: the Case of Germany and Scandinavia* (with Lars Trägårdh, 2002) and *Cultural Origins of the Norwegian Regime of Goodness* (2011). Nina Witoszek is also a fiction and film script writer (known as Nina FitzPatrick), whose work includes, among others, *Fables of the Irish Intelligentsia* (1992), *The Loves of Faustyna* (1995) and *Daimons* (2003).

SELECTED BIBLIOGRAPHY

Afari, Janet, *The Iranian Constitutional Revolution: Grass Roots Democracy, Social Democracy, and Origins of Feminism.* New York: Columbia University Press, 2005.

Aijmer, Göran and Virgil K.Y. Ho, *Cantonese Society in a Time of Change.* Hong Kong: Chinese University Press, 2000.

Allan, James and Lyle Scruggs, "Political Partisanship and Welfare State Reform in Advanced Industrial Societies." *American Journal of Political Science* vol. 48, no. 3 (2004).

Allan, Sarah, *The Way of Water and Sprouts of Virtue.* New York: State University of New York Press, 1997.

Allan, Stuart and Einar Thorsen, eds. *Citizen Journalism: Global Perspectives.* New York: Peter Lang, 2009.

An-Na'im, Abdullahi, "Global Citizenship and Human Rights: From Muslim in Europe to European Muslims," in *Religious Pluralism and Human Rights in Europe: Where to Draw the Line?* eds. M.L.P. Loenen and J.E. Glodschmidt. Antwerp and Oxford: Intersentia, 2007: 13–55.

Anheier, Helmut, Glasius Marlies, and Mary Kaldor, eds. *Global Civil Society Yearbook 2001.* Oxford: Oxford University Press, 2001.

Anton, Thomas J., *Administered Politics: Elite Political Culture in Sweden.* Boston: Martinus Nijhoff, 1980.

Archarya, Amitav B., Michael Frolic, and Richard Stubbs, eds. *Democracy, Human Rights, & Civil Society in Southeast Asia.* Toronto: Joint Center for Asia Pacific Studies, 2001.

Arendt, Hannah, *The Promise of Politics.* New York: Schocken, 2005.

———. *The Origins of Totalitarianism.* New York: Harcourt Brace, 1979.

———. *On Revolution.* London: Penguin Books [1963], 1990.

———. "'Action' and 'The Pursuit of Happiness,'" in *Politische Ordnung und menschliche Existenz. Festgabe für Eric Vögelin zum 60. Geburtstag,* ed. A. Dempf. München: Beck, 1962.

Avineri, Shlomo, *Hegel's Theory of the Modern State.* Cambridge: Cambridge University Press, 1972.

Baogang, He, *The Democratic Implications of Civil Society in China.* London: Macmillan, 1997.

Bayat, Asef, "Activism and Social Development in the Middle East." *International Journal of Middle East Studies* vol. 34, no. 1 (2002): 1–28.

———. "Un-Civil Society: The Politics of the 'Informal People.'" *Third World Quarterly* vol. 18, no.1 (1997): 53–72.

Baron, Barnett F., "Deterring Donors: Anti-terrorist Financing Rules and American Philanthropy." *International Journal of Not-for-Profit Law* vol. 6, no. 2 (2004): 1–32.

Berger, Peter, "Religion and Global Civil Society," in *Religion in Global Civil Society*, ed. Mark Juergensmeyer. Oxford: Oxford University Press, 2005.

Berggren, Henrik and Lars Trägårdh, *Är svensken människa? Gemenskap och oberoende i det moderna Sverige*. Stockholm: Norstedts, 2006.

Berkes, Fikret, *Sacred Ecology: Traditional Ecological Knowledge and Resource Management*. New York: Routledge, 2008 [1999].

Berman, Sheri, "Civil Society and the Collapse of the Weimar Republic." *World Politics* vol. 49, no. 3 (1997): 401–429.

Brand, Philip W. and Paul Yancey, *In His Image*. Grand Rapids, M.I.: Zondervan Pub. House, 1984.

Breckman, Warren, *Marx, the Young Hegelians, and the Origins of Radical Social Theory: Dethroning the Self*. Cambridge: Cambridge University Press, 1999.

Bush, Evelyn L., "Measuring Religion in Global Civil Society." *Social Forces* vol. 85, no. 4 (2007): 1645–1665.

Camus, Albert, *Neither Victims nor Executioners*. Chicago: World Without War Publications, 1972 [Originally published in *Combat*, 1946].

Castells, Manuel, *The Internet Galaxy: Reflections on the Internet, Business, and Society*. Oxford: Oxford University Press, 2001.

——. *The Rise of the Network Society*. 2nd ed., Oxford: Blackwell, 2000.

Catton, William, *Overshoot: The Ecological Basis of Revolutionary Change*. Urbana & Chicago I.L.: University of Illinois Press, 1980.

Chambers, Simone and Jeffrey Kopstein. "Bad Civil Society." *Political Theory* vol. 29, no. 6 (2001): 837–865.

Chesler, Philis, *The Death of Feminism*. New York: Palgrave, Macmillan, 2006.

Clark, Janine A., "Islamic Social Welfare Organizations in Cairo: Islamization from Below?" *Arab Studies Quarterly* vol. 17, no. 4 (1995): 11–17.

Clark, John and Nuno S. Themudo, "Linking the Web and the Street: Internet-Based 'Dotcauses' and the 'Anti-Globalization Movement.'" *World Development*, vol. 34, no. 1 (2006): 50–74.

Clark, John, *Worlds Apart: Civil Society and the Battle for Ethical Globalization*. Bloomfield, C.T.: Kumarian Press, 2003.

Coase, Ronald H. "The Problem of Social Cost." *Journal of Law and Economics* vol. 3 (1960): 15–25.

Cohen, Jean, "Civil Society and Globalization: Rethinking the Categories" in *State and Civil Society in Northern Europe: The Swedish Model Reconsidered*, ed. Lars Trägårdh. New York: Berghahn Books, 2007.

Congjie, Liang and Yang Dongping, eds. *The China Environment Yearbook (2005): Crisis and Breakthrough of China's Environment*. China: Brill Academic Publishers, 2007.

Crone, Patricia, *Slaves on Horses: The Evolution of the Islamic Polity*. Cambridge: Cambridge University Press, 1986.

Curtis, Devon, "Politics and Humanitarian Aid: Debates, Dilemmas, and Dissension." *HPG Report* 10. London: Humanitarian Policy Group, Overseas Development Institute, 2001.

Dagron, Alfonso Gumucio, *Making Waves: Stories of Participatory Communication for Social Change*. New York: The Rockefeller Foundation, 2001.

Dahl, Robert, *Polyarchy: Participation and Opposition*. New Haven: Yale University Press, 1971.

Dahrendorf, Ralf, *After 1989: Morals, Revolution, and Civil Society*. New York: St. Martin's Press, 1997.

Dean, Jodi, Jon W. Anderson, and Geert Lovinck, *Reformatting Politics: Information Technology and Global Society*. London: Routledge, 2006.

Dembe, Allard E. and Leslie I. Boden, "Moral Hazard: A Question of Morality?" *New Solutions* vol. 10, no. 3 (2000).

Diamond, Jared, *Collapse: How Societies Choose to Fail or Succeed*. New York: Viking, 2005.

Diamond, Larry, *Developing Democracy: Toward Consolidation*. Baltimore: Johns Hopkins University Press, 1999.

Duara, Prasenjit. "Knowledge and Power in the Discourse of Modernity: The Campaigns against Popular Religion in Early Twentieth Century China and Campaigns against Popular Religion." *Journal of Asian Studies* vol. 50, no. 1 (1991): 67–83.

Dunlop, John, *The Rise of Russia and the Fall of the Soviet Empire*. Princeton: Princeton University Press, 1993.

Easterly, William, *The White Man's Burden: Why the West's Efforts to Aid the Rest Have Done So Much Ill and So Little Good*. New York: Penguin Press, 2006.

Edwards, Michael, *Just Another Emperor: The Myths and Realities of Philantrocapitalism*. New York: Demos, 2008.

Egeland, Jan Olav, *Impotent Superpower—Potent Small State*. Oslo: International Peace Research Institute, 1985.

Ellen, Roy F., Peter Parkes, and Alan Bicker, eds. *Indigenous Environmental Knowledge and Its Transformations*. Amsterdam: Harwood Academic Publishers, 2000.

Elliot, Charles, "Some Aspects of Relations between the North and South in the NGO Sector." *World Development* vol.15 (Supp.) (1987): 57–68.

Esposito, John L. and Francois Burgat, eds. *Modernizing Islam: Religion in the Public Sphere in the Middle East and Europe*. London and New Bunswick: Hurst Publications and Rutgers University Press, 2003.

Evans, Alfred B., Laura A. Henry, and Lisa McIntosh Sundstrom, eds. *Russian Civil Society: A Critical Assessment*. New York: M.E. Sharpe, 2006.

Falk, Richard, *On Global Governance: Toward a New Global Politics*. University Park, P.A.: Pennsylvania University Press, 1995.

Ferris, Elizabeth, "Faith-Based and Secular Humanitarian Organizations." *International Review of the Red Cross* vol. 87 (2005): 312–25.

Fish, M. Steven, *Democracy Derailed in Russia: The Failure of Open Politics*. New York: Cambridge University Press, 2005.

——. *Democracy from Scratch: Opposition and Regime in the New Russian Revolution*. Princeton: Princeton University Press, 1995.

Foyer, Lars, "The Social Sciences in Royal Commission Studies in Sweden." *Scandinavian Political Studies* vol. 4 (1969): 183–204.

Fung, Archon and Erik Olin Wright, eds. *Deepening Democracy. Institutional Innovations in Empowered Participatory Governance*. London and New York: Verso: 2003.

330 • Selected Bibliography

Frankfurt, Harry G., *On Bullshit*. Princeton and Oxford: Princeton University Press,
2005.
Gellner, Ernest, *Conditions of Liberty: Civil Society and Its Rivals*. New York: The Penguin Press, 1994.
——. *Nations and Nationalism*. Oxford: Blackwell Publishers, 1983.
Gorbachev, Mikhail, *Memoirs*. New York: Double Day Press, 1996.
Grodzins, Morton, *The Metropolitan Area As A Racial Problem*. Pittsburgh: University
of Pittsburgh Press, 1958.
Gunderson, Lance, and C. S. Holling, *Panarchy: Understanding Transformations in Systems of Humans and Nature*. Covelo, C.A.: Island Press, 2002.
Hall, John, *Powers and Liberties: The Causes and Consequences of the Rise of the West*.
Harmondsworth, U.K.: Penguin, 1985.
Hall, Wendy and Stuart Weir, *The Untouchables: Power and Accountability In the
QUANGO State*. London: The Scarman Trust, 1996.
Halliday, Fred, "The Politics of the Umma: States and Community in Islamic Movements." *Mediterannean Politics* vol. 7, no. 3 (2002): 20–41.
Hann, Chris and Elizabeth Dunn, *Civil Society: Challenging Western Models*. London:
Routledge, 1996.
Hardin, Russel, *Distrust*. Russell Sage Foundation Series on Trust, vol. 8. New York:
Russell Sage Foundation 2004.
Hardt, Michael and Antonio Negri, *Commonwealth*. Cambridge, M.A.: Harvard University Press, 2011.
——. *Multitude: War and Democracy in the Age of Empire*. New York: Penguin Books,
2004.
Hart, H.L.A., *The Concept of Law*. Oxford: Clarendon, 1961.
Hardin, Garrett, *Stalking the Wild Taboo*. 3rd ed. Petoskey, M.I.: Social Contract Press,
1996.
——. *Living Within Limits*. New York: Oxford University Press, 1993.
Havel, Vaclav, "Anti-Political Politics" in *Civil Society and the State*, ed. John Keane.
London: Verso, 1988.
Heckscher, Gunnar, *Staten och organisationerna*. Stockholm: KFs bokförlag, 1946.
Homer-Dixon, Thomas, "Across the Threshold: Empirical Evidence on Environmental Scarcities as Causes of Violent Conflict." *International Security* vol.19, no. 1
(1994): 5–40.
——. "On the Threshold: Environmental Changes as Causes of Acute Conflict." *International Security* vol. 16, no. 2 (1991): 76–116.
Homer-Dixon, Thomas and Jessica Blitt, eds. *Ecoviolence: Links among Environment,
Population, and Security*. Lanham, M.D.: Roman & Littlefield, 1998.
Homer-Dixon, Thomas, J. H. Boutwell, and G.W. Rathjens. "Environmental Change
and Violent Conflict." *Scientific American* vol. 268, no. 2 (1993): 38–45.
Hegel, G. W. F., "Elements of the Philosophy of Right," in *Elements of the Philosophy of
Right*, ed. Allen Wood. Cambridge: Cambridge University Press, 1991.
Heidal, Brian, *The Growth of Civil Society in Myanmar*. Bangalore: Books for Exchange,
2006.
Henderson, Sarah L., *Building Democracy in Contemporary Russia*. Ithaca: Cornell
University Press, 2003.
Heinrich Boell Stiftung, ed. *Active Citizens under Political Wraps: Experiences from Myanmar/Burma and Vietnam*. Chiang Mai, Thailand: Henry Boell Foundation, 2006.

Holmstrøm, Bengt, "Moral Hazard and Observability." *Bell Journal of Economics* vol. 1 (1979): 74–91.

Holt, Clare, ed. *Culture and Politics in Indonesia.* Ithaca: Cornell University Press, 1972.

Huntford, Roland, *The New Totalitarians.* New York: Stein and Day, 1971.

Huntington, Samuel, P., *Political Order in Changing Societies.* New Haven, C.T.: Yale University Press, 1968.

——. *Clientelism: A Study in Administrative Politics.* Ph.D. diss., Harvard University, 1950.

Husseini, Nahid, *Impact of Culture on Iranian Female Education.* London: Satrap Publishing, 2010.

Ibrahim, Saad Eddin, "Egypt's Islamic Activism in the 1980s." *Third World Quarterly* vol. 10 (1998): 632–657.

International Crisis Group, *Crisis Report. Turkey's Crises over Israel and Iran.* ICG Europe Report, 2010.

Isaac, Jeffrey C. "A New Guarantee of Earth: Hannah Arendt on Human Dignity and the Politics of Human Rights." *American Political Science Review* vol. 90, no. 1 (1996): 61–73.

James, Jeffrey, "Information Technology and Mass Poverty." *International Journal of Development Issues* vol. 5, no. 1 (2006): 85–107.

Jarque, Arantxa, *Repeated Moral Hazard with Effort Persistence.* Richmond, V.A.: Federal Reserve Bank of Richmond, 2008.

Javeline, Debra and Sarah Lindemann-Komarova, "Rethinking Russia: A Balanced Assessment of Russian Civil Society." *Journal of International Affairs* vol. 63, no. 2 (2010): 171–188.

Johannes, R.E., ed. *Traditional Ecological Knowledge: A Collection of Essays.* Geneva: International Union for the Conservation of Nature, 1989.

Jonsson, Michael and Svante Cornell, "Countering Terrorist Financing: Lessons from Europe." *Georgetown Journal of International Affairs* vol. 8, no. 1 (2007): 69–78.

Kadioglu, Ayse, "Women's Subordination in Turkey: Is Islam Really the Villain?" *Middle East Journal* vol. 48, no. 4 (1994): 645–660.

Kaldor, Mary, Helmut Anheier, and Marlies Glasius, eds. *Global Civil Society 2003.* Oxford: Oxford University Press, 2003.

Kamali, Masoud, "Civil Society and Islam: A Sociological Perspective." *Archives Europeennes De Sociologie* vol. 42, no. 3 (2001): 457–482.

Kaplan, Robert D., *The Coming Anarchy: Shattering the Dreams of the post–Cold War.* New York: Random House, 2000.

Katouzian, Homa, "The Iranian Revolution at 30: the Dialectic of State and Society," *Critique* vol. 19, no. 1 (2000): 35–53.

Keane, John, *The Life and Death of Democracy.* London: Simon and Schuster, 2009.

Keck, Margaret E. and Kathryn Sikkink, *Activists beyond Borders: Advocacy Networks in International Politics.* Ithaca: Cornell University Press, 1998.

Klein, Naomi, *The Shock Doctrine. The Rise of Disaster Capitalism.* New York: Metropolitan Books, 2008.

——. *No Logo: Taking Aim at the Brand Name Bullies.* Toronto: Vintage, 2000.

——. "Reclaiming the Commons," *The New Left Review.* 9 May 2001.

Korten, David C. *Getting to the 21st Century: Voluntary Action and the Global Agenda.* West Hartford, C.T.: Kumarian Press, 1990.

Krafess, Jamal, "The Influence of Muslim Religion in Humanitarian Aid." *International Review of the Red Cross* vol. 858 (2005): 327–342.

Kubba, Laith, "The Awakening of Civil Society." *Journal of Democracy* vol. 11, no. 3 (2000).

Lagerlöf, Selma, *The Wonderful Adventures of Nils*, trans. Velma Swanston Howard. New York: Doubleday, Page & Company, 1907.

Lansing, Stephen S., *Priests and Programmers: Technologies of Power in the Engineered Landscape of Bali*. Princeton, N.J.: Princeton University Press, 1991.

Lanting, Frans, *Eye to Eye: Intimate Encounters with the Animal World*. Köln, Germany: Taschen, 1997.

Laski, Harold, et al., *The Future of Democracy*. London, 1946.

Leader, Nicholas, *The Politics of Principle: The Principles of Humanitarian Action in Practice*. London: Overseas Development Institute, 2000.

Lewin, Moshe, *The Gorbachev Phenomenon: A Historical Interpretation*. Berkeley: University of California Press, 1988.

Lomborg, Bjørn, *Cool It: The Skeptical Environmentalist's Guide to Global Warming*. New York: Alfred A. Knopf, 2007.

Lewis, Bernard, *The Shaping of the Modern Middle East*. New York: Oxford University Press, 1994.

Locke, John, *The Legislative, Executive, and Federative Power of the Commonwealth; Second Treatise of Government*. Clifton, New Jersey: Barnes and Noble Books, 2004 [1690].

Lorch, Jasmin, "Civil Society under Authoritarian Rule: The Case of Myanmar." *Journal of Current Southeast Asian Studies* vol. 2 (2006): 3–37.

Lundström, Tommy and Filip Wijkström, "Från röst till service? Den svenska ideella sektorn i förändring." *Sköndalsinstitutets skriftserie* vol. 4 (1995).

Mann, Thomas, *Goethe and Democracy*. Washington, DC, 1949.

Maathai, Wangari, *Unbowed: A Memoir*. New York: Knopf, 2006.

Martens, Bertin, *The Institutional Economics of Foreign Aid*. New York: Cambridge University Press, 2002.

Matsson, Helena and Sven–Olov Wallenstein, ed. *Swedish Modernism: Architecture, Consumption, and the Welfare State*. London: Black Dog Publishing, 2010.

McFaul, Michael, *Russia's Unfinished Revolution: Political Change from Gorbachev to Putin*. Ithaca: Cornell University Press, 2001.

Meadows, Donella, Jørgen Randers, and Dennis L. Meadows, *Limits to Growth: A Report for the Club of Rome's Project on the Predicament of Mankind*. New York: Universe, 1972.

———. *The Limits to Growth: The 30–year Update*. White River Junction, V.T.: Chelsea Green, 2004.

Mertha, Andrew C., *China's Water Warriors: Citizen Action and Policy Change*. Ithaca: Cornell University Press, 2011.

Midttun, Atle and Anne Louise Koefoed, "The Effectiveness and Negotiability of Environmental Regulation." *International Journal of Regulation and Governance* vol. 1, no. 1 (2001): 79–111.

Milani, Abbas, *The Shah*. New York: Palgrave, Macmillan, 2011.

Miller, James, "Daoism and Nature," in *The Oxford Handbook of Religion and Ecology*, ed. R. S. Gottlieb. New York: Oxford University Press, 2006.

—— ed. *Chinese Religions in Contemporary Societies*. Santa Barbara, C.A.: ABC–CLIO, 2006.

Millet, Kate, *Going to Iran*. New York: Coward, McCann, & Geoghegan, 1982.

Milov, Vladimir and Boris Nemtsov, *What 10 Years of Putin Have Brought: An Expert Evaluation*. Moscow: Novaya Gazeta, 2010.

Mishal, Shaul, and Avraham Sela, *The Palestinian Hamas: Vision, Violence, and Coexistence*. New York: Columbia University Press, 2006.

Montesquieu, Baron de., *The Spirit of the Laws, Vol. 1*, trans. Thomas Nugent. London: J. Nourse, 1777.

Morozov, Evegny, *The Net Delusion*. London: Allen Lane, 2011.

Mouffe, Chantal, ed. *Dimensions of Radical Democracy: Pluralism, Citizenship, Community*. London and New York: Verso, 1992.

Moyo, Dambisa, *Dead Aid: Why Aid Is Not Working and How There Is A Better Way for Africa*. New York: Farrar, Straus, and Giroux, 2009.

Natsoulas, Theodore, "The Politicization of the Ban of Female Circumcision and the Rise of the Independent School Movement in Kenya. The KCA, the Missions, and Government, 1929–1932." *Journal of African Studies* vol. 33, no. 2 (1998): 137–158.

Nabavi, Negin, *Intellectuals and the State in Iran: Politics, Discourse, and the Dilemma of Authenticity*. Gainsville, F.L.: Florida University Press, 2003.

Niebuhr, Reinhold, *The Children of Light and the Children of Darkness. A Vindication of Democracy and a Critique of its Traditional Defenders*. London: Nisbet & Co., 1945.

Nilsson, Bengt, *Sveriges afrikanska krig*. Stockholm: Timbro, 2008.

Norton, Augustus R., ed. *Civil Society in the Middle East*. Leiden: Brill, 1996.

Nustad, Knut G., *Gavens makt: norsk utviklingshjelp som formynderskap*. Oslo: Pax forlag, 2003.

Østerud, Øyvind, "Lite Land som humanitær stormakt." *Nytt Norsk Tidsskrift* vol. 23, no. 4 (2006): 306–316.

Palmer Harik, J., *Hezbollah: The Changing Face of Terrorism*. London: I.B. Tauris, 2004.

Pedersen, Morten B., *Promoting Human Rights in Burma. A Critique of Western Sanctions Policy*. New York: Rowman & Littlefield, 2008.

Pelczynski, Zbigniev A., ed. *The State and Civil Society: Studies in Hegel's Political Philosophy*. Cambridge: Cambridge University Press, 1984.

Petersen, Charles, "Google and Money." *New York Review of Books*, 10 December 2010.

Piattoni, Simona, *Clientism, Interests, and Democratic Representation: The European Experience in Historical and Comparative Perspective*. Cambridge: Cambridge University Press, 2001.

Pliatzky, Leo, "QUANGOs and Agencies." *Public Administration* vol. 70, no. 4 (1992): 555–563.

Polman, Linda, *The Crisis Caravan: What's Wrong with Humanitarian Aid?* New York: Metropolitan Books, 2010.

Portis, Edward B., Adolf G. Gundersen, and Ruth L. Shively, *Political Theory and Partisan Politics. SUNY Series in Political Theory*. Albany, N.Y.: State University of New York Press, 2000.

Posey, Darrell A. *Cultural and Spiritual Values of Biodiversity*. Nairobi, Kenya, United Nations Environmental Program, 1999.

Premfors, Rune. "Governmental Commissions in Sweden," *American Behavioral Scientist* vol. 26, no. 5 (1983): 623–642.

Przeworski, Adam, Susan C. Stokes, and Bernard Manin, eds. *Democracy, Accountability, and Representation.* New York: Cambridge University Press, 1999.

Przeworski, Adam, *Democracy and the Limits of Self–Government.* New York: Cambridge University Press, 2010.

Reichel–Dolmatoff, Gerrardo, *Amazonian Cosmos.* Chicago, I.L.: University of Chicago Press, 1971.

——. "Cosmology as Ecological Analysis: A View from the Rainforest." *Man* 2.3 (1976): 307–18.

Riedel, Manfred, *Between Tradition and Revolution: The Hegelian Transformation of Political Philosophy.* Cambridge: Cambridge University Press, 1984.

Robinson, J. A. and T. Verdier, *The Political Economy of Clientelism.* London: Center for Economic Policy Research, 2002.

Rodriguez, Francisco and Ernest J. Wilson, *Are Poor Countries Losing the Information Revolution?* Report. University of Maryland, 1999.

Rosenau, James, *Along the Domestic–Foreign Frontier.* Cambridge: Cambridge University Press, 1997.

Rothstein, Bo, *Den korporativa staten.* Stockholm: Nordstedts, 1992.

Sanasarian, Eliz, *Women's Rights Movement in Iran: Mutiny, Appeasement, and Repression from 1900 to Khomeini.* New York: Praeger Press, 1982.

Scholte, Jan Aart and Albrecht Schnabel, eds. *Civil Society and Global Finance.* London: Routledge, 2002.

Schudson, Michael, *The Good Citizen: A History of American Public Life.* New York: The Free Press, 1998.

Sen, Amartya, *Identity and Violence: The Illusion of Destiny.* New York and London: W. W. Norton & Company, 2006.

Schafer, Edvard H., "The Conservation of Nature under the T'ang Dynasty." *Journal of the Economic and Social History of the Orient* vol. 5 (1962): 279–308.

Schak, David C. and Wayne Hudson, eds. *Civil Society in Asia.* Aldershot, U.K.: Ashgate, 2003.

Shapiro, Judith, *Mao's War against Nature: Politics and the Environment in Revolutionary China.* Cambridge: Cambridge University Press, 2004.

Shields, Michael P., *Foreign Aid and Domestic Savings: The Crowding Out Effect.* Melbourne: Monash University, 2007.

Simensen, Jarle, Arild E. Ruud, Frode Liland, and Kirsten. A. Kjerland, *Norsk utviklingshjelps historie.* Bergen: Fagbokforlaget, 2003.

Sidel, Mark, "The Third Sector, Human Security, and Anti-Terrorism: The United States and Beyond." *Voluntas: International Journal of Voluntary and Nonprofit Organizations* vol. 17, no. 3 (2006): 199–210.

Singerman, Diane, *Avenues of Participation: Family, Networks, and Politics in Urban Quarters of Cairo.* Princeton, N.J.: Princeton University Press, 1995.

Smith, Steven Rathgeb and Michael Lipsky, *Nonprofits for Hire: The Welfare State in the Age of Contracting.* Cambridge M.A.: Harvard University Press, 1993.

Snyder, Jack L., *Myths of Empire: Domestic Politics and International Ambition. Cornell Studies in Security Affairs.* Ithaca: Cornell University Press, 1991.

Somers, Margaret, "Narrating and Naturalizing Civil Society and Citizenship Theory: The Place of Political Culture and the Public Sphere." *Sociological Theory* vol. 13, no. 3 (1995): 229–274.

Sperling, Liz, "Public Services, QUANGOs and Women: A Concern For Local Government." *Public Administration* vol. 76, no. 3 (1998): 471–487.

Spiro, Melford E., *Buddhism and Society. A Great Tradition and Its Burmese Vicissitudes.* New York: Harper & Row, 1970.

Springborg, Robert, "Patterns of Association in the Egyptian Political Elite" In *Political Elites in the Middle East,* ed. George Lenczowski. Washington D.C.: American Enterprise Institute Press, 1975.

Steinberg, David I., *Burma/Myanmar: What Everyone Needs to Know.* Oxford: Oxford University Press, 2010.

Sörensen, Jens Stillhoff, ed. *Challenging the Aid Paradigm.* London: Palgrave Macmillan, 2010.

Sørensen, Øystein and Bo Stråth, eds. *The Cultural Construction of Norden.* Oslo: Scandinavian University Press, 1997.

Tacchi, Jo, "Supporting the Democratic Voice through Community Media Centres in South Asia?" *3CMedia Journal of Community, Citizen's, and Third Sector Media* vol. 1 (2005): 25–36.

Talhami, Ghada Hashem, "Whither the Social Network of Islam?" *Muslim World* vol. 91, nos. 3 & 4 (2001): 311–324.

Taylor, Bron, *Dark Green Religion: Nature Spirituality and the Planetary Future.* Berkeley, California: University of California Press, 2010.

——. "On Sacred or Secular Ground? Callicott and Environmental Ethics." *Worldviews* vol. 1, no. 2 (1997): 99–112.

—— ed. *Ecological Resistance Movements: The Global Emergence of Radical and Popular Environmentalism.* Albany, N.Y.: State University of New York Press, 1995.

Taylor, Charles, *Philosophical Arguments.* Cambridge: Harvard University Press, 1995.

——. *Hegel and Modern Society.* Cambridge: Cambridge University Press, 1979.

Taylor, Robert, *The State in Myanmar.* Honolulu: University of Hawaii Press, 2009.

Tischner, Jozef, *Etos Solidarnosci.* Krakow: Znak, 1981.

Toje, Asle, *The European Union As a Small Power: After the Post–Cold War.* New York: Palgrave Macmillan, 2010.

Tullock, Gordon, *Public Goods, Redistribution and Rent Seeking.* Cheltenham, U.K.: Edward Elgar Publishing, 2005.

Turner, Graham, M., "A Comparison of the Limits to Growth with 30 Years of Reality." *Global Environmental Change* vol. 18 (2008): 397–411.

Tvedt, Terje, *Utviklingshjelp, utenrikspolitikk og makt: Den norske modellen.* Oslo: Gyldendal Akademisk, 2009.

Trägårdh, Lars, ed. *State and Civil Society in Northern Europe: The Swedish Model Reconsidered.* New York and Oxford: Berghahn Books, 2007.

——. "Rethinking the Nordic Welfare State through a neo-Hegelian Theory of State and Civil Society." *Journal of Political Ideologies* vol. 15, no. 3 (2010): 227–239.

Van Dijk, Jan, *The Network Society,* 2nd ed., London: Sage, 2006.

Vattimo, Gianni, *A Farewell to Truth.* New York: Columbia University Press, 2011.

Vitousek, Peter M., Jane L. Mooney, and Jerry M. Melillo, "Human Domination of Ecosystems." *Science* vol. 277, no. 5325 (1997): 494–499.

Vitousek, Peter M., Paul R. Ehrlich, Anne H. Ehrlich, and Pamela A. Matson, "Human Appropriation of the Products of Photosynthesis." *Bioscience* vol. 36 (1986): 368–73.

Wa, Thiongo Ngugi, *Decolonising the Mind: the Politics of Language in African Literature.* London: Heinemann, 1986.

Waggoner, Paul E. and Jesse H. Ausubel, "How Much Will Feeding More and Wealthier People Encroach on Forests?" *Population and Development Review* vol. 27, no. 2 (2001): 239–257.

Waszek, Norbert, *The Scottish Enlightenment and Hegel's Account of "Civil Society."* Dordrecht, Netherlands: Kluwer Academic Publishing, 1988.

Watt, William M., *Islamic Political Thought.* Edinburgh: Edinburgh University Press, 1968.

Weir, Stuart, "QUANGOs: Questions of Democratic Accountability." *Parliamentary Affairs* vol. 48, no. 2 (1995): 306–322.

White, Anne, *Democratization in Russia Under Gorbachev, 1985–1991: The Birth of a Voluntary Sector.* New York: St. Martin's Press, 1999.

Wiktorowicz, Quentin, *The Management of Islamic Activism: Salafis, the Muslim Brotherhood, and State Power in Jordan.* Albany, N.Y.: State University of New York Press, 2001.

Wiktorowicz, Quintan and Suha Taji Farouki, "Islamic NGOs and Muslim Politics: A Case from Jordan." *Third World Quarterly* vol. 21, no. 4 (2000): 685–699.

Wittfogel, Karl A., *Oriental Despotism.* New Haven, C.T.: Yale University Press, 1957.

Wood, Allen, ed. *Elements of the Philosophy of Right.* Cambridge: Cambridge University Press, 1991.

Yanacopulos, Helen, "The Strategies that Bind: NGO Coalitions and Their Influence." *Global Networks* vol. 5, no. 1 (2005): 93–110.

Yang, Goubin, "Weaving a Green Web: The Internet and Environmental Activism in China." *China Environment Series* vol. 6 (2003): 89–92.

Yue, Pan, *Thoughts on Environmental Issues.* Beijing: China Environmental Culture Promotion Association, 2007.

Zhu Tuofu, Bette T. Korber, Andre J. Nahmias, Edward Hooper, Paul M. Sharp and David D. Ho. "An African HIV–1 Sequence from 1959 and Implications for the Origin of the Epidemic." *Nature* vol. 391 (5 February 1998): 594–597.

Žižek, Slavoj, *Living in the End Times.* London: Verso, 2010.

Zubaida, Sami, "Islam, the State, and Democracy." *Middle East Report* vol. 179 (1992): 9–27.

INDEX

A

Abdi, Ali, 246
adaptive management, 195, 205n41
adultery. *See* Iran
African Awakening, 250
African Biodiversity Network, 191, 203n25
African traditional religions. *See* religion
agenda chasing, 15, 270, 276–278, 284
Ahmadinejad, Mahmoud, 244, 249
aid industry, 15, 269, 270, 274–7, 279–282
AIDS/HIV, 76n1, 89, 96–98, 193, 194, 204n33, 204n34, 204n35, 205n36
Akasaka, Kayo, 92
Al Jazeera, 87
Al Qaeda, 3, 62, 84
American Enterprise Institute, 80n68, 228n9
American Red Cross, 54, 76n3
Amnesty International, 5, 41, 47, 128
Angola, 97, 292, 296–299, 303, 308n18, 308n19
animism. *See* religion
An-Na'im, Abdullahi, 220, 230n41
anti-globalization movement/"the Movement," 55–59, 75, 77n15, 77n26, 91
Arab Spring, 103, 104, 250
Ardalan, Parvin, 233, 245, 252n24
Arendt, Hannah, 11, 14, 232, 233, 240, 243, 247, 249, 250, 251n3, 252n17, 253n28, 253n31, 253n32, 253n33

Assange, Julian, 18, 254
associative democracy. *See* democracy
Ataturk, Kemal, 237
ATTAC, 77n21
Australia, 35, 49n1, 51n10, 55, 65, 92, 106n15, 288n66, 300, 301, 313
authoritarian government, 150, 173
autonomy, individual, 213, 259, 265

B

Baab, 234, 235, 237, 251n4
Baabi movement, 235, 251n7
balance of powers, 11, 15, 303
Bangladesh, 12, 95, 99, 217
Baogang, He, 156, 160f, 176n12, 177n23, 177n24, 177n26, 177n27
Baraghani, Fatemeh, 234
Baron, Barnett F., 63, 78n46
de Beauvoir, Simone, 248
Beckett, Charlie, 101, 109n93, 109n94
Behbahani, Simin, 244
Belarus, 65, 84
Belgium, 300, 301
Bellona, 284
Benn, Hillary, 299
Berezovsky, Boris, 119, 126
biodiversity (biological diversity), 185, 191, 203n24, 203n25, 205n43
Blair, Tony, 268n30, 299
bloggers, 18, 86
BONGOs (business organized NGOs). *See* Non-Governmental Organizations (NGOs)

spaces, 105
uncivil society, 114
voluntary character of, 83
Clark, John, 5, 11, 52f, 91, 107n38,
107n40, 107n45
clash of civilizations, 61, 78n35. *See
also* Bernard Lewis
clientelism, 15, 271–274, 284,
286n13, 286n14, 286n24
climate change, 4, 52, 66–73, 76n1,
80n64, 80n66, 80n69, 81n73,
81n74, 139, 181, 187, 202n19,
205n39, 277, 311, 314, 317,
319n3
Climate Research Unit, 69, 70. *See
also* Phil Jones
climate skeptics, 70
Club of Rome, 187, 202n16. *See also*
Limits to Growth
Coase, Ronald, 294f, 308n14
Cold War, 36, 37, 60f, 163, 202n18,
226, 271, 286n32
colonialism, 190, 192, 196
commissions, 24, 26, 28, 35, 131,
260–266, 267n11, 267n12,
267n13, 267n15
Communist Party. *See* China
Confucianism, 143f
Congjie, Lian, 143, 148n20
Congo, Democratic Republic of, 97
consciousness-raising, 185
and Wangari Maathai, 185, 189,
199f
Constitutional Revolution. *See* Iran
Copenhagen Consensus Center, 68,
79n63
Cordoba House, 61
corporate social and environmental
responsibility (CSR), 5, 289, 291,
294, 307n11
corporatism, 9, 15, 160, 256, 257,
262, 263
corruption, 6, 16, 17, 24, 26, 35, 44,
45, 56, 76n1, 124, 126, 128, 131,
132, 135n31, 184, 186, 197, 199,
202n13, 208, 281, 285, 286n25,
292, 296, 298, 299, 303, 306
cosmopolitanism, 3, 310, 311

Council on Foundations (U.S.),
76n13, 79n48
Crone, Patricia, 212, 228n7
crowding out, 11, 270, 282–284,
288n66
Cuba, 2, 21n5, 65, 139
Cull, Nate, 57, 77n24
cultural revival, 189–94, 203n22
and conservation in Africa, 189–94
Cultural Revolution, 139
cyberspace, 5, 90, 107n44

D

Dahl, Robert, 112, 134n2
Dahrendorf, Ralf, 18, 21n25
Dalai Lama, 147
Danesh ("Knowledge," Iranian feminist
journal), 237
daoism, 142–144, 148n18
daoist nun, 146
dark green religion. *See* religion
Dean, James, 86, 104, 106n21, 109n72,
109n82, 109n86, 110n100
deliberative democracy. *See* democracy
democracy
associative, 254–268
cross-border, 35f
deliberative, 24, 265
democratic governance. *See*
governance
democratic participation, 84, 97,
139, 317
democratizing force, 84, 85
elections, 4, 23, 26, 28, 30f, 35, 38,
44, 112, 119, 121–123, 125, 126,
128, 130, 131, 133, 134, 149,
150, 152, 153, 164, 165, 171,
175, 178n37, 178n43, 181, 184,
186, 231, 239, 246, 251n4
Folkrörelsebaserad demokrati, 262
"managed," 11, 13, 14, 74, 111–136
monitory, 4–6, 11, 13, 16, 18, 22f,
53, 73f, 111, 113, 115, 121, 133,
134, 134n1, 137–148, 176n5,
208–209, 227, 250, 254, 256,
291, 307n3, 310f, 319
monitory mechanisms, 25